T0247604

FOREIGN
AGENTS

ALSO BY CASEY MICHEL

American Kleptocracy

FOREIGN AGENTS

• • •

HOW AMERICAN LOBBYISTS AND
LAWMAKERS THREATEN DEMOCRACY
AROUND THE WORLD

CASEY MICHEL

ST. MARTIN'S PRESS
NEW YORK

First published in the United States by St. Martin's Press, an imprint of St. Martin's
Publishing Group

FOREIGN AGENTS. Copyright © 2024 by Casey Michel. All rights reserved. Printed in
the United States of America. For information, address St. Martin's Publishing Group,
120 Broadway, New York, NY 10271.

www.stmartins.com

The Library of Congress Cataloging-in-Publication Data is available upon request.

ISBN 978-1-250-28605-5 (hardcover)
ISBN 978-1-250-28606-2 (ebook)

Our books may be purchased in bulk for promotional, educational, or business use.
Please contact your local bookseller or the Macmillan Corporate and Premium
Sales Department at 1-800-221-7945, extension 5442, or by email at
MacmillanSpecialMarkets@macmillan.com.

First Edition: 2024

10   9   8   7   6   5   4   3   2

To my brother Norwood,
the best man I know

Law? What do I care about Law? Hain't I got the power?

—Cornelius Vanderbilt[1]

Ladies. Gentlemen. You have eaten well. . . .
Your feast is nearly over.

—Frank Miller[2]

CONTENTS

CONTENTS

FOREIGN AGENTS BY THE NUMBERS

- Decline in staff overseeing foreign lobbyists in the United States before 2016: 43 percent[1]
- Decline in inspections and audits of foreign lobbyists before 2016: 86 percent[2]
- Total convictions for foreign lobbying crimes in the half century before 2016: 3[3]

- Number of former members of Congress who became foreign agents, 1990-2016: 114[4]
- Foreign principals registered to lobby in America since 2016: 1,040[5]
- Amount foreign principals have spent to lobby in America since 2016: $4.1 billion[6]
- Growth of Chinese expenditures on foreign lobbying, 2017-2021: 476 percent[7]
- Growth of Russian expenditures on foreign lobbying, 2017-2021: 584 percent[8]

- First year American officials called for a ban on lobbying for foreign governments: 1869[9]
- Decline in Clinton Foundation donations after 2016: 75 percent[10]
- Undisclosed funds received by American universities from foreign sources: $6.5 billion[11]
- American president with the greatest number of advisors indicted for secretly working as foreign agents: Donald Trump

FOREIGN
AGENTS

Prologue: Bad Business

The first thing I learned at school was that some people are
idiots; the second thing I learned was that some are even worse.

—Orhan Pamuk[1]

On May 19, 1934, a man named Ivy Lee sat in front of a row of American congressional officials, all of whom were trying to determine whether Lee was secretly working for a new regime in Germany known as the Nazis.

Lee wasn't an unknown figure to these officials. There in his starched collar and his pinstriped suit, his heavy cheeks beginning to sweat in the stuffy room, Lee cut a familiar look. By the early 1930s, Lee was already an American celebrity: a man close to politicians, tycoons, and cultural icons alike, steering their careers and their policies—and the direction of the country writ large. Not long before, Lee had launched a brand-new industry, which quickly roared across the nation. To his proponents, this new enterprise was the savior of American capitalism: an amalgamation of advertising and advice, useful to both business owners and political forces trying to navigate the strains of the early twentieth century. To his detractors, it was simply an excuse to plaster decorum on outright deceit, spinning lies in the service of deep-pocketed clients who were trying to protect their wealth from the masses.

The field was still hazy to most Americans, including those congressional officials now peering down at Lee. "Your business is what?" asked John McCormack, a Democrat who chaired the committee Lee sat in front of, known as the House Un-American Activities Committee.[2]

Lee looked back at him. "It is very difficult to describe, Mr. Chairman," he replied. "Some people call it 'publicity agent.' Some people call it 'counsel in public relations.' But that would give you a general idea of it."[3] Even Lee may not have known what he'd launched.

But others noticed. This new industry—this new field of "public relations," as it was eventually described—had brought Lee clients from across the country. There were the giants of the Gilded Age who'd turned to Lee to help bury controversies—people like the Rockefellers, who relied on Lee to help cover up some of the worst massacres in American history. There were the copper and steel and banking magnates, turning to Lee to thwart any kind of regulatory oversight. There were the plutocrats of the railroad industry, who still maintained a stranglehold on American transit, depending on Lee to retain their monopolies. And there were the politicians of the era, deep in the pockets of these American oligarchs, relying on Lee's assistance in blocking the progressive forces rising around the nation.

But they weren't the only ones. As Lee found success after success in America, international clients came calling, from across the political spectrum. The forces of fascism gaining ground in Italy welcomed Lee with open arms. Rising totalitarians in Moscow were likewise eager to see what kind of opportunities Lee might be able to unlock.

And there, in Germany, was a client who recruited Lee in the early 1930s: a company named I.G. Farben, which was concerned, as Lee told American officials on that day in 1934, with how Germany was perceived in the United States—and how Lee might be able to improve things.

The higher-ups at I.G. Farben knew Lee's talents. They'd read about his connections and his cant, his willingness to open doors for—and whitewash—whichever clients were willing to pay the most for his services. As Lee revealed to congressional investigators, I.G. Farben was happy to pay for Lee's work, for some of these "public relations" services they'd heard so much about, if only he'd make it easier for Germany to improve its image in the United States—and expand the efforts and success of a new dictatorship building in Berlin. "The directors of the

company told me they were very much concerned over the German relationships with the United States, and antagonism toward Germany in the
United States," Lee admitted during the hearing. "They wanted advice as
to how those relations could be improved. So they made an arrangement
with me to give them such advice."[4] And that, to Lee, was all it was: an
honest arrangement, based on honest advice. He'd broken no laws. He'd
committed no crimes. And he was happy to take payment—the equivalent of more than half a million dollars, adjusting for inflation—for just
such assistance.

Lee claimed that the guidance he offered was only to I.G. Farben—
not that such advice was especially controversial, anyway. He told his
German counterparts that if they wanted the regime in Berlin—which
Lee preferred to refer to as the "German government" rather than Nazis—to succeed, they should avoid blatantly obvious propaganda. "Our
people regard it as meddling with American affairs, and it was bad business," Lee claimed. (When McCormack asked if Lee would ever consider acting as a mouthpiece for propaganda, Lee stiffened, saying that
he'd "taken the position long ago that I would not disseminate anything,
any [propaganda], however innocuous.")[5] Instead, Lee advised that the
Nazis should "establish closer relationships . . . with American press
correspondents located in Germany" and try to get those journalists to
disseminate Nazi messaging. That, Lee told his German partners, was
key: finding trusted mouthpieces and middlemen who could blast Nazi
messaging far and wide, all for the sake of improving relations between
the United States and Germany.

But as the questions continued, Lee revealed that it wasn't just advice he had provided. He admitted that he'd also charged one of his employees to monitor American media for "what they are saying about
Germany." Lee would then relay the themes, as well as his thoughts, to
his German contacts. All the better for German counterparts to craft
their messages for American audiences—and for American audiences
to understand that this new regime in Berlin was one worth supporting.

The hearing never grew heated, never grew especially raucous. (As
Lee cooed at one point, "My dear sir, I am perfectly delighted to cooperate.") His polished demeanor, though, belied a tension Lee had never
known: a tension suddenly bubbling to the surface, breaking around

Washington, spilling across Europe. Because no matter how much Lee tried to deny any connection between the Nazis and I.G. Farben, the American legislators refused to bite. "In other words, the material that was sent here by [I.G. Farben] was material spread—we would call it propaganda—by authority of the German Government," Rep. Samuel Dickstein said at one point, pointing to items I.G. Farben had shipped to Lee. "But the distinction that you make in your statement is, as I take it, that the German Government did not send it to you directly; that it was sent to you by [I.G. Farben]." As Dickstein laid out, Lee's claims that he'd advised only I.G. Farben were a deflection. In reality, the company—a conglomerate later responsible for, among other things, producing the poison gas that would slaughter millions of Jewish victims—was simply a cutout, a middleman between Lee and his ultimate Nazi clients. As Lee mumbled in response, "Right."[6]

As the hearing wore on, and as the connections between Lee and the Nazis became obvious, Lee's defenses began to slip. He admitted he'd been recruited by I.G. Farben chief Max Ilgner, a Nazi collaborator who would later oversee key pieces of Germany's economy during the Second World War. He admitted meeting directly with Nazi propaganda chief Joseph Goebbels and having a "very interesting conversation" with the war criminal. He'd even met personally with Adolf Hitler, telling the tyrant that he'd "like better to understand him if I could"—all the better to help craft the Nazis' message for American audiences. And he admitted that he'd advised the Nazis—via their I.G. Farben cutout—on the best way to spin Germany's growing stockpile of military weaponry, "to make clear to the American people" that these arms weren't actually a threat.[7]

As Lee finished testifying, he thanked the officials, once more with the kind of obsequious, oleaginous manners that had served him so long. His body, and especially his scalp, ached, and he'd already begun making plans for a trip back to Germany, hoping to enjoy the soothing spa treatments that he thought might help. At fifty-seven, he deserved a breather, a break from this sudden pressure from Americans wondering just who he was working for, and just what impact he might be having on American policy. Plus, he wanted to check in on those clients he'd just described: those Germans who'd paid him phenomenal sums to help open doors, crafting messages for unsuspecting audiences—crafting messages that would help the Nazis rise, reign, and wreak havoc across the European continent.

Lee left that afternoon, sweat curdling around his collar, preparing for projects and clients to come. He had no inkling that the fallout from the hearing he'd just participated in would, in only a few short months, kill him, detonating the reputation he'd spent decades building—or that, nearly a century later, the kinds of links he'd created with the Nazis would come roaring back and nearly undo American democracy in the process.

* * *

IN EARLY 1986, just over fifty years after Lee's hearing, a man named Jonas Savimbi touched down in Washington. Even among the characters and charlatans bouncing around the U.S. capital, Savimbi brought an odd, conspicuous look. With a bushy black beard and slanted red beret, he preferred the kind of revolutionary attire made famous by communist guerillas elsewhere. And that made a certain sense: Savimbi had risen to prominence among the leftist anti-colonial movements blooming throughout southern Africa, espousing the kinds of pro-communist rhetoric that were anathema to America's geopolitical ends.

But Savimbi had since gone through a complete change, transforming from his communist chrysalis into a supposed "freedom fighter" in the new nation of Angola, then emerging from centuries of Portuguese colonization. Backed by the far-right apartheid regime in South Africa, Savimbi turned against his former leftist comrades who'd seized power in Angola. And he'd had more success than most anticipated, with his insurgents clawing territory from the Angolan government—launching Savimbi into a new role, as one publication called him, as the "Che Guevara of the right."[8]

That success came saturated in horrors, with Savimbi authoring appalling crimes across the country. His forces had not only "committed atrocities against children," as one journalist later recounted, but had even "conscripted women into sexual slavery."[9] Even during an era of Cold War proxy wars, Savimbi stood apart. As one analyst described, the warlord was unique in African history "because of the degree of suffering he caused without showing any remorse."[10] (To take just one example, Savimbi "personally beat to death a rival's wife and children," as *The New York Times* reported.[11]) Thanks to his efforts, Savimbi almost singlehandedly extended Angola's post-colonial civil war—a war that would claim the lives of hundreds of thousands, decimating the new nation in the process—for a new generation.

By the mid-1980s, though, Savimbi's forces were running low on arms and ammunitions. The Americans had cut him off years earlier, unwilling to work with a man who, among other things, bombed civilians and Red Cross facilities alike. He'd already traveled to Washington multiple times, seeking to lift the ban on American support for his forces, without success. No doors opened. No help came.

But he'd try once more, beret in hand, looking for whatever aid he could find: Searching for the kinds of heavy arms that the United States doled out to other anti-communist leaders around the world. Looking to convince American policymakers that his was a worthy cause, and that concerns about atrocities against children and women were mere rumor—or that even if they'd happened, well, they'd been for the greater good, hadn't they?

Landing in Washington, Savimbi hopped in a waiting stretch limousine, beginning his tour of the American capital. And it didn't take long for him to realize that this time would be different—that unlike those previous trips to the United States, doors now opened wherever he went, with praise and promises flooding this supposed "freedom fighter."[12]

There were stops at multiple think tanks, including the American Enterprise Institute, where prominent conservative Jeanne Kirkpatrick dubbed Savimbi a "linguist, philosopher, poet, politician, warrior" and "one of the few authentic heroes of our time."[13] There were interviews with major American newscasters, including ABC's *Nightline* and CBS's *60 Minutes*, and even chatter about potentially landing on the cover of *Time* magazine.[14] And at the Washington Hilton, Savimbi gave the keynote speech at a lavish banquet for the American Conservative Union, where he shared the dais with then–vice president George H.W. Bush. Both men received raucous applause from the crowd, with Savimbi joking that he'd "been following [Bush's] career for a long time, from afar, from the bush!"[15]

It was, all told, a publicity coup for Savimbi. As *The Washington Post* wrote, it was "a welcome . . . unlike anything Washington has ever seen for an African guerrilla leader."[16]

The trip not only ushered Savimbi into halls of power long blocked to the warlord, but it immediately jump-started the flow of arms Savimbi had long demanded—all the better to beat back his communist opponents, regardless of the women and children caught in the crossfire. As a capstone to his trip, Savimbi received a "bootlegged copy" of President Ronald Reagan's forthcoming State of the Union address, where the American president would specifically mention Angola and would pledge that, moving forward, America would "support with moral and material assistance [Angolans'] right not just to fight and die for freedom, but to fight and win freedom."[17]

The trip was an unmitigated success—and couldn't have been more different from Savimbi's previous, futile efforts to curry favor with the Americans. For observers, the shift appeared abrupt, almost jarring. With one trip, a decade's worth of regional policy—which had effectively blocked all aid to Savimbi—had flipped, for no obvious, exogenous reason. It was enough to give observers whiplash.

Yet Savimbi hadn't accomplished this transformation alone. He'd had help from a new figure, and a new force: a man who'd taken gargantuan sums from the guerrilla leader and become Savimbi's Svengali in the process, steering the warlord through Washington. A man who, like Lee before him, preferred the shadows and the back rooms, whispering advice and navigating unseen hideaways. A man who cultivated links with powerful figures in America and then took his talents global, working for the most authoritarian, fascistic clients he could find in the process. And a man who would later watch everything he'd worked for collapse in infamy—but not before devastating, perhaps fatally, American foreign policy in the process.

It was a man who reignited Lee's legacy, ushering in a new age of unrepentant Americans willing to sell their services to dictators and autocrats abroad. Mercenaries cloaked in three-piece suits and gleaming loafers, skirting and subverting regulations in the service of madmen

and tyrants, adding a sheen of respectability to those behind the greatest global horrors of the past half century. Men who, in another age,
might be considered traitors, and yet who remain welcomed by polite
society, spinning their clients and shifting the direction of American
foreign policy—and American democracy—in the process.

Men who are considered, to use the technical term, "foreign agents."
And men who have all followed in the footsteps of the foreign agent
who helped Savimbi and who continued Lee's legacy: Paul Manafort.

* * *

THE NARRATIVES OF Lee and Manafort are cornerstones of a far broader
story: the creation and expansion of the world of foreign lobbying in
the United States, and the transformation of American industries into
platforms for foreign governments trying to upend and redirect American policy. And it's the narratives of those men that highlight the contours of this transformation—and reveal how they followed remarkably
similar paths, from distinction to disaster.

Lee, still considered the "father of public relations,"[18] blossomed
into one of the most influential voices of post–World War I America.
He then took his services abroad, and watched his reputation crash on
the shoals of rising fascism.

Likewise, Manafort, the man who first brought the worlds of lobbying and political consulting together, built a sterling reputation for
success in post–Cold War America. He then took his services abroad,
and watched his reputation crash on the shoals of rising fascism.

Yet this book isn't just about these two men, each acting as a dark
mirror of the other. It's also about how they each ushered in unprecedented interest in how foreign governments actually try to shift
American policy, and how those Americans working for these foreign
regimes actually operate—and succeed—in the United States. It's about
all those Americans who've opted to take their talents to the despots
and dictators willing to foot the bill, and degrade American democracy
in the process.

This book is also about the decades-long effort to shine a light on
these operations. Because the third central character in this book is
not a person but a piece of legislation. Dubbed the Foreign Agents

Registration Act (FARA), the legislation came into force as a direct response to Lee's pro-fascist efforts, part of a broader slate of progressive reforms in the 1930s aimed at bringing transparency to the burgeoning world of foreign lobbying. This book tells the story of how FARA was then, for three-quarters of a century, all but forgotten and ignored— and how that lack of enforcement ushered in an explosion of foreign agents who saturated Washington, all in the secret service of foreign benefactors around the world. It's about how America learned, and then promptly forgot, the lessons of Lee's debacle—and how Manafort rose to remind Americans of all the threats these foreign lobbyists truly represent.

If you've heard of FARA, or about the broader threats of unchecked foreign lobbying in Washington, it's likely thanks not to Lee or Manafort but to Donald Trump and Trump's 2016 election. As with so many other topics—kleptocracy, election integrity, the safety and future of American democracy writ large, and plenty more—Trump's success brought a sudden salience to the threats of foreign lobbying in the United States. And understandably so. No president has seen so many members of his inner circle—former campaign managers and national security officials, former fundraisers and political advisors—indicted for or convicted of secretly working on behalf of foreign dictatorships, all while pushing Trump to do their foreign clients' bidding. Not that this reality is especially surprising; Trump was, after all, the first American president to openly accept the aid of foreign governments in order to get elected.

But Trump was hardly an outlier. By the mid-2010s, American politicians of all stripes—conservatives, liberals, and even outspoken progressives—had all welcomed help from foreign lobbyists or foreign governments looking to build these kinds of opaque, subterranean links. Nor were these bit players. They included Bill and Hillary Clinton, whose Clinton Foundation soaked up millions in foreign financing—only to watch that financing collapse following Hillary's 2016 election loss, making a mockery of claims that the funding was somehow apolitical. They included figures like Bob Dole, a doyen of Republican politics and a supposed patriot, who left office in 1996 and immediately began shilling for foreign dictatorships, becoming a courtier to autocrats in the process. And they also included those like

Bernie Sanders, whose chief strategist during the 2016 presidential campaign had just finished off a project helping elect a pro-Russian thug in Ukraine—a project overseen by, of all people, Manafort. (Naturally, Manafort was by then working as campaign manager for Trump's 2016 campaign.)

Yet as this book will detail, these politicians were hardly the only ones profiting from the tsunami of foreign financing targeting Americans, all aimed at manipulating American policy for foreign governments' ends. There were American universities and academics feasting on foreign financing and ignoring basic disclosure requirements, transforming into mouthpieces for autocratic forces in the process. There were American think tanks flowering across the United States, nominally dedicated to independent research while nonetheless spewing messaging favoring their foreign benefactors. There were white-shoe American law firms who had abandoned any interest in American clientele, slobbering instead for the opportunity to work for the dictators and autocrats looking for help.

There was industry after industry after industry, all of which pointed to an additional reality: Even though this book is nominally about lobbying, the people and institutes detailed in the following chapters aren't those we'd recognize necessarily as lobbyists, per se. Indeed, even among experts, "lobbying" is something of a slippery term. "No definitive definition [of lobbying] has ever been agreed upon," Lionel Zetter, author of one of the few textbooks on lobbying, wrote in 2011. To Zetter, lobbying is simply "the process of seeking to shape the public policy agenda in order to influence government (and its institutions) and the legislative program." It is, in other words, "the art of political persuasion."[19] Or as Manafort once said, "You might call it influence-peddling. I call it lobbying."[20]

And that influence-peddling is something anyone can attempt, without being part of any firm, any consultancy, or any body of accredited colleagues. This influence-peddling—this lobbying—is available to any and all. It's also something that in the United States is a constitutionally guaranteed right. As the First Amendment of the U.S. Constitution stipulates, all Americans are assured the right "to petition the Government for a redress of grievances."[21] Alongside the freedoms of speech and religion, the freedom to lobby is a core, constituent part of the American story.

And for centuries, that was a freedom used almost exclusively by Americans, on behalf of American clients, for American ends. In recent decades, though, that freedom has been abused by foreign forces looking to circumvent things like diplomacy and transparency, all in order to manipulate American policy and American national security to their own ends. It's a practice that has become, in many ways, shockingly normalized—as if despots who assassinate political opponents, tyrants who lead campaigns of mass murder and mass rape, and dictators responsible for authoring genocides are no different than American clients.

That process of normalizing this practice is one of the topics this book will examine. But we'll also look at how this entire process has exploded what we traditionally understand as lobbying, or as lobbyists. Because in twenty-first-century America, the world of lobbying now involves the law firms and think tanks mentioned above. It involves the political leaders and staffers who can navigate the halls of Congress and who can usher clients directly into the White House. It involves nonprofits and universities—those nominally dedicated to the pursuit of knowledge or the pursuit of a more democratic American polity— who have discovered just how much foreign financing awaits, if only they'd open their doors. And it involves some of the most nominally pro-American figures of the past decade, all of whom have decided that they'd rather surreptitiously work in the pay of foreign patrons instead.

These, then, are the foreign agents of this book: Those Americans selling their services to the highest bidders abroad, all in order to entrench and enlarge the most brutal governments on the planet—the Americans who, as one scholar wrote, help "make the world safe for dictatorship." Safe for the regimes responsible for ethnic cleansings and genocides. Safe for the world's most horrific environmental crimes and anti-LGBTQ abuses. Safe, in sum, for the most successful expansion of dictatorship the world has seen in nearly a century.

* * *

BEFORE BEGINNING THIS book in earnest, there are a couple of signposts to be aware of. While this book is about the foreign agents working and operating in America, it is *not* a book about espionage. There are innumerable books written on foreign spies operating in America and their effect on everything from American national security to global stability. Those figures, though, are purposely clandestine, purposely operating in the hidden crevices of society, infiltrating institutions and exfiltrating information alike. These are not figures who would ever register their work with federal authorities or disclose their meetings and efforts in accordance with something like FARA. These spies may work for the same governments, but they are a distinct group from these foreign agents—the latter of whom haven't seen nearly as much attention but have done arguably just as much damage.

And while this book is largely chronological, it's not necessarily comprehensive. With hundreds of entities, thousands of filings, millions of data points, and billions of dollars spent, the eruption of what we recognize as foreign lobbying in recent years is far too big for any one book. But that doesn't mean that kind of encyclopedic work isn't being done elsewhere. Civil society organizations like the Project on Governmental Oversight, OpenSecrets, and a handful of others are doing the kind of granular work necessary to make some of the connections I detail throughout this book, creating the databases and organizing the filings that allow journalists and researchers to actually put these stories together. And they are the ones providing and collating the material for future authors to build their own stories, craft their own narratives, and further highlight how these foreign lobbyists have done untold damage to not only American policy but also democracy as we know it.

As such, since this book is about such a broad (and understudied) phenomenon, not every country behind foreign lobbying campaigns will be mentioned in this book. Some countries that make headlines—including Israel, Japan, the UK, and others—won't necessarily be featured heavily, while others—such as Azerbaijan, the United Arab Emirates, and Rwanda—will feature more than expected, for reasons that will become clear.

Meanwhile, one country in particular will thread the entire chronology of this book: Russia. While many Americans learned of Russia's subterranean lobbying efforts only in the mid-2010s, bundled alongside hacking and disinformation campaigns, the Kremlin's efforts to secretly influence American officials stretch all the way back to the middle of the nineteenth century, culminating in the greatest foreign lobbying scandal of the entire century—and arguably the greatest foreign lobbying scandal the United States had seen until Moscow's interference campaign in the mid-2010s. And it's that campaign that begins the next chapter, setting the stage for all that followed.

In many ways, it's Russia's most recent efforts at subverting American democracy—and using foreign agents to achieve the Kremlin's ends—that was the impetus for this book. As a graduate student at Columbia University's Harriman Institute during the mid-2010s, focusing on how post-Soviet dictatorships manipulate Western (and especially American) audiences, I had a front-row seat to watching the Kremlin's interference efforts play out in real time. Not only was I among the first to catalog and report on things like Russia's social media interference campaign, but I even ended up on the receiving end of these foreign agents' efforts, some of which are scattered throughout this book. And my graduate research focused specifically on all of the topics that would become suddenly, stunningly relevant in the aftermath of Trump's election, diving as it did into topics like FARA and even intersecting with figures like Manafort, long before Trump hired the foreign agent as his presidential campaign manager.

But that was then. In the years since, these topics—foreign lobbyists, foreign funding, and the transformation of industry after industry into foot soldiers for dictatorships and mafia-states around the world—have only grown more relevant, and more pronounced. And that, in many ways, is what *Foreign Agents* is about. It's about the broader history of foreign governments specifically, and secretly, lobbying American officials to do their bidding. It's about how a man like Lee—still revered in certain quarters for birthing the public relations industry—ended his career by working to entrench fascism, and ended up with a legacy he never anticipated. And it's about how, with the end of the Cold War, a new figure extended that legacy for a new generation, expanding it around the world and lighting a fuse that would detonate in the election of Donald Trump, that would shatter American foreign policy, and that threatens to destroy American democracy yet.

PART I

POISON

Where the crowd is, there is tyranny.

–Everett Dean Martin[1]

1

Dire Consequences

If I brought up repentance, the response would be, "What do I have to repent for?" Everyone thought of themselves as a victim, never a willing accomplice.

—Svetlana Alexievich[1]

While the rise of foreign lobbying and foreign agents is a relatively modern phenomenon, they both have their roots in the earliest days of the United States—and with the men who looked to take advantage of the new rights a new country promised to offer.

In late 1792, near the end of George Washington's first term as the first president of the United States, a man named William Hull traveled from Virginia to the budding nation's capital in Philadelphia. He had a plan: test the limits of the nascent U.S. Constitution, implemented just three years prior, and see how far the rights laid out in the First Amendment truly stretched. Specifically, Hull wanted to test the proposition that Americans had a right—a "freedom," as the Constitution described it—to lobby, or to "petition," any and all government officials. To pressure them, as a mere citizen, into passing the kinds of policies they wanted.

A vain man—a "proud-looking sort with luxuriant hair," as one writer described him—Hull arrived in Philadelphia with an impressive pedigree. A former Revolutionary War officer, he reportedly "talked to President Washington as often as he liked."[2] And it was that relationship that Hull counted on. Because he hadn't traveled to Philadelphia just for himself. Instead, he came at the behest of a group of Virginia military veterans who'd fought under Washington during the recent war for American independence. Years after thrashing the British, they were still waiting on compensation for their services. But the finances of the early American republic were in shambles, held together with little more than dreams and promises, with American veterans often going without pay while the country found its fiscal footing.

Hull wrote to other veterans groups, calling for "agents" to help him push for a wartime compensation bill to help these former soldiers.[3] After arriving in Philadelphia, he buttonholed federal legislators, arguing his case, familiarizing himself with the workings of this new national government. And he highlighted the fact that, without those veterans, these legislators wouldn't even have their jobs—and might well have been strung up by British authorities looking to decapitate this rebellious American nation.

Hull, though, couldn't argue against the state of federal finances. The country remained effectively broke, and his compensation bill died. The Revolutionary War veterans lost out on the payment they demanded.

But in Hull's failure, something else emerged. A new model for how Americans—regardless of profession, regardless of political persuasion—could try to reach their legislators. It was something untested in this new republic. It was something we would, in years to come, call "lobbying." And like those clients of Hull, it was, in many ways, revolutionary.

*   *   *

HULL, OF COURSE, was hardly the first person to try to influence policy. "For as long as empowered individuals and groups have been responsible for governing societies, others have sought to influence them and their decision-making," scholar Tarun Krishnakumar wrote in his 2021 history of lobbying in America.[4] But unlike European monarchies, the new American government was hardly some outpost of far-off elites, where distant politicians claimed to wield power through some kind of divine right. Access to officials in Philadelphia, or to any of those in the state capitals dotting the expanding country, was far easier than anything the Western world had seen to that point. (If anything, the American model of influencing politicians—of bending the ears of

local leaders, pushing them to preferred policies—was far closer to the governance structures of the Indigenous nations the Americans would soon decimate.)

And even with Hull's failures, it didn't take long for Americans to recognize that difference—and to begin using it to their advantage. Soon, those looking to push and provoke legislators began scouring across the American capital. "In 1795, a Philadelphia newspaper described the way lobbyists waited outside Congress Hall to 'give a hint to a Member, teaze or advise as may best suit,'" one synopsis found.[5] And as the country's finances began stabilizing, and as the country began surging westward during the early nineteenth century, those throngs looking to sway legislators began to find success. From tariffs to fiscal policy, from railroad construction to industrial development, America's expansion in turn expanded the opportunities for these Americans to sway politicians.

Much of such lobbying focused initially on domestic affairs. But soon, these self-styled lobbyists began skirting into foreign policy, too. In 1798, amidst a fraught standoff with France, one senator welcomed "a large committee of Philadelphia citizens" into the halls of Congress to "present a petition" backing his colleagues' position on the potential war with Paris. Another senator, however, objected to saturating the Senate floor with Americans clamoring for certain foreign policy positions, and "won passage of a resolution to prohibit individuals or delegations from presenting such petitions in such a way in the future."[6]

Indeed, even with the allowances in the Constitution, that opposition to free-for-all lobbying was baked into this American experiment from the beginning. Even from these earliest days of the United States, there was concern that these freedoms to petition—these freedoms to lobby—were too broad. That they were too widely available, or that they were too open for potential abuse. "One of the weak sides of republics, among their numerous advantages, is that they afford too easy an inlet to foreign corruption," Alexander Hamilton wrote in the Federalist Papers, considered one of the seminal documents of America's founding. America's openness, Hamilton worried, would provide avenues for foreign powers to meddle, to infiltrate, and to steer policy—without Americans ever being aware. History, as Hamilton added, "furnishes

us with so many mortifying examples of the prevalenc[e] of foreign corruption in republican governments."[7]

And Hamilton was right to worry—not least since the man who later killed him, Vice President Aaron Burr, ended up working alongside foreign agents to try to splinter the United States. (One of Burr's secessionist allies was James Wilkinson, the commander of the U.S. Army, who secretly served as an agent of the Spanish monarchy.) Ironically, though, those "inlet[s] to foreign corruption" didn't come via foreign lobbying during the early decades of the American republic. While there were instances—in 1796, in 1812—of attempted foreign interference in American elections, the first half of the nineteenth century saw surprisingly little in terms of threats of unchecked foreign lobbying in the United States. Americans freely lobbied, exercising their new rights—but almost always for domestic affairs rather than anything international.

But then the Civil War came, and everything changed.

*   *   *

DURING THE CIVIL War—while the American government beat back a group of white supremacist traitors aimed at fracturing the country and expanding the enslavement of millions—foreign governments watched and waited. In Paris, French officials toyed with recognizing the Confederacy, which would have delivered a fatal blow to the Americans. In London, British officials flirted with arming the Confederates outright, all the better to gut their American rivals. In the end, though, the United States' victory over the separatists ended any discussion of European interference. And it instantly opened a new era of foreign lobbying in the United States—and a scandal that, 160 years later, now looks oddly, unsettlingly familiar.

In the immediate aftermath of the American victory, U.S. officials looked for opportunities to patch the country together. One potential outlet: expansion. As some American officials thought, if the United States could conquer or seize new lands, perhaps it could patch over its domestic disputes, at least for a bit. And as Secretary of State William Seward saw it, one region provided the perfect opportunity not only to improve America's global (and economic) standing but to further tether a fractured country together: Alaska.

At the time, the vast expanse we now know as Alaska was a colony of tsarist Russia. Indigenous Alaska Natives had suffered for generations at the hands of Russian settlers, with massacre after massacre aimed at cementing Russian rule in the province. By the mid-1860s, though, the province was little more than dead weight for the Russian regime. It was too far, with too little infrastructure, for Russia to keep pumping it with money and men. And with Russia's own finances slowly imploding, tsarist officials began casting about for someone to take Alaska off their hands.

There were only so many options. Selling to the British, which still controlled the adjacent Canadian provinces, was a nonstarter; Britain was Russia's primary colonial rival, and anything that could strengthen London's hand was to be avoided. The Americans, though, presented an attractive alternative. Selling Alaska to the United States would allow Washington to act as a counterweight to British influence in the region. Plus, in Russia's eyes, America appeared set to eventually conquer the entirety of North America—why not sell out early, and at least make a bit of money along the way?

There was only one problem. Few Americans outside of Seward saw any reason to purchase Alaska from the Russians. "American interest in Alaska wobbled between ho-hum interest and disinterest," one scholar described it.[8] To many Americans, Russian Alaska in the 1860s—in the years before the discovery of the gold and the oil that would eventually make Alaska one of the wealthiest American states—was little more than an empty tundra. It was an "icebox," a "polar bear garden" that the United States didn't need.[9] Plus, Washington had more pressing issues, from the military occupation of the former Confederate states to the passage of basic civil rights protections for Black Americans. Alaska would have to wait.

But the Russians couldn't. Selling the province—and convincing the Americans to spend a gargantuan sum on something almost no Americans wanted, just as the country was trying to get back on its feet—was one of the easiest ways to help stabilize Russian finances, if only Washington could be convinced. Something had to be done.

Fortunately for the Russian government, their ambassador in Washington, a man named Edouard de Stoeckl, had an idea for how to circumvent American opposition—without the American populace, or even much of the American government, realizing what was happening.

In 1867, Stoeckl—who'd somehow earned the nickname "The Baron," despite lacking any kind of actual title—began working. Huddling with Seward, the two hammered out a tentative deal. For $7.2 million in gold, the United States would take Alaska off of Russia's hands. But Seward would still need to overcome congressional opposition, as only Congress could appropriate the funds. Nor did the issues stop there. Seward's primary ally, President Andrew Johnson, began facing a tornado of criticism for his racist policies—and suddenly saw himself the target of the country's first impeachment crisis, which sucked up all of the energy, and all of the focus, in Washington.[10]

By early 1868, Seward's deal appeared all but dead. Which is when Stoeckl stepped in, and set a playbook that would roar back to relevance in the mid-2010s, when Russia once more attempted to direct American policy while remaining completely out of the public eye.

First, Stoeckl hunted down an American who could help rally the congressional votes to actually fund the purchase. He targeted Robert J. Walker, a former Mississippi senator and treasury secretary, as someone who could help. To Stoeckl, Walker was someone who could pose as an independent voice to pressure American legislators to back the funding—without anyone realizing that Walker had become a secret mouthpiece for Russia. Bankrolling Walker with the modern equivalent of a half million dollars, the Russian official "paid Walker to use his influence wherever and however he could."[11]

And Walker was happy to oblige. The former senator and White House official began planting anonymous articles with unsuspecting newspapers, including front-page columns denouncing opponents of the projected sale. (Walker, never known for his creativity, signed his anonymous articles as "Alaska.") He also publicly defended both Stoeckl and the Alaska purchase, predicting "dire consequences" if the purchase fell through. He pushed for the purchase in Washington wherever and however he could—and when questioned, Walker denied that any of his efforts ever qualified as "lobbying."[12]

With Stoeckl funding him behind the scenes, Walker's effort

appeared to succeed. By the middle of June 1868, enough congressional officials had changed their mind and tossed their support behind the appropriations. Suddenly, and unexpectedly, the funding measures passed—and suddenly, and unexpectedly, the United States saw its second-largest expansion in the country's entire history.

In fact, the move was so sudden, and so unexpected, that something seemed off. And soon, details began leaking out confirming opponents' suspicions. One journalist, Uriah Painter, reported that thieves in New York had supposedly stolen thousands of dollars from Walker—but when authorities nabbed the thieves, Walker refused to press charges. (A handy move, Painter pointed out, to transfer money without anyone being able to track its ultimate destination.) Painter also reported that "large sums" from the purchase funds had disappeared months before the formal purchase.[13]

In sum: money was missing all over the place. Combined with new rumors of bribery swirling Congress, all of it pointed to the "biggest lobby swindle ever put up in Washington," as Painter said.[14]

The accusations of financial malfeasance grew so pronounced that shortly thereafter Congress opened its first formal investigation into foreign lobbying. And it didn't take long for congressional investigators to confirm that the entire affair was a swindle, and a scandal. As they found, millions of dollars (adjusted for inflation) was somehow unaccounted for, disappeared into the financial ether. And all signs pointed to one inescapable conclusion: bribery, combined with clandestine foreign lobbying, all on behalf of Russia.

There was, naturally, one person who could help reveal what happened to the missing money: Stoeckl. Yet by the time congressional investigators discovered the disappearance, the Baron himself had vanished, heading back to Russia. As Ronald Jensen, author of the most detailed analysis of the scandal, wrote, "The Russian minister was probably the only man who knew the destination of all the missing funds from the Alaska appropriation, and that secret apparently left with him."[15]

To this day, questions remain about what happened to the missing millions. But as Jensen detailed, there seems one obvious answer. Tucked amidst President Johnson's papers was a memo outlining a conversation the president had with Seward—the man who'd jump-started the Alaska purchase in the first place. As the two sat in a "shady grove," Seward revealed to the president that Stoeckl himself had "bought the support" of one major American newspaper—and that Stoeckl had directly bribed congressional officials to flip their votes, with a total of ten total congressional officials taking Russian funds.[16] Nor were these anonymous officials. Among those bribed to support the Alaska purchase were the "incorruptible" Thaddeus Stevens, best known as one of the era's greatest proponents for civil rights protections for Black Americans.[17]

Unfortunately for investigators, even while the bribery became an open secret in Washington, no hard proof ever emerged. Seward denied any knowledge, and Johnson refused to comment publicly. The congressional investigation concluded in frustration. As the committee report found, the inquiry ended "barren of affirmative or satisfactorily negative results."[18]

Still, even while no convictions ever emerged—and even as Alaska became part of America proper—investigators wanted to make a stand. Members of the investigative committee chastised Walker "for representing a foreign power without public knowledge," calling the former senator and cabinet member out for working as an agent for a foreign government. And a few of the investigators even floated a potential solution: banning former American officials outright from ever working as lobbyists for foreign governments. As congressional investigators wrote: "Certainly no man whose former high public position has given him extraordinary influence in the community has the right to sell that influence, the trust and confidence of his fellow-citizens, to a foreign government, or in any case where his own is interested."[19]

As these officials saw it, no American official, once out of office, should work as a foreign lobbyist or a foreign agent for any other government. It was, in many ways, a statement ahead of its time, pointing directly to the kinds of foreign lobbying practices that would emerge in the decades to come. But it was also a statement that gained little notice, and that went nowhere.

And that was it. In this first foreign lobbying scandal in American history—in which a Russian official had bribed American officials and journalists and hired a former high-level American official to act as his mouthpiece in Washington, all aimed at secretly directing U.S. policy—no one was found guilty. No one lost their job, or ended up in prison. No one, aside from the Russian official in question, even ended up having the full picture of the funding mechanisms, or where all the missing millions ended up.

To modern eyes, maybe that's understandable. After all, the Alaska purchase is now recognized as one of the great successes of American foreign policy: as a pennies-on-the-dollar purchase of a territory that enhanced American power, American finances, and American influence in ways that are still paying off. But it was also something else: a story whose lessons, not least as they pertained to foreign lobbying (and bribery) of American officials, were promptly forgotten. And it was a formula that in coming years would only become more and more familiar—and that would, in the decades to come, reach directly from foreign governments into the White House itself.

* * *

DESPITE THE MAGNITUDE of the scandal, Americans largely shrugged at the allegations and revelations surrounding the purchase of Alaska. And not without reason. Because by the early 1870s, a Russian agent secretly steering American foreign policy—and blanketing Washington with secret payments in the process—was simply one of a far broader range of lobbying scandals saturating Washington.

In fact, it was in the immediate aftermath of the Alaska scandal that the word "lobbying" came into existence in the first place. With President Ulysses S. Grant now in the White House, rising American industrial interests spied an opportunity. As these businessmen knew, Grant made a habit of taking presidential breaks to wander across the street from the White House to a new, sprawling building called the Willard Hotel. There, Grant would head through the hotel's spacious, colonnaded lobby and sit at the hotel's circular bar, enjoying a tipple. It's unclear how many drinks Grant would down—his memoir unfortunately doesn't discuss his presidential years—but, after he'd had his fill, Grant would wander back to the Oval Office, heading back to continue repairing a fractured country.

But on those walks, Grant wasn't alone. As Zetter, the author of the best-known lobbying textbook, recounts, "Those seeking to influence [Grant] would congregate in the lobby of the Willard Hotel and try to attract the great man's attention." All the better, they thought, "to raise specific areas of concern."[20] Flagging down the president, bending his ear, these men could plead their clients' case. Maybe it was the railroad concerns who needed a new route approved. Or the industrialists who needed a new tariff implemented. Or the banking conglomerates who needed federal policy on gold loosened, or restricted, or whatever the day demanded.

There was always something. And there was always something that Grant specifically could help with. And if the president had had a few drinks, well, all the better.

Grant detested these moments he spent navigating the Willard lobby, trying to simply find his way to or from a drink. These men were all vultures, trying to pry loose a preferred policy—all buzzards, looking to extract another favor, all on behalf of their clients.

They were, as Grant would gripe, a group of "lobbyists," all waiting to pounce on the president whenever he wandered through the Willard. "Crawling through the corridors, trailing its slimy length from gallery to committee room, at last it lies stretched at full length on the floor of Congress," as one contemporary newspaper described it, "this dazzling reptile, this huge, scaly serpent of the lobby."[21]

Again, these kinds of attempts to pressure politicians weren't new, per se. "Lobbying has been going on since time immemorial, and there is certainly a case for saying that lobbying is one of the world's oldest professions," Zetter wrote.[22] But by the time of Grant's presidency, lobbying was transforming into something far more organized than its previous iterations—and something far closer to its modern equivalent. Similar to the corporate structures rising elsewhere—the holding companies and shell corporations and the offshoring tools, all helping build up corporate America—lobbying in post–Civil War America was becoming something recognizable. Under Grant, lobbying finally came into its own.

Not that everyone was a fan. As *The Nation* wrote, these new lobbyists were men "whom everybody suspects . . . and whose employment

by those who have bills before a legislature is only resorted to as a disagreeable necessity."[23] They were, in other words, becoming a necessary
evil—as a means to an end, even if few enjoyed their presence.

But it didn't take long for that "disagreeable necessity" to manifest
far more disastrously. Not long after the Alaska controversy, a new,
darker scandal emerged—one that led directly to the first genocide that
foreign lobbyists helped author, and that remains largely ignored by
Americans to this day.

* * *

IN THE EARLY 1880s, while European empires carved up nation after
nation in Africa—claiming their rights to colonization, regardless of
the human costs associated—one small European country in particular eyed a swath of the continent to call its own. For Leopold II, the
haggard, hatchet-faced king of Belgium, the Congo basin would make
a perfect colony for his country. It stretched nearly a million square
miles and hosted bottomless riches—and with Leopold's more militant
neighbors already claiming the right to rule neighboring regions of Africa, the Belgian king wanted his slice.

But Leopold would need help. He couldn't rely on his minuscule
Belgian army to muscle in, beating back more powerful rivals. And
residents of the Congo basin would hardly consent to a distant sovereign, one bent solely on pillaging the region. In order to claim the
Congo, Leopold would have to be creative.

So the Belgian king sketched out a plan. Instead of relying on his
own military force, Leopold would turn to an unlikely ally: America.
Specifically, Leopold thought, if he could obtain American recognition
of Belgium's right to rule the Congo, other European powers wouldn't
challenge his claims. America could effectively act as a mediator,
backing Belgium against all comers. But how could Leopold convince
Washington that he should be the man to control the lives of tens of
millions of Congolese residents?

One man came to mind. Years earlier, Leopold had befriended an
American named Henry Shelton Sanford, who'd served as U.S. ambassador to Belgium during the 1860s. A bespectacled businessman,
interested primarily in land speculation and residential development,

Sanford also envisioned precisely the kind of colony Leopold wanted to build in the Congo. And he wanted to help. As he saw it, he could be the king's man in Washington, convincing American legislators to back Leopold's Congolese strategy—convincing America to effectively gift the Congo to Belgium.

The king agreed. Sanford could be Leopold's mouthpiece in Washington. No one would need to know their arrangement—or what the king truly had planned for the people of the Congo.

In early 1884, Sanford returned to the American capital with a new mission. He began touring Washington, claiming that "entire territories" in the Congo had already been "ceded by Sovereign Chiefs" to Belgian authorities. Naturally, those supposed treaties also promised that U.S. citizens could likewise purchase seized Congolese lands—a nice benefit for Americans on the fence about potential Belgian recognition.[24]

But it wasn't all about business. As Sanford added, Belgian sovereignty over the region would allow Leopold to bring a "civilizing influence" to the region. A touch of Christianity, a dose of civilization, and the Belgians would transform the local populations, as Sanford claimed, into a "United States of the Congo." And he didn't hesitate to pander to legislators' white supremacy. Belgian Congo, Sanford claimed, could provide an outlet for newly freed Black Americans—as "ground to draw the gathering electricity from that black cloud spreading over the Southern states."[25]

Congressional legislators, feasting at Sanford's house, nodded along, sipping his wines, ingesting his arguments. For American officials, it all sounded fantastic, even if the details were all a bit hazy. (As historian Adam Hochschild wrote, "everyone was left pleasantly confused.")[26] Congressional resolutions and reports soon began circulating, backing Leopold's claims. One proclaimed that "no barbarous people have ever so readily adopted the fostering care of benevolent enterprise as have the tribes of the Congo [under Leopold], and never was there a more honest and practical effort made to . . . secure their welfare."[27] The primary author of the text: Sanford.

Sanford didn't just target congressional officials. He also turned to American media, which began highlighting Leopold's "philanthropic work" on behalf of Congolese residents. Rather than a craggy, distant monarch, American media began portraying Leopold as an empathetic emperor, simply looking out for the best interests of the Congolese nations. (Readers were left unaware that the positive coverage was secretly bankrolled "by quiet payments from Sanford.")[28]

But the key relationship Sanford fostered was with the American president, Chester Arthur. Just a few months earlier, Sanford, who was close with Arthur's Republican Party, had hosted the president at his Florida hotel. Soon, with Sanford whispering in his ear, Arthur started regurgitating the Belgian king's talking points. From his perch in the White House, Arthur began his own campaign to back Leopold's claims in the Congo.

Leopold could hardly have asked for more. The American president, thanks to the work of a single foreign lobbyist, had hopped directly into the Belgian king's pocket. At one point, Arthur even directly inserted text Sanford had written, with a few small tweaks, into his State of the Union address. As the American president proclaimed to Congress:

> The rich and populous valley of the Kongo is being opened by a society called the International African Association, of which the King of the Belgians is the president. . . . Large tracts of territory have been ceded to the Association by native chiefs, roads have been opened, steamboats have been placed on the river and the nuclei of states established . . . under one flag which offers freedom to commerce and prohibits the slave trade. The objects of the society are philanthropic. It does not aim at permanent political control, but seeks the neutrality of the valley.[29]

For the Belgian king, it was a coup. A foreign lobbyist had transformed the American president into an effective sock puppet, all with the aim of expanding a colonial empire. A foreign government, using an American lobbyist, had manipulated an entire American presidency into doing its bidding. "Leopold was delighted to hear his own propaganda coming so readily from the president's mouth," Hochschild noted. As the king cabled to Sanford, Leopold was "ENCHANTED" by the entire affair.[30]

Needless to say, everything Sanford claimed—about Leopold's

"philanthropic" aims, about the Belgians never seeking "permanent political control" of the Congo—was a hideous lie. But that didn't matter. When the United States announced formal recognition of Leopold's claims in 1884, Washington effectively sealed Belgian reign in the Congo. All told, it was "probably the most sophisticated piece of Washington lobbying on behalf of a foreign ruler in the nineteenth century."[31]

It was also, as we now know, a prelude to a holocaust. Because of American recognition, Leopold cemented his grip over the millions living in the Congo basin. And over the next quarter century, the Belgian king oversaw one of the most devastating, genocidal campaigns of the entire era, and arguably in the entire history of the African continent.

As a direct result of Belgian cruelty—not least their habit of taking women as hostages and forcing children into effective slave labor—millions of Congolese inhabitants died under Leopold's reign. The best estimates place the total fatality count at approximately ten million dead, or approximately half of the region's total population before the Belgians' arrival. And that's not even including the thousands, and potentially millions, who ended up maimed—losing hands, arms, legs, and more—as a result of Belgian rule.

Thanks to Leopold and Sanford's lobbying successes—thanks to the most sophisticated foreign lobbying campaign of the nineteenth century—Belgian sovereignty was confirmed over the Congo. Belgians and Americans both grew astronomically wealthier. And one out of every two Congolese inhabitants died.

Many in the United States, of course, ignored these developments. (To this day, the Belgian genocide in Central Africa remains largely overlooked.) But not long later, the kinds of tactics Leopold and Sanford pioneered began filtering back into the United States proper—and a new force began to emerge in America, leading to just as much disaster along the way. And all of it was propelled by a man named Ivy Lee.

2

What Is a Fact?

Journalism is printing what someone else does not want printed; everything else is public relations.

—Anonymous[1]

Lee never participated in any of the Congolese schemes. Instead, while Congolese inhabitants began dying by the millions, Lee was half a world away, fine-tuning a craft that would help American corporations cover up the deaths of Americans—and creating a playbook that future regimes would use to spin their own crimes.

In early April 1914, a group of nearly a thousand coal miners and their families began their day in a makeshift tent city near the southern Colorado town of Ludlow. They'd lived in the region for months, developing the area's mining industry. Mostly immigrants, they'd moved to Colorado to help fuel America's industrial rise, and to help fuel their own American dreams.

Recent months, however, had grown tense. Facing dangerous work and paid next to nothing, the miners called a strike. Demanding "improved conditions, better wages, and union recognition," the miners' representatives were confident, announcing that they were "sure to win" the standoff with management.[2] And there was reason for optimism. While company management and the Colorado state government both tried to block the strikers' efforts—even hiring "Texas desperadoes and thugs" to form militias and assault the striking workers—the miners' demands were hardly radical.[3] They simply wanted eight-hour workdays, a nominal pay raise, and the right to move as they pleased. That is, they simply wanted the things that were, as one journalist said, already "required by law."[4]

On that bright, blustery day in early 1914, however, something cracked. While women stoked fires to cook breakfast for their children, and while the men began plotting out the day's events, members of the Colorado National Guard began massing just outside the camp. Suddenly, machine gun fire raked the tents. Screams and thickening thuds—the sounds of bullets hitting limbs, hitting torsos, hitting heads—crackled across the camp. Bodies fell. The state militiamen started torching the tents, with fires racing through the encampments. Smoke mingled with shrieks, and hundreds of miners and their families scrambled to outrace the gunfire shredding their homes.

When the guns finally quieted and the smoke drifted into the nearby mountains, the tent city lay in ruins. Bodies sprawled across the charred ground. Nor were the striking miners the only victims. Wives and children scrambled into holes to try to escape the shooting, inadvertently trapping themselves when the fire reached them. One pit alone contained the remains of two women and eleven children, all of whom had died, according to one description, "like trapped rats when the flames swept over them."[5]

The total number of victims remains unclear, with estimates ranging as high as multiple dozens killed in the assault. Regardless of the final number, the Ludlow Massacre was, as *The New York Times* wrote, a "story of horror [un]paralleled in the history of industrial warfare."[6]

The national response was swift. Hearings opened into the killings, with officials demanding answers on "one of the bleakest and blackest episodes of American labor history." But rather than appear contrite, officials from the Colorado Fuel and Iron Corporation—which oversaw the region's mining operations, and which was ultimately overseen by American tycoon John D. Rockefeller, Jr.—denied that any massacre had even taken place. Rockefeller even told legislators that the company's anti-union stance was a "great principle"—even if it "costs all your property and kills all your employees."[7]

The nation was aghast, first at the slaughter, and then at the denials. Legendary journalist Upton Sinclair launched a public campaign against Rockefeller and his colleagues, announcing that he "intend[ed] to indict you for murder before the people of this country."[8] Quickly, the massacre and its aftermath spiraled into something that threatened not only Rockefeller's company and Rockefeller's wealth but the broader balance of industrial America writ large.

Thankfully for Rockefeller, the tycoon had one last tool up his sleeve: a man who'd rescued the fortunes of plutocrats elsewhere, and who'd helped whitewash and cover up the controversies that might otherwise damage other oligarchs' reputations and fortunes. A man who, Rockefeller thought, might be able to mitigate the fallout of the Ludlow Massacre—and potentially even spin the situation to the industrialist's favor. A man who had invented something called "public relations," which industrial America simply couldn't get enough of.

It was a man named Ivy Lee. And it was Lee whom Rockefeller called on to help spin the most horrific industrial carnage America had ever seen—and who soon took his talents to the most horrific governments on the planet.

*　*　*

LEE NEVER INTENDED to build a career aiding and abetting the worst industrialists, and regimes, of the era. Born in 1877 in the small town of Cedartown, Georgia, Lee always had an inquisitive mind. If anything, he always wanted to be a journalist, or at least an author. According to one academic, he "wanted to write the great American novel."[9]

And indeed, in his early years, that appeared to be the path Lee was on. Attending Emory College in Atlanta, Lee was voted both the "best writer" and "best read" in the school, eventually serving as the college editor of Atlanta's main newspaper. He even managed to land national scoops along the way. After transferring to Princeton University for his final years of college, Lee developed a close relationship with former U.S. president Grover Cleveland, then living near campus. At the start of the Spanish-American War, launched only a year after Cleveland left office, Lee snagged the first comments from the former president. (Not that it was much of a quote; as Cleveland told Lee, "This is terrible!"[10])

Even after graduating, while working as a reporter in New York in his first few years after college, Lee stood apart. He "did what most newspaper men don't," said one fellow journalist in New York, noting that Lee not only created his own filing system but routinely spent hours in the library or a law office for background research. With a stark work ethic—and often seen with multiple books under his arm—Lee found early success writing for a range of outlets, including *The New York Times*.

But if you squint, there were other elements that pointed to how Lee would end up in the pockets of oligarchs and despots, rather than as a great American novelist. As a white child of the Deep South, born to a pastor and a thirteen-year-old mother, Lee was attracted early to apologists for some of the most racist, retrograde political forces in America. His childhood icon was a man named Henry Grady, one of the best-known defenders of the Jim Crow South—a "prophet" who "drew a rosy picture of Southern race relations," selling white supremacy to Americans across the country. Saturated in the white supremacist rhetoric of the era, Lee adored Grady, who was "not only a hero but [an] idol" for the young Lee.[11]

Indeed, there was a clear patriarchal bent to Lee, evident even in his younger years. In college, Lee shared none of the progressive social stances of the era. He was a "puritan," especially when it came to things like women's suffrage. (Lee at one point declared that he was "horrified" when he learned that female students were reading newspapers from the library.) He combined that rank misogyny with an angry streak, routinely overcome by "rages" that were "terrifying," all while proclaiming that "stupidity is the prevalent characteristic of mankind."

But what he lacked in social graces, Lee more than made up for in ego—which his classmates gleefully mocked. At one point, his peers penned a "class prophecy" highlighting how well Lee thought of himself, his intellect, and his "worship of important people." "Our Lee! Our Great Lee! Hail! Hail! Hail!" as his classmates' text read. "The great Lee bestowed a benignant smile upon [his classmates]. Under his arm he carried a book which had made him famous, entitled 'Great Men Who Have Met Me.' As he proceeded with great condescension to join his classmates, he hummed to himself a little song of his own composition, entitled, 'Only Me, Ivy Lee.'"[12]

Rampant ego, chauvinistic views, affection for any and all powerful men: Lee's youth was a cauldron of factors that would, in time, help him climb the eventual ranks of corporate America. And they were also factors that helped him worm himself into regime after regime abroad—especially when he encountered leaders who shared many of these same traits.

First, though, he had to get his start. And after four years of working as a journalist for a range of New York papers, Lee made a move that set the course for the rest of his career—and that turned corporate America on its head.

* * *

IN 1903, THE mayor of New York needed help. Seeking reelection, Mayor Seth Low—a former Columbia University president, who'd successfully run on an unorthodox Fusion ticket—faced down the entrenched Tammany Hall machine. And as it often did, Tammany Hall appeared to be winning.

Low, though, had an idea. If he could find someone to help push his message to new audiences, perhaps he could circumvent the money and the means that Tammany Hall, one of the most corrupt political rings in America, had at its disposal. If only he could find, as he called it, a "publicity manager," perhaps he had a chance.[13]

In stepped Lee. In a theme that would follow Lee's career, he didn't care about Low's politics, per se. Rather, he was simply looking for a bit higher paycheck than his journalism job could provide. The great American novel would have to wait. For now, Lee would get paid.

Leaping into Low's campaign, Lee hit the ground running. Preparing campaign materials, Lee authored a 160-page book, a piece of campaign propaganda claiming that Low had overseen "the best administration New York had ever had."[14]

As Lee and others would later relate, though, it was less the content than Lee's presentation that stood the book, and Low's campaign, apart. To modern readers, the campaign booklet may appear anodyne, even dull. But to those in turn-of-the-century America, Lee's book was striking, containing "many of the features that were to be common" in the future for both Lee and political campaigns alike. Tapping into his experience in media, Lee leaned into dramatic typography—fonts with a flair. Numerous headlines and highlighted sections, bold typeface and simple sentences: Lee simply transferred his journalistic skills, meant to attract readers' eyes, to campaign literature.

But it wasn't enough. Tammany Hall ousted Low. And Lee's career as a "publicity manager"—as someone who'd already proven himself as an innovator of message management, and of understanding what the crowd would want—appeared over before it began.

Yet that innovation caught eyes. Shortly thereafter, a man named George Parker, then working as the so-called "press agent" for the Democratic National Committee, contacted Lee.[15] Would he consider bringing his talents to a national campaign? And would he consider trying to help oust President Teddy Roosevelt in the 1904 election?

Lee agreed. Soon, anti-Roosevelt literature began blanketing Americans. Mailed cards highlighted Roosevelt's supposed "dream of war." Press releases were "printed exactly like regular newspaper columns . . . making it easy for editors to use."[16] Suddenly, years into his presidency, anti-Roosevelt tracts were sliding into major media outlets as never before.

Roosevelt, of course, took the vote and won reelection. And Lee had, yet again, lost a campaign. But Parker thought he had something, and he made a proposition: What if the two of them took their talents to the private sector?

Lee pounced at the idea. In 1905, the two moved to Manhattan and opened a new firm, Parker and Lee. The firm's motto: "Accuracy, Authenticity, and Interest."[17] It was a motto Lee carried with him for decades—and which launched a career that would take him into the annals of political power, into the highest rungs of corporate America, and, eventually, into congressional hearings that exposed his work for a new regime in Germany.

* * *

AT THIS POINT, it's worth pausing on Lee's career for a bit of context. Lee, as mentioned above, was already recognized by the mid-1900s as an innovator, as someone applying a journalistic eye and a journalistic skill set to this world of publicity. But that doesn't mean that he was the only one working in this field, or that he was the only "publicity manager" around.[18]

In fact, campaigns and organizations around the United States had figures they'd hired to generate "publicity," and to attract anything they needed. Maybe it was voters. Maybe it was customers. Maybe it was just positive press, hoping to improve a firm's standing. Whatever it was, those helping these efforts were known by all kinds of names: "publicity managers," "publicity advisors," "press agents," and more.

By the time Lee entered the field, these efforts were all scattershot, barely organized, and rarely cohesive. They were often run without giving much attention to what would actually work. Part of that was the lack of things like scientific polling, figuring out what crowds would actually respond to. But part of it was also that, at least in corporate America, there remained this idea that the public simply didn't matter. What the public thought, what the public felt, how the public responded: it was all immaterial.

After all, with American plutocrats dominating American politics, why would things like corporate responsibility, corporate transparency, or corporate governance actually be important? "The public be damned," Cornelius Vanderbilt, one of America's original oligarchs, once said. "I don't take any stock in this silly nonsense about working for anybody's good but our own—because we are not."[19] Crowds might consume, and crowds might vote—but the crowd's views, and the crowd's perceptions, hardly mattered.

Yet by the early twentieth century, things had started to change. The crowd had begun taking on a life of its own. And the only one who realized that was, by all appearances, Lee. "Lee observed that the rise of national newspaper chains and syndicated journalism in America since the 1880s, combined with the extension of the franchise, had profoundly changed society," *The Economist* once wrote. "Now, for the first time, there was something that could accurately be called 'public opinion,' a shared consciousness and conversation across the country."[20] And that phenomenon—that "public opinion," presenting a kind of coherent consensus, a kind of mass consciousness—was something that could be targeted. Could be harnessed. Could be redirected for corporate America's benefit—if only they'd let it.

So Lee began sketching out a path, and a philosophy. He wouldn't be a simple press agent, a kind of charlatan-cum-carnival-barker trying to con customers. He would use, as he called it, a new playbook of "public relations" to take advantage of this new "public opinion." The public is "the foundation of all power," Lee would later write. "We have substituted for the divine right of kings, the divine right of the multitude. The crowd is enthroned."[21] And as Lee saw it, he could be the one to connect the public to these corporations. He would be—as the title of his lone biography, written in 1966, read—a courtier to the crowd.

In 1906, Lee laid out a series of principles that would define him, his firm, and his career. "This is not an advertising agency," Lee wrote. "Our plan is frankly, and openly, on behalf of business concerns and public institutions, to supply the press and public of the United States prompt and accurate information concerning subjects which it is of value and interest to know about."[22] For Lee, the key to managing this new relationship with the public lay in transparency. In earnest, forthright honesty, regardless of the topic. And Lee could help guide that transparency, could help shape it for a separate, distinct public. "[Lee] often thought of himself as a new kind of lawyer, one representing his client in the court of public opinion, which in a democratic society made judgments with as much certainty and finality as any court of law," one writer summarized.

And it was that distinction that set his new role apart. His work would be "the art of influencing men's minds," he wrote, "the sum of all the arts used to influence public opinion and move it in a desired direction."[23]

All of this was fine in theory. Yet Lee also had plans for how to translate this new philosophy into practice. Viewed from nearly a century later, his ideas appear "blindingly obvious," as *The Economist* described it.[24] But at the time, his tactics—just like his broader formulation of "public relations" writ large—were revolutionary.

Instead of simply dismissing allegations and scandal, Lee told corporate clients to meet controversies head on. Instead of keeping the public at arm's length, Lee taught his clients how to draft things like "press releases," inviting reporters to cover the issues or disputes in question. Instead of scurrying away, closing doors, and shunning the public, corporations should welcome their consumers in—or at least welcome them to the facts and the details and the stories as the corporations saw them.

If the public used to be damned, as Vanderbilt once argued, now it was to be courted. And Lee would be the man to help industrialists and corporations do so.

*　*　*

IT DIDN'T TAKE long for new clients to realize that Lee might be onto something. Mining magnates came calling, asking for his advice on how to spin strikes and work stoppages. Bankers requested his thoughts on how to address financial scandals. Railway operators sought his help when legislators began making noise about potentially breaking up their monopolies.

Indeed, it was that latter industry that got Lee his first glimpse of fame—or notoriety, depending on the audience. In the early 1900s, the United States was firmly in its Progressive Era. Propelled by forward-thinking politicians and a new generation of investigative journalists (known as "muckrakers"), Congress passed bill after bill protecting consumers. After decades of rapacious, unregulated capitalism, Americans finally realized there was a place for governmental oversight in the economy. Food, medicine, trusts: industry after industry suddenly had to think about things like consumers' rights and financial transparency.

And the railroad industry was no different. In 1906, the passage of the so-called Hepburn Act increased the size of the federal commission overseeing America's railway system, providing far more resources for regulators. Suddenly, the federal government could cut down on the crony capitalism and debilitating monopolies that defined America's railroads (and which made the rails one of the deadliest professions in the United States). Railroad management whined about government interference, claiming the new regulations were "strangulation." But there was little they could do.[25]

Then Alexander Cassatt, the head of Pennsylvania Railroad, remembered Lee. He knew that this new "public relations" specialist had previously worked on pro-railway efforts. Would Lee consider bringing his skills to the industry once more?

Lee obliged. Initially, he offered sound advice. He told the railroad executives to provide greater transparency, including by doing things like inviting reporters to the scenes of accidents. As Lee saw it, there was little use trying to cover up an accident that everyone—and every journalist—could see anyway.

Then, he began spreading pro-railway messaging, placing articles in newspapers and leaving leaflets in rail cars. Industrial talking points, these pieces of literature all framed the rail companies and their managers in the best light possible, highlighting just how much economic benefit the country had seen without any railway regulations. As audiences read, new restrictions would only hurt the industry—which would only hurt the customer.

Again, to modern eyes, these lines all appear completely unsurprising, almost obvious. But at the time, Lee's literature campaign was unlike anything America had seen before. It was, said one senator, "the most comprehensive, energetic, and persistent campaign . . . ever witnessed."[26]

But it wasn't just leaflets and press releases. Because even while Lee publicly spread the gospel of transparency—even while he professed to be interested only in principled, accurate information—Lee also pointed his talents in a different direction. While highlighting the rail industry's supposedly benign influence, he also published slashing criticisms against those supporting increased regulation, alleging that they failed to understand basic economics.

Lee specifically turned against officials like famed reformer Robert La Follette, a Wisconsin senator responsible for some of the greatest progressive gains of the era. But Lee saved most of his ire for another group: investigative journalists. To Lee, these muckrakers weren't figures unearthing corporate malfeasance or identifying those responsible for fatalities due to rail companies' gross negligence. Instead, they were people who "suppressed information about worthwhile accomplishments of the railroads," blowing concerns about railway safety out of all proportion. (At the time, fatalities on American railroads were comparable to wartime casualty rates.) These journalists had "prejudices" that "outlive facts," Lee claimed. They were, as he thundered, "demagogues."[27]

The muckrakers responded in kind. One journalist described Lee as a "poisoner of public opinion." Another, in a fit of creative sarcasm, described him as someone who "devoted his energies to proving, by insidious leaflets and gentle epistles, that the present capitalistic system is really a branch of the Quaker Church, carrying on the work begun by St. Francis of Assisi." Most memorably, Upton Sinclair—still considered one of the greatest American investigative journalists, even a century later—provided the sobriquet that would last longest. To Sinclair, Lee was simply "Poison Ivy."[28]

Even with all of these barbs, though, Lee pushed on. And a few years later, he and the railroads proved successful. The federal commission charged with overseeing the new rail regulations reversed course, removing all of the regulations that were supposed to keep American railways both safe and affordable. It was a complete, almost shocking, about-face.

And it didn't take long to track much of that success back to Lee. La Follette called Lee's efforts a "monument of shame," denouncing him on the floor of Congress. And La Follette wasn't wrong; instead of transforming American rails into a clear success story, Lee's work kept the railroads as one of the most dangerous areas of American life—so much so that so-called "railway surgeons" of the era are considered the world's first trauma surgeons.[29]

Lee, of course, didn't seem to mind. He'd done his job—and the plutocrats of the day noticed. With his success, new doors suddenly opened, ushering him into new industries and new opportunities, providing new chances to test his new theories of "public relations." His roster of clients ballooned yet again.

And then, in 1914, Lee received a call that would cement his reputation. A massacre—an unprecedented bloodletting, leaving dozens of immigrants and their family members dead—had taken place near a town called Ludlow. Could Lee help?

* * *

BY THE TIME John D. Rockefeller, Jr.—the son of John Rockefeller, Sr., the arch-tycoon and wildly wealthy founder of Standard Oil Company—called on Lee to help with the Ludlow Massacre, he'd already developed a reputation similar to his father's. Aloof and distant, Rockefeller Jr. remained a closed, cloistered figure, out of sight from the broader public. Not that he would have it any differently. He'd always preferred boardrooms to broad adulation, private conferences to public conversations. Whenever Rockefeller or his father came in for criticism, they "lifted their faces and turned the other cheek," as one hagiographer described it.[30]

But that was before the slaughter in Colorado, where the Rockefellers oversaw mining operations. The carnage was unlike anything the Rockefellers had seen—or been responsible for—before. Dozens dead, hundreds more injured, the fault clearly lying at the feet of the local militias and officials serving the Rockefeller family: all of it was, for the Rockefellers and America alike, unprecedented. There were only so many cheeks the Rockefellers could turn. The public, and legislators, demanded answers. They wanted someone's head to roll. And either Rockefeller would do.

Enter Lee. Immediately after Rockefeller called on him, Lee recommended an about-face. He began drafting pro-Rockefeller language and literature—press releases, opinion articles, and the like—but the Rockefellers would also have to open themselves up and step into the public spotlight. They would have to provide, as Lee said, "absolute frankness." The tycoons were taken aback. "This was the first advice I have had that does not involve deviousness of one kind or another," Rockefeller Jr. later said.[31]

Some of the tactics bordered on the smarmy, even cheesy. On Lee's advice, Rockefeller Jr. flew to Colorado, meeting with some of the miners who survived the massacre. At one point, he even joined an evening dance, twirling with miners' wives. (It's unclear how his dance partners felt about two-stepping with the man largely responsible for the recent massacre.) Lee told Standard Oil to hire "staff journalists" in order to "paint themselves in a favorable light using the language and tools of objective journalism."[32] Elsewhere, Lee began highlighting the Rockefellers' philanthropy, their donations to universities and nonprofits, their love of church and community alike. Not that everything was successful; at one point, Lee commissioned a book-length biography of Rockefeller Sr. that whitewashed the businessman to such a ridiculous extent that they had to scrap the project entirely.

But the rest of the campaign worked. Headlines that once vilified the family (ROCKEFELLER, MAN OR MONSTER?) had transformed into little more than glorified press releases themselves (HOW THE ROCKEFELLERS GIVE MILLIONS).[33] Rockefeller Sr.—a crotchety, cantankerous man at the best of times—suddenly became a benign, grandfatherly patron. "The figure of the striding, ruthless monopolist in high hat and long coat gripping his walking stick and entering a courthouse has been replaced by pictures of a frail old man, playing golf with his neighbors, handing out dimes to children, distributing inspirational poems, and walking in peace amid his flowers," one writer hummed.[34]

The shift was jarring. The elder Rockefeller, as *Time* wrote, "metamorphosed from a corporate monster into a benevolent old philanthropist."[35] And it stemmed almost entirely from Lee. Frankness, honesty, transparency: all of the pillars of Lee's philosophy had, as far as anyone could tell, worked wonders.

But there was a separate, subterranean campaign that paralleled Lee's public-facing efforts—and which proved even more effective. It was one that had nothing to do with honesty, or frankness, or even the Rockefellers themselves. It focused instead on the victims—and on Lee's moves to spread "egregious lies about the strikers and the cause of their deaths."[36]

As Lee wrote in bulletin after bulletin, it wasn't the Rockefellers who were actually responsible for the Ludlow Massacre. Instead, it was the strikers. It was the strikers who'd fired first. It was the strikers who'd instigated the violence. Further, the deaths of women and children weren't actually the fault of the rampaging militia. Instead, they were victims of simple kitchen accidents, of overturned stoves that incinerated the camp.

It was, in other words, hardly a massacre at all. But Lee didn't stop there. Another bulletin argued that editors of Colorado newspapers vindicated the Rockefellers—but omitted the fact that these editors were directly bankrolled by the mining companies. And yet another claimed that prominent strikers were actually millionaires, with legendary union organizer Mother Jones little more than a "prostitute and brothel-keeper."[37]

Lee made sure the bulletins were never linked back to the Rockefellers. Indeed, it's difficult to discern all the things Lee was responsible for. Despite boxes and boxes of folders in his archive detailing his work elsewhere, the section on Lee's work covering up the Ludlow Massacre remains missing.

Still, it wasn't difficult to figure out who was behind the smear campaign aimed at the strikers and the victims. One newspaper described Lee as a "paid liar," a "human snake" with "poison scattered by [his] subtle tongue." Lee's work for the Rockefeller empire was "done by the cunning, slimy brain of a cunning, slimy charlatan . . . [Lee's] sense of right and wrong is a worse force in organized society than that of the murderers who shot women and burned babies at Ludlow."[38]

The combination Lee perfected after Ludlow—laundering the reputations of executives, overseeing smear campaigns against opponents, all in order to cover up revolting crimes—was a playbook he created almost whole cloth. And it's a strategy that has remained with us for a century since. As one analyst recently said, modern spin campaigns use "the same tactics Lee used to rehabilitate Rockefeller's image way back then: fake news, crisis actors, corporate philanthropy as a PR move, all to shift the public focus away from a company's bad behavior."[39]

Another of Lee's legacies also appears familiar to modern audiences, especially following the rise of rhetoric surrounding so-called "fake news" in the 2010s.[40] In the congressional hearing following the Ludlow slaughter, legislators tried to pin Lee down on his dishonest tactics. Would Lee at least admit, for instance, that some of the claims he authored—say, that women and children had actually died in kitchen accidents—weren't even factual?

"What is a fact?" Lee responded. "The effort to state an absolute fact is simply an attempt to . . . give you my interpretation of the facts."[41] As Lee saw it, facts were simply in the eye of the beholder. There is no reality—there is only perspective. And the Rockefellers' perspectives— the Rockefellers' facts—were worth just as much as what might have actually happened at Ludlow.

And that was good enough for Lee. When stunned legislators asked

Lee what efforts he made to find out what actually took place at Ludlow, he responded, "None whatever."[42]

* * *

THE RESPONSES, AND the campaign writ large, were appalling to activists and legislators alike. But there was nothing illegal about what
Lee had done. He'd broken no laws, committed no crimes. And—most
importantly for him and his clients—he'd succeeded. The Rockefellers
avoided any reprobation, and emerged from the scandal with their reputations somehow more sparkling than before.

From there, the list of Lee's clientele exploded. It's not worth listing
all of the new corporate clients that sprinted to Lee's office, that offered
millions (in modern dollars) for his help. There were steel and copper
barons, holding monopolies of their own across the American West.
There were nascent automobile companies, looking for ways to direct
crowds to their "iron horses." There were public utilities and sugar car-
tels, shipping interests and investment houses, food and rubber conglomerates, all competing for Lee's ear. Every industry from breakfast
cereals to Hollywood wanted his perspective. Everyone from Henry
Luce and Woodrow Wilson to George Westinghouse and Charles
Schwab wanted his help. The head of the American Tobacco Company
once revealed that he paid hundreds of thousands of dollars just "to be
able to talk with Ivy Lee."[43]

By the early 1920s, Lee's own Manhattan office expanded, with
dozens of aides now reporting directly to him. He had become a "man
who wields an influence exceeded by few men in America," as one
writer said. And Lee appeared happy to let the new sway go to his
head; as he wrote to his father, "You will understand that I am fully
occupied with work of the greatest importance for some of the largest
interests in the world."[44]

And at some point, Lee realized there were only so many clients—
and only so many opportunities—available in the United States. There
were only so many corporate criminals he could whitewash, only so
many massacres he could spin. There were only so many American industries whose reputations he could launder. There were only so many
ladders he could climb domestically.

But what if he didn't have to remain in America? What if he could take his playbook abroad? And what if there were regimes looking to improve their own images—to undercut critics, to excuse their crimes, and to shift American policy in the process—who wanted a bit of this "public relations" magic as well?

3

Master of Publicity

The sight of an American makes me feel like eating little kids.
—Juan Cortina[1]

In 1923, still saturated in American clients, Lee announced he'd be leaving the country. He needed a break, a breather from the corporate campaigns buttressing his business. He'd be departing on a European vacation, skipping across the continent, taking a tour through country after country still trying to rebuild in the aftermath of the First World War.

It was hardly Lee's first trip abroad. Earlier in the century, Lee had traveled extensively, making it as far as tsarist Russia. He'd even visited Europe during World War I as part of a publicity tour for the Red Cross. Now, though, amid the rubble and the ruin, there was new potential— new areas that could use Lee's playbook to gain more American aid and more American support, and that could present a new challenge for Lee.

Following World War I, Europe had a wide range of scuffling, struggling governments looking for this help. There was a new Weimar government in Germany, battered by rampant inflation and revanchist nationalists burning with frustration over the war's end. There were nascent democracies in newly independent countries like Poland and Czechoslovakia, emerging after decades of occupation. Around the continent, there was government after government that could use Lee's services, and could use him as a springboard for accessing American audiences, and even American financing.

But it was in Italy that, as Lee saw it, something truly unique was emerging. Something untested. Something that, to observers like Lee, provided a kind of order that maybe the Europeans needed. Something that the new regime rising in Rome described in a single word: "fascism."

The man leading this new movement—this agglomeration of government-sponsored violence, state-centric economy, and hyper-masculinity, all gathered under a single strongman—was a young, heavy-browed Italian named Benito Mussolini. For those in the West, and especially in America, little was known about Mussolini, or about this so-called "fascism" that Mussolini claimed to embody. It was an ignorance that Lee sought to change—and in the process convince Americans that there was, despite what critics might say, promise in Mussolini's movement.

Arriving in Rome in 1923, Lee arranged a "private conference" with the new Italian leader. He drove to Mussolini's office, where an aide invited him in.[2] "I was ushered into a huge room about 30 feet square [sic], where [Mussolini] sat with his secretary and an interpreter at his shoulder," Lee later wrote. "I told him we in America had watched his leadership of the [fascist] movement with the keenest interest and delight and we felt he was working out a situation here which offered a lesson to the whole world."[3]

But Lee wasn't there just to gab with the dictator. As Lee told him, he wanted to convey Mussolini's thoughts to the people of America. The dictator was delighted. Running through the details of his fascist playbook—claiming his government, unlike the mewling, decadent democracies elsewhere, was "stable" and "responsible"—Mussolini stated that Italy had become a "country where great liberty was permitted to its people." As Mussolini told Lee, "I am for the working man, but I am not for destruction."[4]

Lee was, by all appearances, smitten. "As he indicated these various thoughts his facial expression was in constant mobility and I was impressed with the common sense which was uttered, not only in his words but in his manner," Lee swooned. "My general impression of Mussolini was most satisfactory. He thinks very quickly, expresses himself tersely and has a very evident grasp of the whole situation."[5]

And Lee wanted to help. He promptly began advising Mussolini on how to craft his message, and how to transmit it most effectively—how, in other words, to gather the most support in America possible. One of Lee's key pieces of advice centered on a new technology: movies. Already, these motion pictures were spreading across America, gathering new audiences eager to learn about foreign affairs. It was a perfect opportunity for Mussolini to attract eyeballs. As Lee saw it, Mussolini should create a range of films highlighting the different facets of his fascist program. And in order to have the most impact, each of these propaganda clips should personally feature Mussolini, telling audiences that the films presented "Italy's own interpretation of itself." As Lee counseled, "Such frankness would be refreshing."[6]

But Lee didn't keep his thoughts on improving Mussolini's image to himself. He immediately reached out to his press contacts at places like *Time* and *The New York Times* to relay his positive impression of the rising fascist. Mussolini, Lee claimed, was a "people's leader," who "takes pride in being accessible to the common folk of his realm."[7] (Years later, after Italy's defeat in the Second World War became clear, Italian partisans shot and killed the dictator, leaving his body hanging upside down off a metal girder.)

Nor was that all. Lee preened that Mussolini was, like him, a "master of publicity." That may have been a bit closer to the truth, insofar as Mussolini invented many of the trappings of fascism that imitators would follow in decades to come, from jutted chins and thrust chests to constant refrains of reclaiming national greatness.[8] Lee further asserted that Mussolini "offered an image of an efficient authoritarian" who "appealed to Italians as one who embodied their aspirations." Lee even went so far as to stake that nearly every American who visited Mussolini's Italy was "full of enthusiasm for the dictatorship of Mussolini."[9] (The idea of Mussolini's efficiency—including the notion that Mussolini's trains all ran on time—was, as one writer said, "a myth, spread by propagandists.")[10]

It was, altogether, the first impression many Americans had of the Italian despot, blasted in the biggest American publications of the era. And it was all the fascist could have hoped for. To Lee, Mussolini was a paragon of efficiency—maybe a bit rough, maybe a bit outré, but a

man worth following. A man America should get to know. And a man
America should, in time, come to support.

* * *

NONE OF THIS means that Lee was necessarily a fascist himself, or that
he was someone who even naturally gravitated toward dictatorship
over democracy. There's nothing in Lee's writings or in his extensive archives detailing why fascism should be replicated in America (or elsewhere). Lee was never a would-be totalitarian, or someone necessarily
opposed to America's democratic project.

For Lee, the reason he visited Rome and sat down with the dictator
was simple: understanding. Understanding who Mussolini was, and what
propelled him. Understanding what Mussolini wanted, both in general
and from America in particular. Understanding what Mussolini—this
man who supposedly "embodied" the aspirations of Italians—could
offer the United States, if only Americans would listen.[11]

And it's not that Lee was wrong, per se; understanding dictators,
despots, and tyrants as they are is a necessary step to combating their
insidious, inhuman efforts. But to Lee, when it came to foreign policy,
understanding wasn't a means to an end—it *was* the end. When it came
to relations between countries and regimes, there was no room for anything beyond conversation, beyond mediation, beyond mutual understanding. For Lee, a "complete knowledge of the truth will make people
understand each other."[12] And that extended to every nation around
the world, regardless of the type of government they had. To Lee, every government—the dictators and the democrats, the fascists and the
fundamentalists—represented the broader wills of their populations.
And Lee viewed the world as one of "reciprocal relationships under
which each nation really wanted to understand [the others]," and where
"each government was prepared to give to another the privilege of ex-
pressing their views with freedom."[13] With this kind of understanding,
wars could become a thing of the past. It was "now necessary to speak
loudly and clearly," Lee said, "without carrying any sticks at all behind
one's back."[14]

On the one hand, Lee's views on international relations were bizarrely naïve, bordering almost on utopian. In Lee's archives, a series

of documents detail his off-the-record comments with a range of foreign policy experts, whose bemused, confused responses still ring true. One "doubted if Mr. Lee's faith that the governments of the world were based on the support of the masses was well-founded." Another "doubted whether it was merely a question of getting people to understand one another," wondering aloud if "the Russo-Japanese War [would] have been avoided if each had understood the other's aims and aspirations?"[15] It was as if Lee had never heard of imperialism, or never considered colonization, or had missed the mutual oppositions that sparked the First World War. Lee seemed to think that conversation, and nothing else, could solve all of the world's problems.

Then again, there's another viewpoint that might explain Lee's thoughts: pure, unadulterated cynicism—and rank, globe-spanning business opportunities. After all, if the most important thing needed was someone to build and bridge conversations, wouldn't someone have to be hired to help? Wouldn't someone have to be that go-between, gathering governments together, translating their wants and needs, bringing the most powerful men in the world to the table?

And wouldn't someone like Lee be the perfect fit for just that role?

Mussolini certainly thought so, as did other governments. Officials in Hungary came knocking, with Lee offering thoughts on how to create an image of a regime that was "thoroughly stable and highly civilized."[16] A new government in Argentina turned to Lee, with the American recommending, among other things, that the Argentines send their polo team to the United States. ("Polo is not played except where there is a very high degree of civilization and a stable society," Lee explained.[17]) Over and again, in a pattern that mirrored his domestic clients, foreign governments raced to Lee, searching out his thoughts, his advice, his perspective. Asking him to help open doors, and open access to American audiences in the process.

But there was one regime in particular that was looking not simply for advice, but for perhaps the greatest foreign policy success possible: formal recognition from the American government. And when that new regime, gathering its bearings in Moscow, connected with Lee, they knew they'd found just the man who could help.

* * *

WHILE LEE CHATTED with Mussolini in Rome, a new government hundreds of miles to the east staggered to its feet, struggling to cement its new rule. By the mid-1920s, following years of horrific civil war, the Soviet Union finally began taking shape, and finally began broadcasting its revolutionary message to the world. Slowly, the Soviets rebuilt links with Western partners.

But while Moscow had patched relations with plenty of Western governments, there was one domino left to fall. Years after Soviet rule first solidified, America still failed to offer formal recognition to the USSR, blocking trade, aid, and anything that could provide the Soviets with a financial lifeline.

From the outside, the Soviet government was hardly a likely client for Lee. Founded on little more than bloodshed and anti-capitalistic rhetoric—and already resorting to the kinds of tyrannical crimes that would define the regime for decades to come—the USSR stood, in many ways, as the antithesis of Lee's entire philosophy. Silencing critics, executing opponents, seizing any and all resources they could find: the communists rampaged, reformatting the Russian empire to their own ends.

But where others saw human rights atrocities, Lee saw an opening. Where others spied the contours of the looming Cold War developing, Lee spied a chance for partnership. All he would have to do is convince the American government to end its policy of Soviet nonrecognition—and open up new potential business streams for him in the process.

So Lee got to work. In the mid-1920s, he began running through his list of contacts, reaching out to try to convince them to back American recognition of the Soviet regime. Lee was "so greatly interested that he has sent out a series of 'confidential letters' to prominent men in relation to [Soviet recognition]," *The New York Times* wrote. Lee's reasons were clear, if generic. "Some day Russia has got to come back into the family of nations," Lee wrote, "and we ought to try to help her to get back rather than to force a great nation like Russia to come back on her knees and in sackcloth and ashes."[18]

As Lee saw it, even with the new communist regime in place, the

Soviet Union still presented potentially trillions of dollars in wealth. The type of government in the Kremlin hardly mattered. All that was important were the resources still buried, still untapped, still waiting to be extracted across the USSR. "The trade of Russia is of great importance to this country," Lee wrote.[19] (Lee decided not to mention the fact that Standard Oil, still overseen by the Rockefellers, had "large holdings" that the Soviets had confiscated, which they were hoping to get back.[20])

It was, in Lee's mind, a simple playbook. The communists might be a cantankerous, rowdy bunch, and their rhetoric might not be ideal. But keeping the Soviets at arm's length—keeping a policy of isolation, or of containment—was doomed to fail. "The policy of simply standing pat and doing nothing has been shown to be futile," Lee wrote. Bridges needed building. Trade needed expanding. The United States should recognize the Soviet regime—and Lee could be the man to help make it so. "The problem posed by the emergence of the Soviet Union could be solved, in other words, by the influence of capitalism . . . through the wise counsel of public relations," Lee thought.[21]

But Lee ran into headwinds. Some of those he contacted—businessmen, investors, former officials, and more—publicly blasted his efforts, highlighting the fact that the Soviet regime was publicly dedicated to overthrowing the American government. "For the United States to recognize Russia would be to publicly acknowledge that the avowed purpose of the present Russian Government to overthrow by force our system of government is consistent with international friendship," former secretary of state Elihu Root said. "Of course, that would be a lie. . . . If the American people lose their sincere belief in their own institutions and fall into a weak milk-and-water indifference toward the principles on which our Government is based, we are going to have very serious troubles ahead of us."[22]

American officials refused to budge. Despite Lee's efforts—and despite being "notoriously the most expensive as well as the most high-toned . . . 'public relations counsel' in active practice," as one newspaper described him—he couldn't move Washington.[23] Even with Lee's efforts, the United States still refused to recognize the Soviets.

But Lee wasn't done. And while his wheels spun, he had an idea.

Perhaps, instead of leaning on his contacts in the United States, he should visit Moscow itself—and see what services, and what advice, he could provide to the Soviets.

*   *   *

AFTER A MULTI-DAY excursion involving planes, trains, and boats—and including at least one emergency landing in a small Soviet city when his aircraft ran out of fuel—Lee finally arrived in Moscow in 1927. His rationale for visiting was simple. "My sole purpose, I stated, was to regard the situation 'objectively' . . . and that I wanted primarily to see people rather than things," Lee later wrote. "And above all I wanted to see responsible representatives of the Government or the Communist Party, who would be in a position to give me candidly their own personal interpretation of the philosophy underlying their regime."[24] If only he could talk with the communists steering the country, perhaps he could find a way to convince the American government that there was a way out of this standoff. If only he could convey the communists' messages, perhaps he could find a way around this precursor to the later Cold War.

He immediately began his tour of the new Soviet capital. As he wandered Moscow, he found a mix of the memorable and the bizarre, the inspiring and the ineffective. There was caviar and vodka, Rolls-Royces on roads that weren't even paved, "soft collars" and "silk stockings" and, unexpectedly, jazz, which "had invaded the Bolshevik capital." Moscow was, naturally, drenched in memorials and paeans to the recent revolution, with statues and placards everywhere singing the communists' praises. But there was, as he found, a surprising orderliness, at least in certain areas. "The visitor to Russia today is both surprised and delighted with the signs of almost complete absence of vandalism in relation to all matters of art," Lee later recalled. "I was struck with the large number of groups of children visiting these museums, and the minute care with which the significance of all of these things [were] explained to them."[25]

But these weren't simply aimless strolls. At one point, Soviet authorities invited Lee into a secret, barricaded vault, where the new government held the tsarist jewelry collection. There, on the table in front of him, splayed one of the most breathtaking jewelry holdings on the planet, now under communist lock and key. Lee wasn't alone; he was surrounded by a number of Soviet guards milling about, "dressed in overalls." As his guards watched, Lee picked up and ogled the tsarist crown, the royal scepter, the famed orb of Catherine the Great, and plenty more. The collection was of "such number and such magnificence as to make one lose all sense of the fact that jewels are rare," he remembered.[26]

It was clear that the Soviets didn't allow just anyone to handle the deposed tsar's collection, worth hundreds of millions of dollars, if not more. As Lee said, "So rarely are these jewels displayed that the fact that my party was permitted to see them evidently got spread abroad in the neighborhood of the building where the jewels are kept, and when we emerged a little crowd had gathered." Lee was, in fact, one of the few foreigners to ever see the jewels during the entire Soviet reign.[27]

But then, given the role Lee had already played in the United States and elsewhere, perhaps inviting him into the most secluded of Soviet spaces shouldn't have been surprising. Because the Soviets recognized who Lee was, and what he could provide. And they made sure that all doors would remain open for him in Moscow. Unlike other Americans who visited the Soviet Union, Lee ran into no difficulties, no obstacles, and no trouble while in the Soviet capital. Moscow could be his playground in a way it was to almost no other American of the era.

And that extended far beyond the vault of tsarist jewels. While in Moscow, Lee soaked in opera and ballet performances (the latter of which saw him sit next to the widow of famed Russian writer Anton Chekhov). He visited the office of one of the primary Soviet propaganda programs, listening in "to news being given out from a station in London." He met directly with Soviet financial advisors, whose "very existence," Lee proclaimed, "offers hope for the future."[28]

And then there were the political leaders. Over the course of just ten days in Moscow, Lee visited with nearly every major Bolshevik figure still in the country (and not yet killed). He met with Alexei Rykov, the nominal head of the Soviet Union, who, as Lee recounted, "asserted his extreme eagerness to develop an understanding with the Government of the United States." He met with Soviet trade union chief Mikhail

Tomsky, who said the Soviet Union was "quite prepared to negotiate with anyone who wants to do business in Russia."[29]

Somehow, Lee earned sit-downs with all the major Soviet voices and forces trying to construct this communist superpower. The only one Lee missed out on was, somewhat ironically, Joseph Stalin, who failed to show at his appointment with Lee for reasons that remain unclear. Even though the two failed to connect, Lee nonetheless viewed the rising Soviet leader as a man of "extraordinary cleverness," a figure who "works silently and away from the public gaze." In Lee's eye, Stalin "represents a moderating or compromising policy"—one whose "judgment upon policies is regarded as sound."[30] (Shortly after Lee departed Moscow, Stalin would directly oversee famines that killed millions of Ukrainians and Kazakhs, followed by a series of high-profile show trials that culminated with the signing of a military pact with Nazi Germany.)

The reason Soviet officials greeted Lee with such aplomb was simple. The Soviet Union was, for all intents and purposes, broke, and required any aid and trade it could find—even if it meant turning to the dastardly West. And Lee appeared as a figure who could help open those doors. He was, in Soviet eyes, a man who could solve the riddle of American recognition and help rescue the listing Soviet regime.

And they weren't wrong. When Lee returned to the States, he immediately published a 206-page treatise outlining why the Soviet experiment wasn't one to be feared but one worth supporting, even embracing. It was, at worst, a government that was simply misunderstood. As Lee wrote, "The real spirit of [Vladimir] Lenin was common sense—and common sense is getting hold of the Russian people."[31] (Lee's book wasn't his only means of helping the Soviets; he also advised his contacts in Moscow to launch an advertising campaign in the U.S. press, with advertisements "signed by Stalin himself.")[32]

Lee's book, which he immediately sent around to his contacts, had one clear thesis: the only thing that could repair the breach with the Soviet Union was for America to finally recognize the regime. Isolation would never work. Nor would containment. Opening our doors, and our pocketbooks, to the Soviets would be the most effective means of overcoming this impasse. Plus, if Western companies could make a bit of profit along the way, who were we to complain?

It was one long, dry exercise in regurgitating Soviet propaganda—in whitewashing a regime set to unspool decades of horrors across Europe and Asia alike. Some of Lee's lies were fairly obvious, such as the claim that Stalin was "doing his utmost . . . to encourage capitalistic enterprise." But some verged on the outright odious. Lee wrote, for instance, that "no innocent person need any longer have any fear" of the Soviet secret police, adding that the "right to vote [in the USSR] is very broad." In Lee's writings, the Soviet Union wasn't a rising totalitarian system. Rather, it was one that just needed a bit of help—one that needed a bit of American capital, with Lee acting as a middleman between the two countries. Further, should Americans fail in attracting the Soviets, that might just "drive Russia toward Asia."[33] And no one would want that, would they?

Page after page, chapter after chapter, Lee sang the Soviets' praises. Moscow wasn't perfect, sure—but, then, neither was the United States. As Lee explained to Leon Trotsky, he penned the book "in the hope of improving . . . the relationships not only between the United States and Russia but also between the rest of the World and the Russian people."[34]

* * *

THE INITIAL RESPONSE on the American side was clear, combining resounding fury with outrage that Lee would even attempt to spin the Soviets for American audiences. And not just because of all the crimes for which the regime was already responsible—but also because of who Lee was. "In instinct, doctrine, career, [Lee] is the ultimate, the absolute capitalist of them all," an editor at *Business Week* wrote. "Sophisticated managing editors frankly do not believe a word of [his book]. It is impossible that Ivy Lee, aide to millionaires and millionairedom, should be serious in all this stuff about Soviet Russia."[35]

Nor was the book well received on other grounds. One reviewer from the University of Chicago dubbed it a "superficial" read, noting that "as a travel narrative the book is without merit. As a contribution to current knowledge about Russia, it is of little value to the social scientist and in many respects misleading to the layman."[36]

And then there were questions: Who paid for Lee's travels? Who paid for this book? Who was actually funding Lee's pro-Soviet work?

"To many it seemed that Russia had simply hired Ivy Lee as its propagandist," Lee's 1966 biographer, Ray Hiebert, wrote.[37] When the editor
in chief of the *Wall Street Journal* asked Lee directly who bankrolled
his pro-Soviet writings, Lee responded with characteristic cant. "I
am doing it for the same reason that you are raising Guernsey cows,"
Lee said. "That's your hobby. Some people collect first editions, some
people collect postage stamps, I collect information about Russia.
That is the whole of my relationship to the problem."[38]

Lee long denied, both publicly and privately, that he ever received
a cent from the Soviet regime. And to be fair, there's no evidence the
Soviet Union actually paid Lee outright for his services. But then again,
if Lee was willing to do so for free—if he did so to create future business
opportunities for himself, opening doors for American clients to tap
into potential Soviet wealth—why would they?

Yet the rumors never died. And they began bleeding into Washington. Not long later, Rep. Hamilton Fish publicly claimed that Lee
was a "notorious propagandist for Soviet Russia."[39] Another official,
Rep. George Tinkham, assailed Lee for blasting related pro-Kremlin
material to members of Congress. Lee was now an "open [propagan-
dist] against the interests of the United States." He was a man with "no
country, no flag and no allegiance except the power of money, and what
money can compel or buy."[40] Documents even circled claiming to out-
line Lee's payment scheme with the Soviets (though they were eventually shown to be fabricated).

But Lee didn't slow his campaign for Soviet recognition. Embargoes
on the Soviet Union were "futile and unwise," Lee said in one lecture,
claiming that "there is no threat in industrial expansion in Russia."[41]
Over and over, Lee spun his arguments to new audiences, new officials,
and new policymakers. "Russia can never be beaten by fighting," he
added in early 1932. "The only thing for the [West] to do is to acknowledge the Soviet government and let in the sunlight."[42]

Slowly, Lee began changing minds. And by 1933, with a new administration sweeping through Washington, Lee finally found success.
Some sixteen years after the Bolsheviks first seized power, the United
States, at long last, recognized their rule—and normalized ties with a regime then in the midst of genocidal famines and unprecedented purges.

There was a broad range of factors that led to American recognition, from the domestic to the geopolitical. But one figure stood at the center: Lee. Thanks to his years-long campaign, Lee had helped turn the tide in the United States in favor of Soviet recognition, playing a "key role" in the process.[43]

And the Soviets understood that role. Immediately after the United States announced formal recognition, Soviet foreign minister Maxim Litvinov dictated a cable directly to Lee. As the telegram read, Litvinov wanted to "express . . . appreciation for the part [Lee] had played in paving the way for a closer Russian-American relationship."[44]

Lee was giddy. He'd succeeded where no American had prior. He had, for the first time, bridged the gap between Moscow and Washington—and set a playbook that future foreign lobbyists would follow when trying to convince America to recognize some of the most loathsome regimes on the planet.

But all that would come decades later. Because by 1933, the Soviets were no longer the only dictatorial government Lee wanted to help usher into Washington. He'd met with, and introduced Americans to, Mussolini. He'd opened doors for Moscow, singing the Soviets' praises to American audiences wherever he could. Now, there was just one regime left he wanted to help—one final piece of this totalitarian triumvirate, which had just taken power in Berlin, and which needed Lee's help.

4

Broken

What is fascism but colonialism at the very heart of traditionally colonialist countries?

—Frantz Fanon[1]

While Lee was opening new doors to Soviet authorities, he was also expanding his search for new international clients elsewhere. He had already helped Hungary, and had already built out links with officials in
places like Argentina. He'd begun working with governments in places
like Poland and Romania. His foreign client roll kept expanding and
expanding.

And then, shortly after he'd finished his tour of the Soviet Union, Lee
linked up with a corporate conglomerate in a place he'd never worked
before—and in a place that would, in just a few years, prove to be his
downfall: Germany.

Created in 1925, the German-based company I.G. Farben dominated the country's markets, expanding into everything from banks
and electricity to coal and iron. It was, in many ways, less a company
than a commercial empire unto itself. To outside observers, it proved
to be one of the few success stories in a nation still reeling from the
transformations following the First World War.

But as future historians and officials would discover, I.G. Farben
was also a—perhaps *the*—key commercial cog in the rise and reign
of the Nazi regime. "Qualified observers have argued that Germany
could not have [launched the Second World War] without I.G. Farben,"
historian Antony Sutton wrote. "Without [the company's] immense

productive facilities, its intense research, and vast international affiliations, Germany's prosecution of the war would have been unthinkable and impossible."[2] While I.G. Farben was nominally a distinct entity, it was in reality—like all supposedly independent companies in dictatorships, both then and now—a foot soldier for the regime, there to do the Nazis' bidding whenever asked.

Not that I.G. Farben's leadership ever had any concerns about what the Nazi regime might be doing. The company "not only directed its energies toward arming Germany, but concentrated on weakening her intended victims," Sutton continued. "The proof is overwhelming that I.G. Farben officials had full prior knowledge of Germany's plan for world conquest and of each specific aggressive act later undertaken." And this included not just shoring up Hitler's dictatorship but also expanding all of the tools available to Hitler's troops in their genocidal campaigns. With "ultimate control of the German war economy," I.G. Farben produced all of the poison gas Nazis employed in their death camps. As one commission later uncovered, the company's directors "had precise knowledge of the Nazi concentration camps and the use of I.G. chemicals." The Nazis may have authored the Holocaust, but I.G. Farben was the company that willingly provided the tools for the Nazis' genocide.[3]

But that was all in the future. In the late 1920s, I.G. Farben simply wanted to access more American markets, more American consumers, more American resources. So they reached out to Lee for his expertise—for his ability to navigate American markets and American politics alike.

Initially, Lee's work for I.G. Farben appeared straightforward: setting up meetings, monitoring media, highlighting the benefits of potential partnership with the company. Lee, as one historian said, was "chosen for the job of selling the I.G. Farben combine to America."[4] It was something Lee had been doing for other companies for decades. And, as with most campaigns Lee launched, it succeeded. I.G. Farben retained Lee year after year, even as Germany's democracy began crumbling, and as fascists in Berlin began tasting power.

And then, in 1934, something changed. I.G. Farben executives came to Lee with a new request. They told Lee they were "very much concerned over . . . antagonism toward Germany in the United States."[5] They "wanted advice as to how these relations could be improved."[6] It was no longer about commercial contracts or building an American consumer base. Now, it was about how Berlin could improve its image in the United States—and how Hitler, who'd risen to power in Berlin only a year prior, could gain new audiences in America.

I.G. Farben had long paid thousands for Lee's services. But now, with these new requests, they upped the ante. Offering the modern equivalent of half a million dollars, I.G. Farben practically begged Lee for his advice about how to help Hitler gain new fans in America. The financing would be organized by I.G. Farben chief Max Ilgner, a man who would later oversee the Nazis' war economy.

The company didn't have to ask twice. Lee gladly accepted the new terms. He could be the man to help the führer gain new acolytes—and spread his gospel of fascism to new audiences in America.

* * *

Lee quickly got to work. Traveling to Berlin in early 1934, he instructed his German partners on how to craft Nazi propaganda for American audiences. It was important, Lee advised, to avoid focusing on anti-Semitic rhetoric. Not that the Nazis should actually refrain from bigoted policies, Lee clarified—just that Americans wouldn't be convinced by the Nazis' anti-Semitic claims. As Lee later said, he "told them that they could never in the world get the American people reconciled to their treatment of the Jews—that that was just foreign to the American mentality and could never be justified in the American public opinion, and there was no use trying."[7] The Nazis, he advised, shouldn't waste their breath.

Instead, Lee suggested something different. He recommended that the Nazis should cultivate American press correspondents and use them as a springboard for spreading pro-Nazi messaging in the United States. "They should see to it that the authoritative utterances of responsible Germans interpreting German policy should be given the widest possible publicity . . . with the American correspondents," Lee said.[8] Put another way: the Nazis should target their messaging at American media, and let those journalists—supposedly neutral, supposedly authoritative—push Nazi messaging to American audiences.

One area in particular Lee focused on was Germany's rearmament. After the end of the First World War, Germany was effectively stripped of military hardware. By the early 1930s, though, Berlin had begun reconstructing its armed forces, thanks in large part to secret deals with the Soviet Union. And some of the details of that rearmament had begun spilling into the open, lifting the curtain on Germany's swelling military strength.

As Lee saw it, there was no use denying Germany's rearmament. Instead, the Nazi regime should simply state that such rearming was necessary—and was geared not toward conquest but toward beating back communism. Lee told his German interlocutors that the Nazis should issue a "frank statement" on "Hitler's storm troopers," declaring that they were "physically well-trained and disciplined, but not armed, not prepared for war, and organized only for the purpose of preventing for all time the return of the Communist peril." As Lee wrote in one memo, the Nazis have "repeatedly proclaimed [their] sincere desire for international peace."[9]

But Lee didn't work only in Berlin. Back in New York, Lee tasked one of his employees, a man named Burnham Carter, with monitoring all American media for mention of the Nazi regime. "Mr. Carter's job is to study American newspapers, magazines, and what they are saying about Germany," Lee later revealed. Carter would then "make extracts from them to point out the significance of them, to prepare memoranda setting forth the nature of them, to be transmitted to Germany."[10] Carter, in other words, would analyze what American newspapers were saying about the Nazis, and what parts of the Nazis' messaging needed improvement—all of which would help Lee "prepare suitable pro-Nazi replies."[11]

All of it—the topics to focus on, the slants and the sleights of hand to use—was exactly what I.G. Farben, and their Nazi patrons, wanted. I.G. Farben officials soon asked Lee if he would "repeat that advice" directly to Nazi officers. And Lee, once again, gladly agreed.[12]

Soon, Lee was having direct meetings with the highest ranks of the Nazi regime. He sat with Nazi propaganda chief Joseph Goebbels, walking him through how to fine-tune fascist messaging. Lee told Goebbels—a soon-to-be war criminal who would lead the efforts to spin the Nazis' murder of millions—that Hitler should cultivate foreign reporters "and learn how to get along with them." Lee also said that the Nazis should avoid expelling foreign correspondents, as "such an act would ruin the Nazi movement." And he further advised Goebbels on how to attract supporters in Austria, which the Nazis "would soon win . . . into the German Nazi orbit"—effectively launching the Nazi conquest of Europe.

Lee also began meeting with other Nazi higher-ups: with the foreign minister, with the economics minister, with the vice chancellor. Again and again, Lee huddled with the highest rungs of Nazi officials, detailing how they could, and should, win over foreign audiences, especially in America.

And then, in early 1934, Lee had a private meeting with the head of the regime himself. As Lee later said, he was "presented" to Hitler in Berlin for a face-to-face with the rising dictator. (Lee said his contacts at I.G. Farben were "anxious for me to meet" Hitler, in order "to size him up.")[13] And Lee quickly got an impression. He "asked [Hitler] some questions about his policies, told him I would like better to understand him if I could." The tyrant, in turn, "made quite a speech."[14] As Lee later remembered, Hitler pontificated for thirty minutes, with the American unable to get a word in. "You don't have interviews with people like that," Lee later said. "Mussolini was just the same. They make speeches and a visitor must listen."[15]

And yet, just as with Mussolini, Lee appeared to speak out of both sides of his mouth about the despot, depending on the audience. Buried in Lee's archives in New Jersey, an unsigned memo from July 1934 describes Hitler as "an industrious, honest and sincere hard-working individual."[16] Another memo written a day later claimed Hitler is "personally sincere," with an "unerring loyalty to his friends."[17] Hitler might appear publicly revolting, and his policies anathema to much of American democracy. But to Lee, he presented a promising partner, especially in private. As Lee later told Rockefeller, "Hitler would do much to restore German confidence, and . . . a confident and

successful Germany was a prerequisite to a healthy Western economy."[18] And it was that "confident and successful" Nazi regime that
Lee could help.

*   *   *

LEE'S FAITH IN the Nazi project shone through in his conversations
with others, including American officials. For instance, around the
same time that he met with Hitler, Lee sat down for lunch with William
Dodd, the American ambassador to Germany. The meal was the first
time the two had met. And according to Dodd, it didn't take long for
Lee to make an impression—especially as it pertained to Lee's outsized
sense of his accomplishments and talents. Lee "told stories of his fight
for [Soviet] recognition," the ambassador later wrote in his journal, and
was "disposed to claim credit" for the United States' decision.[19]

Yet Lee wasn't lunching with Dodd just to discuss his achievements
in Moscow. He wanted to chat about something else: German politics.
Specifically, Lee wanted to talk about the Nazis he'd begun liaising with.
As Dodd later wrote in his journal, Lee saw plenty of promise in the
Nazis' new political playbook. And just as he'd done in Rome with Mussolini, Lee wanted to see if he could help jump-start yet another fascist
movement, this time in Berlin—all while making a tidy fee along the
way. Lee "showed himself . . . a capitalist," Dodd wrote, as well as "an
advocate of Fascism."[20]

It's unclear if Lee laid out any specific Nazi-related projects for the
American ambassador; Dodd's journal remains vague about the details. But one week later Lee met with Dodd again (and once more did
"nearly all the talking"), cheerily detailing all of his recent meetings
with Nazi higher-ups. [21]

To Dodd, Lee appeared excited, almost buoyant, in describing his
recent sit-downs with Nazi officials, leaving the American ambassador nauseous. Lee, thought Dodd, was little more than a "big business
propagandist who has been trying . . . to sell the Nazi regime to the
American public." And Lee was clearly having an effect. A few weeks
later, after his own meeting with the Nazi propaganda chief, Dodd
wrote that "it was plain [Goebbels] was trying to apply the advice
which Ivy Lee urged."

As his meeting with the U.S. ambassador closed, Lee shared that he was returning to America, at least for a spell. He was "on his way back home," the ambassador concluded, "to continue his strange work."[22]

It was, for Lee, a well-earned break. By the middle of 1934, he was, in many ways, untouchable: an effective one-man diplomatic corps, traveling the world, helping despots and dictators crack open access to American audiences, assisting them in navigating the contours of American power and policy. All of it while Lee built his own personal fortunes in the process.

But unbeknownst to Lee, those final months in Berlin would be the apogee—or nadir, depending on your vantage—of his career. Because while Lee had transformed into a consort for Nazi officials, a new committee back in Washington had formed that, in an impressively short time, would uncover Lee's efforts and implode his entire legacy in spectacular fashion.

*   *   *

IN LATER DECADES, the House Un-American Activities Committee (HUAC) would become one of the most notorious congressional committees in U.S. history, launching the careers of American villains like Richard Nixon and wreaking devastating civil liberties violations in the process.

But when the committee first began, it had a far clearer purpose. Formed in 1934, the HUAC was tasked with investigating organizations and networks that might affect "internal and external" policies of the federal government. Specifically, the committee would begin investigating how new fascist and communist regimes—most especially those in Rome, Berlin, and Moscow—were targeting Americans and attempting to spread their messaging to audiences in the United States.

As the initial hearings made clear, there was a fertile field to examine. Led by a pair of Democrats, Massachusetts's John McCormack and New York's Samuel Dickstein, the committee swiftly uncovered numerous campaigns from rising totalitarians looking to sway American audiences. And these weren't just one-off propaganda efforts. Instead, these were programs that involved Americans of all stripes—and models that, in the early twenty-first century, would return with vigor.

For instance, the committee dove into Rome's extensive efforts to whitewash its fascist dictatorship. Reporting revealed that Mussolini had secretly funded Columbia University's Casa Italiana—then the largest Italian organization housed at any American university—in order to "carry on fascist propaganda among the Italian American population of New York."[23] And from Moscow, the committee heard testimony about the Kremlin's involvement with the American branch of the Communist Party, with one party official telling the HUAC that they directly followed the diktats of the Soviet-sponsored Communist International.

Over and over, the committee heard stories about how totalitarian regimes were increasingly targeting audiences in the United States, increasingly innovating new tactics to sway unsuspecting Americans. American legislators knew that fascist and communist movements kept gaining supporters across the country, and around the world— and now they were finding out how exactly these regimes expanded their foreign, and especially American, bases of support.

But it was with Nazi Germany that the hearing found the most success—and, in many ways, its longest legacy. As testimony from the HUAC hearings detailed, committee members heard tale after tale of pro-fascist movements across the United States working to spread pro-Hitler propaganda, pro-Berlin agitation, and pro-Nazi messaging. The Nazis had only been in power for a year when the HUAC first formed, and already they were successfully cultivating support across the United States.

The Nazis' campaigns were varied. One plot involved a German Nazi member infiltrating the United States, posing as a clergyman, and rising to the leadership ranks of an American group dubbed the "Friends of New Germany." One estimate later placed the group's total membership around fifteen thousand people, forming a leading part of the "American section of the Nazi movement"—all of it secretly led by a member of the actual Nazi Party.[24]

Another group, the German-American Bund—which professed "the biggest respect for Hitler"—operated pro-Nazi "summer camps" across America. ("For some reason, the Bund seems to find that New Jersey offers a peculiarly congenial climate for its activities," the committee found.) And as the committee uncovered, much of the funding for these camps came directly via Nazi officials. These Nazis, posing as simple diplomats, "violated the pledge and proprieties of diplomatic status and engaged in vicious and un-American propaganda activities, paying for it in cash, in the hope that it could not be traced," the committee detailed.[25]

The picture the HUAC painted was bleak. As they unearthed, regime after regime had successfully built out American audiences, masking their financing in the process. Shortly after launching the HUAC, congressional officials had already interrogated numerous Americans who "represent[ed] foreign governments or foreign political groups"—all for the purpose of "influenc[ing] the external and internal policies" of the United States, and all without other Americans being aware. The evidence, as U.S. officials described it, was "incontrovertible."[26]

But there was one figure the committee couldn't quite get a handle on. A figure who, as the committee heard, might be serving at the behest of the Nazi dictatorship in Berlin, but who denied under oath ever pushing anything anti-American—or even admitted working on behalf of foreign regimes in the first place.

*　*　*

WHEN LEE WAS called before the HUAC on May 19, 1934, he appeared unruffled. Not that that was any different from his other public appearances; for years, these kinds of hearings and committees had been routine affairs for Lee. He'd been subjected to hearings in the past, about his clients, about their controversies. This would be, as Lee saw it, just another perfunctory meeting, something to keep him busy in between trips to Berlin.

And to be sure, that's how the hearing initially started. Seated in front of a range of American legislators, all tasked with "conducting an investigation of the extent, character, and objects of Nazi propaganda activities in the U.S.," the conversation was initially cordial.[27] Lee was, in many ways, a known quantity, his career and prominence predating the tenures of many of the members of the committee. Still, his foreign work remained, for many, a mystery. And it was that foreign work—especially for a Nazi regime clearly interested in swaying American audiences—that the committee wanted to discuss.

So the committee began. McCormack opened the questioning, asking Lee to detail his business structures and services provided. (As we saw in the prologue, Lee believed his work was "very difficult to describe.") But McCormack then turned to Lee's German work. And it didn't take long for Lee to start trying to slip past the questions—to obfuscate, and throw up smokescreens about what, precisely, he was doing in Berlin.

When McCormack asked if Lee worked directly for the Nazis, Lee demurred, saying, "I have no contract with the German government."[28] He was technically right; just as with many future foreign lobbyists, Lee never signed a contract directly with the regime, but with a company that was an effective regime proxy. But McCormack and his colleagues didn't stop there. Soon, the legislators began probing for information about I.G. Farben, about Lee's specific role for the conglomerate, and about the company's ties with Nazi officials. Question after question, the officials tried to get a clear answer from Lee: What did he do for I.G. Farben? What kind of links did I.G. Farben have with the Nazis? And why, if Lee didn't have any formal contract with the German government, did he keep turning up time and again to provide his advice and efforts for the highest rungs of the Nazi regime?

Lee ducked and dodged. He claimed he traveled to Germany solely to discuss I.G. Farben's "world relationships"—as if I.G. Farben was a company simply interested in global affairs, and not some kind of cutout between Lee and the Nazis. He claimed he couldn't produce a written contract, as all of his arrangements had been "verbal." He maintained that his links with I.G. Farben were no different than his "advisory relations with a great many American corporations," pitching the company as simply the German equivalent of Ford or General Electric.[29]

But the legislators kept circling. Lee tried to put on his best front, especially as his questioners got closer and closer to finally uncovering the details of his pro-Nazi efforts. "I am very anxious to cooperate with you, because I realize the delicacy of this situation and have realized it all the time," Lee purred at one point. He denied that he'd ever participated in any Nazi propaganda schemes, saying he told his German partners it was "very bad business." (At one point, he told the committee that the only document he'd ever produced for anyone in Germany was help with a pamphlet about driving on German roads.)[30]

Soon, though, the committee noticed openings in Lee's defense. Dickstein got Lee to admit that his firm had created memos describing American media coverage of the Nazis, monitoring for what kinds of fascistic messaging worked best. He also got Lee to admit that his German partners had sent him a wide range of anti-Semitic literature—though Lee downplayed its significance. "It would be very inaccurate, Mr. Dickstein, to say that there is very much of that," Lee proclaimed.[31]

But when Dickstein turned back to who, exactly, Lee worked for—and who paid for his services—Lee evaded yet again. "I have no relation with the German government," Lee declared over and over, each denial less and less believable than the previous.[32]

At a certain point, frustration began creeping into the committee's questions. Dickstein tried a different tack. Lee admitted that he'd worked with I.G. Farben for years; had anything changed since the rise of Hitler? "Had [I.G. Farben] given you any money before Hitler came into power for any kind of work of the nature you're now doing?" Dickstein asked.[33]

Suddenly, Lee was stuck. "Not for the advisory services in connection with political relationships," Lee mumbled. "No, sir."[34]

There was the inch the committee needed. If Lee wouldn't provide the answers they sought, maybe the money could speak for itself. Another committee member, Georgia senator Thomas Hardwick, asked Lee to describe his payment schemes with I.G. Farben—and, especially, how much Lee started making after Hitler's rise. When Lee admitted that his income had exploded since Hitler grabbed power, Hardwick responded, "Did it not occur to you that such an enormous increase in compensation . . . was rather unusual, [or] that as a corporation they could very ill afford to pay that much money for that kind of service if they had only an indirect interest?"[35]

Lee blanched. "Well, Senator, that is not the largest contract I have had of an advisory character, by any means," he bumbled. Hardwick

pressed on. I.G. Farben "gave you a compensation more than 800 percent larger than the compensation justified previously; did it occur to
you that they were acting at least indirectly" on behalf of the Nazis?
"No, sir," Lee fumbled in response.[36]

Suddenly, the scheme came into focus. Lee still technically worked
for I.G. Farben—but since Hitler's rise, Lee's income had seen an as-
tronomical leap, all predicated solely on improving Germany's image
abroad. And as congressional officials made clear, whatever independence I.G. Farben maintained was long gone. "Since Hitler came into
power the German government has assumed a pretty thorough control
of private business in Germany, has it not?" Hardwick asked. When Lee
agreed, Hardwick responded, "It did not occur to you for that reason
that they might be acting [on] behalf of the government?" Lee again
claimed ignorance, saying he simply had no idea that I.G. Farben might
be a mere extension of Hitler's regime.[37]

Few on the committee, though, believed Lee at this point. The idea
that a man who'd advised tycoons and politicos, who'd been for years a
fixture of the American industrial establishment and international set
could simply not know what was happening in Berlin was preposterous,
almost offensive. The notion that Lee was some kind of political naïf—
someone who'd *accidentally* ended up advising the Nazis, through no
fault of his own—beggared belief. As one historian later said, Lee was
peddling claims of "naivete to the point of absurdity."[38]

And the committee kept pushing. They forced Lee to admit he'd
met directly with Goebbels, and then directly with Hitler, and that he'd
advised his German partners about how to spin the Nazis' rearmament
program. The conclusion was clear: I.G. Farben was little more than a
front for the Nazis—and Lee had taken staggering amounts of money
to refine Nazi messaging, propaganda, and policies.

Hours passed, and the answers kept spilling out, Lee's defenses collapsing in the process. When the committee finally felt they had a full
picture—of what Lee had done, of how much he had been paid, and
who he was, in reality, working for—they let him go, and moved on to
the next witness in their hearings.

It was the last time Lee would be in Washington—and the last time
legislators would see him alive.

* * *

WHEN LEE LEFT Washington that May, he knew the hearing hadn't gone well. But he didn't seem to be overly worried, as he was under the impression his testimony would be kept secret. The committee was simply looking for insight, for information about what the Nazis were doing. As American officials told him, they didn't see any reason to reveal Lee's comments—at least not yet.

And that, for Lee, was for the best—and not just in terms of his career. For some time, Lee had felt his work catching up with him. New aches, new pains, the wear and tear of working without respite for decades: it had all piled up, without any breaks. A few weeks after the hearing, Lee told his friends he was traveling to the German resort of Baden for its healing spas. The trip could, as Lee wanted, also double as a chance to check in with the German partners he'd described in his hearings.

But before Lee could make it to the spas, Hitler unleashed the spasm of violence that many had long feared. Known as the Night of the Long Knives, Hitler sicced his thugs on his remaining political opponents. Hundreds died, with hundreds more injured. Germans across the country—and regime opponents around the world—realized that the concerns about the Nazis, even as early as 1934, were absolutely warranted. From that point on, there was nothing left to stop Hitler's march, wherever it took him.

It's unclear how Lee reacted to the news. His cloying biographer, Ray Hiebert, wrote that Lee was "fully aware of the disastrous turn of events in Germany."[39] But there's no indication the massacres gave Lee any pause about working with the regime, or that any of Hitler's actions caused Lee to back out of his arrangements with I.G. Farben.

Things in Washington, though, had changed. Shortly after the slaughter in Germany, the HUAC decided to release testimony from their hearings into pro-Nazi efforts in the United States. And among the hundreds of documents released was page after page of testimony from Lee, all dedicated to spinning the fact that he'd become an effective proxy for a regime that was just starting its bloodletting.

It didn't take long for American media to realize what the testimony contained. There was Lee meeting with Hitler, advising Goebbels, taking breathtaking sums from a pro-Nazi conglomerate. There was Lee—Poison Ivy, as American media still remembered him—taking his talents to a monstrous regime, and then trying to claim he had no idea the Nazis would be using his tactics and advice.

And the American media immediately responded. Headlines across the country were unified: LEE GIVES ADVICE TO THE NAZIS, LEE'S FIRM REVEALED AS REICH'S PRESS ADVISOR, LEE EXPOSED AS HITLER PRESS AGENT.[40] Lee's testimony sprawled across the front page of *The New York Times,* blaring out the details of how he "drafted statements to guide [Hitler's] Reich," working directly as an "adviser to the Nazis."[41]

The conclusion was, to everyone reading the testimony, inescapable. As *Time* summed up, the committee "got the impression that Mr. Lee might just as well have been retained by [Hitler] himself."[42] The impact was immediate—and devastating. "How ironic it is that [Lee] managed to give an honest, genuine, and convincing performance on behalf of his clients and failed for himself," the president of Chase Bank said about the testimony. "Maybe it's the old dictum that a lawyer should not conduct his own defense."[43] Or as one scholar later wrote about the revelations, "Lee had served as the hidden propagandist in concert with the Reich; he was the unknown source, that root of propaganda evil that he had warned against."[44]

Still in Germany, Lee continued to defend himself. From his perspective, he had "done nothing wrong." A client had called, and he'd provided the best advice and the best services that he could. And he wouldn't stop. That August, *Time* reported that Lee continued to work for I.G. Farben—and, by proxy, for the Nazis. As he said during his visit to Germany, he "found that everything was quiet and peaceful."[45] He never commented on Hitler's sprint toward dictatorship, or on the fact that his work had helped make the German fascists' rise easier.

But Lee also had other things on his mind at that point. The public relations guru, whose headaches never seemed to abate, had recently learned he had an inoperable brain tumor. The stopover in Baden would soothe his pains, but it wouldn't save his life. Even as he continued working, the physical toll kept piling up. And as his reputation collapsed, so, too, did his body.

And few saw that collapse more clearly than Dodd, the American ambassador. Amidst the revelations about his Nazi work, Lee returned to Berlin and called on the ambassador once more. When they met, Dodd was shocked by Lee's transformation. Instead of the confident, striding inventor of public relations, Lee now slumped, looking wan and worn. Dodd confronted an "old man," he wrote, who "looked broken."[46]

But if Dodd was surprised by Lee's shattered appearance, he wasn't surprised by the cause. As Dodd well knew, Lee's pro-fascist efforts were now an open book that all of America was reading. "He has made his millions the last twenty years," Dodd wrote, "and now the world knows how it was done."[47]

The conversation between the two didn't last long; Lee had only so much stamina, and Dodd had even less interest. As they parted, Lee asked Dodd if he would write something favorable to the American secretary of state on his behalf.

Dodd pondered for a moment, and shook his head. He wouldn't help this "advocate of Fascism," especially now that his motives were out in the open. Lee's story was "only another of the thousands of cases where love of money ruins men's lives," Dodd later observed in his journal. "I cannot say a commendatory word about him to the State Department."[48]

So Lee slouched off, his reputation, his body, and any prospects now in tatters. The world would spin on, and Lee's friends and clients in Rome and Moscow and Berlin would spin that world toward a war in which tens of millions would die. But Lee would not be around to see it. That November, wracked with pain, Lee died. He was only fifty-seven.

* * *

LEE'S LEGACY LIVED on—but not in a way he would have ever expected. Just over a decade later, with Europe and East Asia lying in ruins, the Nuremberg trials attempted to identify the parties responsible for the horrors of the Second World War. Lee never featured prominently in the trials, but he did receive specific mention for advising his German partners about the "'line' to follow to influence public opinion in the United States."[49] There, aside names like Hitler and Goebbels and so many other Nazi monsters, once again stood Lee.

Back in the United States, congressional officials tried to sort through the findings about how the Nazis had targeted American populations, had attempted to influence and upend American policy on Germany's march toward genocide. They brainstormed new policies, and began cobbling together new legislation. They settled on one solution in particular. It would be something called the Foreign Agents Registration Act. And it would, these American officials hoped, prevent the rise of another figure like Lee—and perhaps even help prevent the rise of another regime like the ones in Moscow and Rome and Berlin.

It was a nice thought, and an elegant solution to a problem they thought they'd solved.

But they would be wrong.

PART II

MONSTERS

I asked those nearest, "What have you come for?"
They answered, "We have come to devour you!"
"Oh," I said, "let me help you first."

—Aiṅanwa't[1]

5

Secret Handshake

What's the harm of a difference over the Constitution among
friends!

—Frederick Merk[1]

By the time Lee's work on behalf of the Nazis spilled out, Washington
had already begun moving toward something unheard of: regulating
lobbyists.

After decades of Americans exercising their right to petition however they pleased—and on behalf of whichever clients they wanted—
American policymakers realized that the time had come for greater
oversight. In 1928, the Senate passed a bill that would have required all
lobbyists to register with Congress (though that proposal later died in
the House).[2] A few years later, after investigators discovered lobbyists
for public utility companies had secretly steered a pro-industry propaganda campaign, legislation finally began moving in both houses of
Congress. Bit by bit, industry by industry, Congress started slapping
new transparency requirements on lobbyists, revealing what they were
actually up to. No "sordid or powerful group," one senator said, would
any longer be allowed to hide "behind a mask concealing the identity
of that group."[3]

It was in this increasingly regulatory atmosphere that Lee sat down
for his hearing and revealed all he'd done on behalf of Germany. Once
the furor died down, and once Americans fully digested what Lee
had been doing for the Nazis, the legislative response was unsurprising. Regulations had already begun tightening up domestic lobbying

industries. Now, U.S. officials would apply the same solution to those
with foreign clients, hoping to prevent another figure like Lee from
operating in the shadows.

Following recommendations from the HUAC, legislators introduced
a new bill aimed at doing just that. Dubbed the Foreign Agents Registration Act (FARA), the bill would force the reveal of anyone who was
"engaged in this country by foreign agencies to spread doctrines alien to
our democratic form of government, or propaganda for the purpose of
influencing American public opinion on a political question."[4] Anyone
who was lobbying, anyone who was propagandizing—any Americans
who were secretly working on the dole of foreign governments, in order to push policies those regimes wanted to see enacted—would finally
be forced to reveal themselves. They'd have to disclose their activities.
They'd have to disclose their foreign patrons. They'd have to reveal—to
legislators and to the public alike—just how much they were being paid
along the way. And they would thereafter be known, as the bill dubbed
them, as foreign agents.

The bill wended its way through Congress, bolstered by more evidence coming out on how Nazis were targeting American policymakers. After fits and starts, trying to fine-tune the final language, Congress
passed the legislation over to the White House in 1938, where President
Franklin D. Roosevelt signed it. FARA was now law.

It was, in many ways, the single-most progressive piece of lobbying
regulation the country had ever seen—and would see for decades to
come. And it would also eventually become the most disappointing—
and most frustrating, and most neglected—piece of lobbying restrictions the nation had ever known.

* * *

INITIALLY, FARA WAS geared toward one thing alone: propaganda.
FARA "was conceptualized as a propaganda statute," Tarun Krishnakumar, the foreign lobbying scholar, told me.[5] And that comes through
clearly from the rhetoric of the era. "We believe that the spotlight of piti-
less publicity will serve as a deterrent to the spread of pernicious propaganda," Rep. Emanuel Celler, one of FARA's earliest supporters, said.[6]

To combat such propaganda, legislators loaded FARA with all kinds of disclosure requirements. Any American receiving funds from foreign sources to propagandize Americans, regardless of the regime, would have to disclose their activities to the State Department, which would oversee FARA compliance. This included all the efforts, payments, and publications related to any and all foreign lobbying work. Every "essential detail," as the State Department said, would have to be included in these disclosures, from contracts signed to meetings held to campaigns both previous and proposed.[7] From there, the State Department would organize and disclose that information to Congress—and to the American people.

The solution was, all things considered, a deftly creative one.[8] Rather than banning such foreign propaganda efforts outright, FARA allowed Americans to continue working at the behest of foreign patrons if they so pleased. The only thing the bill required was a rundown of what that work actually entailed—and who was footing the bill. "[FARA's] basic strategy was not to limit or deter speech but to provide additional information 'so that hearers and readers may not be deceived by the belief that the information comes from a disinterested source,'" one later examination found. "[FARA] would rob subversives of secrecy, their most potent weapon."[9] As legislators figured, if Americans knew who was really behind these campaigns—if they knew which regimes were the secret paymasters—they could make informed judgments themselves. And since the work was still permitted, there were no concerns about abridging those sacrosanct First Amendment rights.

This was all fantastic in theory. What Americans wouldn't want to know more about the sources of foreign propaganda? What Americans wouldn't want more insight into which of their fellow nationals were being secretly paid by the Nazis, or by the Soviets, or by any of the other totalitarians rising around the world?

At first, FARA, which came with a five-year statute of limitations, seemed to fulfill its promise—not least because those who ignored the law could face years in prison. Almost immediately after its passage, the United States launched its first FARA-related case against a trio of New Yorkers, all of whom posed as independent booksellers—but all of whom also moonlighted for Moscow. Charged with being paid to spread pro-Soviet propaganda, a court found all three guilty of failing to register their work with FARA.[10] ("After listening to the trial it is my conclusion that the defendants were all so anxious to make money that they forgot their obligations to their country," the presiding judge said.[11]) Another pro-Soviet organization, posing as a tourist agency, was likewise found guilty of failing to register. So too was a former German literature professor at Columbia University, whose pro-isolationist group was caught taking Nazi funds.[12]

But not long after FARA passed, it was clear there was a problem with the legislation. Just because a law is enacted doesn't mean it will be effective, or that the issue in question will be solved. And for as much promise as FARA initially showed—and as the country trundled closer and closer to the Second World War—reality quickly crashed down around it. Despite those first few prosecutions, it was increasingly obvious that the bill was of "no practical importance in exposing the propaganda activities it was designed to expose." By the early 1940s, just a few years after being introduced, FARA had already become effectively a "dead letter."[13]

The sources of the bill's failure weren't mysterious. For one, even with FARA's passage, pro-Axis propaganda kept flooding American audiences. And since much of it was simply mailed out, circulating via the U.S. postal system, there was little way for American authorities to actually track its source—or uncover which Americans might be involved in spreading it in the mails.

More broadly, the officials at the State Department, tasked with overseeing and implementing FARA, were, according to one analysis, "amazingly inept."[14] To be fair, the department had not exactly lobbied to administer FARA; Congress had simply decided that, since the State Department oversaw foreign relations, it made the most sense for them to also take charge of FARA. But it quickly became apparent that the department, overstretched and understaffed as it was, was in no fit state to steer the new regulations. It didn't help that almost all State Department employees were located overseas, anyway. (How were Americans operating in the United States supposed to disclose their work to officials in places like Tokyo or Buenos Aires?)

To take just one data point, the State Department didn't even have resources to alphabetize the disclosures coming in, let alone track down any missing or suspect information. "If an agent of a foreign principal is kind enough to step up to the counter and register, he will do so," the assistant secretary of state later testified. "If he does not, there is not very much that we can do about it." State Department officials were, in other words, hamstrung.[15]

So in 1942—shortly after Pearl Harbor, and as pro-Axis propaganda kept saturating America—the federal government made a move. The United States shifted the responsibilities for administering FARA to the Justice Department—which, with its focus on prosecuting crimes in the United States, made far more sense than the State Department ever had.[16] Regulations were broadened even further, with American officials demanding copies of "nearly anything that a [registered foreign agent] distributed," and requiring that everything that a foreign agent published or produced be publicly labeled as "foreign propaganda."[17]

The reformed legislation also took on an even clearer national security bent, coming as it did in the middle of America's entry into the Second World War. The purpose of FARA, as the amended language read, is to "protect the national defense, internal security, and foreign relations of the United States." And it would do so "by requiring public disclosure by persons engaging in propaganda activities and other activities for or on behalf of foreign governments, foreign political parties, and other foreign principals." FARA, in other words, would now have a new role to play in American defense.[18]

The new reforms appeared to work. With far more manpower available from the Department of Justice, U.S. officials took aim at the foreign propaganda still swirling through the American postal system, with more resources to seize and track the sources of the pro-Axis propaganda. Even after the war, U.S. officials still stepped directly into American mails, using FARA to try to root out propaganda during the early Cold War. "During the 1950s and 1960s the government took full advantage of FARA's broad definition of political propaganda," one analysis found. U.S. officials "engaged in a large-scale program of seizure and destruction of publications mailed from foreign, and particularly Soviet-bloc, nations."[19] (Not that everything was exactly efficient; one part of the effort involved a non-Russian-speaking official being "handed a Russian-English dictionary and told to search a warehouse full of detained material for 'Communist propaganda.'"[20]) Even after President John F. Kennedy tried to end the mail-seizure program in 1961, Congress immediately reinstated it. This, they thought, was FARA's mandate: protect the mails, and protect the country.

Yet once more, it soon became clear that FARA was falling short of its promise. Despite a range of convictions (plus one accused foreign agent who fled the country after charges), legislators by the mid-1960s realized that FARA's writ was still, if anything, too narrow. The world—of superpowers and spreading revolution, of proxy wars and propaganda—was changing. And the scope of Americans secretly working on behalf of these foreign regimes was growing wider, far beyond anything the postal service offered.

Those in Washington knew it. American officials have "become aware of persistent efforts by numerous agents of foreign principals to influence the conduct of U.S. foreign and domestic policies using techniques outside the normal diplomatic channels," Senator William Fulbright said in 1965. But these weren't simply the propaganda campaigns of years past. By the mid-1960s, the techniques Fulbright and his colleagues outlined were largely novel—even if, to modern eyes, they appear oddly familiar. As Fulbright continued, "This trend has been accompanied by an upsurge in the hiring within this country of public relations men, economic advisers, lawyers, and consultants by foreign interests."[21]

Lawyers. Consultants. Advisors. Suddenly, a new crop of white-collar Americans had emerged to help their foreign patrons. But since that work was nominally beyond the scope of propaganda, these Americans had escaped FARA registration—and American voters and legislators alike had little idea what these lawyer- and consultant- and advisor-based campaigns actually involved. As a 1965 Senate report found, "The place of the old foreign agent has been taken by the lawyer-lobbyist and public relations counsel whose object is . . . to influence its policies to the satisfaction of his particular client."[22]

The world of foreign agents was opening up. But one thing was increasingly clear. Even if Americans still enjoyed First Amendment protections—including the right to speech and the right to petition—those rights were being increasingly abused by non-Americans. Most importantly: those rights, given their constitutional basis, obviously didn't extend to foreign regimes. "The Constitution, which protects the right of U.S. citizens to petition their Government, does not afford the same protection to the citizen who exercises that right at the direction of or in the interests of a foreign principal," the Senate report continued. "Not only does he no longer have the same protection of the Constitution, but he has also placed himself in a most sensitive position between his own governmental institutions and a foreign principal."[23]

Constitutional rights were sound, and remained sacrosanct. But they ended at America's borders. Americans couldn't simply sell these constitutional rights to the highest bidder abroad—and then become mouthpieces for foreign regimes and foreign autocrats who wanted to use and abuse those constitutional freedoms in the process.

* * *

IT WASN'T ESPECIALLY difficult to see why foreign governments had turned to this new crop of white-collar Americans. The United States, by this point, had become a superpower, and accessing its byzantine network of committees and governmental branches was a necessary component to influencing American policy. The sheer breadth of the United States was, for many foreign governments, bizarre. "Few foreigners understand the subtleties of our major governmental institutions, particularly the interplay between the executive and legislative branches in the formulation of national policy," the aforementioned Senate report continued. And that was even before factoring in the private sector, especially when it came to things like American media: "Also difficult for most to comprehend is the multiplicity and independent status of our news media which supply information to the public."[24]

Instead, foreign governments needed help. And these "lawyer-lobbyists and public relations counsels" could be their guide. These Americans could navigate the contours of the increasingly complex hallways of power and influence in the United States. And where decades before there had been only one Ivy Lee willing to take on foreign clients, by the middle of the Cold War, far more Americans appeared willing to sign up.

At least, that's what policymakers thought. But because FARA had focused so exclusively on propaganda alone—and not on the increasing scope of services available to these foreign regimes, primarily from the American white-collar sector—legislators really had no idea. Foreign lobbying once more seemed to be on the rise, but there was no way to actually track if that trend was true—or who was behind it.

So once more, American policymakers adjusted FARA. This time, they hoped, the changes would stick, and FARA would finally live up to its promise.

The most prominent change, which came in 1966, amended FARA "in the hope of changing its focus from propagandists to lobbyists," as a later examination described.[25] FARA's structure would be effectively the same. Those working on behalf of foreign regimes would have to submit documents to the Department of Justice, describing their work, payments received, and audiences targeted, all on behalf of their foreign patrons (now called "foreign principals").[26] Copies of contracts and communiqués would still have to be disclosed and made available for the American public to look through.[27]

But rather than center on propaganda, FARA would now focus on something called "political activities."[28] According to the new language, "political activities" were anything "that the person engaging in believes will, or that the person intends to, in any way influence any agency or official of the Government of the United States or any section of the public within the United States." Anything that involved shifting American policy, or that furthered the interests of a "foreign principal"—anything that involved, in the broadest sense, lobbying—would now be captured by FARA.[29]

For anyone sifting through this dry, bureaucratic language, the implications were clear. Anyone engaged in any kind of lobbying or influence-peddling on behalf of foreign regimes, companies, and politicians would now have to register their work. This included public relations counsels, publicity agents, and political consultants—as well as the "lawyer-lobbyists" suddenly sniffing around Washington. (One other, smaller change in these amendments banned political donations from foreign nationals—a topic we'll revisit in later chapters.)

In many ways, the shift was revolutionary—and one Lee would have recognized. No longer were American policymakers interested in propaganda for propaganda's sake. Now, as lobbying began coming into its own in the mid-twentieth century, legislators realized that foreign interests might be taking advantage. These shifts in 1966 set the blueprint for foreign lobbying regulations that, in many ways, are still with us. Suddenly lawyers, consultants, and others who weren't generally lumped in with lobbyists were on notice.

But with the hindsight of decades, the amendments also presented a pair of issues that would only grow more glaring in the years to come. The first centered on exemptions included in the new language. While the changes aimed FARA primarily at secretive lobbying efforts, officials decided to exempt certain individuals and organizations that fell nominally outside FARA's focus—and that, officials were sure, wouldn't need any further transparency.

For instance, foreign-owned news organizations would not have to register as foreign agents, so long as they produced "bona fide news or journalistic activities." Diplomats likewise wouldn't have to register, nor those engaged in "private and nonpolitical activities," including academics and scientists.[30]

Most notably—and perhaps ironically, given the new interest in "lawyer-lobbyists"—legislators provided an exemption for lawyers "acting in the course of legal representation."[31] So long as U.S. attorneys limited their work on behalf of foreign clients to the confines of the courtroom, they wouldn't have to register their work with the federal government. "Lawyers represent clients who may or may not be guilty, and when the evidence against them is clear, the clients almost always go to prison," one comparison later read. "Lobbyists for dictators are working for people whose crimes are generally documented beyond dispute, and when they succeed, they enhance their clients' grip on power and ability to continue oppressing their citizens and pillaging the national treasury. The only people at risk of going to jail are political dissidents opposing the dictator-clients."[32]

At the time, these exemptions all made a certain sense. Journalists doing their jobs, scholars and researchers interested in the pursuit of knowledge, lawyers offering their clients the best representation they could: all of these were anodyne, apolitical issues. All of them could, and should, be exempted from FARA registration. Because surely, no foreign regime would ever try to use these exemptions and loopholes to their advantage, right?

* * *

THE SECOND ISSUE with the new amendments was a familiar one: resourcing. While the new amendments expanded the punishments that prosecutors could pursue against those violating FARA—now including both civil and criminal penalties, as well as potential years-long imprisonment—they did nothing to actually beef up oversight of FARA registrations. That is, legislators told the Department of Justice to expand its FARA focus—but then didn't actually provide any expanded funding or personnel to follow through on it.

This issue wasn't immediately apparent. As with other FARA-related shifts, the amendments initially appeared to work. Shortly after the new regulations passed, the number of FARA registrants peaked, with an all-time high of 511 foreign agents registered with the Justice Department by early 1966.[33] With hundreds of Americans and firms now disclosing their foreign lobbying work, FARA finally appeared to be living up to its potential.

But some American officials wanted to be sure. After all, FARA's promise had floundered in years past. History could yet repeat itself.

So in 1974, the U.S. Government Accountability Office (GAO)—the federal body tasked with making sure legislation is actually working as planned—authorized a study of the effects of FARA's shift.[34] And what researchers found stunned them.

On paper, the amendments appeared successful, gathering a steady stream of registrants and disclosures. But just as in the first few decades after FARA was first enacted, there was a stark difference between rhetoric and reality. And one thing was eminently clear: the Department of Justice still didn't have the resources, funding, or personnel to do its job, at least when it came to enforcing FARA. "Since [the] enactment of the 1966 amendments, the Department has not adequately monitored foreign agents' activities nor adequately enforced the act and related regulations," the GAO report summarized.[35]

The reasons for this lack of enforcement were obvious. The new

FARA amendments had increased the workload for those at the DOJ—but hadn't bothered to provide any kind of commensurate rise in personnel or funding. If anything, the DOJ staff tasked with monitoring FARA compliance had actually *shrunk*. "During the last 10 years, staffing . . . has decreased despite significant increases in its administrative workload," the GAO report continued. Where there had once been more than a dozen Justice Department employees who could regularly monitor the FARA submissions, including eight different lawyers, the group had since contracted by nearly half. All of this, while the total submissions had grown by some 20 percent over just a decade.[36]

Thanks to this implosion in personnel, the DOJ "made little use of" its new powers to punish those who failed to disclose their foreign lobbying work. The GAO conclusion was blunt: "Staffing problems are the underlying cause for the Department's inability to monitor and enforce provisions of the act."[37] More paperwork, fewer people, and even less funding—it was a clear recipe for failure. The GAO called for a simple solution: increased funding to hire more DOJ personnel to monitor the rising flow of foreign agents. If the United States wanted to tackle foreign lobbying, it would need the people to actually do so.

The conclusions were straightforward, and hardly controversial. But the rest of the federal government apparently missed the memo. Distracted as the United States was with nuclear crises, rogue states, and rising terrorism targeting America and its allies around the world, unregistered foreign lobbyists didn't appear to be a priority for anyone in Washington.

Once again, FARA became more and more of a forgotten entity. A few years later, in 1980, the GAO published another study on FARA enforcement and came to almost the exact same conclusions as it had in years prior. Barely half of the FARA registrations contained all the necessary filings, with the "lawyer-lobbyist group . . . [having] one of the lowest levels of adequate reporting." If anything, things had gotten even worse. Over the course of just a few years, FARA-related investigations had plummeted, with barely any inspections by the end of the decade. (As the 1980 report read, "with all the [DOJ] lawyers tied up on court cases, the inspections stopped.") Even those few investigations hardly bore any fruit; in the two decades after the 1966 amendments, only two foreign lobbying criminal cases were pursued—neither of which were successful.[38]

Again, the GAO made the same recommendations. More money. More manpower. More enforcement, and more investigations. Otherwise, FARA would hardly be worth the paper it was written on.

And again, the federal government all but ignored the recommendations. Caught up in the Cold War, when the geopolitical camps were clear-cut, there appeared to be little worry about foreign lobbyists covertly working at the behest of foreign regimes, let alone concern about what threats they might pose. Everyone knew where everyone else fell. And the cycle—recommendations going nowhere, FARA slowly falling into oblivion—continued once more.

*   *   *

By 1990, the findings from yet another GAO report, completed just as the Cold War raced to a close, were completely predictable. Again, only half of the registered foreign agents had fully disclosed all their activities. More than half failed to meet even basic filing deadlines, with a significant chunk not even bothering to include all the required documents. Details of meetings, description of lobbying campaigns, overall payments from foreign regimes: time and again, these most important details weren't even disclosed. And Americans were completely in the dark as to what campaigns might be in the offing.

Not that the GAO—or anyone else—was surprised. As the 1990 report found, "the Department of Justice has not implemented the recommendations we made in our [previous] report." Even worse: the team tasked with overseeing FARA implementation kept shrinking. By the early 1990s, the number of lawyers helping oversee FARA enforcement was *half* what it had been decades prior.[39]

All of which is to say: by the end of the Cold War—fully a half-century after FARA promised to finally shine light on the foreign lobbying and foreign influence campaigns targeting Americans—FARA was little more than a shell of its former self. It was an afterthought. A backwater. Something the DOJ rarely considered, let alone enforced. Few were even familiar with FARA, or why successfully implementing and enforcing it would actually matter.

And maybe that's understandable. By the early 1990s, after all, it was clear that the United States had won the Cold War—and had done so without bothering to enforce something like FARA. There was no clear and present threat from ignoring these lobbying regulations; unlike the 1930s, it's not like there was another world war on the horizon. If you squint, you could almost see how this logic might work.

But it's also possible there was another reason for this lack of interest in any basic upkeep of FARA, or of monitoring foreign lobbying campaigns more broadly. Because as the Soviet Union headed toward disintegration, and as the United States headed toward hyperpower status, Americans and foreign regimes alike realized there were new opportunities ahead. New contracts to be signed. New partnerships to be formed. New governments, new regimes, new despots to whitewash—and new lobbying campaigns to launch, whether or not Americans were even aware.

Because even if Americans more broadly didn't realize it, lobbyists were increasingly becoming the key cogs in the new, emerging post–Cold War era—the "crucial conduit through which pariah regimes advance their interests in Washington," journalist Ken Silverstein once wrote. As one lobbyist of the era said, "It's like the secret handshake that gets you into the lodge."[40]

And there was one man who wanted to make sure as many despots and dictators as possible knew that secret handshake: Paul Manafort.

6

Wise Men

A dread of internal division bred a fear of foreign manipulation.
—Alan Taylor[1]

There are many things to know about Paul Manafort, and the impact that he's had on the direction of American foreign policy and American politics writ large. But one of the first things worth noting about him—and about how he became the man that the world's tyrants and despots, in America and elsewhere, turned to—is that he's not the first Manafort to bend the law to his own bidding, and to end up targeted by prosecutors as a result.

Manafort grew up in the mid-twentieth century in the small, blue-collar township of New Britain, Connecticut. Much like today, New Britain was an overlooked outpost, a small, insular town whose better days never seemed to arrive. Its demographics pointed directly to the waves of immigration in the late nineteenth and early twentieth centuries: Irish abutting Ukrainians, Italians rubbing shoulders with Poles, all of them looking to stake their place in a rising America.

Paul Manafort would later write that his grandfather arrived in the United States from Naples at the age of ten, speaking not a single word of English. But the family soon made its mark. As discovered by journalist Franklin Foer—the author of the only cover feature to ever run on Manafort, published in *The Atlantic* in 2018—the Manafort Brothers construction company had already become a "force" in the local community by the time Manafort was born in 1949. They had plenty of work; with the town dubbed "Hardware City," New Britain needed all the factory space and housing it could get. Soon, that economic heft translated to political power. In 1965, the voters of New Britain elected a new mayor: Manafort's father, Paul Manafort, Sr.[2]

Manafort Sr., as Foer wrote, "had the schmoozing gene, as well as an unmistakable fierceness." "It was like going to the bar with your grandfather," one former member of the New Britain city council recalled. "He knew almost everybody in town."[3] With the town's population peaking at nearly a hundred thousand residents, Manafort Sr.'s politicking skills were obvious for all to see. He was, as his supporters saw it, someone who "believed deeply in equality, fair treatment, and in making life in New Britain better for everyone."[4]

But it wasn't just glad-handing that launched Manafort Sr. to political power and kept him as one of the longest-serving mayors in New Britain's history. In 1981, following rumblings and rumors of organized crime infiltrating the city, prosecutors charged Manafort Sr. with committing perjury. The particular case centered on illicit gambling and police corruption, with Manafort Sr., according to prosecutors, specifically misleading investigators trying to crack local gambling rings. Nor was that all. A whistleblower further testified that, in addition to lying to investigators, Manafort Sr. also slid answers to cadets taking police exams, allowing them to cheat. (Manafort Sr. claimed the answers were simply "boning-up materials.")[5]

The charges in the case ultimately failed, partially due to statute of limitations restrictions, and Manafort Sr. never ended up convicted for either perjury or helping officers cheat on their police exams. But the allegations provided an opening for Manafort Sr.'s critics to flood in. As Foer wrote, the local *Hartford Courant* newspaper compiled a roll of allegations and abuses of office during Manafort Sr.'s tenure. The details ranged from self-dealing ("steering contracts to Manafort Brothers, whose stock he owned while mayor") to kickbacks and manipulating permitting processes. Added Foer, "Even before this scandal broke, a former mayor of New Britain blasted Manafort for behavior that 'violates the very essence of morality.'"[6]

By the end of his tenure, there was no doubt about Manafort Sr.'s guilt. But to Manafort Jr., who "idolized" his father, all of the kinds of dealings and connections that came with his father's political power seemed to be worth emulating.[7] And to Manafort Jr., that was a legacy worth carrying far beyond New Britain—and something he could build upon to change the fortunes of entire nations and eras in the process.

* * *

WHILE THE YOUNGER Manafort watched and learned from his father in New Britain, a pair of developments in Washington pointed to the loopholes, trends, and trajectories that he would later use to catapult himself to prominence, and eventually to prison.

There had been, as seen in the previous chapter, a declining interest in things like monitoring foreign lobbying networks. FARA came, and then faded, and then bounced back, and then receded once more. All of this even while lobbying in the mid-twentieth century was slowly coming into its own, as both a practice and industry unto itself.

Looking back from the twenty-first century, the lobbyists of mid-century America seem quaint, almost dowdy. They were hardly the modern, slick-coiffed and silk-suited figures that would dominate more recent decades. But their image—in their brown, boxy suits, preferring backroom conversations to anything splashy—also fit their ethos. Indeed, that image points to the initial distinction between lobbyists, then busy cornering politicians in congressional hallways, and the public relations industry, whose specialists were far more public-facing. (It was a distinction that, as we'll see in later chapters, eventually faded to the point of disappearance.)

At the time, Washington was still very much a closed, cosseted affair. Television had barely made inroads, and populism (at least at the national level) was a distant phenomenon. Lobbying during these middle decades of the twentieth century was a far more hushed undertaking, with lobbyists who whispered and suggested, nudged and prodded, and who understood the limits of their efforts. Lobbyists of this era were, as Foer later wrote, men (and they were all men) who weren't "grubby mercenaries" but who "transcended the transactional nature of their profession."[8]

It was, in many ways, a strangely elite profession: a conclave of "wise men" who were "elegant avatars of a permanent establishment."[9] There were no mercenaries or guns-for-hire, no showmen who preened for cameras. There were no pinstriped consultants looking to flip from one client to the next, all in the service of making more and more money. More often than not, lobbyists of the era didn't even see lobbying as their primary profession. "At that point in time, lobbying was really lawyers practicing through their connections," Manafort Jr. himself once wrote. "There were no political consulting firms, and no one was practicing lobbying in the strategic sense. They practiced it in the back-room sense, but under the cover of the prestige of a law firm."[10]

And it was all—again, to modern American eyes—strangely ineffi-cient. "To the extent that businesses did lobby in the 1950s and 1960s (typically through associations), they were clumsy and ineffective," political scientist Lee Drutman observed.[11]

Drutman cited a pair of "landmark" studies from the era that con-firmed his point. One found "lobbyists wielding little direct influence" in Congress, often failing to make even nominal impact on an issue. The other concluded that lobbying in Washington was "a sporadic, tinpot, and largely reactive activity." Lobbyists "were on the whole poorly financed, ill-managed, . . . and at best only marginally effective," the study's authors found. "When we look at the typical lobby, we find its opportunities to maneuver are sharply limited, its staff mediocre, and its typical problem not the influencing of Congressional votes but finding the clients and contributors to enable it to survive at all."[12]

None of the refinement or the prominence that would grow in years to come was present in midcentury America. Lobbying was hardly a dirty word, and wasn't yet a strategic profession catering to clients in America and abroad. It was, in many ways, something of an after-thought.

But that would soon change. Part of that, as we'll see, was due to figures like Manafort. But part of that was also due to foreign powers re-alizing just how open American elections were to potential interference.

*　*　*

FOR MOST AMERICANS, the revelations of the Kremlin's political inter-ference efforts during the 2016 elections (which will be detailed further in the second half of this book) came as a shock. The United States stood, in the eyes of many Americans, as something of an untouchable citadel: as a nation whose elections remained sacred, and immune to broader geopolitical realities. There might be too much money, there might be disputed results, there might be far more mudslinging than anyone would be comfortable with—but American elections were generally viewed as a purely domestic affair, insulated from any kinds of foreign forces.

And then 2016 happened. And that image—that mirage—quickly faded. Suddenly, American elections were just like any other: susceptible to foreign manipulation, with foreign actors tilting things as they wished. The revelations of Russia's interference efforts in the 2016 elections—just like the outcome of the election, landing Donald Trump the presidency—stunned many.

But 2016 was hardly the first time a foreign power had meddled in American politics. And it was hardly the first time the Kremlin had done so.

Since the earliest days of the American republic, in fact, foreign governments have sought to bend American politics and elections. And just as we saw in 2016, Americans have long been happy to assist in these efforts.

The earliest evidence of foreign manipulation of American elections stretches back to 1796, as George Washington wrapped up his second term as president. At the time, tensions continued to roil American relations with France, with Paris peeved at the United States' lack of support for its fellow revolutionaries. With a new administration set to take power in the United States, the French government "decided it needed to play an active role in choosing [Washington's] successor."[13] Just a few weeks before the election, French officials publicly announced that the election of Thomas Jefferson—instead of Washington's presumed heir, John Adams—would help avert war between the two countries. As such, Paris proclaimed, Americans should elect the Francophile Jefferson.

Jefferson's supporters reacted with glee, and responded in kind. Back in the United States, a group of pro-Jefferson campaign officials reached out to French counterparts to ask them to intervene more forcefully, and to help prevent the accession of the president's preferred successor.

None of the efforts worked. Adams narrowly won the election—and quickly unleashed his animus on France. During his inaugural address, Adams took direct aim at the notion of foreign electoral interference. If American election outcomes "can be obtained by foreign nations by flattery or menaces, by fraud or violence, by terror, intrigue, or venality, the Government may not be the choice of the American people, but of foreign nations," Adams intoned. "It may be foreign nations who govern us, and not we, the people, who govern ourselves."[14]

Adams's warnings had an effect. The next few rounds of elections saw surprisingly few efforts from foreign powers to meddle in American elections, caught up as they were in the Napoleonic Wars. In 1812, however, things boiled over once more. Riven by the War of 1812, America's partisan splits spilled outward. In the lead-up to the presidential election that year, high-ranking Federalist opponents of incumbent president James Madison once more looked abroad for help. This time, however, they turned to London. Senior Federalists "seem to have secretly tried to persuade the British government to intervene in their favor in some manner in the run-up to the 1812 election," historian Dov Levin wrote. "As the British Ambassador to the United States described it, the Federalists were 'despairing of overthrowing the [Madison] Administration in any other way.'"[15]

Again, though, these foreign flirtations failed. Madison remained in power (and continued the U.S. war against Britain for two more years). And as America began its march toward the Pacific, European powers shied away from further interference. Indeed, for over a century after the 1812 election, there is little record of foreign powers directly intervening in American elections.[16] There were the lobbying scandals mentioned earlier—involving Alaska, involving the Congo, involving the Nazis[17]— but nothing that centered specifically on American political outcomes.

And then, in the immediate aftermath of the Second World War, a new geopolitical rival strode to the stage. And decades before the 2016 vote, the Kremlin began meddling in American elections.

* * *

HENRY WALLACE HAD tasted the presidency. Serving as vice president under the ailing Franklin Roosevelt, the wan, waifish Wallace watched as the man leading America during the Second World War slowly faded as the war came to a close. But by the time Roosevelt, then in his fourth term as president, finally died, Wallace didn't ascend to the presidency. Instead, it was the man who'd replaced Wallace only a few months beforehand as vice president: Harry Truman.

That Wallace had come so close to the presidency, only to see (in his eyes) an incompetent haberdasher move into the White House instead, left a bitter taste in his mouth. So when Wallace, whom Truman kept on as commerce secretary, decided to run against Truman for the presidency in 1948, he opened the door for foreign powers who might be able to provide some electoral aid. And it wasn't difficult to see why one government in particular—the Kremlin—would want to help Wallace.

Broadly sympathetic to Soviet designs, Wallace's pro-Moscow views were an open secret. In fact, they long predated the 1948 election. A few years earlier, while still in Truman's cabinet, Wallace had reached out to the head of Soviet intelligence in the United States. Wallace was "basically telling him that the people who support him are fighting for Truman's soul, and that other people in the Truman administration are more anti-Soviet," Levin, the lone scholar to research foreign political interference in the United States, told me. "He basically asked, 'Come and help me—I'll be an agent of influence to make sure there will be better policies.' He basically believed that [Soviet dictator Joseph] Stalin and the Soviets had benign intentions."[18]

Wallace carried those beliefs into the 1948 campaign. As the head of the third-party Progressive Party, he made rapprochement with the Soviets his key plank. Before the election, Wallace thundered in New York's Madison Square Garden about the need to decrease tensions between Moscow and Washington. And he immediately got a public show of support from the totalitarian presiding over the Soviet Union: Stalin.

Stalin wrote a letter, published in newspapers across the United States, that claimed Wallace's call for easing tension was the "most important" political platform of the entire campaign. "As far as the government of the U.S.S.R. is concerned, we believe that the program of Wallace could be a good and fruitful foundation for such understanding and for the development of international cooperation."[19]

The Soviet tyrant's praise immediately reverberated. "It was a big commotion," Levin said. Stalin's letter "dominated news for a whole month, with some people hoping it would end the Cold War before it started."[20] It was a show of rhetorical support from the Kremlin, just a few months before a pivotal election. More importantly—and in a nod to the kinds of Kremlin interference set to come in later elections—Wallace wasn't surprised to receive Stalin's backing. Thanks to back channels between Wallace's supporters, members of the U.S. Communist Party, and Soviet partners, Stalin had alerted Wallace beforehand that the letter was in the works.

The missive didn't do much for Wallace's chances; his campaign failed to carry a single state, and he soon faded from the American political scene. But to Moscow, that didn't necessarily matter. The seeds of interfering in American elections were planted—a strategy that would be attempted time and again in decades to come.

* * *

IN 1960, WITH the Cold War in full bloom, Moscow tried again. The Soviet ambassador, Mikhail Menshikov, arranged a sit-down meeting with perennial Democratic candidate Adlai Stevenson. Stevenson was hardly a peacenik or a closet communist. But the Kremlin had an offer, and wanted to sound Stevenson out.

According to Stevenson's recollections, Menshikov began by reading a note dictated by Soviet premier Nikita Khrushchev. The Soviets, according to Khrushchev, were "concerned with the future, and that America has the right President"—and "because we know the ideas of Mr. Stevenson, we in our hearts all favor him." The note instructed Menshikov to ask Stevenson directly how the Kremlin could be of "assistance."[21]

As the Soviet ambassador kept reading, a pall fell over Stevenson, realizing what he was listening to. But Menshikov continued, floating ideas for how the Kremlin could aid Stevenson: "Could the Soviet press assist Mr. Stevenson's personal success? How? Should the press praise him, and, if so, for what? Should it criticize him, and, if so, for what? (We can always find many things to criticize Mr. Stevenson for because he has said many harsh and critical things about the Soviet Union and

Communism!) Mr. Stevenson will know best what would help him."
Khrushchev just needed Stevenson's assent, and the Kremlin could begin its help.[22]

Stevenson, according to his notes, blanched. He responded politely,
offering his thanks for "this expression of Khrushchev's confidence." But
the red line Menshikov had crossed was undeniable. "[I detailed my]
grave misgivings about the propriety or wisdom of any interference, direct or indirect, in the American election," Stevenson recalled. "I said
to him that even if I was a candidate I could not accept the assistance
proffered."[23]

Rejected by Stevenson, Moscow turned elsewhere. As Christopher
Andrew detailed in *The Sword and the Shield,* his seminal work detailing documents smuggled from former KGB archivist Vasili Mitrokhin,
the Kremlin especially feared the election of Republican nominee and
Cold War hawk Richard Nixon. And they were willing to go to any
length to stop Nixon's election—especially when it became clear that
Nixon would face off with Democratic nominee John F. Kennedy.[24]

As the 1960 election came closer, the KGB chief in Washington, Alexander Feklisov, received orders from the Kremlin to "propose diplomatic or propaganda initiatives, or any other measures, to facilitate
Kennedy's victory." As Feklisov added in his autobiography, his mission
centered on providing ideas "to Moscow that could help secure a Kennedy victory."[25]

The details on Feklisov's and Moscow's ideas remain scant, still
buried in the closed KGB archives. We do know that, as part of his
mission, Feklisov reached out directly to those surrounding Robert
Kennedy, JFK's lead campaign surrogate. But the Kremlin again got
nowhere; as Andrew wrote, Feklisov and his team's offers of help were
"politely rebuffed."[26] To both Stevenson and Kennedy, accepting aid
from Moscow was a bridge too far, regardless of the benefits.

* * *

NIXON, OF COURSE, lost that 1960 election. But when he stood again
eight years later, with Leonid Brezhnev now overseeing the Kremlin,
Moscow recognized another opportunity. As Anatoly Dobrynin, Moscow's ambassador in Washington, detailed in his 2001 memoir, the

Kremlin cooked up an idea to tilt the election once more in the Democrats' favor.

"Our leadership [in Moscow] was growing seriously concerned that [Nixon] might win the election," Dobrynin wrote. "As a result, the top Soviet leaders took an extraordinary step, unprecedented in the history of Soviet-American relations, by secretly offering [Democratic candidate Hubert] Humphrey any conceivable help in his election campaign—including financial aid."[27] Even after striking out in 1948 and 1960, Moscow would try to tilt the American electoral field once again.

Dobrynin led the effort, meeting directly with Humphrey himself over breakfast. As the conversation wound toward Humphrey's campaign finances, the candidate immediately figured out the point of the meeting—and immediately put a stop to it. "He knew at once what was going on," Dobrynin remembered. "He told me it was more than enough for him to have Moscow's good wishes which he highly appreciated. The matter was thus settled to our mutual relief, never to be discussed again."[28] Like the other candidates before him, Humphrey quickly swatted down the Kremlin's offer of financial assistance.

Amazingly, even with all of these disavowals, the Soviets weren't yet done trying to influence American elections. Shortly before the 1984 American elections, with a new premier in Yuri Andropov, Moscow began trying to oust Ronald Reagan from the White House. As Andrew, the KGB historian, writes, Andropov directed those overseeing American operations to "begin planning active measures to ensure Reagan's defeat." KGB agents were directed to "acquire contacts on the staffs of all possible presidential candidates and in both party headquarters." And it wasn't just limited to the United States; KGB residencies "outside the United States were told to report on the possibility of sending agents to take part in this operation. [KGB leadership] made it clear that any candidate, of either party, would be preferable to Reagan."[29]

As with the entreaties to the Kennedy campaign, the details of these 1984 operations remain murky. (One of the few particulars we know about, according to Andrew, involved KGB agents around the world being "ordered to popularize the slogan 'Reagan Means War!'") However, there's no evidence that any campaigns opposing Reagan ever took the Soviet bait. If anything, Andrew added, "Reagan's landslide victory in the 1984 election was striking evidence of the limitations of Soviet active measures within the United States."[30]

The Soviet Union, weighed down by a crumbling economy and fractured by anti-colonial separatist movements, didn't last much longer. But Moscow's presence in American elections, even during the 1990s, didn't fully disappear. In the lead-up to the 1992 American elections, a trio of Republican representatives came to President George H.W. Bush with an idea. Why not reach out to Russia directly for dirt on Bush's opponent, Bill Clinton, who had previously visited Moscow? Why not see what the Kremlin might be able to offer?

But like Stevenson, Kennedy, and Humphrey before him, Bush and his inner circle balked. "They wanted us to contact the Russians . . . to seek information on Bill Clinton's trip to Moscow," James Baker III, Bush's White House chief of staff, wrote in a memo. "I said we absolutely could not do that."[31] Baker shut the conversation down, and with it any consideration of reaching out to Russia for help in tilting an American election. It would be Moscow's final involvement in an American presidential election.

Until 2016, that is—and until Manafort oversaw a presidential election of his own.

* * *

BACK IN NEW Britain, while Moscow flailed and failed to tilt any American elections, Manafort waited for opportunities. He knew he didn't want to follow into the family construction and salvage business; childhood punishments had involved pulling nails from trashed lumber, leaving him "angry as hell" at the pointlessness of it all.[32]

Instead, Manafort found himself tugged in his father's direction. "From the very beginning, I was drawn to the contest of politics," Manafort would later recount.[33] It was a path his father coaxed him along. One of Manafort Sr.'s initiatives was opening local politics to young New Britons. The program was simple: each of the town's four major high schools would select four students to comprise a city council. From there, those student city councilmembers would vote for a mayor—a single student who could become New Britain's leader for a single day, replacing Manafort Sr. for twenty-four hours.

It was a title Manafort Jr., then in high school, knew he wanted. He coaxed and cajoled, flirted and finagled, trying to land the majority of the votes to become mayor (if only for the day). "With nine of the sixteen votes committed to me, I believed I was on track to win the election for mayor," he remembered. He could already taste victory. And then the results came in—and another student landed the mayorship. "A distant relative of mine cut a deal behind my back," Manafort said. "I lost." The votes had been there—until they weren't.[34]

It was a moment, and a lesson, Manafort could still recall nearly six decades later. "Having the votes isn't enough until people have voted," he would later explain. And all that's very true, if slightly obvious. But there was another, deeper lesson buried in the outcome of a single election, in a small school in a small town in a small state. Somehow, the other students had outfoxed Manafort. And it got him "thinking about the organizational and management aspects of politics, not just the service."[35] It got him thinking less about the *why* of politics, and more about the *how*. How campaigns might be won. How votes might change hands.

And how elections might be stolen.

7

Excess Is Best

Be virtuous and you'll never be happy.

—George Armstrong Custer[1]

During the late 1960s, there was little to distinguish Manafort from the rest of the white, semi-affluent baby boomers then cycling through American universities. He wasn't a hippie, per se; there are no photos of Manafort in tie-dyed shirts flashing a peace sign. But having moved to Washington to study at Georgetown University, he rode the tides of the era.

There he was, for instance, at 1969's seminal Woodstock music festival, watching Jimi Hendrix unleash his legendary "freak flag" rendition of "The Star-Spangled Banner." There he was, a year later, participating in the United States' first Earth Day, trying to heighten awareness of the environmental crimes wracking the nation and the planet. And there he was, as an undergraduate in the nation's capital, watching a frothing Nixon administration lurch toward outright authoritarianism, gunning down anti-war protesters and discussing how to assassinate investigative journalists, all while Nixon himself slouched toward impeachment.[2]

At a quick glance, Manafort—shaggy hair, thick-rimmed glasses, navigating a shifting nation—appears prototypical of his generation. But there was another reality, a subterranean current that also flowed through the era, especially among those of a similar age—one that has only gained attention in recent years, thanks in no small part to figures like Manafort. It was a countervailing reaction, building in response to the progressivism bursting forth. The hippies may have gotten the headlines, but they weren't alone. Even while coming of age "when the civil rights movement and opposition to the Vietnam War animated many of the nation's youth," *The Washington Post* later wrote, Manafort "went in a different direction."[3]

As Manafort recalled it, one book in particular steered him through his undergraduate years at Georgetown. While his peers were reading tracts like *Silent Spring* or *The Electric Kool-Aid Acid Test,* Manafort discovered Barry Goldwater's *Conscience of a Conservative.* Published in 1960, the book served as a launching pad for Goldwater's ill-starred 1964 presidential effort, widely viewed at the time as the most extremist major presidential campaign in American history. Part fundamentalist (the "laws of God" have "no dateline," warned Goldwater) and part anti-statist (government was "the chief instrument for thwarting man's liberty"), the book offered broadside after broadside against the kinds of policies ensuring racial equality, equitable voting, and basic civil rights protections. In many ways, it laid the groundwork for the lurch to the right the Republican Party would experience in the decades to come—and the kind of victory-at-all-costs ethos that flowered during the Trump era.[4]

But that was years in the future. At the time Manafort was in college, the book was read only by certain subsets of students of the late 1960s and early 1970s—those especially, as the *Post* continued, who hailed from "northern, Roman Catholic suburbia," and whose "colleges were not Ivy League."[5] Especially those who may have a bit of a chip on their shoulder, or who didn't get nearly the press, or see nearly the success, that the hippies enjoyed.

Especially those, in other words, like Manafort.

* * *

IN ORDER TO trace Manafort's transformation from a college student to a consigliere for despots, it's worth revisiting not only what he read— but whom, from his earliest days after finishing school in Washington, he worked alongside.

When Manafort graduated from Georgetown as a business major in 1971, and then from Georgetown Law School in 1974, there were no immediate opportunities. He still had a political itch, an interest fueled by his father's reign in New Britain. He could faintly see the contours of a kind of conservative rise rumbling across the nation, even if the chattering classes focused on Nixon's downfall couldn't see it themselves. But a year passed, and then another, and Manafort waffled through Washington, still trying to find a toehold.

And then, in 1976, he received a phone call. An old contact named Peter McPherson had become a special assistant to President Gerald Ford and was looking for help in wrangling delegates to make sure Ford landed the 1976 Republican nomination. Despite Ford's incumbency, this was no sure thing; out in California, a politician named Ronald Reagan was openly flirting with trying to unseat a sitting Republican president.

McPherson, though, had heard of Manafort's interest in political management, in political organization. And he knew Manafort was looking for work. Did Manafort want to help? Did he want to make sure Ford retained the nomination—and potentially the White House?

Manafort quickly agreed. But the work he did during the 1976 convention—where he "actively pursued delegates and kept track of their standing," McPherson later remembered—was arguably less important than whom he did it alongside: James Baker III, who was running Ford's campaign.[6] In later years, Baker would stand as the doyen of the Republican foreign policy establishment, serving as George H.W. Bush's secretary of state and directing America's emergence as the victor of the Cold War. (And, as we saw in the previous chapter, swatting down offers of using Russian help for an election.) Baker was no ideologue; he was almost a throwback, a manager and mediator in his own right, preferring backroom decisions to the cameras-and-klieg-lights of modern American politics.[7]

But Baker was also, first and foremost, a politician. He might present a demure, somewhat detached façade, but behind the scenes he was happy to drop the pretense and cut down rivals wherever, and however, he needed. "Despite his patrician manner he could swear like a Texas roughneck," *The Economist* wrote, adding that during Baker's time "ratfuck" became the "favorite term for Washington backstabbing."[8]

Baker was also something else: "an avid collector of young talent," as an article in *Slate* noted. And Baker spied the talent bubbling in Manafort. They both shared a "pragmatic conservatism and [a] thirst for politics." They both saw politics—and especially the kind of skull-duggery made famous during the Nixon years—as a means to an end, rather than the end itself. They both saw how many doors could open with the right connections, with a bit of organizational talent, and with a mixture of outward modesty and backroom mischief. As Manafort would later write, the two developed "strong personal ties," built on the backs of the 1976 campaign.[9]

And Ford couldn't have asked for a better pair. Holding off the Reagan surge, Ford secured the Republican nomination for president in 1976. He, of course, lost to Jimmy Carter, an upstart from Georgia; not even Baker or Manafort could remove the stench of the Nixon years from Ford's reelection campaign. But Manafort had gotten his taste. He'd gotten the opportunity he'd needed—the toehold he'd sought in the Washington, and especially Republican, establishment.

Before he vacated the presidency, Ford welcomed Manafort into the White House, as a small show of thanks for his efforts. A colorless photo shows Manafort, in that shaggy hair and those thick-rimmed glasses, reaching out to shake Ford's hand. It was the first time a sitting U.S. president had welcomed him into the White House, using Manafort's advice and efforts to try to win a presidential election.

It wouldn't be the last.

*　*　*

SHORTLY AFTER CARTER's victory, Manafort began plotting his next steps. He didn't have to wait long. One year after the election, using his new GOP contacts, Manafort took his organizational talents to the Young Republicans. The group, a cohort of right-leaning twenty-somethings, not only was a testing ground for future Republican figures and forces, but it already had an outsized reputation, having helped push Goldwater to his 1964 nomination.

And Manafort had help. Joining him in the Young Republicans was Roger Stone, a freakish, almost grotesque figure who personified the "ratfuck" culture then gurgling among younger Republicans (and those like Baker). A few years younger than Manafort, Stone would grow notorious in later decades, partially for his efforts to install Donald Trump in the presidency and partially for his softball-sized tattoo of Nixon on his back. At the time, though, Stone was something of an ego to Manafort's id; as flamboyant as Manafort was reserved, as outspoken as Manafort was reticent. Stone played the political jester to Manafort's political advisor. And the two immediately hit it off. "They shared a home state, an affection for finely tailored power suits, and a deeper love of power itself," Foer, the best chronicler of Manafort's early years, wrote in 2018. "Together, they campaigned with gleeful ruthlessness."[10]

In the aftermath of Ford's loss, Stone, still in his mid-twenties, sensed which way the Republican winds should blow. As he'd later say, "Traditionally, Young Republicans have been a leading indicator of the direction of the party."[11] And by 1977, Stone wanted to steer that trajectory. He wanted the Young Republicans, and the party overall, to follow his lead. He wanted to seize the leadership of the Young Republicans outright—and he wanted Manafort's help in doing so.

So he and Manafort concocted a plan. Manafort would wrangle the votes—the hundreds of Young Republican delegates necessary to elect Stone to the group's presidency—while Stone would squeeze rivals out of the race. The playbook worked. Though one rival complained that the outcome had "been scripted in the back room," Stone, with Manafort's help, proved victorious. Suddenly, the Young Republicans were in Stone's and Manafort's hands.[12]

But they didn't stop there. Two years later, after injecting Goldwaterite policies into the group, the pair plotted Stone's successor. They landed on Neal Acker, a lawyer from Alabama, whom they groomed to take over. But Acker made one mistake: he failed to "swear loyalty" to Ronald Reagan, the clear favorite to land the 1980 Republican nomination. "When Acker ultimately balked—he wanted to stay neutral—Manafort turned on him with fury," *The Atlantic* reported. As a result, "Manafort and Stone set out to destroy Acker's candidacy."[13] Acker's campaign promptly crumbled, with Manafort carving up the remains.

It was further proof of Manafort's ruthlessness, there for all to see. The position belonged to Acker, until Manafort decided it didn't. The leadership of the Young Republicans was heading in one direction, until Manafort decided it wasn't. Manafort's move against Acker was, as one witness told Foer, "one of the great fuck jobs."[14] It was also a sign of things—of campaigns, of elections, of entire countries—to come.

And the Reagan team noticed. The campaign tapped Manafort to oversee its operations in the South during the Republican primary, with Stone running operations in the Northeast. The outcome was never in doubt. Reagan proceeded to dominate the Republican convention (with Manafort elevated to convention director), and then the election. Nor was the Reagan team done with Manafort yet. During the presidential transition, Manafort landed the position of personnel coordinator in the Office of Executive Management, helping line up the actual people who would flesh out Reagan's right-wing revolution.

In just a few years, Manafort had gone from a wayward twenty-something to a man helping launch, and staff up, one of the most impactful presidencies of the twentieth century. It was more than he could have imagined. And it was all a testament to his organizational skills: calling and cajoling, pushing and pursuing, helping hew the kinds of coalitions and messaging to thrust Reagan toward and into the presidency.

Following Reagan's victory, a new future—for both Manafort and the country—suddenly opened up. But with the election over, Manafort spied another direction. It was one that, in time, would change both the nature of lobbying and the nature of politics as Americans and others knew it.

*   *   *

WITH REAGAN IN the White House, leading the conservative backlash Goldwater had first described years before, Manafort sidestepped out of the campaign. He wouldn't remain with the rest of the Reagan bureaucracy; instead, he'd join the conservative surge on a parallel track. And he'd do so with a pair of friends: his old accomplice Stone and a new contact named Charlie Black.

Black and Manafort had actually known each other since the Young Republican "wars" a few years before.[15] Like Manafort, Black rode the crest of the conservative counterrevolution, joining the 1980 Reagan campaign as a field director. And also like Manafort, Black saw an opening in Washington for his talents, collecting clients looking to navigate the new right-wing waters.

In many ways, Manafort's jump into the lobbying space after the 1980 campaign can be directly attributed to Black. The year Reagan dominated the election, Black launched a consultancy firm to help clients mimic the new president's successes. And in order to build up the new firm, Black recruited two names to join him: Manafort and Stone. They were the "young Turks of the Reagan revolution," as one newspaper described them.[16] After all, Reagan's victory spoke for itself—and anyone associated with that success was suddenly in demand.

It didn't take long for clients to turn to Black's new firm. Business was "steady, if unspectacular," reporter Kenneth Vogel observed.[17] It helped that the firm didn't maintain any kind of strident ideological approach; segregationists like Senator Jesse Helms and moderates like New Jersey governor Tom Kean were both clients, and both came away happy with the firm's electoral advice.

If anything, that ideological slipperiness only expanded over the next few years. Manafort may have had his political preferences—and Reagan was certainly an embodiment of such a political credo—but by the mid-1980s, the trio realized that there was more business to be had if they kept expanding their political horizons.

To that end, they "reached across the aisle," as Foer writes.[18] Their first recruit: Peter Kelly, the former finance chair of the Democratic National Committee. The thought process was simple. If Republican candidates would pay for advice from Reagan's campaign officials, wouldn't Democratic candidates pay for advice about how to undercut Reagan-like tactics? That is, if Manafort and Stone and Kelly knew the secrets to victory—if they understood the strategy of success in early 1980s Washington—wouldn't *either* side pay for those answers?

The answer was, apparently, yes. ("Why have primaries for the nomination?" one congressional aide asked, half-jokingly. "Why not have the candidates go over to Black, Manafort & Stone and argue it out?")[19] With Kelly aboard, the consulting firm was filled with "young tough, savvy political operatives," *The Washington Post* reported at the time, who could "move into the political market and make big bucks."[20]

The Reagan team didn't seem to mind Kelly's hiring, or the fact that Manafort, Stone, and Black made noise about bringing other Democrats aboard. With the 1984 election nearing, the White House brought Manafort and his colleagues back on. Manafort's specific task was organizing the 1984 Republican national convention, with Black as senior election strategist and Stone as the Eastern regional director of the campaign. The three, and the overall campaign itself, succeeded beyond what anyone expected, with Reagan winning nearly every state in one of the most lopsided elections in American history.

That victory not only added another notch to the firm's credentials but also brought aboard the final voice that would launch Manafort's work from regional to global. Lee Atwater, another thirtysomething rising the conservative ranks, served during the election as Reagan's deputy campaign manager. In time, Atwater would grow infamous for outlining how he and his colleagues cultivated support from white supremacists, but at the time he was seen as something of a campaign savant for Republican candidates.[21] He represented, as one outlet reported, "the cream of Republican inside operatives,"[22] a figure who, as *Politico* added, was already "legendary" in his own right.[23] And by 1985, having worked alongside them during Reagan's reelection, Atwater was now connected at the hip with Manafort, Stone, and Black.

If there had been a steady flow of clients beforehand, the stream now turned into a deluge. And it wasn't just political hopefuls looking to tap some of that Reagan-era magic. Suddenly, corporations looking to build links in Washington came calling as well. There was Bethlehem Steel, the metals conglomerate that had, generations earlier, hired Ivy Lee for similar purposes. There was Salomon Brothers, the scandal-laden financial giant whose higher-ups referred to themselves as the "Big Swinging Dicks" (and later inspired Tom Wolfe's *Bonfire of the Vanities*).[24] There were household names, like Johnson & Johnson, and there were social pariahs, like the Tobacco Institute. All of this while political candidates from around the country kept turning to Manafort and his team for electoral advice and campaign consulting.

By 1986, the firm wasn't just servicing players in and around

Washington—it *was* a player in its own right. And reporters began to notice. In 1986, *Time* dubbed Manafort's team the "slickest shop in town." "A lobbyist can perform no greater favor for a lawmaker than to help get him elected," the magazine wrote. "It is the ultimate political IOU, and it can be cashed in again and again." And with Manafort's team launching victories up and down the American political ladder, "[n]o other firm holds more of this precious currency than the Washington shop known as Black, Manafort."[25]

* * *

BUT IT WASN'T just the firm's connections, or the successes it scattered across American politics. It wasn't even just that, with Kelly as a formal partner, the firm also serviced Democratic candidates, even fundraising outright for Democratic campaigns. It was that the firm had clearly filled a niche—offering political advice, consulting, and strategizing that few others could match—and had then innovated in a way few anticipated. Much as Ivy Lee, decades prior, had effectively invented the public relations industry, Manafort and his crew used their firm as a sort of petri dish for ushering lobbying into the modern era. Much as Lee had innovated the tools and tactics—the public statements, the image-crafting, the spin and the denials and the cover-ups—that would come to embody public relations, Manafort crafted his own innovative tools and tactics, cracking apart the staid playbook and developing something entirely new.

There was no easy descriptor for what Manafort and his team began refining. "The technical term for what we do . . . is 'lobbying,'" Manafort would later say. "I will admit that, in a narrow sense, some people might term it 'influence peddling.'"[26] But as with Lee, the terms were less important than the tactics themselves. And for those in Washington in the mid-1980s, it was clear to see that something new was emerging—and was changing American politics in ways they couldn't yet decipher.

Manafort's basic innovation was relatively simple. His firm was, in reality, *two* firms. While the entities were effectively indistinguishable in terms of personnel, or even structure, they served a pair of distinct ends. The first was known formally as Black, Manafort, Stone

& Atwater, and worked as "a political-consulting firm." This was the group that helped launch Republican (and some Democratic) candidates to power, seeding them across the American political landscape. This was also the firm that tapped the specific organizational talents Manafort displayed during Reagan's elections.

The second was dubbed Black, Manafort, Stone & Kelly, serving primarily as "a lobbying operation." This firm worked with clients (especially the corporate kind) to draft specific regulations, push specific industrial policies, and open doors to specific policymakers in the process. This was the firm that entities like Bethlehem Steel and the Tobacco Institute worked with, and the one that resembles modern lobbying in its purest sense.

Again, from the outside, the two firms appeared almost identical. But their functions were more than just nominally distinct. Instead of simply launching candidates to power, or helping clients pursue their interests in Washington, Manafort and his team did *both*. Put another way: the first team helped place political clients in power, and the second team then helped corporate clients access and influence those original political clients. This effectively closed the lobbying loop, allowing Manafort's team to work every step from the beginning of campaigns to the passage of legislation, building bridges and alliances—and getting paid—all the way. It was a model that, as one paper put it, "would have a transformative effect on the capital, nudging Washington into a generation-long evolution."[27]

A passage from *Time* is worth quoting in full:

[Manafort and his team] say that the lobbying and political-consulting functions are kept separate. "It's like a grocery store and a hardware store," insists Black. "You can't buy eggs at a hardware store and you can't buy tires at the grocery." Yet these are but fine distinctions in Washington, where the firm is considered one of the most ambidextrous in the business, the ultimate supermarket of influence peddling. "You are someone's political adviser, then you sell yourself to a corporation by saying you have a special relationship with Congress," says Democratic Media Consultant Robert Squier, who does no lobbying himself. Is it proper to get a politician elected, then turn around and lobby him? "It's a gray area," sidesteps Squier. Charges Fred Wertheimer, president of the public-interest lobbying group Common Cause: "It's institutionalized conflict of interest."[28]

It was in that marriage—that combination of candidates and corporations, of clients in both the public and private sectors—that Manafort and his colleagues helped create the lobbying industry as we now know it. "I don't think they invented the swamp," one former colleague told *The Washington Post.* "They invented an innovative way to navigate the swamp." It was that innovation that set Manafort and his team apart: the melding of multiple parts into one globular, mucous whole. As another former colleague said, Manafort created "the epitome of everything everybody wants to clean up [in Washington]."[29]

To modern eyes, Manafort's innovation appears almost obvious, a kind of vertical integration that makes logical sense. But at the time—when "no one was practicing lobbying in the strategic sense," as Manafort would later say—it was an opening just waiting for the right minds. And just as with Lee decades previously, Manafort appeared the right man, at the right time, with the right idea.[30]

*   *   *

DURING REAGAN'S SECOND term, business boomed. Not only did the firm's political bona fides expand with Atwater's addition, but client after client came away satisfied, with groups like Chrysler-Mitsubishi and Johnson & Johnson saving tens of millions of dollars from legislation Manafort lobbied for on their behalf. "In just five years, Black, Manafort and Stone—and now Atwater—has become a major new presence in the capital, specializing in connections, influence and hardball politics," one newspaper reported.

As business rolled in, so did compensation. Crunching the numbers, reporters found that Manafort and his partners were "aiming at incomes of $450,000 each" per year—or over $1.2 million annually in modern dollars. It was more money than Manafort had ever seen, and a far cry for a boy whose previous alternative was working at a salvage business.[31]

And it had an effect. Personal drivers, polished suits, a new "lobbying palace" in Washington—Manafort quickly began enjoying the spoils of his work. He and his team were, as one report detailed, "randy, flashy and flush with cash."[32] They certainly weren't shy about it. As *The Atlantic* reported, Manafort came up with the themes for the firm's annual meetings. First came "Excess." Then: "Exceed Excess." And then, at last: "Excess is Best."[33] In the era of Wall Street scandals and grubby greed, few themes could have been more appropriate.

Meanwhile, the political connections kept coming. With Reagan grooming George H.W. Bush as his successor, Atwater stepped in as 1988 campaign strategist, helping steer yet another victory, keeping the White House open to Manafort's clients for another four years. (In building as many allies as possible, Stone even advised the campaign of one of Bush's Republican rivals.)

In that midst, Manafort also made a political connection that would pay off decades later. A real estate developer had hired his firm not to obtain the presidency, but for something far more local: to help prevent the expansion of Native American casinos. While the developer claimed that "nobody likes Indians as much as" he did, he also claimed that this Native American casino expansion would be, for reasons unclear, "the biggest scandal ever, the biggest since Al Capone."[34] The developer was so concerned with the potential expansion that he secretly bankrolled a fake anti-gambling group, claiming that the Indigenous figures involved were harbingers of "increased crime, broken families, bankruptcies and . . . violence."[35]

It was all an exercise in absurdity—and the fact that this developer had significant interests in nearby Atlantic City casinos was left unmentioned. But it was also a project that interested Manafort. The developer quickly hired his firm to stop the casino expansion. Manafort himself provided ideas and advice for how to counter the expansion of the Indigenous casinos, pitching everything from increasing regulations to eliminating tax breaks. And just as with so many other campaigns, they were ultimately successful. "In the end," one newspaper reported, the proposed Indigenous casino plan "fell apart."[36]

Much of that, it should be said, had to do with disorganization and infighting among the Indigenous casino proponents. But to Manafort, a win was a win. More importantly, Manafort had a new client in the developer who viewed him positively—and who would, as he said, be "very loyal" to Manafort in the future.[37]

The developer was, of course, Donald Trump. And it wasn't the last time Trump would come to Manafort with an issue that, as he saw it, only Manafort could solve.

* * *

BY THE END of the decade, Manafort stood in a position that Ivy Lee would have recognized. Like Lee, Manafort schmoozed with presidents and politicians, launching political careers and reaching across the aisle when necessary. Like Lee, corporate titans rushed to Manafort's firm, looking to access the policymakers in its debt. Like Lee, Manafort had reformed American lobbying, bringing it into a new era, molding new systems and finding new services to provide.

As with Lee, there was a distinct era *before* Manafort's arrival, and a distinct era *after* his work began. And that can be seen in the numbers alone. Following Manafort's entrée, the entire lobbying industry exploded, with thousands of Americans flocking to Washington. Following Manafort's lead, "the double-digit list of registered lobbyists [beforehand] had swelled to more than 10,000," *The Atlantic* reported.[38] Lobbying had, in many ways, come into its own, swept into the modern era thanks to the work of Manafort and his colleagues.

And like Lee, Manafort appeared to enjoy the status that such work—such innovation—could bring. Excess, as Manafort liked to say, was best—and it wasn't reserved only for his clients. "We fondly used to refer to him as 'The Count'—'The Count of Monte Cristo,'" one colleague told *Politico*, pointing to an air that seemed to swirl around Manafort wherever he went. (Another colleague claimed the nickname "came from Manafort's penchant for swirling his coat around his shoulders dramatically.")[39]

But then, the similarities between Lee and Manafort didn't end with the proximity to presidents, or with the clear stamp both left on the American lobbying complex. Because, by the turn of the decade, Manafort butted into a similar reality Lee had once experienced. He had, in many ways, conquered the domestic set. He'd become the titan of American lobbyists, the king of American influence-peddling writ large.

But America was only one country. And an entire world, far beyond the United States, beckoned. A world of clients, looking to tap
Manafort's talents. A world of contacts, waiting for Manafort's services.

A world of autocrats and dictators, itching for a bit of Manafort's
help in accessing America, in strengthening their own grip on power,
and in upending American democracy in the process.

8

Shame Is for Sissies

We Americans have yet to really learn our own antecedents.
—Walt Whitman[1]

In early 1992, the latest issue of *Spy* magazine hit newsstands. The edition splashed as a time capsule of the era, with a cover featuring the characters from *Wayne's World*, an explainer on the controversy surrounding Michael Jackson's latest music video, a look at George H.W. Bush preparing for post-presidency life, and even a dig at then-senator Joe Biden's inability to form concise, coherent sentences.[2]

At the time, this is what *Spy* was largely known for: snarky cultural commentary interspersed with scathing political critiques, all of it without ever forgetting a punchline. Its ethos was less of a traditional news magazine, hewing closer instead to the kind of character and comedy later embodied in things like Jon Stewart's *The Daily Show.* And that comparison's not far off the mark, as the now-defunct *Spy* had at the time a similar impact as Stewart's later run on Comedy Central. When *Spy* spoke, people listened.

Which is why in early 1992—with Bill Clinton gearing up for the White House, Clarence Thomas ascending to the Supreme Court, and Wayne Newton emerging as the king of Las Vegas—*Spy* decided to devote a significant chunk of its latest issue to a topic suddenly growing in prominence: foreign lobbying.

The timing couldn't have been better. With the Cold War barely in America's rearview mirror, and with a flood of new states and new regimes trying to sift the shifting geopolitics—and make sure they stayed in America's favor—foreign lobbyists in Washington watched their client rolls explode.

But that trend, and its implications, would only become apparent in the years and decades to come. For the time, *Spy* just wanted to get a feel for this foreign lobbying industry finally finding its feet. It wanted to survey what the industry could do, and who it would service, and who was leading this new industry into the future.

We'll revisit this *Spy* feature later in this chapter, but for now, it's worth flagging just one thing. In the middle of its ten-page spread, *Spy* organized an ad hoc ranking of the new firms building links with the nascent despots and dictators seizing the reins of their countries. The ranking, and the question, was simple: Which of these foreign lobbying firms in Washington displayed the most "moral turpitude," boasting the broadest array of rights abusers and criminals against humanity among their clients? As *Spy* asked, "Who's the Sleaziest of Them All?"[3]

There was plenty of competition. Some firms *Spy* fingered represented dictatorships like those in El Salvador or Sudan, or juntas like those in Myanmar or Pakistan, or even kleptocratic maniacs like Haiti's Jean-Claude Duvalier. One even repped Iraq's Saddam Hussein, fresh off defeat in the Gulf War.

But there was one firm that topped the list, representing tyrants, whitewashing warlords, and servicing those who specialized in the abuse of women and children and entire nations alike. One firm that topped *Spy*'s "Blood-on-the-Hands Index," and that was dragging the foreign lobbying complex into a bright, bloody future.[4]

At the helm? Paul Manafort.

*   *   *

BY THE EARLY 1990s, Manafort's team had been dabbling in foreign clientele for a handful of years. It's difficult to identify Manafort's first foreign clients; as we saw in Chapter 5, FARA by this time was a ghost of itself, the skeletal remains of a once-promising piece of lobbying regulation and transparency. Its scattered, slipshod records from the era are difficult, if not impossible, to sort through, full of missing documents and glaring gaps. But even in that detritus, there are a few filings that can give us an idea of when Manafort began casting his gaze abroad—and the kinds of regimes that caught his eye.

For instance, in 1985—just after Manafort's firm rose to the top of the American lobbying-cum-consulting industry—Manafort inked a contract with the government of Nigeria. While it's unclear what, exactly, he did for the Nigerian regime, we know that his firm made $1 million from the deal, in which Manafort agreed to "lobby, represent, advise and assist" in promoting the "political and economic objectives" of the Nigerian government.

On its face, the contract—with Manafort's signature scrawled all over—appears perfectly straightforward. But that's only if you overlook the fact that, a few months prior, the Nigerian military had launched a successful coup against the sitting regime, jump-starting one of the longest-ruling military dictatorships in the country's history. The "objectives" of this new Nigerian regime, which Manafort freely represented, included barring political parties that weren't explicitly backed by the government, as well as nullifying the lone peaceful presidential election of the era.[5]

These details are, of course, not mentioned in Manafort's filings. But they are of a piece with the kinds of regimes Manafort and his team gravitated toward as they began searching out international clients, cultivating links with foreign regimes and opening doors for them in Washington—and making millions in the process.

We saw in the prologue the kinds of services Manafort provided for a brute like Angola's Jonas Savimbi. But Savimbi was hardly the lone African autocrat Manafort wanted to help. There was, for instance, the regime of Mobutu Sese Seko in the Democratic Republic of Congo, then known as Zaire. The crimes linked to Mobutu—a man who lorded as Congolese despot for over three decades—are enough to make other dictators blanch, from torturing political opponents to massacring university students. Mobutu's reign over the former Belgian Congo was, *The Atlantic* reported, "an African horror story" (and one that Belgium's King Leopold would likely have approved of).[6]

As the Cold War spun to a close, the nominally pro-American Mobutu sought out allies in Washington to make sure he'd retain power through the geopolitical transition—and that all of the United

States' talk about expanding democracy didn't extend to his country. In stepped Manafort. Inking another $1 million contract, Manafort met personally with Mobutu, sketching out meetings and policies the former would push in Washington. Even after a separate domestic scandal rocked Manafort's consulting firm—a scandal that forced Manafort to admit he'd engaged in "influence-peddling"—Mobutu hardly paused, saying that the controversy "only shows how important they are!"[7]

Simultaneously, in Southeast Asia, another longstanding dictator sought help navigating the new geopolitical landscape. Indonesian despot Suharto had already overseen slaughter after slaughter of anti-regime forces, including up to one million opponents during the mass killings of the 1960s. And now, he wanted to make sure he remained in America's good graces. So, à la Mobutu, he turned to a man who could help: Manafort. It remains unclear what Manafort actually did for Suharto—media reports are the only documentation linking Manafort with the Indonesian tyrant—but there's little reason to think it differed from his services elsewhere.

Not all of Manafort's international clients had been in power for decades. In the shattered nation of Somalia, a lanky figure named Siad Barre had recently risen to the top of a claque of competing warlords, thanks in large part to his Red Berets death squad. Barre knew that American support would be the key to eliminating any opposition from his rivals. Enter Manafort, who immediately snapped up the budding tyrant. When one of Manafort's aides expressed uncertainty with the million-dollar contract drawn up between the firm and Barre, Manafort responded, "We all know Barre is a bad guy. . . . We just have to make sure he's our bad guy."[8]

Some countries were even cursed with experiencing Manafort's help *twice*. A few years after hiring Manafort, the Nigerian junta collapsed, shredded apart by competing generals. One of those military despots, Sani Abacha, eventually rose to the top of the post-regime struggle, founding his own junta in Lagos. Just like his predecessors, the scar-faced Abacha engaged in routine brutality, with his personal security force having trained in North Korea. And just like his predecessors, Abacha wanted to convince the Americans to stand by him. To that end, he "turned to Manafort's team to help clean up his public

image," with Manafort "personally handl[ing]" Abacha's account.[9]
Soon Abacha, via Manafort's help, "engaged in an aggressive public
relations and lobbying campaign to persuade Americans that he was
the leader of a progressive emerging democracy," *The New York Times*
reported.[10] (It's unclear if Abacha personally considered jailing and
hanging regime opponents "progressive.")

Again and again, wherever a ruling despot smothered opposition
and suffocated democracy, it seemed Manafort stood in the middle.
There was business in the bloodshed. There were doors to be opened
for these despots, regardless of what it cost regime opponents, be they
gender rights activists or environmental campaigners or simply families trying to escape persecution. Despite all of America's triumphalist
talk of democracy and freedom, Manafort's clients all remained close
to Washington for years—and remained in power just as long.

Not that Manafort saw anything wrong in what he was doing. "Dictators," as Manafort's colleague Stone would later say, "are in the eye of
the beholder."[11] Or as one congressional staffer would add, Manafort's
view was, "To hell with the facts, fuck the world."[12]

*   *   *

WE'VE ALREADY SEEN the details of how some of the campaigns of this
era played out, as when Manafort transformed Savimbi from a blood-
sotted monster into a supposedly democratizing force. (Who says con-
scripting child soldiers is anti-democratic, anyway?) And if we tried to
detail every facet of every campaign Manafort worked on during this
initial foray into foreign clientele, we'd never get to the twenty-first century, let alone examine how the scope of foreign lobbying has exploded
over the past two decades.

But it's worth pausing on at least one campaign, detailing the minu-
tiae of at least one client, to get a sense of the kinds of services Manafort
and his colleagues provided—and how that began shifting U.S. policy
more broadly, tilting international relations and draining American
coffers in ways few realized.

Much like Mobutu's Zaire or Suharto's Indonesia, the Philippines of
the late Cold War had been dominated—and decimated—by a single
dictator. Ferdinand Marcos may be remembered best for his wife's shoe

obsession (her thousands of pairs are now housed in a new museum), but he was arguably one of the most important American allies during the Cold War in both Asia and the Pacific. And he was also, perhaps unsurprisingly, one of Manafort's most lucrative clients.

Manafort actually arrived in Manila to service Marcos relatively late into the tyrant's rule. Where previous administrations had overlooked Marcos's rank ruthlessness—not least the thousands of extrajudicial killings directly attributed to his reign—things began changing as the Cold War wound to a close. After assassins dispatched Benigno Aquino, Jr., Marcos's leading political rival, officials in Washington began raising noise about potentially slashing aid to Marcos's regime. They even talked about simply cutting loose the despot, who was largely reliant on American largesse.

But an American named Paul Laxalt had different ideas. Laxalt had helped oversee Reagan's multiple elections, and knew how positively the conservative establishment viewed Marcos. He also understood that a successful foreign lobbying campaign could stanch much of the burbling criticism—and how much someone like Manafort could help to keep Marcos in power. "Everybody needs a Washington representative to protect their hind sides, even foreign governments," Laxalt once said. "So the constituency for these [foreign lobbyists] is the entire free-world economy."[13] (Despite the distinct lack of even basic freedoms, Marcos's Philippines was still considered part of this "free-world economy.")

With Laxalt connecting Marcos and Manafort—and all of them getting the go-ahead from the Reagan administration, which continued to view Marcos as a key ally—the lobbyist got to work. Technically, Manafort's firm agreed to work for a separate, nominally distinct Filipino corporate client: the Chamber of Philippine Manufacturers, Exporters & Tourism. (As Ivy Lee knew well—and as we'll see time and again in the second half of this book—corporations working under dictatorial regimes are always effective proxies for the regimes in question.) The contract was worth nearly $1 million, with the first tranche personally delivered to Manafort's firm by Marcos's wife.[14]

Manafort's aim was clear: keep Marcos, now running against Aquino's widow, in power at all costs. He immediately "revved into high gear," *Politico* reported. On the image-management side, Manafort linked Marcos officials with a range of conservative, and sympathetic, American journalists. Manafort "worked to seed the idea in Washington conservative circles" that Marcos's political opposition "would not be a reliable U.S. ally." Politically, Manafort and his colleagues also targeted specific American officials, meeting with everyone from congressmen and staffers to State Department officials overseeing American aid to Manila.[15]

Meanwhile, back in the Philippines, Manafort and his colleagues viewed the upcoming presidential election as a key inflection point for Marcos's reign. They knew full well that in modern dictatorships, tyrants need to "win" even sham elections in order to retain power. And they also knew what kind of electoral strategy was worth pursuing. As Manafort let slip to *Time,* "What we've tried to do is make it more of a Chicago-style election and not Mexico's"—alluding to Chicago's reputation for electoral shenanigans, which appeared mild compared to Mexico's outright single-party rule.[16]

All of this—crafting a new public image, setting up high-level meetings in Washington, directing the election overall—looked like a winning strategy on paper. And it may well have been, allowing Manafort to successfully pocket another dictator. But Manafort's plans failed to account for one factor: Marcos himself. On the day of the election, Marcos unleashed a wave of voter intimidation on a "grand scale," from eliminating thousands of names on voter rolls to beating poll workers outright. *The Los Angeles Times* even reported that "masked men fired M-16 rifles at cripples and nuns trying to guard the polls."[17]

Despite the rain of criticism following the vote—and despite the fact that Aquino's widow clearly had majority support—Marcos claimed victory. It was "wholesale fraud," as one local said.[18] But Marcos didn't claim victory alone. While the Filipino dictator "barricaded himself in the presidential palace," Manafort's team "repeatedly lobbied" allies in Washington, reporter Kenneth Vogel found, working "to perpetuate the idea that . . . Marcos had prevailed."[19] With Marcos holed up in his estate, Manafort could be his man—and his mouthpiece—in Washington.

Initially, the White House appeared to back Manafort's and Marcos's claims, announcing tentative support for their flailing ally. But with daily details emerging of Marcos's electoral brutality—and fresh reports of regime proxies also targeting both priests and "wheelchair-bound paraplegics" alike—the fraud became impossible to ignore.[20] Eventually, the Reagan administration shifted its stance. Marcos took the hint, and promptly fled the country.

Technically, Manafort had failed his client. Marcos was out of power and on the run, his decades-long dictatorship crumbling behind him. But that was, in many ways, hardly Manafort's fault. And Marcos's allies appeared to recognize that. Shortly after fleeing, Marcos's wife, finally separated from her sprawling shoe collection, spoke directly with Manafort over the phone. She "thanked Manafort profusely for his services," as *Politico* reported.[21] She knew that he'd done all he could to keep her husband in power, all he could to allow Marcos to continue pillaging Filipinos for years yet.

There were no hard feelings on Manafort's end, either. After all, he and his team made millions from servicing clients like Marcos, helping steer them toward a bright, promising post–Cold War era. Indeed, it was the world's *most* kleptocratic leaders who hired Manafort, time and again. Suharto, for instance, was accused of looting up to $35 billion from Indonesians. Marcos himself allegedly swiped up to $10 billion from Filipinos. Mobutu purportedly thieved $5 billion from Congolese citizens, a similar amount attached to Abacha. According to Transparency International, these figures were the four most corrupt politicians of the late twentieth century, looting health and infrastructure and education budgets alike. And they all used part of that lucre to bankroll the one man they all had in common: Manafort.[22]

* * *

BY THE 1990s, Manafort and his colleagues were sitting pretty. A new crop of dictatorial clients had surged to Washington, looking for Manafort's lobbying and consulting talents, looking to get a lay of the new geopolitical land. The United States stood as the sole superpower remaining. And plenty on both sides of the United States' political divide were happy to toss America's doors open, ushering in a new epoch of globalization, of internationalized capitalism that could supposedly enrich us all—and supposedly help spread democracy in the process. Why bother being concerned about foreign lobbyists? Why let pesky things like regulations and transparency, especially when it came to figures like Manafort, get in the way of America's dawning golden age?

Officials certainly didn't seem to see any reason. Clients continued to flock to Manafort, flooding him with their kleptocratic wealth, watching him open doors in Washington. But amidst the onrush of dictators looking for lobbying help, there were two developments that should have given Manafort and his colleagues pause. While the United States stood triumphant, and while regimes rushed to use American lobbyists to remain in Washington's good graces (and in power), two countervailing elements began swirling, and began showing interest in the burgeoning foreign lobbying industry.

The first group was civil society. These were the American nonprofits and nongovernmental organizations who were actually interested in the pursuit of democracy, rather than just the rhetoric of it all. With post-communist and post-colonial states cracking open, and new regimes sending their representatives to Washington and claiming they were "transitioning" toward democracy, American civil society groups wanted a closer look at how serious these new governments were—and how, in the process, they were actually accessing American policymakers.

One group in particular, the Center for Public Integrity (CPI), decided in 1992 to take a specific look at the role the budding foreign lobbying industry was playing. They knew these lobbyists had begun acting as handmaidens for these "transitioning" regimes, providing them platforms they'd previously gone without. But what they found shocked them.

Over nearly a hundred pages, CPI detailed what it described as "The Torturers' Lobby." In case after case—in regime after regime that claimed to "have begun the long hard march toward democracy"— governments steeped in "oppression and human rights abuses" found willing compatriots in Washington, happy to launder their reputations for a tidy fee. Countries as disparate as Kenya and Peru, supposed partners like Morocco and Egypt, even allies like Turkey and Israel: all of them had found lobbyists in Washington to do their bidding, despite rampant human rights concerns. And they'd done so on a bipartisan basis. As CPI found, "Many of the foreign agents representing countries showing little respect for human rights are Washington insiders who have ties to both Republicans and Democrats in Congress and the executive branch."[23]

Nor was that all. As CPI found, "U.S. taxpayers are indirectly supporting the activities of lobbyists, lawyers and public relations firms who were paid . . . to represent foreign interests"—including those who "are persistent abusers of human rights." The report shone a harsh light on how these regimes redirected American financial aid—money cobbled directly from American taxpayers—to bankroll the lobbyists who could keep them in power. That is, rather than using those funds for, say, hospitals or libraries, the regimes in question directly rerouted that money to the lobbying mercenaries mushrooming through Washington. Think of it as a kind of vicious circle: American taxpayers would fund American aid, which would then go to these revolting regimes, who would then use some of that aid to fund lobbyists—who would then work to keep that aid spigot open and their clients entrenched in power.

The report is an unfortunately dry read, with numbers (Indonesia spending $6.8 million on lobbying, Turkey spending $3.8 million, etc.) interspersed with examples of torture and rampant abuse linked to these regimes (Indonesia massacring independence fighters in East Timor, Turkey using electric shocks and water hoses in its torture regime, etc.). But even so, the report was something of a signal flare. For the first time, American civil society had woken to the phenomenon—and even the threat—of unchecked foreign lobbying, or at least to the reality of why these regimes may be using foreign lobbyists in the first place.[24]

And the report didn't shy away from Manafort. Dubbing him the "quintessential Washington insider," CPI mentioned Manafort some forty times throughout its report. When contacted about why he and his colleagues serviced torturers and human rights criminals, Manafort's spokesperson said the firm doesn't "attempt to explain away" concerns about its clients' human rights abuses. Instead, it simply tries "to open a dialogue."[25]

* * *

THE SECOND GROUP that displayed a sudden interest in the rise of the foreign lobbying complex was the press. By the early 1990s, American writers had begun sniffing out the details of this new force slithering through Washington, of lobbyists acting as foot soldiers for these new mafia-states—acting, as *Spy* dubbed them, as "publicists of the damned."[26]

Indeed, that *Spy* feature mentioned earlier put something of a stake in the ground regarding how American investigative journalists would—and should—treat these lobbying forces. Written by Art Levine, the piece pulled back the curtain on a phenomenon that had seen almost no investigation previously. Never before had any outlet attempted a wholesale examination of the industry, let alone a ranking of the most rotten, most reprobate firms working in Washington.

Levine's piece is, even decades later, a *tour de force*, introducing casts of characters profiting from the new lobbying services Manafort and his colleagues pioneered. Manafort is, of course, featured in the investigation itself. (See the aforementioned "Blood-on-the-Hands Index.") But he's hardly the sole American that foreign regimes raced to. As Levine found, he was one of a sprawling range of figures happily laundering the images of the planet's worst villains.

There was, for instance, a man named Joseph Blatchford, who worked at an American law firm named O'Connor & Hannan. Blatchford had a nominally impressive résumé, having run the Peace Corps during the Nixon administration. At some point, though, Blatchford realized there was more money in representing and entrenching despots (and, it goes without saying, undercutting the Peace Corps's efforts abroad).

As Levine wrote, Blatchford signed a $10,000-a-month contract to represent El Salvador's fascistic ruler Alfredo Cristiani. Organizing meetings between Salvadorian officials and American congressmen, Blatchford downplayed the death squads ransacking El Salvador on Cristiani's behalf, claiming them as simple law-abiding posses working toward Salvadorean democracy. But that work became more difficult after Cristiani's regime, just like Marcos's, openly massacred a half dozen Jesuit priests. (As Levine added, "The defense lawyer for the [murderers] later threatened to have the jury whacked, with the trial judge saying he was planning on fleeing El Salvador for his life.") Not that that stopped Blatchford, who continued to work on his client's behalf in Washington, spinning Cristiani as some kind of democratizing force. As one representative said, Blatchford's arguments were "bullshit."[27]

Levine looked at another American group facing a similar "predicament" to Blatchford. The law firm of Patton Boggs had veered into foreign lobbying toward the end of the Cold War, snapping up the kinds of clients Manafort would recognize. One of those was the autocratic regime in Guatemala, which oversaw "the torture and execution of activists, academics and peasants." Among those targeted by the regime: an American nun named Sister Diana Ortiz, allegedly raped by Guatemalan military personnel and scarred with more than a hundred cigarette burns.

All of these accusations convinced the United States to finally block military aid to Guatemala—a block that Patton Boggs now worked to lift. In meeting after meeting in Washington, Patton Boggs officials spun Guatemala's case. According to the firm, the Guatemalan regime was actually full of reformers, just looking for an opening to implement the kinds of policies and adjustments necessary to get Guatemala back up on its feet. Pulling American support, Patton Boggs argued, would snuff Guatemalan reforms before they could begin.

When American officials didn't bite, the firm's lobbyists tried a different tactic. Setting up a meeting with staffers for the House Foreign Affairs Committee, one of the firm's employees, David Todd, proclaimed that American officials should avoid criticizing Guatemala. According to Todd, the United States had no room to condemn the Guatemalan regime, especially since multiple white Los Angeles police officers had recently been videotaped beating a Black man named Rodney King.[28] The argument was specious, and wildly offensive to the thousands of regime opponents slaughtered by the Guatemalan regime. "I almost hit the ceiling," one committee aide told *Spy*.[29] But it also, in the end, appeared to work. Thanks in large part to Patton Boggs's efforts, the regime avoided the pariah state status it seemed destined for—and still remains a key American partner in the region.

*   *   *

MANY OF THOSE featured in Levine's reportage fit a mold Manafort would recognize: buttoned-up, professional, visually indistinguishable from the legislators and staffers they regularly met with. But there was one other figure worth highlighting, who not only bucked that sartorial trend but arguably did more than anyone else to bring early attention to the industry.

Even in an era when excess, as Manafort saw it, was "best," Edward J. von Kloberg stood apart. He was, as one paper called him, "one of Washington's true characters."[30] Everything about the lobbyist screamed for attention, from his outfit (he was routinely seen in both a bow tie and a cape) to his fake name (which included adding "von," which Kloberg thought "made him sound like European nobility"). As journalist Ken Silverstein wrote, Kloberg "did the devil's work with flair." And he also had a catchphrase that summed up his—and, for that matter, Manafort's—ethos. As Kloberg liked to say, "Shame is for sissies."[31]

That ethos extended to his clientele. Like Manafort, Kloberg serviced any dictator who came calling, from Romania's Nicolae Ceausescu to Liberia's Samuel Doe to Iraq's Saddam Hussein. (In a fit of decorative delusion, Kloberg plastered his bathroom with dozens of photos of him and his despotic clientele.) His mania was so pronounced that *Spy* dubbed him "Washington's most shameless lobbyist."[32] Not that Kloberg minded. "I don't have any problem sleeping at night," he admitted.[33]

That shamelessness was on full display in Levine's *Spy* feature. In preparation for publication, the magazine wanted to see if there was anyone—any figure, any regime, any ideology—that would be beyond the pale for a figure like Kloberg. And they came up with a creative solution: posing as neo-Nazis, and attempting to recruit Kloberg to their cause. Working, in other words, to see how far Kloberg would go to follow in Ivy Lee's footsteps.

The entire transcript of *Spy*'s call with Kloberg is worth reading in full. Posing as representatives from the "German People's Alliance," the journalists told Kloberg that they wanted to ban immigration into Germany, to reconquer Poland, and to amplify their "own voice in the U.S. Congress to counter the pro-Jewish claque."

And they had one question: "Would Edward von Kloberg take on one of Germany's nascent neo-Nazi organizations as a client?"

They didn't have to ask twice. "You see, consulting and lobbying here is what we call a necessary evil," Kloberg told the Nazi imposters. "And I believe in many of the tenets you believe in. . . . You will also find that there are a lot of people in America who feel that way. It has just not been presented to them." Kloberg hit it off with the Nazi poseurs, discussing potential lobbying strategies, discussing lands Germany should recapture from Poland, discussing all the ways, as Kloberg said, "to make Germany great again."

A few days later, *Spy* called Kloberg once more, again posing as German fascists. They wondered if Kloberg had any recommendations for further Americans to link up with. Perhaps former Ku Klux Klan leader David Duke, then running for Louisiana governor? "Yes," Kloberg responded. "No question. [Duke] has opened an entire new chapter." Duke would be a perfect partner for these new clients, the lobbyist said. And Kloberg would be happy to connect them.[34]

Unlike Ivy Lee, Kloberg and the supposed Nazis ultimately failed to finalize an actual contract. (The Nazi reps later called Kloberg and told him they'd "been attacked by anarchists . . . rendering further conversation impossible for the time being.")[35] And they'd never get a chance to revisit their partnership; not long later, Kloberg killed himself by leaping off of Rome's Castel Sant'Angelo, claiming he was depressed over a failed romance.

Kloberg's death left his dictatorial partners in a lurch. (It remains unclear what happened to the bathroom photo albums of Kloberg and his dictator-clients.) But figures like Manafort still operated in Washington and were happy to sweep up Kloberg's erstwhile partners, providing them with all the services they'd need. "They suck in their breath and represent total shits and monsters," Diana McLellan, one of Kloberg's friends, would later say. "That's what Washington is all about."[36]

* * *

THESE TWO ELEMENTS—civil society and journalism, both investigating the scope of rising foreign lobbying in Washington—offered a way to pick up the slack left by FARA's failures. But given the soaring scale of the foreign lobbying industry, they were hardly enough. And, to be fair, there was hardly a demand from American audiences for information about how these lobbyists might be shifting U.S. policy—or about how they might even be directing American taxpayer monies. The United States, after all, had just won the Cold War. Couldn't Americans sit back for a bit? Couldn't Washington just enjoy a few years away from geopolitical worries?

That's certainly what the foreign lobbyists seemed to be arguing, raking in millions as they went. To Manafort, the decision to expand from domestic campaigns to international clientele appeared the right one. Through the 1990s, life for Manafort was like convincing policymakers to hear out his despotic clients, or like working around the bare-bones FARA regulations: easy.

And that can be seen in a clip from the era (and still available online), taped during an episode of the game show *What Would You Do?* on Nickelodeon. The premise of the game was simple. The host, Marc Summers, would select a pair of women from the audience, and proceed to weigh their purses, with the owner of the lightest bag winning a prize. The catch: if they emptied anything out of their purse, Summers would get to keep it.

As viewers watched each woman go through their purse, unloading everything from brushes to makeup kits, Summers honed in on one woman in particular. "Remember, whatever you put [on the table], you gave up," Summers said. He reached down. "And this is her husband's wallet," he continued, hoisting a massive wallet in the air. He turned to someone in the audience behind him, and began speaking. "Sir, how many American Express cards does one person need?" He opened the wallet, and started tugging items out. "Let's count them together. There's . . . three American Express cards: he's got a gold, a platinum, and a corporate. He's got nine Visas, and an AT&T credit card."

As Summers pretended to pocket the cards, the audience began laughing. And the camera panned to the man Summers had been talking to.

It's Paul Manafort, with a giant, almost cherubic grin on his face, sitting in a collared shirt, in the middle of a Nickelodeon audience, watching the host go through his wife's purse—and watching him count out all his credit cards, there for the crowd, and for the rest of us, to see.[37]

PART III

REVOLUTIONS

What do I care for peace?

—Leo Perutz[1]

9

Safe for Dictatorship

I frequently met with human bones during my rambles.
—Thomas Manby[1]

For about a decade after the collapse of the Soviet Union, there was a sense that the new, America-led epoch was something of an inevitability. There might be military flare-ups, as in Kosovo or Moldova. There might even be genocides, as in Rwanda or Bosnia. But the days of international instability—the days of national security crises facing the United States—were over. America's model had, naturally, won out. History, as the phrase went, had ended.

With the United States triumphant, interests and resources that would have previously gone to national security concerns were redirected elsewhere. And that extended to monitoring who was actually lobbying on foreign regimes' behalf, how they were doing it, and how much money was changing hands along the way. FARA's decades-long collapse accelerated with the end of the Cold War, extending well into the twenty-first century, with American officials continually showing little interest in maintaining the Nazi-era lobbying regulations. "FARA enforcement from the 1990s to the 2000s was," as one study charitably put it, "limited."[2]

To take just one data point: From 1992 through 2016, the U.S. Department of Justice didn't bother to block a single lobbying firm from working with any client—even if that firm hadn't bothered to file the right paperwork, or even any paperwork at all. Officials might be aware of a firm's links to a foreign regime, or of documents that were never filed. But that didn't seem to matter. For the first quarter century of the post–Cold War era, American officials sat on their hands. Even with the United States bungling into Afghanistan and Iraq, FARA by the early twenty-first century was hardly worth the legislative paper it was written on.

Then again, maybe that's not fair. After all, there was hardly a surge of demand for answers on who was representing foreign regimes, on what they were doing, on how they were entrenching new dictatorships around the world. Not from legislators, not from the American public—not even from academics. Indeed, FARA, and foreign lobbying more broadly, barely saw any scholarly research after the United States emerged from the Cold War. For three decades after 1990, the number of FARA-related scholarly articles could be counted on one hand. For context, that's fewer academic articles than had been written on things like baseball cards, Batman's mythos, and the legacy of pop groups like the Spice Girls and *NSYNC. Not unimportant topics, necessarily— but perhaps not quite as important as the Americans helping tyrants eviscerate their populations, and bludgeon democracy as they went.

Still, that might not be quite fair, either. Academic research remains contingent not just on scholars' interests but also on things like funding sources and data access. Not only was there little money in actually researching foreign lobbying, but when it came to tracking down data on these schemes—in obtaining details of meetings and payments and actual outcomes—American officials had decided by the end of the century to make gathering such information somehow even more difficult. That is, instead of actually enforcing the extant laws, U.S. officials decided to water them down even further—and provide foreign regimes even more leeway to target Americans without the rest of us being aware.

The biggest blow came in 1995, when Congress passed a new bill dubbed the Lobbying Disclosure Act (LDA). On its face, the LDA was supposed to nominally strengthen American lobbying regulations. And it did, at least in certain respects; the new legislation required domestic lobbyists to finally register their work, their clients, and their contracts with all corporate customers. Like FARA, the LDA didn't *prevent* any lobbying. Instead, it was supposed to simply bring a bit of transparency to the growing, and increasingly opaque, industry—and provide Americans greater insight into machinations in Washington.[3]

But there were two interrelated issues with the LDA's passage that, when combined, not only kneecapped the legislation but gutted FARA even further. The first dealt with the actual new requirements themselves. While the LDA was a clear improvement in terms of corporate lobbying transparency, it wasn't nearly as stringent as previous FARA requirements. For instance, unlike FARA, the LDA didn't require any details on lobbyists' actual meetings with officials. You might learn how much, say, Nike or Tesla was paying a certain lobbying firm—but you wouldn't know who those lobbyists were actually speaking with, or how often, or even what they discussed. And unlike under FARA, not every lobbying firm even had to register; if the contract was below a certain monetary threshold, the lobbyists wouldn't even have to file paperwork on their activities.[4]

The second issue flowed directly from the first. On its face, the new LDA—directed as it was at purely *corporate* clients—shouldn't have had any effect on *foreign* lobbying disclosures. The former focused on those lobbying on behalf of companies, while the latter focused largely on those lobbying on behalf of all foreign entities. But around the same time the LDA passed, legislators decided to amend FARA's language to specifically link it with the new legislation—and ended up dissolving those supposed differences entirely.[5]

The change was simple. While lobbyists for foreign governments and political parties still had to file with FARA, those repping foreign *companies* could now file under the less stringent LDA. The only catch: those companies couldn't operate, or lobby, on behalf of any foreign regime. "In 1995 FARA was amended to exempt those who represent foreign companies or individuals if the work is not intended to benefit a foreign government or political party," the new text read. So long as they claimed they were engaged in "bona fide commercial, industrial, or financial operations," they could skip FARA entirely, and instead "register under the far less transparent LDA."[6]

If you don't bother to think through the implications—which many legislators apparently didn't—you can see the rationale of the new amendment. If FARA was supposed to bring transparency into how foreign *regimes* target American policymakers, why would regulators necessarily care about *companies* from foreign nations? As U.S. officials saw it, these foreign corporations were just trying to follow the American model: corporate capitalism, interested only in bottom lines and commercial growth. These foreign companies wouldn't be proxies for regimes, because that's not how the *Pax Americana* economic model, then swarming around the globe, was supposed to work. And given the broader deregulatory thrust of the era—which, as it happened, helped both American corporations and their political allies line their pockets that much further—it was easy to push the idea that the fewer regulations, the better.

At least, that was the argument behind the LDA. And in a vacuum, maybe that's how these systems could operate. Maybe, in a perfect world, foreign companies could be fully, formally disentangled from the regimes they were trying to work under. Maybe companies in autocracies and hereditary dictatorships and single-party states could fully divest their profits and prospects from the governments ruling their nations.

It's a nice thought. But as we've already seen, and as we'll continue to see throughout this book, it's a fantasy. It was a fantasy when Ivy Lee first signed up to represent a supposedly apolitical firm in Nazi Germany, which acted as a key piece of Hitler's designs. It was a fantasy when Manafort inked his deal with a supposedly apolitical group in the Philippines, which acted as a front for his work on behalf of Marcos. And it was a fantasy as America turned toward the twenty-first century and these foreign companies and corporations erupted around the world—most especially in those countries where, in order to survive, they had to do the regimes' bidding whenever asked.

American legislators apparently missed the memo. But foreign lobbyists, and their clients, didn't. Suddenly, rather than having the lobbyists busy spinning foreign corporations register with FARA, they could hop over to the skeletal LDA and still be following the law. Legislators—who were hardly enforcing lobbying regulations, anyway—had suddenly created a loophole that entire regimes could now barge through, all at the public's expense.

And that's exactly what happened. In the early 1990s, there were just over two thousand registrations with FARA. Just a few years later, after the new LDA legislation was enacted, that number had dropped by nearly two-thirds—an unprecedented collapse, never before seen in FARA's history.[7] All of it because legislators had introduced new lobbying regulations—and helped decimate FARA that much more in the process.

*　*　*

STILL, INFORMATION ABOUT foreign lobbying wasn't a black hole, at least not entirely. And while legislators spent years largely ignoring foreign lobbying campaigns—and, as we'll see in the final section of the book, barreling the nation toward disaster—by the twenty-first century we began to have *some* idea about how these campaigns operated, and why regimes around the world would use foreign lobbyists in the first place.

Much of these insights come from the few academics who *have* dedicated themselves to studying the phenomenon. There may be more scholars devoted to things like fantasy football or the rise of the Marvel Cinematic Universe, but the handful of academics cataloguing the explosion of foreign lobbying have been essential to understanding the topic—and to deciphering the reasons that regime after regime, regardless of region or ideology, turn to American lobbyists for their needs.

According to one academic named Alexander Dukalskis, an American political scientist at Ireland's University College Dublin, the reasons were relatively simple. These despots use lobbying firms in order to, as Dukalskis sees it, "make the world safe for dictatorship." It's all a form of "authoritarian image management," which sees lobbyists transform dictators into supposed democratizers, reprehensible regimes into allegedly reformist governments, tyrants who terrorize populaces into officials who should receive American support and aid.[8]

We've already seen above how this has worked for figures like Savimbi, Barre, or Abacha, all of whom used lobbyists to spin themselves into American allies in the eyes of Washington. But as Dukalskis detailed in his book—entitled, fittingly enough, *Making the World Safe for Dictatorship*—many of these lobbying efforts are actually targeted at the dictators' own *domestic* audiences, and not just U.S. officials per se. There is, to be sure, more American support and American financial aid, as well as American arms, that can be unlocked with these lobbying efforts. But the kind of "image management" these lobbyists engage in on behalf of their dictator-clients further helps entrench their dictatorships, and further helps smother any challenges to their rule domestically.[9]

As Dukalskis wrote, whitewashing a regime abroad aids with "internal security," primarily by "suppressing challenges to [a regime's] legitimacy emanating from abroad."[10] That is, with these lobbyists abroad pushing a regime's arguments and spinning its image for foreign audiences, there is less likelihood that regime opponents—journalists, dissidents, and (actual) democratizers—will be able to get a hearing with Western policymakers. The lobbyists can suck up all of the oxygen and drown out the criticism.

If you think this sounds identical to why American corporations first hired Ivy Lee—using him to both spin their images and undercut those trying to highlight corporate crimes and malfeasance—you'd be right. Only in this case, instead of an oil company or a metals tycoon using the tactic, it is a dictatorship dedicated to immiserating an entire nation.

As Dukalskis continued, these dictators' efforts contain multiple components. They "may involve externally facing media of the authoritarian state disseminating information designed to refute criticism, 'correct' the record, and/or question the credibility of challengers." They may likewise "draw on networks of influential persons with connections to the foreign policy establishment of the host state, fund think tank activities, and retain public relations firms, among other tactics." In effect, these regimes use figures like Manafort and his ilk to overwhelm critics abroad, making sure it's only the regime's message that gets heard—and the regime's preferred image that gets seen.[11]

On its face, this may not be much of an issue. (Isn't the point of the U.S.'s First Amendment the allowance of such competing viewpoints?) But since these dictatorships have already eliminated critics in their own countries—jailing journalists, assassinating opponents, targeting any who may stand in the regime's way—critics based abroad are often the only ones left who can highlight the ruling tyrant's gross crimes.

And by hiring these foreign lobbyists—by using and abusing the American right to freely lobby—these regimes can swamp those remaining critics abroad, dominating the conversation and burying any criticism. They can't eliminate those critics (yet), but they can effectively silence them, and use foreign lobbyists to do so. And this has been happening around the world, including in countries that have supposedly built themselves back from traumatic pasts and are now, as they claim, on their way to becoming democratic success stories.

Few countries have embodied this trajectory, and this reality, as clearly as the Central African country of Rwanda. A few decades removed from a genocide that killed hundreds of thousands, the Rwandan government, led by President Paul Kagame, has gone out of its way in recent years to portray itself as a country emerging into a far brighter future.

But as Dukalskis found, the Rwandan regime—overseen by the increasingly dictatorial Kagame since 2000—has crafted such an image thanks not to any kind of actual democratic reforms but to a remarkable lobbying and public relations campaign that the regime has spearheaded. From sponsoring tours to funding supposedly independent documentaries on the country to launching smear attacks on academics and critics, all of these efforts successfully "promote[d] a positive image" of Kagame's regime.[12]

And the campaign worked. Rather than seen as a "rogue dictatorship," Kagame's Rwanda stands as a supposed success story in the broader world of foreign aid and democratization. "Rwanda is perhaps the most successful example of authoritarian image management in the contemporary world," Dukalskis concluded—even while the regime is responsible for "grave humanitarian and human rights catastrophes," from assassinating political opponents to overseeing the "violent autocratization of politics" domestically.[13] And this image remains even after Kagame's forces effectively kidnapped Paul Rusesabagina—the hero of the film Hotel Rwanda and one of the regime's most outspoken critics—and imprisoned him on sham charges of supposed terrorism.[14]

And all of it has helped Kagame—and similar figures who employed similar tactics elsewhere—remain in power, as other researchers discovered. "Authoritarian leaders use the international recognition they consequently obtain as a means to legitimize their rule at home, by presenting themselves as internationally praised role models and therefore deserving of support by the local population," Adele Del Sordi and Emanuela Dalmasso, a pair of political scientists, wrote in 2018.[15] In other words, the more populations hear about how wonderful—or how reformist, or how savvy, or how benign, etc.—a regime may be, the less likely any audience, either foreign or domestic, will be to challenge that regime's rule. Or as Dukalskis summed up, "The aim of [such] efforts is to secure, at best, active belief in the regime's ideology or, at a minimum, passive compliance among most of the population."[16]

To create, in other words, a world that is fine with their regime—their autocracy, their tyranny, their despotism—remaining in power. "Even if they do not intend to create a world of dictatorships," Dukalskis wrote, "they still want to create a world safe for their own dictatorship."[17]

* * *

BEN FREEMAN IS tall and lanky, someone you might mistake for a cross-country runner, or maybe even a professional lacrosse player. Rather than taking his talents to an athletic field, though, Freeman has become one of the few voices in the United States dedicating himself to uncovering the tides and trends of the world of foreign lobbyists—and how these firms and figures have not only lobbied on behalf of their clients but even injected their foreign clients' wealth directly into the American political system itself.

At least, that's one of the implications of Freeman's work as a doctoral student. While studying at Texas A&M University, Freeman focused his studies not only on the porous history of FARA enforcement but also on the biggest American firms feasting on foreign lobbying monies in the twenty-first century. Later bundling his findings into a book entitled *The Foreign Policy Auction*, Freeman pored through the scant filings in the FARA database to see what he could turn up.[18] In doing so, he took a scalpel to a number of firms and their regime partners to see what, exactly, they were doing—and where some of the money involved actually went.

On the one hand, Freeman's findings confirmed what others—not least the federal Government Accountability Office, whose reports we read about in Chapter 5—had found. FARA was a shell, an after-thought, with foreign lobbying firms running havoc over deadlines and requirements. The topic of foreign lobbying enforcement still "garners scant attention," Freeman wrote.[19]

But it wasn't just that the world of foreign lobbying was largely overlooked. By the 2000s the industry was already worth hundreds of millions of dollars, with "foreign expenditures constitut[ing] approximately 25 percent of all lobbying in the U.S.," Freeman calculated. Yet as Freeman found, that money didn't stay with the lobbying firms. Instead, it had begun "infect[ing] the U.S. political process"—and "systematically undermining United States foreign policy."[20]

American foreign policy, Freeman continued, is "not just altered, shifted, manipulated, or influenced" by such networks. Instead, it's being "sold" outright. As Freeman saw it, by the 2000s an effective "auction" had emerged, with U.S. foreign policy going to the highest bidder, and with American foreign lobbyists acting as the middlemen.[21]

The claims were spectacular—and they weren't wrong. Freeman used a range of examples to inform his conclusions, centering on some of the biggest lobbying firms emerging in Washington. One group Freeman focused on was a law firm named DLA Piper, formed in 2005. DLA Piper wasn't necessarily new to the world of foreign lobbying; one of the firms merged into DLA included a subsidiary that had lobbied on behalf of foreign clients since 1985. But after DLA Piper's launch—and the fact that it boasted American officials like Dick Armey (a former GOP House majority leader) and Dick Gephardt (a former Democratic House minority leader)—the firm began swaggering through Washington, signing deals with some of America's key partners abroad, such as the dictatorial United Arab Emirates and the illiberal Turkish government.

By this point, a bipartisan firm feting dictator-clients was par for the course. But as Freeman found, it wasn't just that DLA Piper began representing autocratic clients in Washington, or that the firm made millions in the process. It was, instead, what the firm ended up *doing* with the millions they made. "The most striking aspect of DLA Piper's lobbying efforts on behalf of their foreign clients is not the amount of money [involved], who they contacted, or the number of times they contacted them," Freeman wrote. "It is the amount of money they gave to legislators they contacted and the timing of these contributions."[22]

As Freeman detailed, DLA Piper wasn't only lobbying legislators on behalf of dictators abroad. The firm and its employees were also sending those legislators money *directly*—funneling them much-needed campaign contributions, even while pressuring them to change American policy on behalf of their foreign clients. They were, in effect, acting as a pass-through for regime-linked monies, which went directly into American election coffers.

Nor were these just a handful of officials that DLA Piper gave money to. Freeman tabulated that over 20 percent of all congressional officials "received contributions from DLA Piper and were contacted by its lobbyists on behalf of foreign clients." And recipients were not only household names, but those charged with directly crafting American foreign policy. Barack Obama, John McCain, Hillary Clinton, Chuck Schumer: presidents and senators, leading voices on both sides of the aisle, all took funds from DLA Piper while simultaneously sitting down with the firm to listen to them whitewash dictators and autocrats. Some of them even met with DLA Piper on the *same day* as the campaign contributions, wasting no time between the two—including figures like Clinton, who did this multiple times as senator.[23]

Think about that for a moment. A foreign dictatorship bookmarks millions of dollars to a lobbying firm, in order to pressure U.S. legislators to pursue pro-regime policies (and smother critics' voices in the process). While the lobbyists spin the regime in question, they also then direct some of those funds directly to the legislators themselves, helping those American officials get reelected in the process. These firms have become, in effect, sieves for the regimes, cutouts that allow them to ricochet the money from the foreign regimes to American politicians directly. And because of the scant oversight of foreign lobbying filings—to say nothing of the wide availability of the campaign funding mechanisms and lack of fundraising limits—the American electorate has little idea of how wide the problem actually is, let alone the impact it's begun having on both American foreign policy and American democracy writ large.

The firms in question deny that their campaign donations are related to the income received from foreign dictatorships; firms like DLA

Piper claim such funding streams are entirely separate. Part of this defense is rhetorical, as no firm wants to be seen funneling dictator-linked wealth directly to American legislators. Part is also out of legal concerns, as it remains a crime for foreign entities and foreign nationals to donate to American officials.

But these disavowals are a sham. These firms may technically be following the law. But as they well know, so long as American nationals, like those at these lobbying firms, act as intermediaries, they can organize effectively unlimited donations to American legislators—all on behalf of foreign clients. And because the foreign regimes in question have access to effectively limitless wealth—thanks to dictators' control over things like national treasuries, allowing them to pillage at will—there's little to stop them from using these lobbying firms as effective fronts, cycling gobs of foreign money directly into American politics.

It's a simple cycle: Regimes bankroll the lobbying firms, who then act as cutouts that can reroute dictators' wealth to legislators, who can then use that wealth to get reelected—and then pursue pro-dictatorship policies that much further. It's a kleptocratic carousel, spun around and around, all for the benefit of the autocrats and dictators in question.

Again, the lobbying firms argue that these tranches of money—income received from foreign regimes, and donations directed toward the officials these lobbyists are hired to pressure—are distinct, without any interplay or overlap. But all of that is ignoring the fungibility of the funds in the first place. As one of the political scientists Freeman cites said, "A dollar is a dollar."[24] The revenue made from foreign regimes directly offsets the donations themselves, even if the accounts are nominally separate.

The data highlights just how specious the firms' defense is. At DLA Piper, for instance, there was a clear, conspicuous preference for donating to officials the firm directly targeted on behalf of dictatorial clients. "For every dollar given to candidates not contacted on behalf of foreign clients, nearly two dollars went to candidates that were of use to DLA Piper's foreign clients," Freeman writes. In other words: DLA Piper's donations were *nearly twice as high* to congressional officials whom it lobbied on behalf of foreign regimes as to those it didn't lobby.[25]

But DLA Piper is hardly alone. They're hardly the only firm taking dictator-linked funds with one hand and shoveling donations to targeted officials with the other. (Though DLA Piper *is* the only major firm that questioned whether or not the Turkish massacre of Armenians constituted genocide.[26]) Another lobbying firm, the Livingston Group, has engaged in the same practice, at perhaps an even greater clip. Founded in 1999 by Robert Livingston, the former Republican chairman of the House Appropriations Committee, the Livingston Group hoovered up millions in the 2000s by taking on dictators that even other firms wouldn't touch, from the Republic of Congo's Denis Sassou Nguesso to Libya's Muammar Gaddafi.

Along the way, Livingston and his employees donated massive sums to the congressional officials they simultaneously lobbied on behalf of their kleptocratic clients. "From late 2007 to late 2009 one in four legislators was contacted by the Livingston Group on behalf of foreign clients and had received a campaign contribution from a member of the firm," Freeman's analysis found. Fully 25 percent of the U.S. Congress, on both sides of the political divide, had taken funds from Livingston Group staffers—and concurrently sat down with those same staffers, all on behalf of the firm's roster of tyrants.[27]

And again, these weren't back-bench, no-name politicos. "This is not a randomly selected group of legislators," Freeman continued. "It is disproportionately stocked with the most important players in the foreign policy arena and party leaders." As with DLA Piper, the Livingston Group's targets were household names, from Obama to former Senate majority leader Mitch McConnell to former House speaker John Boehner.[28]

Nor were these donations subtle; plenty of them took place on the *same exact day* that these legislators hosted Livingston Group lobbyists. In one remarkable instance, Indiana representative Dan Burton met with a Livingston Group representative spinning the dictatorship of Azerbaijan—and, later that day, received three separate donations from three separate Livingston representatives. (Not long later, Burton left office and immediately jumped into a new role as a pro-Azeri lobbyist. When a reporter questioned him about his new gig, Burton snapped at him, saying, "You're a scandal monger and I don't want to talk to you.")[29]

*   *   *

By the mid-2000s, this carousel—this auction, as Freeman dubbed it—was picking up speed. Manafort was no longer an outlier, nor were figures like Savimbi or Abacha. With America retaining its hyperpower status, even as it bled out in Iraq and Afghanistan, regime after regime still cultivated allies in Washington. Maybe it was to try to retain foreign aid. (Every country that lobbied for economic aid during this period received it.) Maybe it was to expand military aid. (Nearly every regime lobbying for military aid during this period obtained it.) "The message is clear: if a country does not want to lose its U.S. aid, it had better be lobbying for it," Freeman summed up. "Diplomacy has been privatized."[30]

The demand was clearly there; every regime—regardless of allegations of genocide, corruption, or crimes against humanity—wanted a representative in Washington. And this isn't an exaggeration. Adversaries like China and Russia, democratic allies like Australia and New Zealand, dictatorships like Saudi Arabia and Kazakhstan and Belarus and Egypt: all of them had their American lobbyists scuttling around Washington, bending legislators' ears, and in plenty of instances, even directing campaign funds their way. An ever-expanding network of American firms were willing to service monsters and madmen, making millions as they went.

Which is why, around the same time that Freeman conducted his research into the regime-to-lobbyist-to-donor pipeline, a journalist named Ken Silverstein launched his own investigation. Silverstein wanted to see just how far these firms would sink to seek business with one of these regimes—and just how much, or how little, the American populace would know about it.

Rather than approach the firms outright, though, Silverstein had a different idea. Concocting a new persona and fabricating an entire backstory—now posing as someone named "Kenneth Case," working not as an American journalist but as a UK-based broker—Silverstein reached out to a range of American lobbying groups. Emailing from his "Kenneth Case" account, Silverstein claimed he was a consultant looking to link the firms with one of the most repressive regimes on the planet. He kept the details vague, dangling the offer to as many lobbyists as he could. As he wrote, "I would pose as the representative of a small, mysterious overseas firm with a major financial stake in the country in question, and which hoped to curry favor with the ruling authorities by retaining a Washington firm to buff their image and improve the regime's ties with the American government."[31]

His preparation wasn't necessarily airtight; as he admitted, his cover was "recklessly thin," with a website registered in Pennsylvania and business cards that were "printed on flimsy cardboard stock," looking "far too cheap for an official from a fancy international energy firm." But Silverstein knew that, by the 2000s, the groups he contacted were happy to supply all lobbying needs for any regime in question. As Silverstein wondered, "If presented with a potentially fat contract to represent a pariah regime, just how low would a well-heeled Washington lobbying firm sink?"[32]

The answer was clear: as low as needed, and then even lower yet. Part of that was evident in the client Silverstein claimed to be helping: the government of Turkmenistan, one of the most thoroughly repressive states in the world. The Turkmen regime at the time was almost a caricature of a totalitarian state, dominated for years by a tinpot, drug-addled dictator who built golden statues of himself while renaming months after his family members. Most bizarrely, the dictator had penned his own religious text—and then forced all Turkmen schools and universities to teach it to students. It was a state and a regime that made North Korea look like a bastion of liberty. And it was a regime that, as Silverstein found, lobbying firms would be more than happy to help—to become, as one firm said, the Turkmen dictator's "eyes and ears in Washington."[33]

One of the lobbying groups Silverstein contacted was APCO Worldwide, a behemoth firm in Washington that had recently been named the "Agency of the Year" by PRWeek, the leading public relations industry publication.[34] APCO was no stranger to servicing despots, having previously worked with Nigeria's Abacha and the kleptocratic mafiosi overseeing the country of Azerbaijan. For them, selling dictators was a familiar field. As APCO responded, they'd be "delighted to put a team together" to help Turkmenistan's regime.[35]

The firm quickly unspooled their strategy for Silverstein, spilling their tactics to the undercover investigator. One of their proposed moves involved hiring supposedly neutral observers—journalists, scholars, former officials, and the like—to spew pro-regime messaging. "We can utilize some of the think-tank experts who would say, 'On the one hand this and the other hand that,'" one of the APCO officials told Silverstein, detailing how to help muddy any criticisms the regime may face. APCO also outlined a pro-regime media strategy. Claiming that they'd already placed "thousands" of op-eds on behalf of clients across all kinds of media, APCO admitted that they "actually wrote the pieces and then went out and found 'signatories'"—a tactic they'd be happy to help reprise for Turkmenistan's dictator.[36]

Another firm, the Carmen Group, responded to Silverstein's entreaties with a similar strategy. The Carmen Group had already serviced a neighboring dictatorship, in Kazakhstan. And they said they'd be happy to pay for American journalists to go on an all-expenses-paid junket to Turkmenistan—and then have those journalists write paeans to just how wonderful the Turkmen regime truly was. (They wouldn't have been the first to represent Turkmenistan in Washington; a few years before, former secretary of state Alexander Haig signed on to launder the Turkmen dictator's reputation, claiming he "should be a hero rather than a pariah.")[37]

Over and over, firm after firm raced to Silverstein's offer, willing to take on the Turkmen tyranny as a client. They were, as Silverstein wrote, "groveling" to work for one of the most heinous dictatorships on the planet, where opponents were regularly tortured and basic freedoms were nonexistent. There were no concerns about human rights abuse, or how the regime immiserated women and children, obliterated local environmental efforts, or engaged in the kinds of corruption and crimes that would have made Mussolini or Mao proud. There was only the promise of a potential contract—of the opportunity to profit from entrenching the Turkmen dictatorship even further.[38]

It was, on the whole, one of the most depressing undercover investigations of the era, highlighting that there was no regime beyond the pale for these firms. As one of the lobbyists told Silverstein, "As I have often said, I would represent the devil himself for the right price—it's not personal, just business."[39]

* * *

WHEN SILVERSTEIN FINALLY admitted his ruse, the firms were predictably embarrassed. But few of them appeared chastened. If anything, the public relations industry sprinted to their defense. Rather than drafting new standards or calling for reforms that might prevent American firms from slobbering to service the most despicable regimes extant, the industry closed ranks around the conned firms. Kathy Cripps—a representative from the Council of Public Relations Firms, which supposedly set industry standards—called Silverstein's efforts "tawdry," recommending his employer, *Harper's Magazine,* "reassess [their] current standards of reporting." To those steering the public relations industry, it was Silverstein at fault, rather than the firms that laid out a roadmap for how to help a neo-Stalinist dictatorship remain in power. Said Silverstein in response, "Where was Cripps when poor Ivy Lee needed her? Had it been the 1930s and the offices of Lee I had infiltrated, one could easily imagine Cripps denouncing me for my 'tawdry' exposure of the führer's man."[40]

And he wasn't wrong. Decades may have separated them, but Ivy Lee's work on behalf of the Nazis was little different than what these modern American firms promised to do on behalf of Turkmenistan's murderous, maniacal dictator. The world may have changed, but the services—and the willingness to serve these despots—remained the same.

But by the time Silverstein published his findings, these firms weren't the only players in Washington courting these dictators. Because by the mid-2000s, a new force had entered the field: America's most prominent politicians, who realized how much money could be made by lobbying directly for these dictators—and who realized how easily they could trade their reputations in for a piece of this growing foreign lobbying lucre.

10

Ukrainian Cocktails

It is madness, but it is a glorious madness.

—Michael O'Rahilly[1]

In the middle of 2003, Oleg Deripaska—one of Russia's original, and most notorious, oligarchs—had a problem. It had little to do with how to manage his billions of dollars, gained through rapacious violence in Russia's so-called "Aluminum Wars" of the 1990s.[2] It wasn't even necessarily related to his relationship with rising Russian dictator Vladimir Putin, for whom Deripaska was a "key ally."[3] It instead had to do with how Deripaska could gain access to the most important country in the world: the United States.

For years, the United States had specifically blocked Deripaska from obtaining an American visa. And with good reason. As the Treasury Department wrote, Deripaska faced allegations that he'd "bribed a government official, ordered the murder of a businessman, and had links to a Russian organized crime group."[4] His presence in Washington—whether to organize investments, to act as an extension of Putin's regime, or both—could only be disastrous.

Deripaska, though, had an idea. If he couldn't reach the U.S. government itself, perhaps he could hire a proxy of his own to push his case. Maybe there was a man in Washington who would act as a front for Deripaska, arm-twisting American officials into letting the kleptocrat into the country. Maybe there was someone who could downplay Deripaska's past, his mounds of dirty money, and his connections to the Kremlin, pushing instead the idea that Deripaska was some kind of "independent" businessman who'd made his wealth perfectly legally. Maybe there was a lobbyist Deripaska could hire, whitewashing his image and ushering him into Washington—and helping open the floodgates for other Russian oligarchs, all of whom owed their wealth to the Kremlin, and all of whom acted as effective foot soldiers for Putin himself.

It didn't take Deripaska long to find someone in Washington to help him. This time, though, it wasn't a former campaign organizer like Manafort, or a public relations specialist like Ivy Lee, or even a savvy consultant like Charlie Black or Peter Kelly. This time, the American who offered his help was one of the most prominent politicians of his age.

It was Bob Dole, senior statesman of the Republican Party, longtime senator, and failed GOP presidential candidate. Recently retired, Dole had transformed himself into one of the United States' most successful (and most lucrative) foreign lobbyists. And as he told Deripaska, he'd love to help the Russian oligarch expand his—and the Kremlin's—tendrils in Washington.

* * *

As we saw in the first section of the book, when a former treasury secretary lobbied on behalf of Russian interests around the Alaska purchase, Dole was hardly the first former official to later sell out to a foreign regime. But he was the most outsized, and easily the most impactful.

Nicknamed the "lion of the Senate," Dole stood for years as one of the towering figures of the American political establishment.[5] He'd steered the Republican Party for decades, first as a senator from Kansas and then later as the Senate majority leader, culminating in the 1996 GOP presidential nomination. He was, as *The New York Times* described him, one of the "longest-serving Republican leaders" in American history, one of the "most durable political figures of the last century."[6] As President Joe Biden said after Dole's death in 2021, the GOP stalwart was "an American statesman like few in our history."[7]

And that may be true. But Dole was something else, as well: the first prominent American politician who, after leaving office, sold his reputation to myriad foreign bidders, opening doors in Washington to regimes and oligarchs around the world. He was the first former presidential candidate to become, quite literally, a foreign agent.

First, there were the foreign governments. Some of those who hired Dole after his 1996 retirement were democratic allies, like Kosovo and Taiwan.[8] But some of them were outright dictatorships, ransacking and impoverishing populations back home—and looking to Dole and his firm (known as Alston & Bird) to shore up support in Washington. Dole worked on behalf of the anti-democratic government of the United Arab Emirates, directly lobbying his former colleagues as part of the Emirati regime's broader efforts to infiltrate Washington. Dole also signed on with the autocrats following in Mobutu's footsteps in the Democratic Republic of Congo, with his firm promising to help with "strategic communications" and "policy issues" regarding the DRC's upcoming elections. According to the letter of engagement, Dole would play a "lead" role in the arrangement.[9] (Left unmentioned was the fact that the incumbent Congolese autocrat had already delayed elections multiple times, hoping to cling to power as long as possible.)

Then there were the oligarchs. Deripaska, for instance, hired Dole and his firm to specifically lobby the U.S. State Department to obtain an American visa. As *The Wall Street Journal* reported, Dole then tried to "persuade U.S. officials his client isn't a criminal and that his business operations are transparent."[10] (Deripaska's corruption and Kremlin links were so flagrant that he would later end up specifically sanctioned by the United States, as well as by Britain and the European Union.) American officials were apparently convinced: thanks to Dole, Deripaska soon had his visa—setting the stage for Russia's 2016 interference operations, as we'll see later.

Nor did Dole limit himself to kleptocrats in places like Russia or Central Africa. Around the same time, he joined the board of a bank in Kyrgyzstan called AsiaUniversalBank (AUB). According to extensive reporting from both journalists and pro-transparency groups like Global Witness, the bank was one of the most crooked institutions the region had ever seen. AUB acted as an effective money laundromat for the ruling, brutal Bakiyev family, allowing them to pilfer millions while turning Kyrgyzstan into their own personal fiefdom. As Global Witness wrote, the bank maintained "significant indicators that suggest

money laundering: hundreds of millions of dollars seemed to be moving through their accounts while they were not engaged in any real
business activity." AUB was regarded as so corrupt that even the Russian Central Bank recommended against working with it.[11]

But then Dole stepped into the breach. He joined the bank's board
in 2007 and began vouching for AUB's credentials. With Dole's help,
AUB staggered on for a few more years—before it collapsed amidst a
bloody revolution that finally ousted the Bakiyev family, who enjoyed
their looted millions in exile. As one Kyrgyz official told me about Dole
joining the bank, "I remember being disgusted by how cheap U.S. politicians [were for] sale."[12]

Russian oligarchs, foreign dictators, money laundromats writ large:
over and again, Dole spent his post-congressional career lobbying on
behalf of some of the most notorious figures and institutions of the era.
While playing up his supposedly patriotic credentials at home, Dole
spun on, year after year, as the go-to foreign lobbyist in Washington.

And it's not difficult to see why he did so. Dole's firm made millions
from the dictatorships and the regimes they represented. Deripaska
himself shoveled more than $560,000 directly from Moscow. The deal
to represent the Democratic Republic of Congo involved a half million dollars, for only three months' work. (As one person familiar with
Dole's foreign lobbying deadpanned, "That's a lot of money.")[13]

It's ultimately unclear how much Dole made from his arrangements
in places like Kyrgyzstan, so it's difficult to tell how much his sum as
a foreign lobbyist totaled. But one thing is clear: Dole made far more
money over just a few years as a foreign lobbyist than he did in his
decades in Congress. As one analysis of Dole's lobbying career found,
Dole "has never been happier—and certainly not more prosperous."
(Despite a lifetime of public service, Dole died with a net worth that
ran into the tens of millions.)[14]

Perhaps more importantly, Dole also opened a new door in Washington, with legislator after legislator following his lead into the world
of foreign lobbying. After all, if the supposed "lion of the Senate" could
sell out to foreign regimes, why couldn't they?

Thanks to Dole, by the 2000s it was entirely normal for former officials to transform into foreign agents, and to do so at a far higher

clip than ever seen before in American history. One analysis in 2016 found that more than 10 percent of legislators who'd left office during the post–Cold War era had immediately flipped into foreign lobbyists, selling their services to dictators around the world. Dozens and dozens of senators and representatives had left Congress and, as if on cue, promptly transitioned into foreign agents.[15]

And this is on both sides of the aisle, and for regimes of all stripes. Senators went on to lobby for Saudi tyrants and Hungary's budding autocracy. House members went on to lobby for entities in Belarus and anti-democratic forces in Qatar. Majority leaders and minority leaders, Democrats and Republicans, single-term politicians and lifelong officials—all of them have left office, only to jump right into a new role as a foreign lobbyist. From GOP leaders—like former House speaker John Boehner, who now works at the firm that represents the genocidal regime in China[16]—to Democratic standard-bearers—like former vice presidential candidate Joe Lieberman, who also worked for a proxy of the same regime in Beijing[17]—America's leading politicos have turned, with increasing pace, to foreign patrons after leaving office.

And that remains thanks to Dole, who made the idea of a former official selling out to foreign regimes far more palatable—and far less treasonous—than it had once been viewed. "Want to be a 'foreign agent'?" one headline on the topic would later read. "Serve in Congress first."[18]

*　*　*

BUT MAYBE THIS shouldn't be all that surprising. When Dole ran for president in 1996, shortly before launching into his career as a foreign lobbyist, he'd turned to none other than Paul Manafort to wrangle the votes needed to land the Republican nomination.

Manafort was "Dole's convention manager," *The New Yorker* reported in 1996, "which means that he is the chief architect of [the 1996] Republican National Convention."[19] Even after Manafort had already signed on with dictator after dictator, even after Manafort had tried to help warlords and tyrants steal elections in their home countries, Dole thought it a good idea to have him help organize Dole's GOP nomination. With Manafort steering the convention, Republicans jettisoned

the hourlong speeches of conventions past and instead issued short
soundbites that could be bundled into later clips. "We're creating political television," Manafort described it.[20] And it worked: the delegates
anointed Dole their nominee, with Manafort overseeing a far more active, and far more interesting, convention than those in years past.

Dole ultimately lost the presidential race. But his links with Manafort
didn't end with the 1996 defeat. In the early 2000s, shortly after Deripaska hired Dole to spin himself as some kind of successful, apolitical
Russian tycoon, Deripaska took on Manafort's services as well, in order
to help Moscow regain control of a country it increasingly eyed with
monomaniacal obsession: Ukraine.

*   *   *

BY THE MID-2000S, Ukrainians were already making clear that they
preferred to join the West—including things like NATO and the European Union—instead of Russia. And they were willing to put their
bodies on the line to do it. After a rigged 2004 election, which saw
a pro-Putin puppet named Viktor Yanukovych supposedly "win" the
vote, Ukrainians took to the streets by the hundreds of thousands to
protest, in an event later dubbed the Orange Revolution. Remarkably,
they succeeded in forcing a re-run of the vote, with the pro-Western
candidate finally proving victorious. (The win was made all the more
remarkable given the fact that the pro-Western candidate had been
nearly murdered via poisoning during the campaign.)

The result was a clear victory for Ukraine's Westernizing forces:
for pro-transparency voices and investigative journalists, for gender
and environmental activists, for those advocating for a more equitable
economy. It was, however, a clear loss for a range of figures who owed
their wealth to both the Kremlin and Ukraine's corrupt claque of pro-
Russian politicians—and to the Russian and Ukrainian oligarchs who
profited along the way.

One of the figures set to lose both influence and income with
Ukraine's pro-Western drift was Deripaska. Which is why, shortly after
the Orange Revolution, the oligarch reached out to Manafort and asked
if he'd be able to help.[21]

According to later investigations from Ukrainian journalists and

American officials, Deripaska hired Manafort in order to "mitigate the dangers [that] Ukraine's political crisis" suddenly posed.[22] But it wasn't just about Deripaska's finances. The oligarch also wanted to know: Could Manafort help return Ukraine to a more pro-Kremlin trajectory? Could he help restore Kyiv's pro-Putin political forces, subverting the country's pro-Western moves in the process?

Manafort quickly agreed. (To Manafort, Deripaska wasn't a glorified mafioso but a "brilliant businessman.")[23] In June 2005, Manafort—whose mission, as American investigators later detailed, would be to help Ukraine's oligarchs and pro-Kremlin forces "avoid future events like the Orange Revolution"—outlined his plan in a strategy memo.[24] As Manafort wrote, he would help "subtly influence the perceptions" of Western governments to create "an acceptable explanation for actions by [the Ukrainian and Russian governments] not totally in concert with Western thinking."[25] That is, Manafort would instruct his pro-Kremlin partners on how to undercut Western concerns about things like democracy and human rights—and to subvert Ukraine's pro-Western forces in the process.

The plans would tap Manafort's well of expertise from similar campaigns elsewhere. This was a man, after all, who had laundered an Angolan warlord into a supposed freedom fighter, a Filipino despot into a supposedly pro-Western ally, a Congolese tyrant into a supposed bastion of stability. There was little reason Manafort couldn't reprise his talents for Deripaska and the pro-Russian forces, and pro-Putin proxies, in Ukraine.

Nor is there any reason to think Moscow didn't sign off on Manafort's efforts. Not only was Deripaska one of Putin's closest allies—he proclaimed at one point that that he was "indispensable to Putin and the Kremlin"—but Manafort began his efforts in clear concert with the Kremlin.[26] "Connections between Manafort's program in Ukraine and Russia's own influence efforts there suggest that they were effectively part of the same campaign to undermine the Ukrainian government and support pro-Russia candidates," as the U.S. Senate Intelligence Committee later found. For good measure, documents seen by American investigators "also [suggest] that Manafort intended to brief the Kremlin on his activities in Ukraine and understood that his activities benefited the Kremlin."[27] (Manafort long denied that he'd ever pursued any pro-Kremlin policies; as he told *The New York Times,* he was simply interested in "teaching [Deripaska] democracy.")[28]

Not that Manafort was ever coy about his willingness to do the Kremlin's bidding; he directly pitched his work to Deripaska as something "to benefit President Vladimir Putin's government."[29] Or as he said in that first memo, "We are now of the belief that [this work in Ukraine] can greatly benefit the Putin Government if employed at the correct levels with the appropriate commitments to success."[30]

* * *

TRAVELING TO UKRAINE, Manafort quickly set down roots. Deripaska, however, was not the only oligarch Manafort immediately linked up with. Another one soon entered Manafort's orbit: a scrub-haired, squint-eyed figure named Dmytro Firtash.

At the time, Firtash's profile appeared almost indistinguishable from Deripaska's. Both were close to the Kremlin, acting as effective extensions of Putin's regime. Both of them engaged in reputation laundering in the West, with the two using public relations firms and strategic donations to gain toeholds in both London and Washington. (Most memorably, Firtash bankrolled Cambridge University's Ukrainian studies program, with the university praising his "generous benefaction.")[31] Both of them owed their wealth to a raft of corrupt networks emerging in the 1990s, with Deripaska focused on aluminum and Firtash working with natural gas. And both of them were directly fingered by American officials as surrogates for the Kremlin, with the United States sanctioning Deripaska for his "malign activity" and indicting Firtash on large-scale bribery charges, describing him as an "upper-echelon [associate] of Russian organized crime."[32]

There was one key difference, however. Deripaska was a Russian national, while Firtash was a Ukrainian citizen. And while Deripaska never publicly posed as someone interested in Ukraine's pro-Western shifts, Firtash long attempted to position himself as a supposed "patriot" for Ukraine, as a purportedly pro-Western figure who dissembled that he was a "major contributor" to Ukraine's pro-European trajectory. It was an image gullible Western media happily lapped up; as one CNN headline read, Firtash was an "oil baron" who "unleashe[d his] vast wealth to fight Putin."[33]

It was all, to use a technical term, bullshit. As *The Washington Post* later (and accurately) described, Firtash has long been a "Putin ally."[34] And as later investigators would discover, Firtash, like Deripaska, would play a key role in the Kremlin's efforts to restore control over Ukraine (as well as Moscow's political interference operations in the West). In fact, Firtash put paid to the idea that there was anything like a "pro-Western oligarch" in Ukraine. He revealed that the term "pro-Western oligarch" was itself an oxymoron: that these oligarchs, whether they're from Russia or Ukraine, are simply looking out for their own interests, which all too often overlap entirely with the Kremlin's.

But those investigations were all in the future. By the time he connected with Manafort, Firtash was simply looking to launch further links across the West: financial anchor points that he and the Kremlin could later build upon to upend Western policy and polities. And Manafort, once more, proved more than happy to help—and had an idea for how to do so.

Linking up with Firtash shortly after arriving in Ukraine, Manafort lofted a proposal: Would the oligarch be willing to use some of his illicit wealth to bankroll a new luxury apartment construct in Manhattan? The proposed building, dubbed the Bulgari Tower, would soar nearly 65 stories high, and would run approximately $850 million in total construction costs. As Manafort saw it, it was the perfect place for Firtash to not only sink his wealth into the American real estate industry—already one of the most kleptocratic, oligarch-friendly industries in the world—but gain further entrée into the United States itself. Meeting multiple times with Firtash, Manafort convinced him to put up over $100 million of his own money to get the project off the ground. It was evidence, said one outlet, of Manafort's "uncanny ability to conjure investors"—especially those with a direct line to the Kremlin.[35]

Unfortunately for the two, the investments came just as the global economy began to crater in 2008. Not even pro-Kremlin oligarchs were fully insulated from the shifting economic winds; Firtash pulled out of the deal, citing the need to stabilize his finances elsewhere. From the outside, it looked like yet another collapsed proposal, yet another victim of a spiraling recession. But shortly afterward, a lawsuit emerged alleging that Firtash, with Manafort's help, had planned to use the investment not as a means of simply gaining Firtash a foothold in the United States—but as a means of laundering hundreds of millions of Kremlin-connected dollars along the way.

Filed in New York by former Ukrainian prime minister Yulia Tymoshenko (who we'll revisit next chapter), the lawsuit alleged that Firtash planned to launder his illicit natural gas profits via American real estate, and then use those clean, untraceable funds to launch a "large bribery and influence scheme" on behalf of pro-Russian forces in Ukraine.[36] The allegations weren't necessarily unique; thanks to a decades-long loophole, American real estate has long enjoyed exemptions from basic anti–money laundering protocols, transforming the entire sector into one of the most popular destinations for transnational money laundering networks.

And Manafort was at the center of it all. The lobbyist "played a key role in [Firtash's] conspiracy and racketeering enterprise," the lawsuit read. According to the filing, Manafort allowed Firtash access to dozens of "U.S.-based companies," giving Firtash "the opportunity to expand the scope of his money laundering activities into the United States."[37] (Until 2021, the United States was the global leader in providing anonymous shell companies to kleptocrats and oligarchs around the world, which Manafort and Firtash well knew.[38]) As one of Manafort's emails read, Firtash was "totally on board" with the plans.[39]

The 2008 recession ultimately scuttled these alleged laundering plans. And the lawsuit—as with so many others dealing with shell companies, real estate investments, and transnational money laundering—was ultimately dismissed following a lack of evidence. (The beauty of these anonymous shells is that they remain ultimately untraceable—helping prevent lawsuits like this from ever succeeding.) But along the way, Manafort had deepened his links with another oligarch who would later play a key role in the Kremlin's designs not only in Ukraine, but in launching an unprecedented interference effort in American politics. And he would also be injected directly into the heart of Ukrainian politics itself—and light a fuse that would eventually detonate the entire country.

* * *

WHEN THE ORANGE Revolution rocked Ukraine's politics in 2004, the collapse of Kremlin influence in the country was seen most spectacularly in the ousting of Moscow's handpicked puppet, Viktor Yanukovych. A thuggish, dim-witted character from eastern Ukraine—a man who'd seen multiple prison stints for petty robberies—Yanukovych appeared to many as little more than a warmed-over Soviet apparatchik. With his blocky stature and stiff suits, with his dull presentations and soporific speeches, Yanukovych had little political skill to speak of. Indeed, his only talent appeared to be a clear willingness to act as a front for Kremlin interests in Ukraine—and to deliver Kyiv back into a Russian embrace.

And yet, thanks to the thousands of Ukrainians demanding a more transparent, more democratic government, Yanukovych couldn't do even that. Rather than acting as a puppet for the Kremlin, Yanukovych was instead tossed out of power. His political future had suddenly shattered, undone by the protesters demanding better governance.

Yanukovych retrenched to eastern Ukraine, licking his political wounds. There, he encountered someone who would change everything: for Ukraine, for Yanukovych's future, for the fate of Europe and Russia and the West more broadly. Shortly after the Orange Revolution seemed to cement Ukraine's pro-Western course, Yanukovych met Manafort.

The two connected via oligarchic intermediaries. As Manafort later revealed, Deripaska had introduced him to Rinat Akhmetov, another billionaire oligarch with his own alleged links to organized crime. From there, Akhmetov brought Manafort into a meeting with Yanukovych, who'd operated as Akhmetov's "key political benefactor" for years.[40]

It didn't take long for Manafort to patch together why the oligarch had introduced him to a politician on his heels—one who, Manafort well knew, presented the Kremlin's best shot at reclaiming control of Kyiv. If Manafort had managed to transform Savimbi into a democratizer, or Marcos into a reformer, or Mobutu into a statesman, what could he do with Yanukovych? Could he, as it were, transform Yanukovych back into a president?

None of this would be easy. As charismatic as a mop, as appealing as a bout of influenza, Yanukovych was saddled not only with his criminal past but also with his clear links to the Kremlin and its proxy oligarchs. But he was also someone who, as his oligarchic backers saw it, held promise. There was a potential buried within his stiff appearance and uncomfortable presence. (There was also the potential for payment, as we'll soon see.) Manafort agreed. Reforming Yanukovych—relaunching him to the presidency, regardless of the consequences—would be his next project.

*   *   *

MANAFORT'S STRATEGY TO return Yanukovych to the presidency in Kyiv involved a number of key interlocking parts. The first dealt with the physical: how Yanukovych actually, viscerally appeared. The Ukrainian would have to ditch the moth-eaten suits, his greased hair, and his habit of standing like he was in a straitjacket. Instead, he would now wear tailored outfits, a bit tighter around the waist and a bit less jarring to the eye. He would visit a proper barber, replacing his "raging bouffant" with something a bit more fashionable. And he would learn the basics of political speeches: about cadence and pacing, about structure and anecdotes, about audiences' expectations and attention spans. He would, in other words, transform into a modern politician—all part of his "Extreme Makeover," as other diplomats described it.[41]

The second element dealt with the actual contents of the Ukrainian politico's talks. Rather than using the kinds of boring, banal figures that characterized his Soviet-era upbringing—total grain yields, average dairy productions, and the like—Manafort taught Yanukovych about the utility of platitudes, of imagery, of promise. Instead of the stale, staid speeches of the past, Yanukovych began plastering bromides throughout his talks. "I understand your dreams," he starting insisting to audiences, adding, "I share in your desire to make Ukraine a land of opportunity."[42] For the first time, Yanukovych would "speak in punchy, American-style sound bites" that could grab listeners—and could end up clipped into nightly Ukrainian newscasts, reaching even more Ukrainian voters.[43]

If this was all redolent of Manafort's impact on the transformation of American, and especially Republican, politics over the past few decades, that's because it was. Similar to his roles with Reagan and Bush, similar to his efforts on behalf of Dole at the 1996 convention, Manafort brought both savvy and style (even flash?) to Yanukovych's life. If it had worked in Washington, then perhaps it could work in Kyiv, too.

But there was also a third, perhaps less public element to Manafort's project. Something that also drew on his success in steering Republican Party politics over the previous few decades, and that allowed Yanukovych to direct his new skills to far more malignant ends. Where Manafort and his colleagues had helped pioneer the infusion of right-wing—even race-baiting—politics into the modern Republican Party, the lobbyist now told Yanukovych that he should reprise something similar.

Ukraine's social axis differed from the United States', of course. It didn't revolve around racial issues, or bigotry from segments of the white population directed at Black citizens, immigrants, and others. Rather, as Manafort saw it, Ukraine's primary social cleavages orbited around ethnic Ukrainians (and Ukrainian-speakers) and ethnic Russians (and Russian-speakers). According to Manafort, "Ukraine is really two different countries."[44] And if Yanukovych wanted to win, he should play up those divisions. Similar to how Manafort's Republican clients had pandered to white grievance politics in the United States, Manafort told Yanukovych he should start hammering on ethnic grievances in Ukraine, focusing on those supposed divisions and splintering the voting bloc his opponents still relied on for success.

Given the deep unity Ukrainians of all backgrounds and languages showed following Russia's 2022 invasion, it's clear that Manafort's prescription was ultimately based on an illusion. But that didn't stop Yanukovych from focusing on trying to pry Ukrainians apart from one another, deepening the kinds of social fracture that could ultimately destabilize a country. (Manafort would later, and bizarrely, claim that Yanukovych was "a Ukrainian nationalist who wanted to protect a multi-cultural society," and that he displayed a "willing[ness] to take on Moscow."[45])

Yanukovych didn't flinch from Manafort's advice. Soon, his talking points began to describe the Orange Revolution—largely cheered on by Ukrainian-speakers, rather than Yanukovych's base of Russian-speakers—not as a pro-democratic revolution but as a "coup." He began portraying ethnic Russians as supposed victims of the new government, with Russian-speakers suddenly supposedly discriminated against. He began, in other words, amplifying the rhetoric coming from the Kremlin, which would ultimately culminate in the portrayal of Kyiv as a government steered and cheered by "Nazis," targeting ethnic Russians who needed Moscow's protection.

* * *

WHILE YANUKOVYCH'S RHETORIC described the country as a whole, there was one area he focused on in particular: the southern Ukrainian peninsula of Crimea.

Years later, in 2014, Putin invaded the Ukrainian peninsula, claiming it as his own and overseeing the first proclaimed "annexation" in Europe since the days of Hitler. When Manafort and Yanukovych linked up in the mid-2000s, though, Crimea was simply another Ukrainian province, populated by ethnic Ukrainians and Russians and Indigenous Crimean Tatars and many more. It was an undisputed part of Ukraine. As such, it was also a destination for American troops taking part in a joint NATO-Ukraine military exercise organized by Kyiv.

Ukraine, of course, was not part of NATO. But its pro-Western government clearly had designs on joining the military alliance. And in May 2006, Kyiv opened its doors to Western troops, who were looking to help Ukraine shore up its national defenses, improve regional infrastructure, and cultivate local support.

The joint exercises planned for Crimea were hardly threatening; they were far closer to goodwill gestures than anything menacing, focusing on things like building playgrounds and soccer fields. Which is why, when U.S. troops arrived on the Ukrainian peninsula, the response they received was alarming. Rather than a warm welcome, or even general apathy, the 113 U.S. Marines and sailors discovered irate crowds lining their path, hurling stones and invective alike. "We had rocks thrown at us," one officer later said. "Rocks hit Marines. Buses were rocked back and forth. We were just trying to get to our base."[46] Prowling the perimeter, some protesters even began filling plastic bottles with diesel, making so-called "Ukrainian cocktails" to launch at the Americans.[47]

Thousands of protesters, seemingly arriving out of nowhere, had greeted the American troops. There had been no warning, no sense that the local populace would turn into a frothing mess. U.S.-Ukrainian relations were, at that point, the best they'd ever been; there was little reason or rationale for the protesters to suddenly metastasize. Yet there they were, blocking the Americans' path, assaulting the Americans' transports, harassing the Americans to no end.

And the protests began to work. "Pinned in by 'thousands' of protesters with loud music, rocks, and ineffective gas bombs . . . the Marines hunkered down in a local sanitorium," one outlet later reported. "And waited. They couldn't reach their supply ship at the port; they couldn't reach their base."[48]

For one week, and then another, the protesters remained. At some point, military higher-ups realized the scene risked turning into a fiasco—or potentially worse. They pulled the plug, and pulled the troops out. "We basically waited out two weeks and under the cover of darkness one night got to an airstrip and flew home," one officer said.[49]

The fallout didn't stop there. President George W. Bush canceled a planned trip to Ukraine, with the military nixing the remainder of the joint exercises entirely. Suddenly, links between Kyiv and Washington were broken, perhaps irrevocably. Rather than building local support, the protests had suddenly fractured ties between the United States and Ukraine.

But there was always something odd, something amiss, about the entire affair. These protesters seemed, as one Marine said, like "their hearts weren't in it."[50] Like they may have been "planted." Like the whole thing was, as one State Department cable read, an "engineered controversy"—not least because "most demonstrators seemed lackluster and only gathered in numbers at times when television cameras were likely to be turned on them."[51] The whole thing appeared to have been fabricated (similar, in that sense, to the sham "referendum" in 2014 in which Crimeans purportedly voted to join Russia).[52] As the U.S. cable continued, "The malicious intent that is ultimately responsible for this ongoing incident is entirely on the side of the political forces that have not wanted to see [the Ukrainian] government succeed since the pro-democracy forces emerged victorious."[53]

Even today, the entire operation remains shrouded in questions. But after the incident, a Ukrainian prosecutor placed one person at the center of the entire affair: Manafort. "It was his political effort to raise the prestige of Yanukovych and [Yanukovych's] party—the confrontation and division of society on ethnic and linguistic grounds is his trick from the time of the elections in Angola and the Philippines," the prosecutor wrote. "While I was in the Crimea I constantly saw evidence suggesting that Paul Manafort considered [Crimean autonomy from Ukraine] as a tool to enhance the reputation of Yanukovych and win over the local electorate."[54] As part of those efforts, Manafort "orchestrated" the protests—and in so doing, forced the evacuation of U.S. troops from Crimea.[55]

Manafort always denied responsibility. But it didn't take much to see who benefited from the debacle. The entire affair resulted in an unprecedented downturn in U.S.-Ukrainian relations, a blow that the pro-Western government in Kyiv never recovered from. And in the process, it strengthened pro-Russian forces on the Crimean peninsula—and helped lay the groundwork for Moscow's invasion in 2014.

* * *

EVEN BEYOND CRIMEA, it didn't take long for Manafort's "Extreme Makeover" strategy for Yanukovych to begin paying dividends.[56] Shortly after Manafort's hiring, Yanukovych's party, known as the Party of Regions, dominated the next parliamentary vote. Because of Ukraine's multilayered governance structure, the Ukrainian legislature then sat to select the country's new prime minister, who would help steer domestic affairs alongside the country's pro-Western president.

And they chose the man who'd just been toppled by the Orange Revolution: Yanukovych.

It was something close to an electoral miracle; Yanukovych had effectively risen from the political dead. The talking points, the flashier suits, the new presence: it had all worked. Yanukovych surged back to prominence, and even popularity. Manafort had succeeded, yet again.

But Manafort wasn't done yet. Soon after Yanukovych rose as Ukraine's prime minister, Manafort began selling him to another constituency: questioning, reticent Westerners. American and European officials had watched Yanukovych's presidential campaign just a few years earlier—especially his reliance on Moscow and the near-fatal poisoning of his opponent—and remained understandably skittish. Some Western officials were even based in Kyiv, and watched firsthand as Yanukovych suddenly began exploiting Ukraine's social tensions. One U.S. official, Ambassador William Taylor, specifically asked Manafort to have Yanukovych "dial back the rhetoric." Manafort demurred; the talking points, one reporter said, "polled too well."[57]

Yet Manafort knew Yanukovych would have to gain at least token Western backing if he wanted to continue consolidating support. So he began setting up meetings for Yanukovych "with a broad range of officials and think-tank experts [in Washington] in an effort to rebrand him as a reformer."[58] Yanukovych's audiences included legislators and analysts, even higher-ups like Vice President Dick Cheney. It was a playbook that had worked with Savimbi, with Abacha, with Marcos. And it began working with a man who'd recently been toppled in the era's most prominent pro-democratic revolution. (One tool that helped: when speaking with American officials, Yanukovych's translator "turned the Ukrainian's crude rhetoric into flowery, high-end English.")[59]

Links between Washington and Kyiv may have soured—thanks to the unseen hand of Manafort's and Yanukovych's allies in Crimea—but Yanukovych had, to gullible Westerners, turned a new page. Manafort "definitely lobbied for him in Washington, that's part of what he brought to the table," one diplomat later said, adding that Manafort "tried to sell Yanukovych as being an advocate of transparency, democracy, and generally pro-American [positions]." And if his American interlocutors didn't buy fully into Yanukovych's supposed transformation, they at least began toning down their criticism. For good measure, Manafort told American audiences that "Yanukovych was more or less the same sort of person" as Manafort's Republican clients, such as Dole and Reagan. Yanukovych brought, as Manafort said, "good-old fashioned Republican values" to Ukrainian politics.[60]

Meanwhile, back in Ukraine, Yanukovych continued unfurling

Manafort's strategy. He cultivated support among a broad array of Ukrainians: elderly pensioners, nostalgic for the Soviet Union; pro-Russian activists, trying to keep Kyiv close to the Kremlin; restive families, dissatisfied with Ukraine's slowing economy. He also sat back, watching his Westernizing opponents collapse into infighting and rising acrimony, undone by ego and a roiling recession.

While the pro-Western government in Kyiv began to falter, Manafort and Yanukovych spied an opportunity. Soon, Ukrainians would return to the polls for the country's next presidential election, scheduled for early 2010. And there was, as they realized, one logical choice for who Ukraine's next leader should be. Not some young reformer, dedicated to taking Ukraine on its pro-Western path—but, instead, the man responsible for sparking a revolution just a few years earlier, propelled by his rank authoritarianism and his clear links to the Kremlin.

As they both realized, Yanukovych should run for the presidency once more—and Manafort could help him win.

But Manafort couldn't do it alone. He'd need a team to flesh out Yanukovych's presidential ambitions. So he began making calls to Americans he'd previously met: experts in organization and polling, media and electoral strategy. Their own ideologies were immaterial. Manafort wanted them for their talents, and not their political preferences. All they needed was a willingness to help a budding kleptocrat seize power in Ukraine and push Kyiv closer to the Kremlin—all while undoing all of the democratic gains of the past few years.

It didn't take long for Manafort to find American allies willing to help him sell Yanukovych. If anything, Manafort's success highlighted just how bipartisan this work of whitewashing despots can be. There was Rick Gates, a lobbyist fresh from a stint running John McCain's 2008 Republican presidential campaign. There was Tad Devine, a prominent Democratic pollster and the future campaign chief for Senator Bernie Sanders's 2016 presidential run. There was even a separate public relations firm, Edelman, tasked with helping to "boost Yanukovych's public image in Europe and the U.S."[61] Across the American political spectrum, aides and experts raced to help Manafort's project—and to help get paid by, among others, the Ukrainian oligarchs funding Yanukovych's political return.

According to one of the Americans who worked for Yanukovych, Manafort and his allies said all the right things: that Yanukovych was interested in Ukraine's democracy, in expanded transparency, in simply bringing the best policies to the greatest number of Ukrainians. Nothing about thieving an election, or bludgeoning opponents, or seizing the levers of power and turning them against journalists and activists and critics alike. Over long conference tables and vodka-drenched dinners, Manafort spun Yanukovych once more. And this new team of Americans—consultants and pollsters, lobbyists and experts—soaked it up.

With Manafort as Yanukovych's "closest political advisor," these new Americans agreed to flesh out Yanukovych's campaign staff.[62] They were, as Manafort told people, the best political consulting talent he could find. And they would all help launch Yanukovych back to the Ukrainian presidency.

* * *

IT'S WORTH NOTING: Much of this was never detailed in any FARA filings. There were almost no documents describing Manafort's meetings, or his campaign work in Ukraine, or his communications with anyone on either side of the Atlantic. There was little about the other Americans he'd recruited or the tools and tactics they used to sell Yanukovych. His work for Yanukovych—alongside Gates, Devine, and a range of other Americans—was an open secret in and around Washington. But for Americans or Ukrainians interested in what Manafort was actually doing, or who was actually paying his bills, FARA was effectively a dead end.

Not that anyone at the time seemed to care. The foreign lobbying industry may have been sprinting toward its zenith, with Manafort at the helm, but legislators couldn't be bothered to reinvigorate FARA. No officials raised the alarm about Manafort's dearth of filings. There was no one person responsible for this failure; everyone, it seemed, was asleep at the wheel of the exploding foreign lobbying industry. Which makes a certain, perverse sense; Manafort's bipartisan team was a microcosm of the industry itself, which attracted talent from across the political spectrum.

There's little indication Manafort even thought about the lack of filings. He, alongside the other Americans he'd recruited, was intent on only one mission: laundering Yanukovych's reputation, and expanding on the electoral playbook that had already succeeded during the past few years. And when the votes began rolling in in early 2010, Manafort's team realized how successful they'd been. Yanukovych won Ukraine's presidential election with nearly a million more votes than his opponent. He'd completed his comeback. And he'd done so with Manafort as his "chief political strategist."

One month later, on a blustery day in Kyiv, Manafort joined Yanukovych at his inauguration. A half decade after Ukrainians had gathered en masse to push Yanukovych out of a stolen presidency, he'd returned, triumphant. And while Yanukovych stood there, roaring about cultural grievances and ending Ukraine's pro-Western path, Akhmetov—the oligarch who had first introduced Manafort to Yanukovych—saw Manafort, smiled, and kissed him on the cheek.[63]

11

Blood Money

That is my country.

—Caqawix[1]

In the early 2010s, shortly after he helped Yanukovych reclaim the presidency, Manafort joined his grateful client just outside Ukraine's capital city of Kyiv. The two met at a new palatial, five-story home Yanukovych had built out for himself. Sprawling alongside the Dnipro River, the building, called "Mezhyhirya," was less a mansion than a castle, rising in the middle of a gargantuan estate.

Stretching over hundreds of acres of green, rolling land, the estate came with everything an aspiring kleptocrat could need. The entire construct, as one visitor said, "is stamped with gilding," from the winding staircases to the marble ballroom. There were multiple chandeliers and ornamental gardens, which included pots "covered with real alligator skin." There was a helicopter pad and a mansion-sized "cabin," a garage to house Yanukovych's seventy different cars, dozens of rooms (fitted with at least one stuffed lion) and an outdoor zoo (fitted with at least one live ostrich).[2] There was even an entire galleon ship anchored in the adjacent river—and, for some reason, a golden loaf of bread that Yanukovych kept in the house.[3] (There was also a nude portrait of Yanukovych, which is probably best not to describe.[4])

Valued at nearly $100 million, the entire residence was, as one analyst said, a "monument to corruption."[5] And it's not hard to see why. Yanukovych lived on an official salary of approximately $2,000 per month before being elected to president—hardly enough to even pay for any of the estate's $100,000 chandeliers (let alone the $115,000 statue of a wild boar he apparently purchased).

But once ensconced in power, Yanukovych—like Marcos and Mobutu and all of the other Manafort-led despots of years past—could grab the levers of national wealth. There was access to Ukraine's treasury, and Ukraine's infrastructure budget, and Ukraine's educational budget. He could even dip into Ukraine's military budget—money that should have gone to shoring up the country's national security but instead ended up funding gold-plated banisters and sterling silver bathroom mirrors instead.

And there was, throughout it all, a potpourri of financial secrecy vehicles freely available to Yanukovych and his kind: the shell companies in Delaware and the Caymans, the anonymous trusts in South Dakota and the South Pacific, all of which kleptocrats like Yanukovych could use to offshore and launder all the money they'd stolen. Regaining power in 2010, Yanukovych rode to the presidency at the height of the offshore boom—and soon joined kleptocrats around the world in laundering billions of dollars, without investigators or journalists having any idea how to trace it.

Yanukovych's story was hardly unique; by the time he was elected, tyrants and autocrats around the world had been using these financial secrecy tools for years, cycling potentially trillions of dollars into the offshore economy. Yanukovych was simply the latest in a long train of crooks dedicated to pillaging and pilfering their populations. Years later, estimates of the wealth Yanukovych and his cronies had looted would reach as high as $100 billion.

And in the months immediately after Yanukovych's election, Manafort wanted his slice. Some of Yanukovych's loot began flowing directly to Manafort—and, in short order, became a bigger pot of money than Manafort had ever seen. Hardware City was the distant past. Thanks to Yanukovych's victory—and the fact that Manafort was now part of Yanukovych's inner circle—Manafort's net worth began running into the tens of millions, jumping him into a financial echelon few could match.

And like Yanukovych, he didn't appear to be shy about spending his new wealth. He began pocketing luxury home after luxury home: a

Brooklyn brownstone, a Manhattan walk-up, estates of his own in the Hamptons and in south Florida. The purchases came so quickly that one colleague described it as a "mania for accumulating property."[6] But it wasn't just the homes. Pinstripes were soon replaced with ostrich-skin jackets. Old cars were swapped out for multiple new Range Rovers. Millions upon millions began pouring into Manafort's pockets—much of it following the same offshore networks that Ukrainian kleptocrats like Yanukovych used, fueling Manafort's "spending spree with money funneled through a network of offshore bank accounts."[7]

It was a simple setup: With Yanukovych ensconced in power, controlling Ukraine's state budgets, he and Manafort could effectively make as much money as they wanted. And because the offshore accounts they used relied on secrecy and anonymity, there was little chance their financial networks would ever be found out. Things like the Panama Papers and Pandora Papers—those massive data leaks that revealed details of myriad offshore networks—were still years in the future. For kleptocrats like Yanukovych, the offshoring world was a black box they could exploit at will.

In fact, there was only one real way for the details of their financial malfeasance to slip out: if Yanukovych ever lost power. Surely, he wouldn't do so for a second time. Surely—with the presidency in hand, and with Manafort by his side—that wouldn't happen again.

All of which is why, when Manafort would visit Yanukovych at his palace at Mezhyhirya, the two would swim in the nude together in one of the Ukrainian kleptocrat's hot tubs, floating next to one another, and talk. Talk about the country they'd just taken over. Talk about their futures to come. Talk about what it would take for Yanukovych to consolidate control in Ukraine—and which Americans could help Yanukovych remain in power, regardless of what Ukrainians wanted.

* * *

IN THIS PUSH to consolidate power, Yanukovych initially followed the playbook of other authoritarians across the region and around the world. He began placing friends and allies in key ministerial positions, ousting independent bureaucrats. He kneecapped rival oligarchs, seizing assets along the way. And he began, in his most important move, weaponizing Ukraine's judicial system and using the courts to target political rivals.

The central component of the new president's power grab came soon after his election. One year into his reign, he ordered the jailing of Yulia Tymoshenko, the pro-Western politico whom Yanukovych had faced in the 2010 election, accusing her of gross corruption and (in a fit of irony) abuse of power.

Tymoshenko, it should be said, was hardly some pristine, unsullied politician in her own right. She was steeped in the corrupt networks of Ukraine's natural gas sector, and there were very real concerns, even in Western capitals, about her own possible financial malfeasance.

But Yanukovych blew past all of those, and directed her straight to where she could no longer be a threat: prison.[8] In late 2011, a court sentenced Tymoshenko to seven years in jail—a transparently anti-democratic move that highlighted not only his power consolidation but also, as one outlet said, Yanukovych's "tight symbiosis with . . . Moscow." Ukraine's democratic hopes had suddenly imploded, undone by Yanukovych—and by Manafort.

But no one ever accused Yanukovych of political savvy; it was clear almost immediately that he had overreached. Tymoshenko, who'd long advocated for greater links between Ukraine and the West, retained key allies in Western governments—all of whom immediately launched vocal opposition to her imprisonment. Suddenly, under a deluge of Western criticism, Yanukovych's efforts to eliminate political rivals appeared wobbly.

Manafort, though, didn't appear to worry. Instead, he began recruiting new Americans to help his client cement his grip on Ukrainian politics. And in so doing, he found an ally who highlighted how an entire U.S. industry had now become the best friend modern kleptocrats could hope for.

*　*　*

BACK IN THE early 1960s, when FARA was amended into something that could target foreign lobbying campaigns (if only it was enforced), legislators wanted to make sure that foreign entities would still receive equal treatment before the law. Lawmakers decided that they didn't want to force all of the U.S. attorneys working on behalf of foreign clients to have to register their work with FARA, and potentially run afoul of due process considerations. As such, they provided an exemption to the new amendments: U.S. attorneys wouldn't have to register their work with FARA, disclosing their clients and their payments and their work, so long as they restricted their efforts to the inside of the courtroom. Lobbying, after all, was different than lawyering—right?

For years, that assumption was broadly correct. And then, like so much else, the end of the Cold War brought a flood of new clients to Washington—and to the law firms that suddenly sat staring at this loophole, realizing there might be an opportunity there. What if, they thought, they could argue that representing clients *outside* of the courtroom was just as important as representing clients *inside* the courtroom? What if they could argue that attorney-client privilege extended to lobbying? Or what if they could simply rely on the fact that no one enforced FARA—and that there was hardly any appetite in Washington to target these white-shoe law firms, anyway?

These factors—the loopholes, the lax enforcement, the onrush of foreign clients looking for any and all lobbying (and whitewashing) help they could find in Washington—all pointed in one clear direction. Shortly after the end of the Cold War, traditional public relations and consulting shops were no longer the only players in the foreign lobbying game. American law firms entered the fray—and brought a range of new legal tools to help flesh out all of the services that kleptocrats could find.

These weren't no-name firms; nearly all of the swaggering giants of the American legal industry started working directly for foreign regimes. Dole's Alston & Bird firm, mentioned in the previous chapter for its work on behalf of Russian oligarchs, is a law firm. So is Patton Boggs (which lobbied on behalf of the Guatemalan officials who allegedly raped an American nun), as well as DLA Piper (the firm at the center of the regime-to-donor pipeline), both mentioned a few chapters ago.

Indeed, it's nearly impossible to find a white-shoe law firm in the United States that *hasn't* transformed into a vehicle for foreign regimes to lobby American legislators. Baker McKenzie (working for the regime in the Democratic Republic of Congo), Hogan Lovells (Saudi Arabia), White & Case (Azerbaijan), Jones Day (China)—all of America's most nominally impressive law firms have turned into happy lobbyists for dictators around the world.[9]

Which is why, when Manafort went looking for help to spin Yanukovych's move to jail his leading political opponent, he didn't go searching for another public relations specialist, or another consultant. He went looking, instead, for a law firm to help. And it didn't take long to find one.

* * *

THE LAW FIRM of Skadden, Arps, Slate, Meagher & Flom is no stranger to the world of foreign lobbying or foreign influence. Founded in the 1940s, the firm joined the tide of law firms racing to the foreign trough in the early 1990s, signing on to lobby on behalf of anti-democratic regimes in places like Kazakhstan and Georgia. For good measure, Skadden was also a key player in one of the biggest transnational money laundering cases the world had ever seen, helping kleptocrats out of the United Arab Emirates and Saudi Arabia who thieved billions of dollars from unsuspecting depositors, launching the greatest Ponzi scheme the world had seen to that point.[10]

All of which is to say: when Manafort went looking for an American law firm to help Yanukovych prosecute his primary political opponents, Skadden was a natural fit. And it didn't take long for Manafort to bring Skadden on board. Inking its initial contract with Yanukovych's government in February 2012, the firm immediately flew some of its most prominent employees to Kyiv for meetings with "interested parties and government decision-makers."[11] The most notable employee Skadden shipped to Ukraine was also one of its most renowned recent hires: Gregory Craig, who had recently finished a stint as the general counsel for President Barack Obama's White House.

It's worth pausing on Craig's involvement for a moment, for two reasons. Firstly, Craig's involvement builds on Dole's legacy, highlighting how some of America's most broadly respected figures could sell out to foreign regimes—especially regimes dedicated to eroding democracy. (As *The New York Times* wrote, Yanukovych's regime

"planned to capitalize on Mr. Craig's luminous reputation."[12]) Yanukovych, after all, was hardly an unknown quantity; his clearly anti-
democratic and pro-Kremlin tilt was obvious for everyone to see. But
according to contemporary reportage and later federal filings, Craig
expressed no concerns about enlisting to help a would-be autocrat
cement his power.

Secondly, Craig's involvement further highlights a point made
earlier: the sheer *bipartisanship* of not only Manafort's network in
Ukraine but the world of foreign lobbying itself. Craig, after all, had
worked hand in glove with the most progressive president the country had seen in decades. (And one who, as a senator, had actually proposed ending foreign lobbying loopholes, to no avail.) Obama and his
staff nominally opposed everything Manafort and his despotic clients
stood for. And yet almost as soon as Craig left Obama's White House,
there he was, jetting to Kyiv to aid Manafort—a prominent Democratic lawyer willing to help a leading Republican lobbyist, all in the
service of undermining both democracy and American influence in
Ukraine.[13]

Craig's mission, on behalf of both Skadden and Manafort, was simple. He would "conduct an inquiry" into Yanukovych's jailing of Tymoshenko, and then "writ[e] an independent report" on the affair.[14] That
report would then be presented to critics of Tymoshenko's jailing, including Western officials and the European Court of Human Rights—
and do so with the full backing of one of America's leading law firms.
Skadden's report would in effect be the final statement on whether or
not Yanukovych was justified in jailing his primary political opponent.

The firm later claimed that it would "reach its own conclusions
based on its own independent work," and that neither Manafort nor
Yanukovych would influence the firm's findings.[15] What Skadden often
failed to mention was that it was being contracted directly by Yanukovych's government—and that it would be receiving millions of dollars in return for its supposedly "independent" work.

At a quick glance, you can see why Manafort and Yanukovych
wanted to bring Skadden aboard. The firm could provide a patina of
legitimacy to Yanukovych's consolidation of power. If it signed off on
Tymoshenko's jailing, lending its imprimatur to Yanukovych's move

to imprison his rival, Western criticism would wane—and allow Yanukovych to continue robbing Ukrainians, continue providing a front
for Russian influence, and continue demolishing Ukraine's nascent democracy. The firm would in turn receive nearly $5 million, presumably
assuming that they would never have to worry about being investigated
for foreign lobbying crimes.

It was a neat, tidy kleptocratic circle. And Skadden was perfectly
aware of its role; as they later admitted, they knew that their report
would be used for "improved PR in relation to [Tymoshenko's] trial."
They could get their slice of this foreign lobbying racket and keep the
industry spinning into the future—all while spinning Ukraine's democracy directly into the ground.[16]

*　*　*

THE REPORT THAT Skadden ended up issuing, published in 2012, is
hardly worth citing. While criticizing Yanukovych for overreach in
certain areas, the report effectively absolved him of any kind of autocratic crimes, and instead accused Tymoshenko of "insulting" the
presiding judge and "making frivolous arguments." Yanukovych's efforts would have been upheld in American courts—and his moves to
consolidate power could continue apace. To Yanukovych, and to Moscow, the millions funneled to Skadden were clearly worth it. Given the
arrangement—in which an American law firm was effectively pocketed
by a nascent autocracy and paid millions to effectively whitewash the
regime—the findings were hardly surprising.[17]

Far more revealing, though, is what Skadden and Craig did in the
lead-up to the report's publication, and how they helped Manafort spin
the report after it was released.[18] Skadden and Craig didn't act as supposedly "independent" analysts, interested in simply discovering the
truth. As federal filings make clear, they worked as effective proxies
for Manafort and Yanukovych. And in so doing, they served as a microcosm for how American law firms had transformed into extensions
of these malignant regimes, and into the latest fronts of the foreign
lobbying complex.[19]

For instance, just two months after signing the deal with Yanukovych's regime—and months before it had completed the

report—Skadden began working with Manafort to identify public relations firms they could hire to help roll out the report's findings. Skadden effectively acted as a liaison between Manafort and other public relations specialists, simultaneously coordinating both the report's language and the public relations spin—even as they publicly claimed that the report would somehow remain "independent."[20] Skadden not only sat down with Manafort in New York to discuss the public relations rollout but even involved its own internal public relations team, plotting out "media briefings" to inject the report's findings into American media.[21]

Indeed, Craig himself appeared to take a lead in the public relations side of the campaign.[22] He not only emailed directly with Manafort about the "communications strategy" for the report, but he also worked with Manafort to coordinate specific phone calls with American journalists. One of the key writers Craig had in mind: *New York Times'* national security reporter, David Sanger. To Craig, Sanger was the key conduit to launching the report's findings into the American media ecosystem—and to making sure it undercut Yanukovych's critics as much as possible. And as Skadden saw it, if they could get *The New York Times* to repeat their pro-Yanukovych findings, their job was effectively complete.[23]

As the report neared publication, the whitewash campaign kicked into high gear. Internal strategy documents specifically named Craig as the primary contact to link up with Sanger and *The New York Times*. According to internal emails, Craig not only took the lead on liaising with Sanger but also told Sanger he'd be "even happier to talk to you about" the report's findings, outlining why Yanukovych should be absolved of accusations of autocracy. Coordinating with yet another lobbying firm, Craig directly emailed Sanger a copy of the report, even offering to "hand-deliver a hard copy of this report to your home tonight"—which, according to a later indictment of Craig, he did.[24]

The next day, *The New York Times* published its analysis of the report. While Skadden found that Yanukovych's prosecution had made mistakes, the firm nonetheless "seemed to side heavily" with Yanukovych. The jailing of Yanukovych's main political rival "was supported by the evidence," and there was "no evidence" to any of the claims that it was political persecution. The imprisonment, Skadden concluded, would be upheld even in American courts.[25]

It was a public relations coup. The law firm had gotten the most prominent outlet in the world to repeat its findings, effectively clearing Yanukovych of his crimes. The piece even quoted Craig, saying that Skadden's assignment "was to look at the evidence in the record and determine whether the trial was fair." Nothing about steering the public relations and spin, nothing about partnering with Manafort, nothing about taking millions of dollars for the entire arrangement. Just a non-partisan, apolitical analysis—all of which just so happened to benefit Yanukovych and Manafort both. "Your [work] has been key to it all," Manafort wrote to Craig. "People in Kiev are very happy. You are 'THE MAN.'"[26]

*　*　*

STILL, IT'S WORTH noting that Manafort didn't rely solely on Skadden to help his pro-Yanukovych campaign. Instead, he had help from other familiar sources. Another prong in Manafort's efforts involved the creation of something known as the "Habsburg Group," a roster of former European heads of state whose main mission would be to spin Yanukovych for other audiences. Figures like former Polish president Aleksander Kwasniewski, former Italian prime minister Romano Prodi, former Austrian chancellor Alfred Gusenbauer: these "discarded European statesmen" would all be part of this new pro-Yanukovych claque, all organized by Manafort in order to push out "commentary and analysis in favor of Yanukovych."[27]

And they would have help from another pair of foreign lobbyists Manafort recruited, yet again illustrating the bipartisan breadth of the American foreign lobbying industry. One of the lobbyists involved in spreading the messaging of Manafort's "Habsburg Group" was Vin Weber, a former Republican member of Congress who'd since become a lead partner at a lobbying shop known as Mercury Public Affairs. The other was Tony Podesta, a leading Democratic fundraiser (and brother of leading Democratic campaign organizer John Podesta) whose foreign lobbying work had catapulted him into becoming one of Washington's premier lobbyists. Coordinating with both Skadden and pro-Yanukovych figures, the two firms launched a joint campaign to help the "Habsburg Group" spread its messaging to unsuspecting audiences.

(Another organization that worked on Yanukovych's behalf was the behemoth American consulting company McKinsey & Company. The organization didn't work for Manafort but instead served in parallel to Manafort's efforts, helping "polish [Yanukovych's] battered image" and working toward "resurrecting Mr. Yanukovych's career." McKinsey has never disclosed how much money it made from its arrangement with Yanukovych, but his government was only one of a range of loathsome regimes that McKinsey worked closely with, as we'll revisit later in this book.[28])

Lobbyists and law firms, former heads of state and former legislators, Republicans and Democrats alike: the roster that Manafort built up to help Yanukovych was an impressive array of malign talent. But there was one additional figure Manafort relied on—a man who not only bankrolled much of the entire effort but also confirms once more that the notion of a supposedly "pro-Western oligarch" is a pernicious oxymoron.

For years, Ukrainian oligarch Victor Pinchuk had positioned himself as the most nominally "pro-Western" of the country's corrupt tycoons. Not only did Pinchuk routinely host conferences that brought Western policymakers to Ukraine, but he further used his deep pockets to build out Western links, especially in the United States.

Pinchuk, for instance, paid then-candidate Donald Trump six figures to speak at his conference in 2015. Shortly before, he had also directed millions of dollars to the Clinton Foundation, the private foundation overseen by powerful U.S. politicians Bill and Hillary Clinton.[29] At one point, Pinchuk lent the Clintons his private jet, and even traveled to Los Angeles "to attend Mr. Clinton's star-studded sixty-fifth birthday celebration."[30] Along the way, Pinchuk also donated significant sums to American think tanks like the Brookings Institution and the Atlantic Council—even joining the advisory board of the latter. (We'll revisit the foreign lobbying roles of both foundations and think tanks in the final section of this book.)

All of these financial links had laundered Pinchuk's reputation from a seedy, crooked oligarch into a supposedly pro-Western figure. Pinchuk had become, said one analyst, "a fixture of the global cultural and political elite," someone who'd used these donations to create a "sparkling, Western-facing reputation."[31] He'd become, said one blinkered analysis in *Forbes*, a "democratic oligarch."[32]

Yet as both federal filings and court testimony later revealed, all of that was a front, providing Pinchuk a cover to do what Ukraine's and Russia's oligarchs had done for years: back Yanukovych, support Manafort, and cement Kremlin influence in Ukraine. Because the millions that Skadden made to help Yanukovych came directly from one person: Pinchuk.

Pinchuk's role in the entire affair was secretive, shadowed in denial and anonymous finance. But as we now know, it had begun early, with Craig agreeing to "seal the deal over breakfast" at Pinchuk's house.[33] Craig later testified that Pinchuk paid Skadden "most of the $4.6 million fee,"[34] with further testimony confirming that "most of the bill . . . was secretly paid for" by Pinchuk.[35] Federal filings likewise revealed that Skadden "understood that its work was to be largely funded by Victor Pinchuk."[36]

Despite the mountain of evidence about Pinchuk's payments, the oligarch has continually denied that he had anything to do with Manafort's efforts. But the payments were an open secret around Kyiv; as *The New York Times* reported, Pinchuk was clearly "footing the bill for the Skadden lawyers."[37] Emails between Craig and Manafort further confirm the arrangement, discussing how Pinchuk wanted his role in the report kept anonymous, with Manafort routing the payments through offshore companies in order to hide the oligarch's tracks.[38]

The entire network can appear, at first blush, overly complicated. But boiled down, it's surprisingly simple. Manafort brought together a team of white-collar Americans to launch a public relations scheme aimed at whitewashing Yanukovych, helping him eliminate political rivals in a bid to stay in power. A white-shoe law firm came aboard, lending its name as a supposedly neutral observer and authoring a report that would absolve Yanukovych of any crimes. High-profile Republicans and Democrats then rushed in to help, providing bipartisan support for the efforts. Behind it all, an oligarch acted as paymaster, moving millions of dollars via anonymous, offshore accounts, making the money effectively untraceable. And at the center stood Manafort, orchestrating this transnational scheme to help his client loot a nation, imprison political opponents, and remain in power as long as possible—all while expanding the Kremlin's influence in Ukraine.

And it would have worked, too—if it hadn't been for those pesky Ukrainian protesters, who just wouldn't give up.

* * *

WHEN SKADDEN'S REPORT came out in late 2012, Manafort and Yanukovych appeared to have succeeded. Their playbook—which, it hardly needs saying, wasn't disclosed in any FARA filings at the time—kept Tymoshenko in prison, and kept Yanukovych on the same path as other post-Soviet autocrats, many of whom have stayed in office for decades.

And then, a few months later, Yanukovych overreached once more and lit the fuse that would detonate in revolution, in revanchism, and in a war in the heart of Europe that still shows no signs of slowing.

In 2013, Yanukovych announced that he was pulling back from a forthcoming trade agreement with the European Union. The move would see Ukraine veer away from the West and lurch far closer to Moscow—and undo years of progress in Ukraine's European path. Immediately, protesters began gathering in the center of Kyiv, hoisting Ukrainian and EU flags alike. One month passed, and then another. Protesters continued to gather, demanding Yanukovych reinstate the trade deal. Encampments went up, with thousands continuing to pour in. International media arrived, and the spotlight turned on Kyiv once more.

At some point, Yanukovych realized the situation was slipping out of his grasp. He unleashed his security services on the protesters, cracking skulls but unable to crack apart the crowds. Soon, pro-Russian goons infiltrated the protests, bloodying those who simply wanted closer links to the European Union. With each assault, the protests metastasized—and soon, protesters began fighting back.

And then, in February 2014, the standoff shattered. Yanukovych organized snipers on nearby roofs, unleashing a hail of bullets on the unarmed protesters. Dozens died. And suddenly, all of Manafort's work—all of his campaign organizing, all of his reputation laundering, all of his efforts at organizing entire teams of Americans dedicated to keeping Yanukovych in power—crumbled.

With a nation suddenly outraged at Yanukovych's brutality, Ukrainians toppled the autocrat once more. Overnight, Yanukovych fled the capital, leaving most of his belongings (including both his nude portrait and his golden loaf of bread) behind in his mansion. He flew to Russia, cowering from a revolution suddenly sweeping the country, claiming all the while that he'd done nothing wrong. Russian state media went into hyperdrive, saying the protesters were American plants, that the entire revolution was a CIA-orchestrated coup—and that Ukrainians and Russians were, in reality, one people. Immediately, Russian troops began scouring through southern Ukraine, destabilizing the country further. Moscow oversaw a sham "referendum" to claim Crimea and began arming separatist proxies in eastern Ukraine, stealing further land for themselves.

Suddenly, for the first time in years, war unfurled in the heart of Europe. Tanks once more rolled across European plains, destabilizing the continent in ways that hadn't been seen since the days of Hitler and Mussolini. It was the start of a war that, years later, has claimed hundreds of thousands of lives, and brought the world closer to nuclear Armageddon than anything seen in decades. All of it thanks to Yanukovych's efforts to cling to power—and thanks to all those Americans who'd helped him along the way.

* * *

YANUKOVYCH WASN'T THE only one cowering from the sudden change in fortunes. With the autocrat fleeing, the secrets of his regime—including who'd helped him try to secure his rule and how much they'd been paid in the process—began spilling out.

His American allies went into overdrive, trying to distance themselves from Yanukovych. Craig immediately scrambled, suddenly claiming that *The New York Times* article he'd tried so hard to seed a year earlier was actually full of "serious inaccuracies"—and that, in reality, Skadden had found "serious violations" in Tymoshenko's prosecution. According to Craig, the idea that Skadden's report was "largely sympathetic" to Yanukovych was now patently false.[39]

Manafort, meanwhile, was nowhere to be found. No reporting places Manafort in Kyiv during the bloodshed, or during Yanukovych's flight to Russia. The man who'd had Yanukovych's ear for years was glaringly absent.

Yanukovych certainly didn't need Manafort's sign-off to unleash his snipers on unarmed protesters. But in the months leading up to the autocrat's crackdown, we know that Manafort had transformed from mere lobbyist into one of Yanukovych's key advisors. He enjoyed "walk-in" rights, meeting with—and advising—Yanukovych whenever he pleased.[40] Part of that was electoral, in order to discuss Yanukovych's political maneuvering. Part of that was geopolitical, about Yanukovych's relations with Moscow, Brussels, and Washington. But part of it was also, according to those who knew Manafort best, about how to disperse the swelling protesters in Kyiv—and how to use the bloodshed to Yanukovych's benefit.

In a series of text messages between Manafort's daughters Andrea and Jessica, hacked and published by a "hacktivist collective" in 2016, the two sisters discuss the mundane, from coffee orders to friendly gossip, to the mendacious, from their father's lack of ethics to his abusive behavior toward their mother.[41] As one of them wrote, their father "has no moral or legal compass."[42]

Such a synopsis is hardly surprising. But there, in the middle of thousands of texts, the sisters start talking about Ukraine's revolution—and their father's role in the middle of it all.

"You know he [had] people killed in Ukraine?" Andrea texted her sister in March 2015. "Knowingly."

Jessica responded in disbelief: "What?!" Her sister continued. "Remember when there were all those deaths taking place? A while back. About a year ago. Revolts and what not. Do you know whose strategy that was to cause that, to send those people out and get them slaughtered?"[43]

There was only one person, according to Manafort's daughter, who was ultimately responsible. And it wasn't Yanukovych, the man in charge of the country's crumbling regime. Instead, it was the American whispering in his ear, guiding the regime, the country, and Europe toward catastrophe.

It was their father.

"Don't fool yourself," Andrea closed. "That money we have is blood money."

12

Not for Profit

Steal from a thief and God laughs.
—Marlon James[1]

As the Yanukovych case study illustrated, by the early 2010s the United States was already sinking under the weight of ever-widening foreign lobbying networks. Manafort's efforts in Ukraine might have been the most expansive—and, thanks to later investigations, the one we have the most details on—but he didn't operate alone. Major U.S. law firms, leading lobbyists on both Republican and Democratic sides, former U.S. officials and political consultants and campaign managers: all of these Americans dedicated themselves to laundering the reputation of the first European leader since Napoleon to be tossed from power not once but *twice*. Manafort's Yanukovych network was an indicator of just how expansive—and just how bipartisan—the foreign lobbying links had now grown in Washington.

And yet, for even how broad Manafort's network ran, it still didn't encapsulate all that the foreign lobbying industry now included. Because by the early 2010s, there were other prongs—and other entire American industries—that had likewise turned themselves into influence-peddling operations, all on behalf of foreign dictatorships, allowing foreign despots to further target and affect American policy.

Interestingly, the latest entry into the world of foreign lobbying was an industry that was, unlike the others mentioned above, one that claimed to be working toward the betterment of society, toward providing opportunities and lifting voices and bringing people together.

An industry that, on its face, was hardly an industry at all: one that was supposedly dedicated to everything *besides* profit.

By the time Yanukovych scurried out of Ukraine, this so-called "non-profit" industry had already swelled into a launching pad for dictators to lobby American officials—and to do so with as little regulation and oversight as possible. Where these nonprofits had once served as ways of organizing charitable contributions (and where many still do), modern American nonprofits had transformed into vehicles for reputation laundering, for granting access to policymakers, and for injecting illicit, dictatorial wealth directly into Washington.

Nonprofit organizations in the United States first came into their own in the mid-twentieth century, following tax regulation reforms that provided a carve-out for groups dedicated to charitable causes. Following the reforms, regulators soon received a "surge in applications" to create new nonprofit groups.[2] And with good reason: Because these organizations, often formed as foundations, were not focused on revenue generation, they received tax-exempt status. Such a designation allowed donors to not only provide funds to nonprofit groups of their choice—to fight cancer, to eliminate homelessness, to support First or Second Amendment causes, etc.—but also effectively write off such gifts.

It was, in many ways, a win-win for all parties involved. Even amidst declining tax rates and exploding wealth inequality, billionaires could use donations to transform into supposed "philanthropists," bankrolling pet causes while claiming to be disinterested donors—all while ducking waning taxation requirements. In so doing, they could transform not only their wealth but their reputations as well. Similar to the Rockefellers' experience of decades prior, American billionaires began using directed donations to become patrons of the arts and education, of medical research and civic renewal, of anything and everything that could improve their reputation in the public eye. Corporations could likewise follow suit, creating their own philanthropic arms to enhance their own standing, burying criticism of environmental- or labor-related misconduct in the process.

As critics have described, the world of billionaire and corporate philanthropy has in recent decades transformed into a vehicle for obscuring corporate and elite malfeasance. In the United States, the most spectacular case of such large-scale donations being used to distract from corporate crimes—call it "donor-washing," if you will—was seen with the Sackler family and its related Purdue Pharma company, responsible for the surge in opioid-related deaths in the United States. Overseeing strategic donations to a range of nonprofits, the family and company spent years undercutting criticism by pointing detractors to its supposed philanthropy. "This family and this company are spectacular examples of how to get away with human destruction on a continental scale and use strategic philanthropy as lubricant in an engine of exploitation and misery making," Anand Giridharadas, author of a 2018 book on billionaire philanthropy, said.[3]

The Sacklers may be the most egregious case, but they are hardly alone. And it's not hard to see why. Such large-scale donations are an easy, and often welcome, mechanism for laundering one's reputation. And nonprofits all too often do little due diligence on the sources of the funds in question—or offer introspection on what role they themselves may be playing in helping donors dodge criticism, or taxes, or both.

By the turn of the century, nonprofits had surged in total worth, with their combined annual intake now running into the tens of billions of dollars, if not more. In recent years, it has become more and more common for billionaires to hire an entire fleet of nonprofit and donation advisors (often in conjunction with a related fleet of lawyers and tax advisors), with corporations following in turn.

All the while, nonprofit organizations have only continued mushrooming, with nearly two million nonprofit entities now in the United States. And some of them, it turns out, have become fantastic vehicles for foreign lobbying—especially if they involve former, and potentially future, presidents.

* * *

WHEN THE CLINTON Foundation first launched in 2001, it was unlike anything seen in American history. Whereas former presidents, from George Washington to Dwight Eisenhower to George H.W. Bush, had retired to their estates, the Clinton Foundation—named after former President Bill Clinton and his wife, Hillary Clinton—provided a vehicle for the Clintons to remain in the public eye, and in the political mix. Its stated mission was a muddy mix of bland centrism and corporate jargon. The former U.S. president "established the Clinton Foundation on the simple belief that everyone deserves a chance to succeed, everyone has a responsibility to act, and we all do better when we work together."[4] Nearly a quarter century later, the foundation remains saturated in these platitudes, with its annual report claiming that the organization focuses on "putting people first," "expanding opportunities," and "taking action together."[5]

Few, of course, could argue against such generic goals. And it's worth noting that the group *is* responsible for much positive work around the world, from expanding medical access to helping small-scale farmers. Propelled by billions of dollars in donations over the past two decades, the Clinton Foundation rose to become a financial juggernaut, and one of the most prominent nonprofits in American— even global—history.

Over that same time, though, one clear pattern emerged. Donations weren't related to the group's success, or even to its aims. Instead, donations to the Clinton Foundation were clearly correlated with the Clintons' proximity to the White House. That is, donations to the Clinton Foundation spiked whenever Hillary Clinton grew close to the White House—and nosedived off a steep cliff whenever her path to the presidency disappeared.

A quick scan through the numbers confirms this pattern. In the late 2000s, as Hillary Clinton stood as the presumptive Democratic nominee—before then-senator Barack Obama stormed through the primary campaign, swiping the nomination—the Clinton Foundation spent multiple years taking in nearly $150 million annually, peaking at one point at $184.1 million in a single cycle. A few years later, the foundation's intake had collapsed by more than 70 percent, amounting to only $51.5 million in donations. Shortly thereafter, Clinton declared her intention to run for the presidency once more—and donations to the Clinton Foundation soared yet again, spiraling up to $172.6 million by 2015. Then, Donald Trump surprised everyone and defeated Clinton—and donations to the Clinton Foundation plummeted once more.[6]

Today, with Hillary Clinton's chances of landing in the White House effectively nil, the onetime flood of donations and gifts to the Clinton Foundation has turned to a trickle. In 2021, contributions were down to only $16 million—fully *90 percent less* than they once were, and a fraction of what the foundation saw when Hillary Clinton still had a clear route to the White House.[7]

In terms of the foundation's actual achievements, there's no clear reason for why the annual donation rates went through such wildly disparate swings. There were no internal scandals, no leadership turn-over, no endogenous explanations. Indeed, for those in the nonprofit space, the Clinton Foundation's fluctuating donation rates border on the bizarre; nonprofits prefer steady, predictable growth rather than something that resembles a peregrine falcon on the hunt, soaring and diving and soaring and diving.

But then, perhaps the simplest description is the right one. The Clinton Foundation may have been interested in "striving to solve problems faster, better, and at a lower cost" (who isn't?), but many of its donors, especially foreign regimes, certainly didn't appear to be. As one pro-transparency group wrote, its pattern of donations—with its steep climbs and the swift drop-offs, all predicated on Clinton's path to the presidency—points to one question: "Were donors more interested in sponsoring the work of a former president—or currying favor with a future one?"[8]

Unfortunately for Clinton, the identities of the foundation's greatest donors provide one clear, dispiriting answer. Rather than being some-thing dedicated to "putting people first," the Clinton Foundation became instead, as anti-corruption expert Sarah Chayes said, "a cover for inter-national influence peddling."[9]

* * *

THIS KIND OF "influence peddling" was especially true for the Clinton Foundation's wide range of foreign donors. Rather than limit accepted donations to democratic allies, rather than turn away funds linked to some of the most repulsive regimes on the planet, the Clinton Foun-dation time and again welcomed all manner of kleptocratic, dicta-torial wealth. Funds that would, in any other context, be considered dirty—the kind of "blood money" Manafort happily accepted—were routinely spun through the Clinton Foundation, opening up untold doors in the process.

A quick skim through the mega-donors to the Clinton Foundation reads like a roster of the world's most reprehensible regimes. The government of Saudi Arabia—known best for, among other things, preventing women from driving, as well as beheading journalists—provided between $10 million and $25 million to the Clinton Foundation. A politically connected Saudi businessman, as well as a group called the Friends of Saudi Arabia, donated an additional $5–10 million each, with the autocracy of Kuwait donating the same amount. The Zayed family, related to the former despot of the United Arab Emirates, donated an additional $1–5 million, with a further $1–5 million coming directly from the Emirati government. Dictatorships in both Qatar and Oman donated millions more, with additional sums coming from Algeria's brutal regime.[10]

Nor was that all. Multiple oligarchs, acting as proxies for their related governments, directed further millions to the Clinton Foundation. Pinchuk, mentioned in the previous chapter, singlehandedly donated between $10 million and $25 million to the Clinton Foundation. But he was hardly the only oligarch who decided to splash funds at the organization. Kenes Rakishev, a notorious Kazakhstani oligarch, donated significant sums to the foundation. So did a company overseen by Viktor Vekselberg, a Russian oligarch considered part of Putin's inner circle—and a man who, a few years later, ended up directly sanctioned by the United States for his role in aiding the Kremlin. Nigerian billionaire Gilbert Chagoury provided between $1 million and $5 million to the foundation—despite having been previously convicted for money laundering.[11] (Years after the donation, Chagoury would also be accused by the Justice Department of trying to route money to illegally fund American elections.)[12]

Time and again, foreign dictatorships and oligarchs fire-hosed tens of millions of dollars toward the Clinton Foundation. Unfortunately, the foundation never disclosed the total amounts donated from any of the figures and regimes mentioned above, instead only offering a range of numbers to describe the donations (hence why Pinchuk is somewhere between $10 million and $25 million). However, when added up, the Clinton Foundation may well have accepted *more than $100 million* from dictatorial and oligarchic sources over the span of just a few short years. And all of it was transparently, even blindingly, pegged to Hillary Clinton's potential presidency.[13]

To its limited credit, the Clinton Foundation at least put on a public show of concern about the foreign donations. After Obama named Clinton as his secretary of state in 2009, the foundation announced a moratorium on donations from foreign governments. But even then, that simply left an oligarch-sized loophole that regimes were happy to drive through. Although the "Clinton Foundation agreed not to accept donations from foreign governments . . . it did accept millions of dollars in contributions from private donors with ties to foreign governments," wrote *Philanthropy News Digest*. These included donations that "were not reviewed by the State Department, as stipulated in an agreement between the Clintons and the Obama administration." Tens of millions of dollars from "individuals, foundations, and corporations with ties to foreign governments" still rumbled into the Clinton Foundation, despite the supposed moratorium.[14]

All of this—the spikes in donations whenever Clinton neared the White House; the apparent lack of concern about dictator- and oligarch-linked funds; the loopholes that the foundation barreled through while Clinton was secretary of state—point in one clear direction. From the late 2000s through the mid-2010s, the Clinton Foundation became perhaps the easiest way for foreign regimes, foreign oligarchs, and foreign tyrants to try to access and influence the presumptive president—all while laundering their own reputations in the process.

"For years, the Clinton Foundation raised ethical concerns and blurred lines between the foundation, private entities, and the State Department," said Scott Amey, general counsel for the Project on Government Oversight (POGO), one of the country's leading anti-corruption watchdogs. "Money was pouring in when Hillary Clinton was a senior official and a candidate for president. The fact that foundation donors received special access to the secretary of state isn't surprising, nor is the fall in foundation funding after her 2016 election loss. . . . It really looks like they were cozying up to who they thought was going to be the future president."[15]

If anything, the Clinton Foundation resembled something far closer to what's usually seen in those same dictatorships that were happily donating tens of millions to the group. "Proudly mixing business, splashy humanitarianism, image enhancement, and personal enrichment, the Clinton Foundation is known for its unsightly smudge of financial and personnel practices," Chayes wrote. "Among its donors and beneficiaries, corrupt and abusive developing-country politicians rub shoulders with Western business executives angling for sweetheart deals, and members of both groups hoping to curry favor with the Clintons." The Clinton Foundation is, Chayes concluded, "the U.S. [version] of the 'charities' run by corrupt ruling families from Honduras to Uzbekistan."[16]

Even with the similarities to other dictators' "charities," the Clinton Foundation existed in a league of its own, a *sui generis* experiment in foreign powers using supposed philanthropy to try to access the highest rungs of American power. In terms of American nonprofits, there was nothing else comparable to the Clinton Foundation's precedent. (For context, the Obama Foundation doesn't have any foreign regimes or foreign oligarchs among its numerous donors.)

But then, by the early 2010s, the Clinton Foundation was hardly the only way foreign regimes used U.S. nonprofits to target and sway American policymakers. Around the same time, a new model had entered the field—one that saw foreign regimes *themselves* steering the American nonprofits in question, and one that led to the greatest foreign lobbying scandal the U.S. Congress had ever seen.

* * *

IN MAY 2013, as Yanukovych's regime began showing cracks and as the Clinton Foundation started sucking up tens of millions of dollars from dictators, I was standing in the kitchen of Houston's newly opened "Azerbaijan House." Based in a small bungalow, this center was dedicated to informing Americans about the history, culture, and impact of Azerbaijan—a former Russian colony located in the Caucasus region, snug between Russia, Iran, and the Caspian Sea. Unsurprisingly, instead of discussing Azerbaijan's decades-long dictatorship or any of the

journalists or LGBTQ activists or ethnic minorities targeted by the regime, the house portrayed the country as a land of splendor and wealth,
buoyed by some of the largest gas reserves in the region.[17]

I'd arrived at the "Azerbaijan House" for a relatively soft story, working as a journalist to introduce Houston audiences to the house's cultural
offerings, including lessons on how to make traditional Azeri dishes.
But as the day wound down—and as Azeri dumplings cooled next to
me, steam coiling to the ceiling—my host, a dark-haired middle-aged
woman who ran the center, had an offer.

In just a few weeks, she said, Azerbaijan would be hosting one of the
biggest congressional delegations to travel abroad in years, and the biggest the Caucasus region had ever seen. Nearly a dozen members of the
House of Representatives, alongside many more staffers, would travel
to Azerbaijan to meet with the country's president and learn about all
of the democratic strides the young nation had made.

As I plopped a dumpling in my mouth, my host asked: Would I like
to go on the trip? Money wouldn't be an issue; it would be all-expenses-
paid, with all travel and hotel and food costs covered. And I could write
as much about the trip as I'd like—especially about all of the wonders of
Azerbaijan that I'd encounter. Wouldn't that be nice?

I reached for another dumpling in response. My host then added
one qualifier, one thing she and her colleagues would ask in return. She
said they'd be happy to cover all of my travel costs, "so long as you don't
write anything negative about our country." Some people, she said, only
want to write about the "bad things" in Azerbaijan: the country's horrific, decades-long dictatorship; the smothering and jailing of nearly all
critics; the violence directed at sexual and ethnic minorities alike. And
surely, if she and her colleagues were paying for everything for me, it'd
only be fair that I don't criticize the country, right?

My eyes opened a bit wider, a half-eaten dumpling suddenly getting
stuck in the back of my throat. It was a kind of *sotto voce* quid pro quo:
if I accepted the offer—enjoying a free trip on the biggest congressional
junket the region had ever seen—the only thing required was positive
spin on Azerbaijan's despotic regime. And no one would ever have to
find out about the arrangement, anyway. What could go wrong?

Shuffling my feet, I muttered something about appreciating the

offer, but insisting that I'd have to decline. I immediately gulped another dumpling, grabbed my bag, and headed for the door.[18]

* * *

THE CONGRESSIONAL DELEGATION that arrived in the Azeri capital of
Baku presented an impressively bipartisan slate. There were hardline
conservatives, such as Oklahoma representative (and future Trump
appointee) Jim Bridenstine, and left-of-center policymakers, like New
York representative Yvette Clarke. It was, all told, one of the "biggest
concentrations of American political star power" the region had ever
seen.[19] And all of the officials were there to learn more about Azerbaijan's role in everything from energy supplies to national security, as
well as Azerbaijan's supposed moves toward democracy.

But as a later congressional investigation into the trip made clear,
the American officials appeared far more interested in sumptuous
dinners, lavish gifts, and parties that stretched deep into the evening.
Rather than exploring how Azerbaijan's decades-long dictatorship had
launched one of the world's most thoroughly kleptocratic regimes—so
much so that Azerbaijan's despotic president had recently been named
as the most corrupt "person of the year" by one of the world's leading anti-corruption organizations[20]—the American officials instead
received gifts they could hardly afford on official salaries.[21] Instead of
demanding meetings with jailed journalists and opposition members,
American officials enjoyed new crystal tea sets, silk scarves, jewelry,
and rugs worth thousands of dollars.[22] (In a sign of the times, they even
received DVDs describing the wonders and magnificence of the ruling
regime.)[23] And instead of publicly criticizing how the Azeri government brutalized ethnic minorities (most especially Armenians), U.S.
officials publicly praised Azerbaijan as a steady, stalwart American
partner worth supporting.[24]

This is all, of course, somewhat par for the course. The 2013 trip
was hardly the first congressional delegation to visit a dictatorship,
or one that spent far less time criticizing a miserable regime than it
should. There was one key difference, however. Where most other congressional delegations are funded by American taxpayers, or by official
government entities, the money for this Azerbaijan jaunt came instead

from a pair of American nonprofits—which, as later investigations would uncover, were little more than fronts for the Azeri regime itself.

The funding scheme was relatively straightforward. Before the congressional trip, a U.S. national named Kemal Oksuz registered a pair of American nonprofits in Houston (including one memorably named "The Turquoise Council of Americans and Eurasians"), and proceeded to set up a pair of related bank accounts. Azerbaijan's state gas company—the ruling regime's primary source of corrupt, unchecked financial flows—then funneled cash to the new nonprofits' bank accounts, secretly pumping them full of nearly one million dollars. From there, Oksuz, on behalf of the nonprofits, began contacting congressional offices, offering to help fund a trip to Azerbaijan, all for the betterment of U.S.-Azeri relations—without ever disclosing that the nonprofits' wealth came directly from the regime itself.[25]

On its face, using American nonprofits as a cover to hide regime-linked wealth shouldn't have been quite so easy. In order to accept travel funds from third parties (such as these nonprofits), members of Congress must first file approval requests with the House Ethics Committee, effectively asking for permission to accept the money. The committee is within its rights to decline the requests. However, the committee can only compel certain financial information—and can't track funding from outside the United States, or anything "protected by the Constitutional protection against self-incrimination."[26] In essence, the House Ethics Committee relies on good-faith disclosures from trip sponsors—on the myopic belief that, surely, those funding these trips would never lie to congressional officials about who might be covertly funding these junkets.

With the Azerbaijan trip, Oksuz and the American nonprofits told the House Ethics Committee that they were the "sole sponsor" of the trip, and that they had not "accepted any funds intended to finance any aspect of the trip, either directly or indirectly, from any other source."[27] There were no details of the hundreds of thousands of dollars from Azerbaijan's gas firm, or that Azerbaijan's corrupt regime was the one organizing and bankrolling the trip, or that the entire purpose of the trip was to use these nonprofits as cutouts in order to whitewash Azerbaijan's ruling dictator.

And there's no evidence the House Ethics Committee bothered to look too far. The committee quickly signed off on the forms, and approved the trip. The misdirection had worked, in spectacular fashion. "This wasn't a case where someone just said, 'Oops,'" Meredith McGehee, policy director at the Campaign Legal Center, later told me. "This was a lot of effort to make this happen."[28]

To be sure, this wasn't the first time that nonprofits had been involved in funding schemes for these kinds of congressional trips. In 2011, one junket saw dozens of U.S. lawmakers tour Israel thanks to a nonprofit closely linked to AIPAC, the pro-Israel lobbying group.[29] Another trip that same year saw legislators visit South Africa and Botswana via a nonprofit with close ties to multiple lobbying organizations.[30] And in 2009, U.S. officials visited Liechtenstein and Germany on a trip sponsored directly by a nonprofit whose president was himself a lobbyist.[31] As Jack Abramoff, one of the most infamous lobbyists in American history, told me, the "practice of using nonprofits to blur transparency for congressional travel is not new."[32]

But this 2013 trip was a step apart, both for its brazenness and for its scope. To Azerbaijan, the trip was a staggering success. Not only was the funding kept hidden, but the American legislators appeared more than happy to sing Azerbaijan's praises and push pro-Azeri policies upon their return. Many of the House members immediately began stumping for Azerbaijan's interests, calling for far closer ties between the United States and Azerbaijan's dictatorship. Some even began calling for the country to be exempted from certain sanctions, clearing the way for both the Azeri government and its gas firm to generate even more illicit wealth.[33] Instead of a mafia-like regime dedicated to pulverizing its population, Azerbaijan was suddenly, in the eyes of many in Washington, a trusted partner worth supporting. The despotic rulers in Azerbaijan couldn't have asked for more.[34]

* * *

AT SOME POINT, though, the contours of the trip—especially given the sudden jolt of pro-Azeri policies in Washington—began raising questions. Soon, the U.S.'s Office of Congressional Ethics (OCE) began poking around the junket's funding. Formed in 2008, the OCE served as

Congress's independent, nonpartisan ethics watchdog, meant to keep tabs on these ethics failings, though usually only for domestic scandals. But with this trip, the OCE had questions. Where did these nonprofits get this sudden influx of wealth from? Who was actually footing the bill for the flights and the hotels and the DVDs praising Azerbaijan's dictator? And why didn't the House Ethics Committee—made up of colleagues of those who went on the trip—demand more information on it all?

A few months went by, and the OCE began putting out feelers. It invited figures like Oksuz and other trip organizers for interviews, asking them to provide further information on the sources of their wealth. And it didn't take much for the questions to transform into alarm. Even though the OCE couldn't compel testimony, overconfident witnesses showed up nonetheless. And they immediately let slip their financial secrets, pointing directly to Azerbaijan's regime as the ultimate funder. As one nonprofit representative memorably (and confusedly) said in response to the OCE's questions about whether he'd accepted money from Azerbaijan's regime, "I mean, to be honest, it seems . . . like so, yes. I mean, we didn't accept it, maybe, but yes we did. What can I say?"[35]

Suddenly, the money behind the trip came into sharper focus—and it was little surprise that it came not via the House Ethics Committee, which showed little interest in the secrets of the trip funding, but via the independent OCE. "The House Ethics Committee is often a puppy dog, rather than a watchdog," one ethics expert told me. "If you're looking for a success story on ethics, the OCE is that success story."[36] Bit by bit, witness by witness, the OCE began piecing together the bigger picture—even as multiple members of Congress who went on the trip refused to meet with the OCE.

And then, two months after it began its investigation, the House Ethics Committee swooped in and demanded that the OCE halt its investigation.

The move, known as "cease and refer," arrived out of the blue.[37] It supposedly came about because the House Ethics Committee had also launched its own investigation into the affair. But it was unclear if the House Ethics Committee even had the right to demand the OCE stop such an inquiry. More importantly, and most jarringly, such a move had never actually been tried before.

According to a letter signed by a number of anti-corruption groups, such a move was "unprecedented"—and would effectively allow the House Ethics Committee to kill any investigation, into foreign lobbying or any other topic, that it wanted. It would "establish a dangerous precedent" for such an "extraordinary order." As the letter pointed out, it didn't help that the chairman of the House Ethics Committee, Pennsylvania representative Charlie Dent, had personally received thousands of dollars from Oksuz—the man whom Dent's committee was supposed to be investigating—or that Representative Clarke, the only House Ethics Committee member who had gone on the Azerbaijan junket, hadn't even bothered to follow the committee's rules about getting prior approval for the trip.[38]

With little warning, the House Ethics Committee had turned its sights on the OCE—one of the few ethics success stories in Washington. And there was little the OCE could do; no one in Congress (or elsewhere) raced to its rescue. The committee smothered the OCE's investigation—and effectively strangled the OCE's ability to actually look into foreign lobbying scandals. "You've got a foreign government participating in trying to lie to the U.S Congress and hoodwink the American public," one ethics expert told me. "[And] the House Ethics Committee tried violating congressional rules and burying the OCE report."[39]

In its own later report, the House Ethics Committee absolved congressional members of any wrongdoing. (Representatives said they were "blindsided" by the secret funding, with one representative claiming he was "furious" at Azerbaijan's shenanigans.[40]) It also avoided taking any specific steps against Oksuz or the nonprofits in question, instead referring the investigation to the Department of Justice. For good measure, and despite requests from the anti-corruption community, it also specifically refused to release the OCE's findings.[41]

Back in Azerbaijan, there was no price paid for such a brazen foreign lobbying scheme. Not only has the United States increasingly relied on the Azeri regime for energy and national security needs—even after its dictator launched multiple armed attacks on neighboring, and democratic, Armenia in 2022—but the country has continued funding undisclosed lobbying assaults in the United States. Even Ok-suz, the mastermind of the entire operation, faced little blowback. He eventually pleaded guilty to misleading congressional investigators—but never faced any time in jail for his crimes.[42]

Meanwhile, there's every reason to think that these kinds of schemes using American nonprofits have continued unabated. And Azerbaijan is hardly the worst culprit, even if its 2013 trip was the most egregious. One investigation from *USA Today* found that numerous Turkish groups had followed a similar playbook—claiming they are nonprof-its but secretly acting as fronts for third parties, all to whitewash the Turkish government. Some of these pro-Turkish nonprofits didn't even go through the bare minimum of actually registering for a nonprofit status with the U.S. government, rightly figuring they'd never face any penalties.[43]

Unfortunately, due to the House Ethics Committee's unwillingness to investigate these kinds of funding sources—as well as its move to gag the OCE, one of the few bodies that's shown any interest in inves-tigating these nonprofit foreign lobbying scams—we have no idea of just how broad this phenomenon is. "I suspect this type of laundering of funds to pay for congressional travel junkets happens uncomfort-ably often," one ethics expert told me.[44] Or as another said, "The Ethics Committee is allowing members to hide behind its so-called approval process to they can take exotic vacations paid for by special interests."[45]

* * *

BY THE MID-2010S, it was clear that American nonprofits—thanks to loopholes, the ease of hiding donations, and legislators' unwillingness to investigate their colleagues—had joined public relations specialists, law firms, and many more in America's swelling foreign lobbying com-plex.

But one thing that wasn't clear: Manafort's future—or even his location. By 2015, Manafort was, as *Politico* reported, the "Invisible Man."[46] Emails from former associates wondered aloud, "Where is Paul Manafort?"[47]

According to Manafort himself, he spent the year following Yanu-kovych's ouster traveling. ("In 2015 I was busy abroad," he tersely writes in his memoir.[48]) But most evidence has Manafort going to ground in the United States, keeping a lower profile than he'd ever known. Where Manafort had once acted as effective kingmaker in both Washington and abroad, his role—and his life—appeared to have shattered.

Part of that was due directly to his work with the oligarchs in Ukraine and Russia. One of them—Oleg Deripaska, the Putin ally who'd allegedly bribed officials and ordered the murder of a business rival—turned his sights on Manafort, claiming that the American had swindled him out of millions tied up in a failed investment. Taking to American courts, Deripaska's lawyers began prying open Manafort's finances, with no end in sight.[49]

Around the same time, Manafort's family learned that he'd been having an ongoing affair with a younger woman. The revelation left Manafort's remaining personal life in tatters. "He has too many skeletons, he can't have a public divorce," one of Manafort's daughters texted, pointing directly to his "legally questionable" payments in Ukraine.[50] (Manafort had, among other things, provided a Manhattan apartment for his mistress that cost nearly $10,000 per month.[51])

All of it—Yanukovych's implosion, Deripaska's lawsuits, his affair suddenly detonating his family—appeared to break Manafort. He "is in the middle of a massive emotional breakdown," Manafort's daughter texted in June 2015. He checked into a psychiatric clinic in Arizona, where he got one ten-minute call per day and, his daughter said, "sobs daily." It was an experience—an isolation—unlike any he'd ever known. And even then, it failed to repair the breach. "I refuse to let him ruin more of my life," his daughter added. "I don't want to hear his apologies. Or tell him the thousands of ways he has hurt me."[52]

Decades after Manafort first began rising through the Republican establishment, decades after he first began laundering the reputations of warlords and oligarchs and dictators alike, his influence had cratered. Huddled in a psychiatric clinic, without a client and in the crosshairs of a furious Russian oligarch, Manafort's story appeared effectively over.

And then, a week after Manafort entered the Arizona clinic, a real estate developer in New York descended a golden escalator, announcing his intention to run for president. A former client of Manafort's, launching one of the strangest campaigns in American history. A reality television star, pledging to change the face of American politics—and the world of foreign lobbying in the United States—forever.

And Manafort had an idea.

PART IV

INSURRECTIONS

May not one single person who voluntarily took up arms against our Flag ever return to his home, but may their bones be left to bleach upon the earth forgotten and alone.

—Byron Strong, Union soldier, Louisiana, April 1865[1]

13

Pot of Gold

The country is full of rebellion; the country is full of kings.
—Ralph Waldo Emerson[1]

Years later, as America suffered through its first non-peaceful transfer of power since the Civil War, the missed signs of the rising threats of foreign lobbying would be clear for all to see. As Donald Trump clung to power and sicced insurrectionists on legislators in Washington, the few voices who'd tried to raise concerns about unchecked foreign lobbyists would be proven right. And as Trump became the first American president to call for the "termination" of the U.S. Constitution, the topics of foreign lobbying regulations and prosecutions and reforms would rise to more prominence than they had seen in nearly a century—and arguably ever.[2]

The price for that relevance was, of course, steep. And while it's not fair to say that greater foreign lobbying regulations might have stopped the rise of Trump—might have prevented the first American president who called for the jailing of his political opponents, or who refused to concede an election loss—it's also not beyond the realm of possibility. If legislators and policymakers had been more focused on the threats of unhindered foreign lobbying in the years leading up to 2016, America might have dodged one of the most destabilizing, most damaging presidencies it had ever known. The United States may have avoided the first president to solicit foreign aid for election help, to be impeached multiple times, and to attempt to overturn a democratic election.

But it didn't. Because by 2016, things like foreign lobbying or foreign influence operations were hardly the primary focus in Washington.

Still, that's not to say no one was focusing on these topics. As we saw in the previous section, a number of scholars and journalists had started congealing around the topic, trying to describe and decipher the phenomenon. And by the early 2010s, they were joined by other investigators and organizations, all of whom realized that the space for researching foreign lobbying was—unfortunately, and distressingly—wide open.

One group, known as the Project on Government Oversight (POGO), initially launched in the early 1980s, focused largely on financial fraud and abuse. But in 2014, the Washington-based group decided to issue a report on a separate topic: FARA. Across nearly forty pages, the group detailed how FARA had long been a rank, rancid failure. Surveying existing FARA filings, POGO discovered that nearly half of the foreign lobbying firms who registered blew past basic deadlines, with more than half admitting they hadn't bothered to follow legal requirements about disclosing their links with foreign clients.[3]

Not that clients needed to worry; according to the most recent data POGO uncovered, there hadn't been a single audit of FARA filings in *years*. POGO didn't mince words in its summary: "We found a pattern of lax enforcement of FARA requirements by the Justice Department," the group wrote, especially since "the Justice Department office responsible for administering the law is a record-keeping mess."[4]

That same year, another group, known as the Sunlight Foundation, issued its own assessment. A group dedicated to improving governmental transparency, the Sunlight Foundation backed up POGO's findings. Their report described the "extremely poor quality" of FARA filings, often resulting in "gibberish." (At one point, the report's authors said they had to "physically cut and paste" some of the filings, just so they'd make any sense.) One of the group's developers offered to help the Justice Department improve the FARA system, streamlining and organizing as much as possible. But they apparently never heard anything back, despite multiple attempts to contact officials in charge of FARA. It was as if a group of undermotivated, easily distracted teenagers—all of whom had absolutely zero interest in actually doing their jobs—were in charge of overseeing America's foreign lobbying regulations.[5]

But even with such scant information available in the FARA filings, both POGO and the Sunlight Foundation still uncovered how foreign lobbyists manipulated American policymaking, all on behalf of their dictator-clients. One case POGO uncovered saw the Livingston Group fighting to make sure a congressional resolution criticizing Egyptian dictator Hosni Mubarak was never published. (The paperwork describing the Livingston Group's efforts was filed well past the FARA deadline—a breach that was, naturally, never punished.) Another case saw American lobbyists protect Libyan tyrant Muammar Gaddafi from paying restitution to family members of those his regime had murdered. The researchers also confirmed findings mentioned earlier, of American foreign lobbyists directly funding the same congressional officials they'd been lobbying. As POGO summed up, these foreign agents "have reported millions of dollars in political contributions annually."[6]

The simultaneous reports were something of a shot across the bow; civil society, it appeared, was finally waking up to the reality of ever-expanding foreign lobbying and foreign influence networks. In conjunction with the other scholarly and journalistic findings mentioned earlier, the new reports put U.S. officials, especially those tasked with monitoring FARA, on notice.

And, in a surprising twist, it all had an effect. Because not long after these groups began publicly slamming the United States for its lax foreign lobbying enforcement, the federal government began its own study of the topic—the first time U.S. officials had examined foreign lobbying regulations in decades, since the waning days of the Cold War.

Conducting internal interviews and combing through their own records, the federal government authored its own report on foreign lobbying oversight failures. Published in September 2016 by the Department of Justice's Office of the Inspector General (OIG), the report backed up everything everyone else had written. FARA was an abject failure. Despite the filing requirements, foreign lobbyists—and foreign dictators—had nothing to worry about. Nearly two-thirds of filings missed deadlines, with filings "ranging from 4 to 251 days" late. And hardly any punishments resulted: as the federal report charitably described, "historically there have been hardly any FARA prosecutions."[7]

To be fair, there was at least *some* good news buried in the report. Thanks to digitization efforts, the FARA database containing all of the foreign lobbyists' scanty filings was now available to anyone and every-one with a computer. Logging onto FARA's website, anyone could scroll through, say, the filings appended to India's lobbying efforts, or Belar-us's influence campaigns, or Mexico's state-funded PR publications in the United States—if, of course, those documents had actually been filed.[8] But as the OIG report made clear, the staff tasked with moni-toring FARA had been sliced nearly in half, continuing to shrink year after year, making it next to impossible to actually track any of these campaigns. And even if those regulators did discover some mishap or missed filing, they still didn't have the ability to compel things like re-cords or testimony.

Starved of resources, starved of solutions, the officials tasked with monitoring FARA were just doing all they could to keep from drowning. And as a result Americans had less and less idea of what foreign lobbyists might be doing—or how widely they might be affecting U.S. policy.[9]

For foreign lobbyists, of course, this lack of transparency surround-ing their work (let alone prosecution for any crimes) was a godsend. They could run rampant, racing around Washington, finding dictator-clients and funding legislators at will. As one analysis said, for these foreign lobbyists working in an industry now worth billions of dollars, it was like "finding an actual pot of gold at the end of a rainbow, just replace the leprechaun with a dictator."[10]

Yet with these new reports by the mid-2010s, there was a slight chance that something could finally change. These reports could, just maybe, jump-start interest in foreign lobbying, FARA, and how all of this impacted American policymaking—and maybe even how it had begun influencing American democracy. Maybe things could finally start to turn.

And, in a sense, that's what happened. Except it wasn't because of these reports. Instead, it was because a prodigal son had returned to Washington—to work on one final political project, and to launch one final president to power, after which nothing would be the same.

* * *

As WE SAW earlier, Manafort and Trump had actually met decades be-fore 2016, when Manafort was still focused on working with domestic

clientele. In the intervening years, though, the two had had little contact. This lack of overlap is somewhat surprising, given how they had
simultaneously turned their sights outward, with Manafort lining up
dictatorial clients and Trump courting kleptocratic investors in his
buildings, from figures in Azerbaijan and Kazakhstan to corrupt businessmen in places like Malaysia and the Dominican Republic.

Still, it's not as if the two spent the decades siloed off from each
other. Manafort's longtime partner, Roger Stone, had worked with
Trump for years, acting as an informal advisor during Trump's occa-
sional political flirtations. More pertinently, in 2006 Manafort spent
$3.7 million on a forty-third-floor condo in New York's Trump Tower.[11]
Hiding the purchase behind an LLC, Manafort enjoyed a 180-degree
view of Manhattan's West Side[12]—and joined a Haitian dictator, multiple Russian organized crime bosses, and plenty more in this small slice
of Trump's real estate empire.[13] Every once in a while, Manafort would
even bump into Trump near the elevators, where the two would talk
about everything from property values to geopolitics.

By the mid-2010s, though, their paths—and their fortunes—had
clearly diverged. Where Manafort's world had crumbled, Trump paired
economic populism with racist conspiracy theories to make more
headway in the 2016 Republican presidential primary than anyone
had anticipated. As Manafort watched, holed up in an Arizona clinic,
Trump rampaged through a primary unlike any other in American history. Ramshackle and haphazard, full of bizarre beliefs and staggering
lies, the early days of Trump's campaign would eventually set the tone
for the presidency—and the cult of personality—that followed.

But in early 2016, that rickety campaign nearly imploded before
Trump could even start. That February, Trump came in a disappointing second place in the Iowa caucuses. Whining about stolen votes,
Trump missed the fact that his opponent, Senator Ted Cruz, had simply out-organized his opponents—and that he would continue doing
so if nothing changed.

One person noticed this reality: Manafort. As Trump continued
whinging about Cruz's supposed election theft, Manafort reached out
to an old friend—one he thought might be able to help. Tom Barrack
is a lithe, balding billionaire, a man who'd made his wealth years earlier

in the private equity market. And Manafort, who'd initially met Barrack decades previously, knew that the financier was advising Trump behind the scenes on both economic and foreign policy—and that he might whisper in Trump's ear about who to hire to help organize his campaign.

Traveling to Beverly Hills in February 2016, Manafort sat down over coffee with Barrack, unwinding his pitch.[14] Barrack didn't need much convincing; thanks to his position as Trump's advisor, he had an inside look at how Trump's primary campaign was suddenly at risk of disintegration. The two quickly hammered out an arrangement: if Manafort could draft a strategy memo, Barrack would slide it in front of the candidate—and do what he could to bring Manafort aboard.

Manafort quickly obliged. In a terse three-page letter, he outlined his plan. Much of the memo was straightforward, bordering on vacuous. ("I can channel my strategic skills, tactical abilities and knowledge of modern political campaign tools," Manafort wrote, and will "apply these skills in helping to shape a national campaign working for the team that Trump has organized."[15]) But a few elements stand out. Manafort added in the memo that he had "not been a part of the Washington establishment since I de-registered as a lobbyist in 1998"—a claim that conveniently elided his lack of registration as a foreign lobbyist in the time since.[16] He also opened the memo with something that no other campaign organizer could match. As Manafort revealed, he wouldn't need to be paid for the position. "I am not looking for a paid job," he wrote.[17]

Barrack immediately pushed the memo to Trump, describing Manafort in a cover letter as "the most experienced and lethal of managers," as someone Trump could use as a "killer."[18] Stone also popped in to recommend Manafort, telling Trump that the candidate had "to bring Manafort on. He understands this stuff."[19]

Trump quickly obliged. Meeting with Manafort in Trump Tower, he peppered the lobbyist with questions about strategy, experience, expectations. He also asked why Manafort wouldn't need any payment. As Manafort later remembered, he responded that Trump "would respect me more and see me as a peer, as someone on his level" if he turned down any income. "I needed to be part of his group, not part of the campaign staff." The answer apparently soothed Trump.

As the candidate responded, "I guess if you can afford a place in this building"—referencing Manafort's multimillion-dollar condo, just a few floors above them—"you don't need to take my money."[20]

Manafort never publicly made the comparison, but it would have been impossible for him to miss the similarities between Trump and Yanukovych. The pinstriped suits and gaudy tastes, the political crassness and disheveled campaigns, the kleptocratic machinations and authoritarian preferences: the parallels were obvious. All that was needed to complete the comparison was for Trump, as with Yanukovych, to bring Manafort aboard—and to have Manafort launch them to power.

One day passed, and then another. And then Manafort's phone rang. It was Trump. "We need you," the candidate said. "We want you. When can you start?"[21]

* * *

Millions of words have already been spilled on the 2016 U.S. presidential campaign. The election remains one of the most bizarre and unexpected in American history—all of which resulted in one of the most bizarre and unexpected presidencies the country had ever experienced.

But even with the piles of books, memoirs, and dissertations that have already been written on the subject, it's worth pausing on Manafort's role in Trump's victory, both in the primary and in the general campaign—and the questions that remain about what he did, how he did it, and who he did it with. Because even with all those millions of words that have already been written about the election, questions— perhaps the *most important* questions—still remain about the campaign itself. And it's worth setting the stage for how the world of foreign lobbying intersected with the Trump campaign, the Trump presidency, and the Trump aftermath—and what that tells us about where the foreign lobbying industry is heading next.

As soon as Manafort joined Trump's campaign in March 2016, he hit the ground running. Working phones and organizing meetings, structuring a strategy and tapping the kinds of Republican contacts still squeamish about Trump's chances, Manafort quickly left an imprint on the campaign. Not that he had much time to waste. With the Republican convention just a few months away, there was hardly a guarantee that Trump would sweep to the nomination—let alone unify a fractured party behind him.

With Manafort as campaign manager, though, those rifts suddenly started receding. He was, as one analysis described, "an elder statesman on a campaign that had lacked such a figure."[22] Consolidating his role internally, Manafort steered the campaign toward the July convention, steadily snatching delegates as he went. Trump's campaign began to gel, resembling something that could actually win.

Along the way, Manafort helped Trump refine his message—and helped the candidate sharpen the kind of divisive rhetoric that could launch him to the White House. Similar to Yanukovych, Trump began elevating cultural grievances, especially among populations nostalgic for some kind of gauzy, glorious past. Similar to Yanukovych, he began openly calling to imprison his political opponent. And similar to Yanukovych, he melded it all with suspiciously, obliquely pro-Russian rhetoric, from backing Moscow in Crimea to supporting Putin's policies elsewhere.

As he'd done with Yanukovych, Manafort polished the candidate, hewing and honing Trump into something far more palatable than anyone thought possible. And that July, at the Republican National Convention, it all paid off. Trump stormed to the nomination, picking up the mantle of the GOP and pledging to restore American "greatness."

For Manafort, it was his "shining moment."[23] Which certainly seems true, both in public and private. Manafort had returned to the nexus of the American political firmament, far more quickly, and far more strangely, than he'd thought possible. Two years removed from Yanukovych's downfall, one year removed from a personal bottoming-out, Manafort was once more at the center of the Republican orbit, and had once more crowned a Republican nominee, helping a candidate unlike anything seen prior.

And he'd done so during a campaign that was already more steeped in abnormal developments and unexpected twists than any in U.S. history. Because by the time Trump cinched the Republican nomination, the candidate and his campaign already had help far beyond the traditional Republican allies Manafort helped cobble together. Suddenly, a new force had entered the American electoral fray: a consortium of hackers and anti-American activists, dedicated to disseminating the most unflattering, embarrassing, and damaging information about Trump's opponent that they could find.

And if Manafort could help these hackers and their allies spread their salacious discoveries, all the better.

* * *

THE RUSSIAN HACKERS who swiped the internal communiqués of both the Democratic National Committee and Hillary Clinton's campaign staff will almost certainly never see prosecution, or any kind of jail time. But they didn't operate in a vacuum, or in conjunction only with other Russians or organizations like WikiLeaks. Instead, as both high-level investigations and court testimony make clear, they had help—and Manafort, despite public disavowals, was clearly privy to at least part of the hacking campaign, while plotting out how the Trump campaign could best capitalize on the revelations.

Much of Manafort's prior knowledge of the hacks came from Roger Stone, the conspiracist court jester later sentenced for witness intimidation and obstructing investigations, among other charges. As Rick Gates, Manafort's former deputy, later testified, Stone immediately called Manafort after WikiLeaks released the initial batch of stolen DNC emails in July 2016. "Additional information would be coming down the road," Stone told Manafort. According to Gates, Manafort "thought that would be great," and told Gates to stay in contact with Stone "about future releases." Manafort "would be updating other people on the campaign, including the candidate."[24]

Soon thereafter, with the emails already damaging Clinton's campaign—though not yet enough to make Trump the favorite—Stone reached back out to Manafort. As he said to Manafort, "I have an idea . . . to save Trump's ass." He told Manafort to call him.[25] While neither Stone nor Manafort revealed the contents of the ensuing call, surmising the topic of their conversation isn't difficult. That same day, Stone said he met with WikiLeaks founder Julian Assange, the man responsible for disseminating the swiped emails. And one day later, Stone publicly predicted a "devastating" release from WikiLeaks—a release that came almost immediately thereafter, when yet another tranche of released emails dominated the news cycle, damaged Clinton further, and propelled Trump that much closer to the White House.[26]

Manafort and Stone have denied any knowledge of, or coordination with, Russian hackers or their WikiLeaks proxies. But given that both were eventually convicted for crimes ranging from things like fraud to outright lying to investigators—to say nothing of their previous history of dissimulation, and the preponderance of evidence pointing to their prior knowledge of the hacks—their denials are hardly worth any weight.

Moreover, it's not like Manafort was averse to working directly with foreign actors looking to benefit from the Trump campaign, and from a potential Trump presidency. Because, as we now know, Manafort maintained a parallel contact in Russia throughout the campaign that left far more of a paper trail—and that tied directly back to the Kremlin itself.

*   *   *

BORN IN 1970, Konstantin Kilimnik is a small, mousy Russian national who'd known Manafort for years. While Kilimnik had spent a spell working with the U.S.-funded International Republican Institute in Moscow, he had far closer, and far more conspicuous, links with the Kremlin and its proxies. Not only did he admit that he learned English at a "training ground for Russian spies," but he had also worked extensively for oligarchs like Akhmetov and Deripaska, helping them expand their fortunes and entrench pro-Kremlin interests in places like Ukraine.[27]

Eventually, in the mid-2000s, Manafort brought Kilimnik aboard his Ukraine team, with Kilimnik becoming one of Manafort's most trusted deputies during their pro-Yanukovych campaigning. And after Yanukovych's ouster, Manafort wouldn't let Kilimnik go. The two remained in contact, even as Manafort once more injected himself into American politics—and especially after Manafort began directing Trump's campaign.

Indeed, after being appointed to Trump's campaign in early 2016, Manafort immediately reached out to Kilimnik, who was then bouncing between Ukraine and Russia. Manafort's communiqués, though, weren't simply to check in on Kilimnik, or to potentially plan out future projects.

They instead centered on one thing: how to erase Manafort's purported debt to Deripaska, the Russian oligarch still hunting for Manafort's assets. As Manafort wrote to Kilimnik, sending along press clippings announcing his new position with Trump's campaign, "How do we use this to get whole? Has [Deripaska's] operation seen?"[28]

Kilimnik responded positively, assuring Manafort that the Russian oligarch was aware of his new role. Surely, there was some way the two could use Manafort's new position to make Deripaska happy. As Kilimnik wrote, "We will get back to the original relationship [with Deripaska]."[29]

On its face, the communiqués were concerning enough. Manafort appeared to be asking how to leverage his new role in Trump's campaign as a way to eliminate his debt to a key Putin ally, a man who was by this point little more than a proxy for the Kremlin. But there was one further complication. Kilimnik wasn't a simple go-between, a former Manafort employee now acting as courier. He was, as American officials would later reveal, a "Russian intelligence officer"—and one who'd been working for Moscow for years.[30]

A few weeks after they reconnected, in early May 2016, Kilimnik joined Manafort in New York in their first—but not last—meeting of the campaign. There, Manafort "detailed Trump's path to winning the election," pointing out which states would prove most critical to their effort.[31] He then passed along proprietary polling data about which states the Trump campaign would target—and how they'd do it. Page after page after page, Manafort outlined Trump's prospective path to the White House. As author Rob Waldeck notes, Manafort "fully expected that Kilimnik would pass this information on" to his contacts in Russia.[32]

Pulling back, Manafort's move was nothing short of a scandal. For the first time in U.S. history, a presidential campaign manager was passing internal campaign data and strategy to a foreign intelligence asset—one working on behalf of an American adversary, no less. Even more concerningly, as investigators later discovered, gaining further insight into Manafort's and Kilimnik's conversations proved nearly impossible. The two used "sophisticated communications security practices,"[33] including "encryption, burner phones, and 'foldering'—writing emails as drafts in a shared account."[34] Messages between Manafort and

Kilimnik were routinely scrubbed, with some messages "deleted . . .
daily."[35] It was less tradecraft and more spycraft—and all completely
beyond the scope of a traditional campaign manager.

Manafort never bothered to explain why he was passing blocks of
pages of the most sensitive polling data and campaign strategy to a
Russian intelligence agent. However, in 2021, the U.S. Treasury Department answered the question for him. Kilimnik, a "known Russian
agent," had been "implementing influence operations" on behalf of the
Kremlin—and had "provided the Russian Intelligence Services with
sensitive information on polling and campaign strategy."[36]

Nor was that all. Soon after pumping Kilimnik with internal campaign data, Manafort hosted the Russian intelligence asset in the
United States once more.[37] In a dark, smoke-swirled meeting in New
York's Grand Havana Room—a "perfect put-up stage set for a caricature drama of furtive figures hatching covert schemes," *The New York
Times*' Jim Rutenberg wrote—the men discussed something far beyond
simple polling data or campaign rhetoric.[38] As they sat surrounded by
velvet draping and leather-lined chairs, they talked about the future of
one country they'd both worked in, which was slowly lurching toward
the center of global geopolitics: Ukraine.

As Kilimnik laid out, a new "peace plan" had begun floating around
Moscow, one that could provide a fix for the supposed "problem" of
Ukraine.[39] The idea was relatively straightforward. The new plan
"would create a semi-autonomous region in Eastern Ukraine," among
the areas already decimated by pro-Russian forces. Yanukovych would
then "get elected to head" these new parts of Ukraine—and proceed to
"reunite the country as its leader."[40] The plan, in effect, would see an
entirely new polity created: a Russia-backed enclave in the Donbass
region of eastern Ukraine, with Yanukovych as its leader—a position
he would then use to return to power in Kyiv.

To outside observers, the idea that Yanukovych could catapult to
power in Kyiv again was ridiculous. (Not even Napoleon returned to
power for a *third* time.) But to Kilimnik, relaying all of this to Manafort,
there was only one step necessary to make it happen. "All that is required to start the process," Kilimnik later told Manafort, "is a very
minor 'wink' (or slight push) from [Trump] saying 'he wants peace in

Ukraine and [the] Donbass back in Ukraine.'"[41] Manafort agreed: the plan would need "Trump's assent to succeed."[42]

Everyone, as Kilimnik saw it, would win. Yanukovych would return from exile and resume power. The Kremlin would have its man once more in Kyiv. Trump would "have peace in Ukraine basically within a few months after inauguration," Kilimnik said.[43] And Manafort would be at the center of it all: a man shuttling between Moscow, Kyiv, and Washington, stitching the geopolitics of the era—a kingmaker crossing oceans, threading the halls of power, and restoring peace in the heart of Europe.

It was a plan that almost certainly wouldn't have worked. And Manafort would later deny that he supported it. But given that he later lied to both investigators and a grand jury about both the peace plan and his meetings with Kilimnik, those denials—just like his denials that he had any foreknowledge of the hacked emails—are hardly credible. Moreover, shortly after their initial conversation, Manafort connected with Kilimnik once more to talk about the "peace plan." And then he did it again. And then again once more. Over and over, Manafort and Kilimnik—this known Russian intelligence agent, actively working as part of a broader Russian influence operation— spoke directly with Manafort about bringing a Moscow-sponsored "peace" to Ukraine, and what Trump could do to make it happen. And they spoke consistently about how Manafort could be the "envoy" in the middle of everything—about how Manafort could be the centerpiece of the entire operation.[44]

But before Trump could offer his "wink" to sign off on the operation, journalists in Ukraine stumbled across a name in Yanukovych's reams of documents that they recognized. It was someone who, as these files described, had secretly siphoned off millions of dollars looted from Ukrainians, splurging on himself, and hiding it all from Ukrainian and American authorities alike. And it was someone who was now running an American presidential campaign unlike anything seen before.

* * *

ON AUGUST 14, 2016, less than two weeks after Manafort hosted Kilimnik for their initial conversation on the "peace plan" for Ukraine, *The New York Times* splashed a headline from Kyiv: SECRET LEDGER

IN UKRAINE LISTS CASH FOR DONALD TRUMP'S CAMPAIGN CHIEF.[45] A new folder, uncovered by Ukrainian journalists and researchers poring through the records Yanukovych had abandoned, listed Manafort as the recipient of millions of dollars in off-the-book payments from the erstwhile autocrat's network.

With Manafort's name appearing nearly two dozen times, the ledger detailed how the lobbyist had received nearly $13 million in "undisclosed cash payments." Line after line, payment after payment, the documents in this so-called "Black Ledger" illustrated how Yanukovych had bankrolled Manafort for his lobbying and consulting work—and had used hidden, offshore networks to do so. As Serhiy Leshchenko, one of Ukraine's leading anti-corruption researchers, said, "This is money stolen from Ukrainian citizens and . . . paid to Manafort for [his work] with our former corrupt president."[46] Hidden behind shell companies, masked via offshore networks, Manafort had made millions as Yanukovych's campaign consigliere—much of which he'd then proceeded to hide from authorities.

The revelations detonated in the United States, even amidst everything else happening in the campaign. Manafort swiftly denied the accusations, claiming the assertions of illicit payments were "laughable" and that someone, somewhere had launched a "deliberate, premeditated attack that showed a high level of sophistication" against him.[47] (Manafort would later blame, among others, financier George Soros for the revelations.[48]) But his denials fell flat. The evidence continued to mount: the confirmation of the shell companies, the continued details of the specific payments, Manafort's slippery unwillingness to provide straight answers. Along the way, Manafort had committed a cardinal sin of the Trump campaign: he'd stolen the spotlight from the candidate.

Three days later, Trump shook up his campaign leadership, demoting Manafort. And two days after that, reading the writing on the wall, Manafort submitted his resignation.[49]

It was over. Just as he'd begun rebuilding his career, just as he'd begun spying a way toward the White House, just as he'd begun plotting out a way to restore both himself and a former client to glory in Ukraine—just as he'd returned to the center of it all—everything fell apart. Yet again.

Manafort slunk away from the campaign, letting Trump race through the final stretches of the election on his own. More email hacks would come, and more questions about Trump's (and Clinton's) foreign entanglements, and more unexpected, inexplicable twists and turns than most Americans could keep track of. But Manafort was there for none of it. Instead, he was back home, watching a case slowly building against him in Ukraine—and realizing that his best chance for evading any potential charges, either in Ukraine or the United States, lay in a Trump victory, however unlikely that might be.

And then, that November, Trump won. And Manafort breathed a sigh of relief. Because, surely, with Trump in the White House, there would be no sudden focus on things like foreign lobbying crimes, or how foreign regimes target lawmakers, or how foreign lobbyists themselves had begun steering domestic politics in the United States. Surely, with Trump in the Oval Office, foreign lobbyists would be able to run riot through Washington, expanding their tools and their networks and their clients around the world. Manafort could be brought back in from the cold—and could even become, perhaps, the "envoy" steering Trump's foreign policy.

Right?

14

Black Hole

It is impossible to destroy men with more respect to the laws of humanity.

—Alexis de Tocqueville[1]

Shortly before the election, when I was still a graduate student focused on what I thought would be the niche topic of how post-Soviet dictatorships manipulate American audiences, I sat in a crowded room at New York's Columbia University, there to listen to a panel on Azerbaijan's supposed importance to the West. The panel featured a trio of voices, joined to discuss why Azerbaijan—whose state-run gas firm, SOCAR, had just sparked the biggest foreign lobbying scandal in congressional history—should be providing America's energy and security needs in the region.

One of the speakers was a member of Columbia's staff, while another was a representative from SOCAR itself. And there, at the center of the table, was a towering, imposing woman named Brenda Shaffer. A Georgetown University professor, Shaffer was widely considered the most prominent expert in the United States on Azerbaijan, having recently written opinion pieces on the country in both *The New York Times*[2] and *The Washington Post*.[3] She'd even recently testified in front of the U.S. Congress on the country's apparent importance. And she would soon join the Atlantic Council think tank, becoming that organization's in-house expert on all things Azerbaijan.[4]

Unbeknownst to the audience at Columbia University that day—and unbeknownst to any of her editors, or any of the members of Congress who listened to her testimony—Shaffer also had another role. As journalists at Radio Free Europe/Radio Liberty discovered, Shaffer had worked as "Advisor to the President" of Azerbaijan's state-run gas company, the source of much of the regime's illicit wealth.[5] That is to say, while Shaffer was writing, testifying, and advising on United States relations with Azerbaijan—while she was speaking glowingly about the country's regime, all from a supposedly neutral, objective stance—she never bothered to disclose that she was also tied directly to the ruling dictatorship and its piggy bank.

Shortly after the revelation, *The New York Times* and *The Washington Post* issued simultaneous corrections, both of them revealing that Shaffer had never disclosed her relationship with Azerbaijan's government. As the *Times* editors wrote, Shaffer had signed a contract promising to disclose her potential conflicts of interests—which she clearly hadn't done. It was, as far as anyone could remember, the first time America's two most important newspapers had ever had to issue simultaneous corrections for the same person. And that day at Columbia, I decided to ask Shaffer about the controversy—and about whether she had any comment about her historic, ignominious achievement.

"Professor Shaffer, I was hoping to address a question to you," I began. "Your name has been in the news a little bit recently. You were a 'strategic adviser,' an 'adviser for strategic affairs,' for the president of SOCAR; you had an op-ed in *The New York Times* that had to issue a correction clarifying that. I was wondering if you might address that, and then whether or not Congress was aware of that relationship when you testified."

Shaffer immediately scowled, locked her eyes on mine, and deflected the question. "If I asked you, Casey, OK, what's your wife's name, what school do you go to, who funds your scholarship right now, where do you work, how do you pay your meals, how do—what's your cholesterol count—there's nothing to be ashamed of in any of those answers," Shaffer started.

Since my cholesterol count and romantic life weren't quite as pertinent to the discussion, I repeated the question, asking again if she had any comment about her lack of disclosure. And Shaffer seized up once more. "Again, like I said, I'm not going to ask you your cholesterol count," she replied. "Who pays your scholarship? How do you pay your tuition here?" The panel moderator tried to interject: "I don't think we need to—" Shaffer cut him off, zeroing in on my finances, voice beginning to boom. "Who pays your tuition here?"[6]

The moderator eventually regained control of the conversation, stumbling back to some sense of normalcy. But Shaffer, despite the questions, never addressed her role with Azerbaijan's gas company, or why she hadn't disclosed that relationship to her editors, to American legislators, or even to the audience that day at Columbia University. To this day, she's never directly addressed her clandestine role working for Azerbaijan's gas firm.[7] (For what it's worth, I still don't know my cholesterol count, either.)

Still, Shaffer's lack of disclosure about her work on behalf of a kleptocratic dictatorship did reveal one thing. With her connections to both Georgetown and the Atlantic Council, Shaffer embodied in a single person how American universities and American think tanks had become their own vectors for these kinds of undisclosed foreign lobbying efforts—an area that got almost no attention, and even less scrutiny, until the Trump administration decided to begin taking a look, and began uncovering just how widespread the rot of undisclosed foreign money in both sectors had become.

* * *

IT IS, OF course, somewhat ironic that American officials largely overlooked the spread of foreign funding and foreign lobbying in both the university and think tank sectors until the Trump administration began focusing on both industries. And for those correctly worried about how susceptible Trump was (and remains) to foreign influence, fear not: for the remainder of the book, we'll be poring through all the ways that foreign regimes targeted and manipulated Trump and his inner circle, launching an unprecedented assault on America's policymaking apparatus.

But credit is due, however surprising it may be. Year after year, administration after administration, U.S. officials effectively ignored how universities and think tanks alike spiraled into centers of foreign influence and foreign lobbying campaigns. Like law firms and public relations consultancies before them, both universities and think tanks provided fonts of supposed expertise, as well as deep connections to officials in Washington. Like nonprofits and foundations elsewhere, universities and think tanks both enjoyed a galling lack of transparency when it came to foreign funders, revealing only what they wished (which was often very little) about their foreign financial agreements. And like all other avenues of foreign lobbying in America, universities and think tanks spent decades flouting basic foreign lobbying transparency requirements, confident that no investigator would come calling, and that no regulator would ever check to see whether or not they were complying with the law.

And for decades, they were right: no investigators came calling, no regulators came knocking. Even journalists showed little interest in how American universities and think tanks had transformed into vehicles for undisclosed foreign lobbying links; you can count on one hand the number of major media investigations into the topic, at least before 2016.

But that would all change with the Trump administration. Despite the morass of foreign lobbying investigations swirling around Trump himself, his administration took an especial lead in investigating how universities and think tanks had transformed into go-to destinations for reputation laundering, for targeting American policymakers, and for tilting American policy toward foreign regimes', and especially foreign dictatorships', benefit. Thanks to the administration steeped in more foreign lobbying scandals than we've ever seen before, Americans have a far better idea of how universities and think tanks joined the flood of foreign lobbying campaigns, opening their doors in ways we've only just begun learning about.

* * *

LET'S LOOK AT universities first. Beginning with legislation enacted in 1986, all American universities were supposed to disclose, twice a year, all foreign gifts and contracts valued over $250,000.[8] As with other nonprofits, receiving such foreign financial gifts wasn't prohibited. Instead, like foreign lobbying contracts in FARA, these arrangements were supposed to be detailed and disclosed for American officials. All the federal government asked for was a bit of transparency.[9]

But for decades, no administration bothered to actually enforce these disclosure requirements, or even check whether any university filings were accurate. Like FARA, these basic transparency requirements were "neglected routinely."[10] The regulations were on the books, but with no one taking a look, they were effectively worthless.

In the late 2010s, though, this began to change. First, a bipartisan investigation from the Senate Permanent Subcommittee on Investigations, focused primarily on Chinese influence efforts in U.S. higher education, found that American universities "routinely" avoided disclosing funding from Beijing-linked sources. To take just one data point, the stark majority—nearly three-quarters—of American colleges and universities that received significant funding from the Chinese education ministry "failed to report as required." Information about these funding streams, worth millions of dollars, was effectively a "black hole."[11] And as the report summarized, such Chinese funding came "with strings that can compromise academic freedom"—such as censorship and silence regarding things like China's Tiananmen Square massacre or Beijing's ongoing colonization of Tibet.[12]

The findings were surprising in scope, if not necessarily shocking; by the late 2010s, concerns had grown across the American political spectrum about Chinese influence operations, which these numbers bore out. However, the Senate investigation sparked a second, broader investigation that revealed far more about undisclosed foreign funding in American universities, and how China was hardly alone. Overseen by the U.S. Department of Education, this follow-up investigation discovered not only just how much further Chinese funding had gone but also how dictatorship after dictatorship had followed a similar model, funding some of America's most prominent universities—and turning them into centers of pro-regime lobbying efforts in the process. Without much attention in wider American media, the Trump White House had become far and away the most successful administration to examine how Beijing, and plenty of other dictatorships besides, had transformed American universities into go-to vehicles for accessing American audiences—and opening untold doors along the way.

Surveying a dozen major U.S. universities, investigators discovered that these institutions had failed to report a staggering $6.5 billion in

"previously unreported foreign money." And it seemed like every major American university had taken part in hiding these financial flows
and ignoring federal transparency regulations. Harvard, Yale, Stanford,
Georgetown: major university after major university had failed in its
basic diligence requirements. "The largest, wealthiest, and most sophisticated of America's institutions of higher education have received . . .
billions of dollars in assets using an assortment of related intermediaries, including functionally captive foundations, foreign operating units,
and other structures," the Education Department's report found. All
of this, while universities "aggressively pursued and accepted foreign
money."[13]

Yale, for instance, failed to report nearly $400 million in foreign gifts
and contracts, admitting that they didn't submit a single report on the
funding for years on end. ("It is hard to understand . . . how Yale University could have simply failed to report any foreign gifts or contracts," the
report read, especially given Yale's "highly credentialed administrators
and ready access to the very best accountants and attorneys.")[14] Other
universities, like Harvard, maintained "inadequate institutional controls
over . . . foreign donations and contracts," while Stanford anonymized
foreign donors, meaning that investigators couldn't track tens of millions
of dollars in funding from Chinese sources. Meanwhile, Cornell University somehow couldn't account for an astounding $760 million in foreign
funding. As the report read, Cornell University officials "chose the word
'dumbfounded' to explain this reporting error and provided no explanation.'"[15]

Again: accepting these funds wasn't illegal. But these universities—
those supposed bastions of free speech and progressive values—
proceeded to blow past all reporting requirements, all while taking
funding from some of the most odious, repressive regimes on the
planet.

Indeed, the investigation found that accepting funds from kleptocrats around the world—money that, in any other instance, would be
considered "dirty"—became a kind of de rigueur habit at these schools.
The most popular sources of foreign financing for American universities were not open, democratic governments, but rather dictatorships in places like the Persian Gulf, as well as Moscow and Beijing. As

American officials uncovered, funding from these dictatorships "rose massively" during the late 2000s and early 2010s. But even getting details about the original source of those dictatorial donations was difficult; as the report concluded, "the evidence shows the industry has at once massively underreported while also anonymizing much of the money it did disclose, all to hide foreign sources." All told, these kinds of anonymous donations from places like China, Saudi Arabia, Russia, and Qatar totaled over $1 billion—and that's only at the dozen schools surveyed.[16]

*   *   *

THANKS TO THESE investigations, we at least know a bit about the kinds of relationships prominent American universities developed with repressive—and, in the case of China, genocidal—dictatorships abroad. For instance, the Massachusetts Institute of Technology (MIT) built links with at least one Kremlin-controlled institute, and apparently had no qualms about signing contracts with high-ranking Russian officials.[17] (One of Putin's closest allies, sanctioned Russian oligarch Viktor Vekselberg, would remain on MIT's board of trustees until 2019—years after the Kremlin first launched its invasion of Ukraine.)[18] And Qatar routed $1.4 billion to not one but *six* different American universities—all while setting up an American nonprofit called the Qatar Foundation International to obscure the source of the funds.[19]

Since these findings were published so recently, we've only just begun learning about what effect these massive donations have had on universities, on related researchers and students, and on U.S. policy writ large. But thanks to a new database on the Department of Education's website, the public can at least see which universities—and which alma maters—have opened their doors to all of this dictatorial wealth. Launched in 2020, the publicly accessible database reveals all the universities who've freely opened their doors to kleptocratic funds. They can see, for instance, Boston University and Johns Hopkins accepting tens of millions of dollars from the dictatorship in the UAE. They can see that places as disparate as Portland State University and West Virginia University have taken in millions more from Saudi Arabia. And they can see that regimes as far-flung as Uganda, Turkey, and Vietnam have even lobbed cash at universities, finding new partners wherever they look.[20]

Thus far, there's been disappointingly little attention paid to things like the new database, and what it reveals about how universities now act as tills for dictatorial money. But given the overlap between higher education and the world of policymaking—with former officials routinely cycling through academia, and with American universities educating rising generations of U.S. officials—it's not difficult to see why foreign regimes may be interested in opening doors at these universities.

Initial reportage indicates that foreign regimes are especially interested in using these donations to both improve their reputation and silence criticism of their policies. With Qatar, for instance, a pair of American universities partnered with a Qatar-funded group "which has been known to silence viewpoints Qatar opposes."[21] (Among other things, the group convinced Northwestern University to block an openly gay artist from speaking on their campus.) And China, Senate investigators found, used the funding to "change the impression in the United States and around the world that China is an economic and security threat"—even while Beijing brutalizes Tibet, threatens Taiwan, and oversees genocidal policies aimed at its Muslim minorities. As one school official told investigators, they "would never even propose to hold an event on Tibet or Taiwan."[22]

Indeed, whitewashing regimes and silencing criticism are hardly mutually exclusive. And it turns out that large-scale donations to American universities are great tools for effecting both. Look, for instance, at Harvard, and at the single largest donation Harvard has ever received in its almost four-hundred-year existence. In 2014, a dual American-Chinese national named Ronnie Chan, who made billions in the Hong Kong real estate industry, announced a $350 million gift to Harvard University. As Harvard president Drew Faust said, the funds were an "extraordinary gift,"[23] with another official describing the donation as "transformational."[24]

All of that may be true. But it's also clear that the funding hardly followed traditional routes of other donations Harvard had received. Rather than one lump sum, Chan used a Massachusetts-based non-profit to parcel out the donation over several years—a convenient

mechanism for, say, maintaining leverage with Harvard officials waiting for the rest of the funds to come.[25] The funds, however, did not
originate with this nonprofit; instead, they originated via a range of
offshore entities. These included a series of Monaco-based companies
that shared the same address as other offshore entities discovered in the
Paradise Papers, one of the biggest leaks of offshore wealth in global
history.[26]

Between the offshore accounts and the decision to parcel the donation out over years, the structure of this "extraordinary gift" was, at the
least, extraordinarily odd. Even beyond that, it's unclear what due diligence, if any, Harvard actually did on the funds. As with most universities, Harvard maintains opaque rules and regulations when it comes
to screening gifts, even after accepting donations worth millions from
figures like Jeffrey Epstein and the opioid-producing Sackler family.[27]

But it's clear that Harvard should have exercised far more diligence
about Chan's donation—not least since Chan is known to be cozy with
officials in Beijing, on whom Chan is reliant in order to maintain his
real estate holdings in Hong Kong.[28] "The thing to note is that Ronnie
Chan is a complete and unreserved supporter of the Chinese Communist Party," one person familiar with Chan told me. "His bread is very
clearly buttered on the side of business with China."[29] That relationship
comes through clearly via Chan's stewardship of an organization called
the Asia Society. In 2017, the group was at the center of a scandal when
it publicly silenced one of Hong Kong's most prominent democracy
activists, Joshua Wong, barring him from speaking at an Asia Society
event.[30] While Chan publicly blamed his staff for booting out the democracy activist, internal documents indicate that Chan himself led
the effort to evict Wong.[31] As one document read, "The press release
of the Joshua Wong incident blamed it on the staff, when in reality it
was . . . Ronnie Chan."[32]

But it's not just the odd structure of the donations, or the fact that
Chan's group stood at the center of efforts to silence anti-Beijing critics.
According to sources familiar with Chan's moves, Chan further used
his donation to Harvard to try to silence Harvard officials—and even
former, and potentially future, American officials.

One figure who asked not to be named told me that after the

donation was announced, Chan sat down with Nicholas Burns, then running Harvard's Kennedy School. Burns is considered one of the United States' leading China scholars—so much so that he is, as of 2023, the U.S. ambassador to Beijing.

According to those familiar with their interaction, Chan wasn't interested in Burns's expertise. Instead, he used his donation to access Burns, and then offer him a position with Chan's Asia Society group— but only if Burns agreed to stop criticizing Beijing. "This is to me quite stunning," the person familiar with the interaction said. "Chan went up and said, if there was any criticism [of Beijing], he'd make sure [Burns] got fired" from the Asia Society position. "That to me was shocking."[33] (Burns declined the offer, and neither he nor Chan responded to my questions.)

This is all from a single donation, to a single university, all related to a single dictatorship. But even with this one donation, we can see the contours of why regimes might launch donation after donation to American universities. Hiding the sources behind offshore vehicles, gaining leverage over the universities, being able to access policymakers (and students), and silencing criticism that might emanate from these universities—all of this, in addition to potentially gaining access to proprietary research and technology—and donations like Chan's suddenly seem unsurprising. Toss in the fact that American regulators were asleep at the wheel, and American universities transform into completely logical destinations for this kind of foreign funding. And given the scope and scale of the financing, the impacts of this money— and how it's allowed foreign regimes to silence, to spin, and to lobby along the way—are going to take years to disentangle.[34]

* * *

But as Shaffer and Harvard illustrated, it's not just American academics and universities who've become vectors for foreign lobbying and influence efforts. Another industry, known colloquially as think tanks, has emerged in recent years as a go-to destination for dictatorial funding—and for upending American policy, all without the rest of us having any idea.

Think tanks are, like universities and foundations before them, nonprofits, nominally dedicated to the study of any range of policy issues. Some think tanks are dedicated to domestic affairs, from housing policy to wealth inequality. But many, especially in Washington, also work on foreign policy—and on drafting papers, conducting research, and hosting meetings and events about how America can and should pursue certain policies vis-à-vis certain governments abroad. Few think tanks, such as the Atlantic Council or the Council on Foreign Relations, are focused *exclusively* on foreign policy. But many of the biggest American think tanks, including ones like the Brookings Institution and the Center for American Progress, have wings dedicated to the topic. And all too often, when legislators—who are rarely foreign policy experts to begin with—are strapped for time and resources, they effectively outsource their policy prescriptions to think tanks, relying on them to provide the most effective recommendations along the way.[35]

It's a sound arrangement, at least on paper. But unlike universities or other foreign lobbying shops, think tanks have never been actually required to disclose sources of foreign funding. And given that so many of them are so intimately tied with America's foreign policymaking apparatus—U.S. officials not only rely on think tanks' recommendations but routinely cycle in and out of these think tanks themselves—they've become go-to vehicles for foreign financing, and for foreign lobbying efforts that can operate without any disclosure requirements.

As researchers have discovered, the amount of foreign funding sprinting toward American think tanks, especially from foreign dictatorships, has positively exploded over the past few years. America's most prominent think tanks have taken in hundreds of millions of dollars, and potentially more, from foreign regimes in recent years, none of it being disclosed in things like FARA. And as we saw with universities, much of this funding comes from kleptocratic dictatorships dedicated to immiserating their populations, imprisoning opposition figures and journalists, and doing everything they can to keep their ruling regime in power.

For instance, the foreign country with one of the highest donation rates to American think tanks is the United Arab Emirates, a repressive autocracy where things like LGBTQ rights, media freedoms, and opposition politics are all oxymorons. According to the most recent findings, the UAE has given millions of dollars to America's most prominent think tanks—all without being required to disclose any of this funding to American regulators, to the American populace, or to the American legislators whom these think tanks influence.[36]

With these donations, the Emirati regime became the single largest foreign benefactor for a number of major American think tanks. Not only did the UAE provide the majority of all foreign funding for think tanks like the Aspen Institute—a group that claims to be "committed to realizing a free, just, and equitable society"[37]—but the UAE is also the largest foreign donor to places like the Atlantic Council, which accepted at least $4 million from the dictatorship. And that money apparently came with strings attached. As one researcher found, the "Atlantic Council's ties to the UAE have given the UAE the opportunity to shape the think tank's reports prior to publication"—effectively allowing the dictatorship to craft the Atlantic Council's supposedly independent analysis before publishing. As leaked emails showed, Atlantic Council officials directly reached out to their UAE patrons with offers to edit their text, including material "that was to be published under the name of" David Petraeus, one of America's most well-known former military officers.[38]

And the UAE is hardly the only foreign government the Atlantic Council—arguably America's most prominent think tank in the foreign policy space—turned to for funds. Up to 20 percent of the organization's budget derives from these kinds of foreign donations. And despite being supposedly dedicated to creating a world that is "more free,"[39] much of the Atlantic Council's funding has come from some of the most stifling, kleptocratic dictatorships and autocracies in the world, such as Bahrain, Saudi Arabia, Kuwait, Azerbaijan, and more.[40]

"Of all entities involved, of all the big think tanks, the one that seems to be the most engaged, the one run most like a bordello, is the Atlantic Council," one researcher focused on foreign funding for think tanks told me. "The Atlantic Council just doesn't seem to care, and they seem to operate by taking huge sums from foreign sovereigns, and then preparing programs for foreign sovereigns. . . . The Atlantic Council is an absolute floozy, and it's completely ridiculous that it doesn't even seem to care."[41] (Another figure connected to the Atlantic Council? Ukrainian oligarch Victor Pinchuk, who somehow remains on the organization's International Advisory Board—despite financial links to Paul Manafort's network.)[42]

To be fair to the Atlantic Council, other think tanks happily gorged on UAE financing as well. (Others also happily placed post-Soviet oligarchs on their boards; the Council on Foreign Relations kept Vladimir Potanin, Russia's wealthiest oligarch, on its board through early 2022.) The Emirati dictatorship also became one of the top donors for the Center for American Progress—a nominally liberal think tank, linked closely with the Democratic Party. Following the UAE's donation, which also ran into the millions, a member of the think tank's staff began helping Emirati officials "organize UAE-sponsored trips" to the country, and began directly advising Emirati officials on how to lobby their American counterparts.[43]

Indeed, it's difficult to find a prominent think tank that *hasn't* been feasting on these foreign—and especially kleptocratic—funds in recent years. For instance, the Brookings Institution is perhaps the United States' most prominent think tank, and certainly its oldest, founded in 1916. Widely viewed as a centrist, nonpartisan think tank, Brookings hosts some of America's foremost scholars and former officials.

It is also the single biggest recipient in the United States of funds from the brutal regime in Qatar. With Brookings having taken in at least $14.8 million from the regime, Qatar is its largest single source of foreign funds—as well as, as far as we can tell, the *only* think tank to which the regime has given funds.[44]

And it's not difficult to see why. For years, think tank officials at places like the Brookings Institution have claimed that their work focuses largely on research and policy, and not on things like advocating for the foreign governments funding their work. But as the case of the Brookings Institution and Qatar illustrates, that line is hardly credible. Like lobbyists elsewhere, American think tanks routinely do the bidding of their foreign patrons—and all of it out of the public eye. As one foreign diplomat said, "Funding powerful think tanks is one way to gain such access [to American politicians], and some think tanks in Washington are openly conveying that they can service only those foreign governments that provide funding."[45]

* * *

IN 2014, *The New York Times* conducted the first—and, to date, only—in-depth media investigation into how American think tanks had begun doing the bidding of foreign dictatorships. But even then, investigators could barely get a handle on the flow of such funds; as the *Times* concluded, the "scope of foreign financing for American think tanks is difficult to determine."[46]

There were a few details journalists managed to uncover, though—especially about the relationship the Brookings Institution had built with Qatar's dictatorship. As the investigators discovered, Brookings began taking a clearly pro-Qatar line after Qatari funds started flowing in. Instead of an open space to conduct research and draft policy recommendations, multiple Brookings affiliates cited an atmosphere of "self-censorship" when it came to their work on Qatar. One even described a "no-go zone when it came to criticizing the Qatari government."[47]

Not that any of this should necessarily be a surprise. One of the few academic studies to survey think tank funding, published in 2022, found that such self-censorship is "common," largely due to fear of running afoul of donors. "A lot of think tank experts posture as experts with complete academic freedom," one interviewee said. "This is absolutely not the case." As another added, "At the end of the day, you work for the funders. . . . What we were producing was not research, it was a kind of propaganda."[48] And as we now know, that goes especially for the foreign regimes blanketing American think tanks with funds—even if they are, like the Brookings Institution, among America's most supposedly venerated institutes. With millions in Qatari funds swamping places like Brookings, this kind of pro-Qatari propaganda and self-censorship could have been predictable.

And yet, it wasn't just Qatari talking points that Brookings began peddling. Indeed, such propaganda appears almost quaint compared to revelations that erupted over the summer of 2022, when the FBI issued a search warrant against John Allen, who had served for years as the Brookings president.[49]

As the warrant detailed, Allen—a retired four-star general who once oversaw all American and NATO troops in Afghanistan—effectively became a liaison for the regime in Qatar. In numerous meetings with Qatari officials and other pro-Qatari lobbyists, Allen directly advised Qatar's dictatorship on how to craft its messaging and lobbying efforts. This even included pushing the use of so-called "black" information operations, which, as one newspaper detailed, "are typically covert and sometimes illegal."[50]

And this wasn't related just to Qatar's funding of the Brookings Institution. In return for his efforts, Allen requested tens of thousands of dollars as a "speaker's fee" for his work on behalf of Qatar, and discussed how they could set up a "fuller arrangement of a longer-term relationship." As the affidavit related to Allen's search warrant detailed, while Brookings rolled in Qatari cash, Allen even "pursued at least one multimillion-dollar business deal with the Qatari government on behalf of a company on whose board of directors he served."[51]

Meanwhile, back in Washington, Allen transformed into arguably the most effective foreign lobbyist working on behalf of his Qatari counterparts. He took part in a range of high-level meetings with White House officials, allowing him to push pro-Qatari policies at the most senior levels of American government. And because Allen never disclosed his arrangements with Qatar, no U.S. officials had any idea that he may have had ulterior motives.

The case against Allen couldn't have been clearer. But after the investigation into his links with Qatar began, it somehow got even worse. When officials subpoenaed Allen's communications, the former general failed to turn over all documents pertaining to his financial arrangements with Qatar, including "incriminating documents" linking him directly with other lobbyists working for Qatar.[52] During questioning, Allen further laid out a "false version of events" about his links to the foreign dictatorship. (Allen's spokesperson has denied these allegations, and the formal U.S. government investigation was dropped in 2023 for reasons that remain unclear.)[53]

* * *

LOBBYING AND LYING, backroom deals and under-the-table arrangements, all on behalf of a regime that routinely jails critics and arrests

pro-democracy activists—the revelations about Brookings were a spectacular look at how even America's most prominent think tank had
succumbed to dictatorial money, and how those regimes could then
access American policymakers. These dictatorships, as *The New York
Times* wrote, had learned how to "buy influence" via these think tank
donations and then capitalize on the connections the think tanks had
in Washington.[54] And since think tank officials claimed they weren't
lobbying, they never disclosed these donations—or what they were
doing on behalf of these foreign patrons.

As with universities, Washington appeared completely fine with
ignoring this rotten revolving-door relationship between foreign regimes, think tanks, and the former officials who passed from one to the
other. And why wouldn't they? Landing positions at think tanks is an
easy, lucrative position for those figures who no longer work in government. These new roles provide those figures an opportunity to continue
to influence American policy and remain in the public eye. All they need
to do is find someone—or some foreign regime—to bankroll their think
tank work. "I am surprised, quite frankly, at how explicit the relationship
is between money paid, papers published, and policymakers and politicians influenced," one lawyer specializing in foreign lobbying law said of
American think tanks and their foreign funders.[55]

Still: none of this is illegal. Even when dictators secretly funnel
funds to think tanks, no crimes appear to have been committed. And
if American legislators didn't seem to mind, why wouldn't this crooked
merry-go-round continue?

And it likely would have if—and, again, ironically—the Trump administration hadn't stepped in. In 2020, Secretary of State Mike Pompeo
announced that the State Department would finally request that think
tanks that engage with U.S. diplomats "disclose prominently on their
websites funding they receive from foreign governments, including
state-owned or state-operated subsidiary entities."[56] As Pompeo continued, "The unique role of think tanks in the conduct of foreign affairs
makes transparency regarding foreign funding more important than
ever," adding that State Department staff would "be mindful of whether
disclosure has been made."[57]

The move wasn't a requirement; rather, it was a simple request. But
it was a clear signal flare. As Pompeo said, "The purpose is simple: to

promote free and open dialogue, untainted by the machinations of authoritarian regimes."[58] It was unlike anything seen previously, taking
direct aim at the "murkiness" surrounding foreign dictators who use
American think tanks to lobby on their behalf. For the first time in U.S.
history, American officials had directly taken on the lack of transparency
about regimes bankrolling think tanks—as well as universities—and finally started raising the alarm about what that geyser of foreign finance
was doing to American policy, and to American democracy.

*   *   *

IN A DIFFERENT world, Pompeo's salvo, as well as the separate investigations into American universities ignoring disclosure requirements,
would have been cause for celebration, and would have been roundly
commended. Looked at in isolation, the moves may have even placed
the Trump administration as arguably the most forward-leaning administration the United States had seen in decades—and potentially ever—
when it came to bringing transparency to foreign influence campaigns.

Because it wasn't just that American officials in the late 2010s were
finally examining universities and think tanks, or looking at the access
they granted foreign regimes. Elsewhere, out of the Department of Justice, prosecutors had finally begun trying to enforce a separate piece
of legislation effectively ignored for decades. Finally, nearly a century
after it was first imposed, an administration in the White House began
using FARA to go after the foreign lobbyists operating in the shadows.

But these moves didn't come in a vacuum. They didn't come because
American officials realized that unregulated foreign lobbying efforts
were some kind of theoretical threat, or that laws on the books are actually worth enforcing. And they certainly didn't come because the president for whom these administration officials worked was some kind of
prophetic politico who recognized how much damage these unchecked,
untrammeled foreign lobbying efforts could do to American policy, or
even democracy.

Instead, these actions came in large part because the president for
whom these officials worked had surrounded himself with far more
foreign lobbyists, and far more foreign agents, than any American president ever before. And all of these covert foreign lobbyists competed

for the attention of a president who, despite everything the State and Justice and Education Departments did to shine a light on new avenues of foreign lobbying, ushered more foreign lobbying efforts directly into the White House than anyone in American history.

15

You're Fucked

Wouldn't it be great if we could get all the Russian billionaires to move here?

—Michael Bloomberg, September 2013[1]

On an early morning a few months after Trump's inauguration, Manafort, lying in his condo in Alexandria, Virginia, heard a muffled noise outside of his bedroom. It was still early, around six in the morning, with the sun lingering behind the horizon. He couldn't see much, but began to swing himself out of bed. And then he heard another noise, this time far clearer, and far closer.

"FBI," the voice boomed. "Hands up. We're coming in—and we have guns out."[2]

Manafort slipped into a robe and scrabbled toward the voice, opening his bedroom door. There, in his living room corridor, were people he never expected to see: a dozen federal agents, clad in flak jackets and carrying sidearms. There, in his house—there for him.

Caught somewhere between confusion and concern—as he later said, the agents had "somehow unlocked my condo door" before he was even out of bed—Manafort stood there, staring at the gaggle of FBI agents suddenly spreading throughout his condo. He searched for words, something to calm his own boiling nerves. "Chill out," Manafort managed. "We will cooperate."

For hours, the agents combed through Manafort's belongings: his computers and his hard drives, his cabinets and his cameras. They searched his kitchen. They searched his bedroom. They pored through as much as they could, for more than twelve straight hours. And they hauled out box after box after box, making a note of every piece that they took.

Manafort watched all of this, there in his bathrobe, there in his living room. It was, as he later wrote, an "out of body" experience, with American agents sifting and sorting through all of his belongings. ("There was nothing they wouldn't look at, including my underwear," Manafort later huffed.) But it was also—which Manafort may not have realized—a piece of history, played out in real time, on that hazy Virginia morning.[3]

For the first time in U.S. history, federal agents barged into the house of a campaign manager for an American president. Moreover, they'd done so not because of some kind of nominally ordinary crime—Manafort was never accused of murder, or aggravated robbery, or some kind of assault—but because prosecutors now had reason to believe that, for years, Manafort had secretly worked as a foreign lobbyist, without reporting his work or his payments to federal authorities. And as evidence began to pile from testimony and discoveries elsewhere, prosecutors also began to suspect that Manafort had used that covert foreign lobbying work to tilt an American election in a way no one thought possible—and to help install a president who carried more concerning, and criminal, foreign lobbying links than anything America had ever seen before.

* * *

AT THIS POINT, it's beyond cliché to note that Trump was unlike any other president previously seen in Washington. To his rabid supporters, that difference centered on Trump's apolitical, business-oriented background. But to the rest of America, that difference stemmed from all of the norms—and laws—Trump shattered before and during his presidency. And one of the key elements of Trump's unique role in American history grew directly from his 2016 campaign: a willingness to call for foreign help during an American election.

As was obvious even before the 2016 vote, Trump openly courted support from backers in and around the Kremlin—figures and forces who were more than happy to launch a broad array of interference and influence operations at the United States throughout the presidential campaign, and well into Trump's presidency. Indeed, the Kremlin's 2016 election interference efforts—almost all of which relied on compliant Americans, acting as fellow co-conspiracists—were not only the greatest influence operations Moscow had ever attempted but also one of the most successful foreign influence operations the United States had ever suffered.

Trying to catalogue the entirety of Russia's influence and lobbying campaigns in the 2010s would be an exercise in exhaustion, and would take up the rest of this book. (There's a reason the Mueller Report, the most comprehensive document we have to date on the topic, is nearly 450 pages long.)[4]

But it's worth at least mentioning the broader contours of the Russian interference efforts, especially for what they revealed about how lobbying and influence efforts evolved through the 2010s. And it's worth focusing on the Mueller Report (named after Special Counsel Robert Mueller) even if only briefly, for a handful of reasons. Even in its redacted form, that report offers deep insight into many of the different factors Russia used to torch the 2016 American election, not least the hacking operation surrounding the Clinton campaign and related DNC emails, which dominated the American news cycle for months. The report also touches on the ways that Russian propaganda—including, but not limited to, the Russian outlet RT—and fake social media accounts disseminated the stolen material.[5]

That said, the Mueller Report was still not necessarily comprehensive, failing to investigate Russian cultivation of American evangelicals[6] or groups like the National Rifle Association (NRA).[7] But there was another blind spot, or maybe false implication, that wasn't necessarily the fault of Mueller and his team of investigators. Because if you read the Mueller Report cover to cover, you may come away assuming that the Kremlin was the only foreign power that launched an unprecedented foreign lobbying campaign surrounding the 2016 election.

But that would be a mistake. It could be argued that the Kremlin wasn't even the most *successful* opaque foreign lobbying campaign of 2016, which then used the Trump presidency to its advantage. In reality, a number of other dictatorships launched their own illicit lobbying campaigns during the Trump campaign and well into the Trump presidency.

And they were in many ways just as effective—and just as insidious—as the Kremlin's efforts.

And they used the one tool that the Kremlin ironically didn't turn to, but which represents one of the emergent vectors of foreign lobbying in the United States: American billionaires.

When FARA was passed in 1938, Americans could count the nation's billionaires on one hand. But by the time of Trump's elections, U.S. billionaires had spread like a fungal rot, riding a combination of globalization, offshoring services, financial secrecy, and collapsing tax rates to accrue more and more wealth, at faster and faster clips.

One of them was, of course, Trump, who became the first billionaire to win the presidency. But many other American billionaires appeared eager to do what they could to help Trump to the White House, and to entrench their wealth that much further in the process. In so doing, these billionaires—increasingly detached from things like democratic governance, or even national identity—appeared all too happy to act as freelance foreign agents, doing the bidding of foreign benefactors in order to help sway Trump to their side.

One key case study in the rise of this kind of billionaire foreign agent is a man we met in Chapter 13: private equity financier Tom Barrack. During Trump's campaign, in which Barrack recommended that Trump hire Manafort, the financier was already one of Trump's key economic and foreign policy advisors, directing Trump on everything from trade policy to national security. In public, Barrack posed as a simple Trump supporter, a patriotic American keen to simply help his preferred candidate win the presidency.

But as later court filings made clear, Barrack hardly worked alone. Instead, as American officials alleged in 2021, Barrack quietly operated at the behest of a foreign regime: the dictatorship in the United Arab Emirates.[8] As federal authorities detailed, Barrack spent years liaising directly with Emirati officials, and then whispering in Trump's ear about why the president should push pro-UAE policies. Nor were his contacts junior, no-name Emirati officials; as investigators laid out, Barrack's efforts were steered by none other than the UAE's de facto dictator. Barrack's work for the Emirati despot, declared prosecutors, "strikes at the very heart of our democracy."[9]

According to prosecutors, Barrack's efforts on behalf of the UAE ran the gamut.[10] He wrote pro-UAE op-eds for unsuspecting American audiences and appeared on multiple television interviews to push pro-UAE policies. But his greatest impact came within Trump's inner circle—and within Trump's White House. As detailed in a forty-six-page indictment, Barrack edited Trump's speeches in order to praise the Emirati dictatorship, lobbying along the way for more pro-UAE policy and staffing decisions.[11] After Trump won the presidency, Barrack then covertly passed internal White House discussions to the UAE regime without the White House being aware. Barrack even gathered a so-called "wish list" of policy decisions from Emirati officials that they wanted the Trump administration to implement, setting up a "secure messaging" stream to communicate without detection.[12]

At first blush, there was no clear, pecuniary reason for Barrack to push pro-UAE policies. Prosecutors never detailed how much money he directly made from the arrangement, if any. But while Barrack—who never told the president or the public about his secret liaisons with Emirati officials—lobbied Trump, his private equity firm just so happened to make a staggering *$1.5 billion* from the UAE and its close ally, Saudi Arabia.[13]

Think about all of that for a moment. With both the president and the public kept in the dark, one of Trump's primary foreign policy and economic advisors was secretly working at the behest of a foreign dictatorship—and stealthily changing White House policy as a result. For the first time in U.S. history—or the first time since at least Chester Arthur, who we met in the opening chapter of this book—an alleged foreign agent had specifically slipped language into an American president's speech to stump for pro-dictatorship interests. And for the first time in U.S. history, this agent had seen his company make over one billion dollars along the way.

As one of Barrack's Emirati contacts told him, the regime "loved" his work.[14] And why wouldn't they? They'd effectively landed a covert ally in the White House—and knew that a billionaire like Barrack would always put profit over patriotism, without anyone suspecting otherwise.

* * *

But Barrack's success is only half of the story. Because, amazingly, he wasn't the only American billionaire in Trump's orbit who turned out to be an alleged foreign agent. Instead, Barrack was joined by another billionaire rising alongside Trump: casino magnate Steve Wynn.

With his unnatural tan, ill-fitting suits, and penchant for bluster—as well as his myriad sexual misconduct allegations—Wynn is, in many ways, a carbon copy of Trump. And like Trump, Wynn in the late 2010s floated to the top of the Republican Party apparatus, being appointed in early 2017 as the finance chairman of the Republican National Committee. In his position, Wynn, worth around $3 billion, was tasked with overseeing campaign financing for Republicans around the country, and especially in Washington.[15]

But as the Justice Department later revealed, Wynn also had another task: working closely with Chinese lobbyists to try to convince Trump to implement pro-Beijing policies, especially by targeting dissidents opposed to the Chinese Communist Party. As U.S. officials uncovered, Wynn strategized directly with Chinese officials about how best to convince Trump to target an unnamed dissident who was then hiding out in the United States. As American investigators detailed, Beijing was "extremely pleased" with Wynn's work.[16]

Understandably so. Throughout 2017, Wynn lobbied Trump multiple times to place pressure on the unnamed dissident, using "what appeared to be unscheduled meetings" with Trump to lobby for Beijing's interests. At one point, the Justice Department says Wynn called Trump from a yacht off the coast of Italy to discuss the matter, roping in Trump's chief of staff and senior national security council figures in the process. Month after month, Wynn—who, of course, told no one of his contact with Chinese officials—tried to convince Trump to target the anti-Beijing dissident, including by revoking the dissident's American visa and placing him on the United States' no-fly list.[17]

Nor did Wynn work alone. In fact, he liaised closely with another American named Elliott Broidy. As the deputy finance chair at the RNC, Broidy, a fleshy financier with a walrus mustache, was supposed to be Wynn's right-hand man in organizing Republican Party finances.

But he also had another role: helping Wynn's pro-Beijing efforts. Using similar back-channel communiqués, Broidy "sought to lobby the highest levels of the U.S. government . . . all the while concealing the foreign interests whose bidding he was doing."[18] While Wynn focused on Trump, Broidy "made direct entreaties to high-level Trump officials," including Trump's chief of staff.[19]

Wynn and Broidy worked closely, routinely texting each other to plot out how to target the dissident. It was, as Broidy wrote, a "matter of upmost [sic] importance" to Chinese officials that they succeed.[20] (Broidy had a habit of working as a secret foreign lobbyist; around the same time, he linked up with officials from Malaysia to privately lobby the Trump administration to drop a money laundering investigation into Malaysian prime minister Najib Razak.)[21]

As with Barrack, Wynn never appeared to take any direct payment from Beijing. But then, he didn't need to. As U.S. officials detailed in their filing against Wynn, in 2016 Beijing began clamping down on Wynn's Chinese casinos, threatening a significant chunk of his revenue stream. A few months later, Wynn's pro-Beijing work began. As if the quid pro quo—of Wynn doing Beijing's bidding in return for relaxing pressure on his casinos—couldn't have been more obvious, Wynn would later spend time on the phone with Chinese officials discussing two things: his work on their behalf, and the fate of his Chinese properties.[22]

* * *

IF IT WAS only billionaires like Barrack and Wynn, the intersection of foreign lobbying and the Trump White House would have already been unlike anything seen in American history. Even if it had been restricted to figures like Manafort, the Trump presidency would have already had more outsized foreign lobbying concerns than any other administration prior.

But the foreign lobbying links didn't stop with Manafort, or with Barrack, or with Wynn. They weren't restricted to campaign chiefs, or to close advisors, or even to billionaires circling the president's orbit. Where previous administrations had largely avoided any taint of foreign lobbying scandals, the Trump administration was positively saturated in covert foreign lobbyists, in a way no previous administration had ever known—and in a way America's Founding Fathers could have hardly imagined.

Look, for instance, at who Trump selected as his closest national security counsel. On its face, the appointment of retired Lt. Gen. Michael Flynn as Trump's national security advisor was a questionable one— not only had Flynn recently appeared in Moscow at a gala honoring the Russian propaganda outlet RT, but he'd also fallen out with the broader military leadership, many of whom were increasingly concerned about his mental stability.[23]

Unbeknownst to anyone, though, was the fact that Flynn had also begun moonlighting as a lobbyist for foreign regimes. As American officials later discovered, not only had Flynn accepted tens of thousands of dollars from the Kremlin to appear at the RT gala, but he and his consulting company also signed a deal to confidentially help the regime in Turkey, making hundreds of thousands of dollars in the process. Flynn, naturally, never disclosed any of this work under FARA, even though his "business relationship with the Republic of Turkey was . . . exactly the type of information FARA was designed to ensure," as prosecutors said.[24]

Or look at who Trump tapped as acting director for national intelligence. Richard Grenell. Before his selection, Grenell was known as a bombastic, buffoonish troll, and his appointment was roundly condemned due to his lack of qualifications. But as investigators at ProPublica discovered, Grenell had one additional role before heading national intelligence for the White House: secretly lobbying on behalf of foreign interests.[25]

In 2016, shortly before he joined the government, Grenell authored a series of op-eds laundering the reputation of a Moldovan oligarch named Vladimir Plahotniuc, one of the most transparently corrupt figures in the entire region. According to Grenell, Plahotniuc had been unfairly smeared as a crooked, pro-Russian lackey, and any allegation that he benefited from money laundering was untrue. (Shortly afterward, the United States specifically sanctioned Plahotniuc for "his involvement in significant corruption.")[26] The writing was bizarre; Grenell had no clear links to Moldova, or any interest or expertise in the country. But ProPublica investigators dug up one link: while praising Plahotniuc, Grenell "did not disclose that he was being paid." In other words, the man Trump selected as director of national intelligence had whitewashed one of the most rancid oligarchs extant—and never bothered to disclose any of the payments involved in the operation.[27]

Or look, if you will, at the man Trump retained as his personal lawyer. During the aftermath of the 2020 election, Trump attorney Rudy Giuliani became something close to a national laughingstock, his hair-dye ink running in rivulets down his face while he peddled conspiracy theories and outright lies. But before helping Trump try to overturn America's democratic election, Giuliani used his perch in the White House to routinely lobby for foreign interests—without ever disclosing to the president or the public whom he was working for.[28]

For instance, like Flynn, Giuliani directly lobbied for Turkish interests, including by pushing Trump to drop federal charges against a well-known Turkish gold trader who had violated U.S. sanctions on Iran.[29] Giuliani also lobbied Justice Department officials to "go easy" on a wealthy Venezuelan businessman under U.S. investigation.[30] Most memorably, Giuliani helped a Ukrainian oligarch named Dmytro Firtash, who had previously worked with Manafort and who had since been indicted by U.S. officials on bribery-related charges. Giuliani aided Firtash's efforts to spread so-called "dirt" on then-candidate Joe Biden—and, in so doing, helped try to get Firtash's charges lifted, and get Trump reelected in the process.[31]

And all of this before accelerating Trump's efforts to overturn the election and drive a spike through the heart of American democracy.

*　*　*

ANY ONE OF these scandals would have set the Trump administration apart in the annals of American foreign lobbying history. Indeed, trying to wrap all of these into one chapter is a nearly futile undertaking. But if we pull back, we can get a sense of just how open the Trump administration was to foreign lobbying efforts—and how successful, and how unprecedented, such efforts truly were.

In tallying them up, those with clear, conspicuous links to undisclosed foreign lobbying campaigns include Trump's campaign chief; his foreign policy and economic advisor; his national security advisor; his director of national intelligence; his personal lawyer; and both the lead and the deputy finance chiefs of the Republican National Committee. All of this in addition to the Americans who aided the Russian foreign influence campaign of 2016 (and beyond). And this isn't even mentioning Trump's deputy campaign manager or his inauguration committee fundraiser, who as we'll see below joined Manafort in also secretly lobbying on behalf of pro-Russian interests in Ukraine.

It's all, in many ways, overwhelming. And it was all entirely unprecedented. But somehow it didn't end there. Because all of these campaigns also existed alongside the fact that, for the first time in American history, foreign regimes could now freely patronize a sitting American president's businesses—and could now use those businesses as a springboard to lobby for their own interests.

As of now, only a few years removed from the Trump presidency, we still know distressingly little about how foreign regimes, ruling families, or their oligarchic proxies patronized Trump's businesses while he was president, and how that may have upturned American policy along the way. Much of that is structural; because of rampant anonymity in the U.S. real estate sector, where much of Trump's business remains, we have only a minuscule look into how regimes used things like anonymous shell companies or anonymous real estate purchases to bankroll Trump's properties during his presidency, and gain access to Trump in the process. To take but one staggering data point, by 2017 *three-quarters* of new sales at Trump real estate properties were going to anonymous buyers—masking not only the purchasers but what regimes they might be connected to.[32]

Still, at least a handful of stories and revelations have begun circulating that highlight how dictators and despots turned to Trump properties not only to launder their illicit wealth but to try to sway his presidency as well. Not only have a range of Trump property purchases already been linked to dictators and their allies, from Russian organized crime heads[33] to Indonesian kleptocrats[34] to families of African autocrats, but congressional investigators have also discovered that Trump's hotels transformed during his presidency into a blinking beacon for any and all wishing to influence his administration.[35] Even from the little that we yet know, it's clear that autocracies around the world spent Trump's presidency stampeding to his hotels, spending millions at his properties while looking to influence the most nakedly transactional president in American history.

Some of those who splurged at Trump's hotels during his presidency were familiar figures, such as Malaysia's kleptocratic leader Najib Razak, who helped loot billions of dollars from the country's sovereign wealth fund (and whom we met above). As investigators discovered, Razak "spent freely" at Trump's Washington hotel, as did his entire Malaysian delegation—all of it to help get them in Trump's good graces, and to try to lift investigations into Razak's rank corruption.[36]

Reading through the Malaysian expenditures, which run over forty pages, is an exercise in preposterous excess. There's nearly $10,000 spent on coffee alone, with thousands more for things like personal trainers and room service. Over just a few days, the Malaysian delegation spent hundreds of thousands of dollars at Trump's hotel—the details of which the American populace learned about only after Trump left office, when a congressional committee obtained the documents.[37]

But from the Malaysians' perspective, the money was well spent. Despite the gargantuan money laundering allegations then hanging over Razak, Trump opened the White House to him, thanking him directly for "all the investment you've made in the United States."[38] (Not long later, a Malaysian court would sentence Razak to over a decade in prison for money laundering and abuse of power.)[39]

Yet these Malaysian expenditures were just a drop in the bucket of the foreign wealth that gushed into Trump properties during his time in the White House. As *The New York Times* reported, in just the first year of Trump's presidency, officials from dictatorships like Saudi Arabia, the UAE, and Qatar all spent significant sums at Trump's Washington hotel, with plenty more coming from regimes in places like China, Kuwait, and Turkey.[40] Even those caught up in congressional investigations into modern kleptocracy couldn't stay away; Nigeria's Atiku Abubakar, at the center of one of the largest American investigations to date on transnational money laundering, was also spotted at Trump's Washington hotel, swimming amidst the tide of other corrupt foreign officials that the building drew in.[41]

All of this was at only one Trump property, in only one city, located in the one country whose real estate sector has become arguably the globe's greatest money laundering market. And despite all of the questionable wealth splurged on the sitting American president's business, these kleptocrats and dictators apparently committed no crimes. Instead, they barreled through an opening without precedent in American history: shoveling staggering sums of cash toward a president's business, without disclosing what they spent, or who they spent it for, or what they hoped to gain from it—or what they *did* gain out of it. And with Trump properties both built and planned around the world—and with any number of them, from Azerbaijan to Panama to Kazakhstan, already saturated in allegations of corruption—there's no reason to think that Trump's Washington hotel was the only Trump property these dictatorships patronized.

Instead, these hotels appeared to be a glimpse into a potential future: how foreign regimes could directly run money through a sitting American president's till, and directly buy influence in the White House, without the American populace ever being aware. It was a model we've caught only fleeting glimpses of, thanks to subsequent investigations and discoveries. But it's a model that makes another reality—that Trump was the president surrounded by more covert foreign lobbyists than any U.S. president before—far more understandable, and far less surprising.

* * *

AT ANY OTHER time, any of these singular revelations would have made for a presidency-defining scandal. When gathered together—the advisors and the appointees, the officials and the billionaires, the hotels and the purchases, all wrapped up alongside the Kremlin's broader interference campaign—it's almost too much to take in.

Yet it was all too real. And if there's a silver lining to this tsunami of foreign lobbying and foreign interference campaigns in and after 2016, it's that, for the first time in nearly a century, the federal government actually responded. Not nearly fast enough, and not with nearly enough resources. But for the first time since Ivy Lee burrowed into Berlin, advising the Nazis on how to sway American politicians and audiences, the U.S. government began viewing the threat of unchecked foreign lobbying networks seriously. With Trump in the White House, the perils of foreign lobbying suddenly snapped into reality.

That response began soon after Trump's election, when the secrets of the Russian interference campaign started spilling out. Flynn, caught out lying to investigators about his conversations with Russian officials, was the first domino to fall, resigning his post in Trump's administration in February 2017. Soon after, with further revelations about how Moscow had spewed hackers and social media bots on the American electorate, the Justice Department appointed Robert Mueller to head up the investigation into Russian interference. And it didn't take long for Mueller and his team of investigators to realize that Russian interference extended far beyond fake Facebook feeds—and instead overlapped directly with figures like Manafort.

As Mueller was investigating Russia's efforts throughout 2017, Manafort maintained a low profile, at least in public. After resigning from Trump's campaign in August 2016, he kept his distance from the president-elect. But Manafort didn't spend the rest of the campaign and the early months of the Trump presidency twiddling his thumbs, or even regretting his decisions. Instead, he leaned into them—and set off another round of spiraling questions and concerns about all of the foreign lobbying avenues that kept intersecting, time and again, with the Trump administration.

As we saw in Chapter 13, Manafort maintained his cozy links with Kilimnik, the Russian agent shuttling between the United States, Russia, and Ukraine. But the two didn't discuss only how Moscow could implement its "peace plan" and regain sovereignty over Kyiv. Rather, they began spinning a new line that would also help things move in Moscow's direction—and that would eventually spark the first serious impeachment crisis in the United States in over a century.

Working alongside Kilimnik once more, Manafort began claiming to contacts throughout Washington, including in the White House, that the hacking campaign at the center of Russia's interference efforts—and at the center of the swelling Mueller investigation—wasn't actually the fault of Moscow. Instead, it was the fault of *Ukraine*. As his former deputy Rick Gates told investigators, Manafort was "insistent" that Ukraine was responsible, and that Russia was being unfairly slandered.[42] Manafort, of course, had no evidence. But as he spun it, the supposed Ukrainian hack job was related to another anti-Trump campaign, also out of Ukraine. As Manafort now claimed, the so-called "Black Ledger" outlining the secret payments he received from Yanukovych was also a fabrication of its own—one created whole cloth by "[Hillary] Clinton's Ukrainian allies . . . to tar Manafort and undermine Trump."[43]

For anyone following Manafort's work, the claims were manifestly ridiculous; the details of Manafort's illicit payment schemes weren't fabricated, nor were they or the hacking campaign the fault of some shadowy cabal of pro-Clinton forces in Ukraine. But with a president like Trump, facts hardly mattered. And Manafort's theory would eventually detonate in Trump's first impeachment, coming in 2019 after Trump threatened to withhold American military aid if Kyiv didn't investigate the claims first propounded by Manafort. All of it ended up weakening U.S.-Ukrainian links that much further—and, thanks once again to Manafort, opening the door for Russian interests in Ukraine in the process.

* * *

ALL THAT, THOUGH, was in the future. Because by the summer of 2017, even with Manafort trying to spin blame on Ukrainian authorities, Mueller and his team of prosecutors realized that so many of the strands of Russia's 2016 interference efforts kept threading back to Manafort. Moreover, they realized that they had a tool in their back pocket, one dusted over and forgotten, that they could use to target him: FARA.

Reading over the decades-old statute, Mueller and his team determined that Manafort had cheerfully ignored even its minimal foreign lobbying regulations. There were no FARA filings detailing all of Manafort's sprawling work on behalf of Yanukovych, or his work to recruit a range of other Americans to his cause. And there was certainly nothing about the millions of dollars that Manafort—who made an estimated $60 million from his time in Ukraine—had squirreled away while working alongside Yanukovych.

There was, in other words, more than enough to prosecute. And that's precisely what happened.

In the summer of 2017, federal agents authorized their "no-knock" raid on Manafort's house, which found the lobbyist groggy and bleary-eyed in bed.[44] Gathering documents and testimony that confirmed all

of Manafort's work—all of his illicit foreign lobbying, all the lengths
to which he went to mask his finances, all his increasingly concerning
contacts with Russian agents along the way—Mueller's team released
their findings. As prosecutors alleged, Manafort had purposely failed
to register as a foreign agent, ignoring foreign lobbying regulations and
strengthening pro-Russian figures in Ukraine in the process. His work
in Ukraine had "generated tens of millions of dollars in income"[45]—
money that, year after year, was laundered and hidden through "scores"
of different shell companies, accounts, and other financial vehicles,
from Cyprus to the Seychelles to the United States.[46]

The charges ran the gamut, from bank fraud to tax fraud to conspiracy against the United States. Most pertinently, prosecutors charged
that Manafort had "knowingly and willfully" acted as an "[agent] of a
foreign principal"—that he had ignored FARA, all in the service of a
pro-Russian autocrat in Ukraine.[47]

To Manafort, the allegations were a joke, especially the FARA-
related charges. But when he faced a judge, claiming his innocence, she
was unmoved. And as his trial date grew closer, Manafort—increasingly
disheveled, increasingly imperiled—realized that a jury might not believe him, either. Just as he'd been a few years prior, when he bottomed
out in an Arizona clinic, Manafort once more found himself staring
up from the abyss. The only difference was that, for the first time in
his life, Manafort—the one-time kingmaker, the one-time presidential
consigliere—was now facing jail time. And with his age already pushing seventy, any conviction ran the risk of becoming a potential life
sentence.

Which is, in effect, what he received. In 2018, buried under the piles
of evidence of his crimes, Manafort pleaded guilty to failing to register
his foreign lobbying work, as well as to tampering with witnesses. With
the plea, Manafort dodged the potential decades-long prison stay staring him down. But the presiding judge nonetheless sentenced him to
seven and a half years in prison. (Manafort had already been sentenced
on separate felony fraud charges, which he would serve concurrently.)[48]

His illicit lobbying campaigns had "infect[ed] our policymaking,"
the judge said, adding that it was "hard to overstate the number of lies
[and] the amount of fraud" attached to Manafort. And as the judge saw

it, it was clear that any sense of remorse Manafort may have had was "completely absent." "Saying 'I'm sorry I got caught' is not an inspiring plea for leniency," the judge told him.[49]

Listening to the ruling, Manafort looked up in stunned silence. It's unclear what, if anything, he was thinking. Perhaps he thought about how he'd just become the first presidential campaign manager ever jailed for acting as a foreign lobbyist. Perhaps he was thinking about the fact that he'd fallen even further than Ivy Lee, who, despite all of his pro-Nazi work, never ended up as a convicted felon. Perhaps he was thinking about how he'd ended up broken and decrepit, without any potential future, suddenly facing the very real prospect of dying in prison.

Or maybe his mind was blank. "I felt fear," Manafort later wrote. "I felt numb . . . I felt like vomiting." One of his friends summed up the moment, and what now lay in store for Manafort. "One of my friends . . . told me plainly, 'You're fucked,'" Manafort said.

"I realized he was right: I was fucked."[50]

* * *

MANAFORT MAY HAVE been, to use his term, fucked—but Mueller and his prosecutors were hardly done investigating all of the crimes surrounding Trump's campaign. Nor were they done using FARA as a cudgel to target all of Manafort's fellow conspirators, and many of the others in Trump's immediate circle who hadn't bothered to disclose their own foreign lobbying links. Much as Manafort set the precedent for modern Americans looking to spin foreign dictatorships for un-suspecting audiences, he also set the precedent for their downfall—a pattern that played out over and over and over again during the Trump years.

Flynn's implosion, for instance, didn't stop with his resignation. In 2017, Trump's disgraced national security advisor publicly admitted that he'd lied to federal investigators, pleading guilty to making false statements to the FBI. As part of his plea agreement, which resulted in a prison sentence, Flynn admitted that he'd "made materially false statements and omissions" about his foreign lobbying work, includ-ing lying about his relationship with the Turkish government—and especially about the fact that Turkish officials "provided supervision and direction" over all of his lobbying efforts.[51]

Others joined Flynn in pleading guilty to similar FARA-related crimes. Broidy publicly admitted that he'd served Malaysian and Chinese interests while simultaneously working as the Republican National Committee's deputy finance chair.[52] And prosecutors also rolled up much of Manafort's Ukraine network, including figures like Gates (Trump's deputy campaign manager) and Samuel Patten (Trump's inauguration fundraiser), both of whom revealed that they'd covertly worked with pro-Russian interests in Ukraine.[53]

Yet prosecutors didn't target only those in Trump's orbit. In 2019, as part of a broader settlement, the Skadden law firm issued a new report, detailing all of the backroom decisions and dealings it had with Manafort: how Skadden had crafted its pro-Yanukovych report, how it had strategized the rollout and fed that report to American media, how it had helped Yanukovych's team figure out the best way to keep their boss in power, all to help pro-Russian interests in Ukraine.[54] Skadden admitted that it had misled American officials about its work in Ukraine. In the end, the firm agreed to make a $4.6 million payment to the federal government, the largest foreign lobbying–related settlement the United States had ever seen.[55] Shortly thereafter, the law firm shelled out an additional $11 million to avoid a lawsuit from Yulia Tymoshenko, Yanukovych's erstwhile opponent. As Tymoshenko said, Skadden's work with pro-Russian interests in Ukraine was a "dirty, dirty, dirty contract."[56]

But it was those closest to Trump who ended up in the center of Justice Department investigations. Figures like Barrack, who was soon indicted for his work on behalf of the Emirati dictatorship.[57] Or those like Wynn, whom the Justice Department later sued to force his registration as a pro-Chinese foreign agent.[58] Or those like Giuliani, who came under investigation for his own work on behalf of foreign regimes—even while he was being investigated separately for his efforts to help end American democracy.[59]

Over and over, these foreign lobbyists whom Trump had invited into the White House began toppling. Over and over, their networks—their efforts and payments, their work on behalf of foreign governments bent on steering American policy—came to light, there for Americans to see and scrutinize for the first time. The investigations, the revelations, the repercussions: it was a crackdown on foreign lobbying unlike anything the United States had ever seen.

Indeed, it was something of a perfect storm: an unprecedented interference effort, which sparked a breathtaking investigation overseen by Mueller and his team, which unearthed a range of illicit foreign lobbying campaigns—all of it roiling a president who had brought more covert foreign lobbyists into his administration than ever before, and who had opened the door via his business enterprises to more backroom dealings than any other. On their own, any of these ingredients may not have been enough to rocket foreign lobbying regulations back to importance. But taken together, bundled into the sordid morass that was the Trump campaign and Trump presidency, they all brought foreign lobbying—and especially FARA—back to a relevance the United States hadn't seen since Ivy Lee, the Nazi regime, and the onset of the Second World War.

And that relevance was reflected not only in the indictments but also in the sudden surge of filings the Justice Department saw from foreign lobbyists across Washington, suddenly realizing they needed to get ahead of potential prosecution. As one analysis found, first-time FARA filings soared an incredible *50 percent* between 2016 and 2017, disclosing far more information about foreign lobbying networks than Americans had ever seen.[60] With one of Mueller's prosecutors, an official named Brandon Van Grack, appointed to oversee the new, muscular unit tasked with administering FARA, it was clear that enforcing foreign lobbying laws had become, as one write-up said, a "priority" for U.S. officials.[61]

Nor was it just Justice Department officials suddenly realizing the relevance of things like FARA. On the political side of things, major Democratic figures were suddenly wondering aloud about the need for foreign lobbying in the first place. Senator Elizabeth Warren, then running in the Democratic presidential primary, pledged to outright ban Americans from "accepting money from foreign governments, foreign individuals, and foreign companies to influence United States public policy."[62] And then-candidate Joe Biden, hardly viewed as a radical, followed suit. As Biden announced in 2020, he saw "no reason why a foreign government should be permitted to lobby Congress or the Executive Branch." Should Biden win the 2020 election, he promised, his administration would "bar lobbying by foreign governments" outright.[63]

After nearly a century of overlooking foreign lobbying regulations, the comments and pledges took direct aim at the foreign lobbying complex itself. They were the kinds of conversations and policy prescriptions American politicians hadn't seen since the 1860s: since Russia first used a subterranean lobbying campaign to sway U.S. policy. And in combination with the new prosecutions, the renewed focus, and the reinvigorated investigations, that foreign lobbying complex was suddenly facing far more pressure—and looking far more unstable—than at any point prior.

There was only one catch, though. Because for as much as the Trump era had seen an unprecedented explosion of focus on foreign lobbying links—and as remarkable as it was that figures like Manafort were jailed for their foreign lobbying crimes—there was still one figure who could undo all of that progress, and all of that potential. And it happened to be the man at the center of it all: Trump.

16

The Republic Itself Is at Risk

As one menace is disposed of, another seems
inevitably to develop.

—Witmer Stone[1]

A few weeks before his sentencing, Manafort's body began to crumble. The trials, the investigations, the lurching reality that he was suddenly staring down years in prison for his foreign lobbying crimes—all of this while his daughter's hacked texts spilled out, revealing both his mental collapse and his alleged spousal abuse—it all slipped beyond simple legal concerns. His body, as he later said, "broke down." He saw it most especially in his legs, which began swelling into Vienna sausages, leaving Manafort unable to walk, reliant on a wheelchair to roll between his cell and his hearings.[2]

Transferred to a prison in Pennsylvania, Manafort tried to settle in with his fellow inmates. He couldn't walk, but he could stew. He still refused to display any chagrin, any regrets about his work in Ukraine, or for any other autocrats and dictators responsible for slaughtering thousands around the world. Like Trump, Manafort claimed he was the victim of a "lynching." Keening about "almost POW-style solitary confinement," Manafort claimed that he was being "persecuted" for his beliefs and for his work. He'd become, as he titled his later memoir, a "political prisoner"— jailed not for any crimes but simply because he helped launch Trump to the White House. "What did I do to get here? I failed to file a FARA form," Manafort bleated, conveniently ignoring that he'd also been convicted of bank fraud, tax evasion, and witness tampering, among other crimes.[3]

Unable to walk, unable to work, unable to do much besides watch his future and his legacy collapse in tandem, Manafort slowly fell apart. A year after his sentencing, with Covid now rampaging through American prisons, authorities announced that Manafort—suddenly frail, suddenly elderly, clearly at risk in a pandemic—could serve out the rest of his sentence under house arrest. It was an improvement, if only to escape exposure to coronavirus. But it was hardly a panacea. "This ordeal," Manafort wailed, "has destroyed my life."[4] (Manafort never shared his thoughts on all the Ukrainians, Angolans, Filipinos, Congolese, Nigerians, and others whose lives had *actually* been destroyed as a result of Manafort's clients, and Manafort's work.)

And then, during the final weeks of 2020, he received a phone call. In Washington—where another of Manafort's clients was attempting to gut democracy in a bid to cling to power, damn the consequences— Trump announced a new round of pardons. And there, on the list of those absolved of their crimes, was one name in particular: Paul Manafort.[5]

It's unclear how much thought Trump put into pardoning Manafort, caught up as he was in conspiring to overturn the 2020 presidential election. (Exactly two weeks after Manafort's pardon, Trump would help sic a deadly assault on the U.S. Capitol in an effort to overturn the election results.) But the implications were impossible to miss. Manafort had conspired to help place a new president in power—and then, after he was found out, his former client offered absolution, expunging his record and setting him free. It was, as one headline in *The Atlantic* read, the "triumph of kleptocracy."[6]

* * *

AND IT WASN'T simply because Manafort was responsible for helping install and entrench autocrats in Eastern Europe and East Asia and Sub-Saharan Africa—and, if Trump had had his way, in the United States. It wasn't even that Manafort was the clearest case study in foreign lobbying crimes, a precedent now undone by Trump's pardon. It was also that, even after his imprisonment, more details had continued spilling out about Manafort's criminal activity—and his central role in opening the floodgates of foreign interference into the United States.

A few months before Manafort's pardon, the Republican-controlled Senate Intelligence Committee had revealed even more details of Manafort's work through and beyond the 2016 campaign. In the final volume of its examination of Russian interference—over nearly a thousand pages of painstaking, eye-watering detail—the committee focused especially on Manafort's alliance with Kilimnik, whom the GOP-led committee identified outright as a "Russian intelligence officer."[7]

As the committee found, Manafort had previously "implemented . . . influence operations" on behalf of pro-Putin Russian oligarchs, making tens of millions of dollars in the process, and had specifically "participated" in efforts to "discredit [American] investigations into Russian interference." Along the way, he'd forged a "close and lasting relationship" with Kilimnik—one that, by the 2016 campaign, culminated in a "grave counterintelligence threat" to the United States, especially once Kilimnik began to "leverage his relationship with Manafort for influence."[8]

The conclusions couldn't have been starker. Manafort had opened the door to the Kremlin's interference operations, ushering a Russian intelligence officer directly into Trump's campaign—all as a direct outgrowth of Manafort's previous lobbying work for Russian oligarchs and pro-Russian politicians in Ukraine. And when investigators tried to untangle these malign connections, Manafort threw up chaff, dipping and ducking, tossing investigators as far off the scent as possible.

As the GOP-led report also found, the relationship between Manafort and Kilimnik remains shrouded in questions. Part of that stems from how the two communicated; using things like encrypted chats and edited email drafts (rather than emails sent back and forth), the two "eliminate[ed] a documentary record of many communications." Even after his indictment, Manafort still hid his communications with Kilimnik, using things like a "pay-as-you-go phone"—also known as a "burner phone," especially popular among those who don't want their communications tracked by authorities.[9]

As the committee described, Manafort "lied so much" to investigators about his links with the Russian agent that it was all but impossible to get to the root of their relationship.[10] "Manafort's obfuscation of the truth surrounding Kilimnik was particularly damaging to the Committee's investigation because it effectively foreclosed direct insight into a series of interactions and communications which represent the single most direct tie between senior Trump Campaign officials and the Russian intelligence services," the report said. In other words: Manafort's lies clouded the investigation to such an extent that the true center, and the ultimate reach, of the Russian interference operations will likely never be known.[11]

And Manafort knew the cost of that misdirection. As the committee found, he was willing to lie about his links with Kilimnik even though it cost him a potential plea deal with Mueller's team. As a result, Manafort spent additional time in prison—and spent more time watching as his body "broke down"—in order to prevent investigators from finding any kind of clarity about the Kremlin's 2016 interference operations.

And then, in late December 2020, Trump announced his pardon. Manafort's record was cleared, his convictions undone. The man in the middle of it all—of the Mueller investigation, of Russia's interference efforts, of the new surge of foreign lobbying threats and investigations and convictions—was free.

*   *   *

IN MANY WAYS, that Republican-authored report was simply a confirmation of what had long been suspected, previously hidden behind redactions or innuendo, previously obscured by so much smoke that you could choke on it. Manafort had directed pro-Russian influence operations, conspiring with a Russian intelligence officer in the process, and had then lied about those links to such an extent that he ended up gutting a potential plea deal—and ended up receiving an effective life sentence as a result.

In that sense, Trump's pardon of Manafort was a stake through the heart of the investigation into Russian interference overall. But it was more than that. With his pardon, Trump effectively undid all of the progress his own administration had made on the fight against foreign lobbying. Not only was it a signpost that those committing foreign lobbying–related crimes could rely on an authoritarian president to absolve them of their crimes, but it was also a move that helped unwind all of the successes the United States had made in recognizing and prosecuting the threats of unchecked foreign lobbying—and that now risked unleashing those threats once more.

Because while the Manafort pardon was shameful enough, it didn't come in a vacuum. Around the same time, Trump announced that he was also pardoning another key vector of foreign lobbying and influence: Flynn. Despite the tens of thousands of dollars Flynn accepted from the Kremlin, despite the hundreds of thousands of dollars Flynn and his company made to secretly represent Turkish interests, Flynn continued to wrap himself in the mantle of supposed patriotism. More importantly, he continued to back Trump's increasingly unhinged claims: of stolen votes, of international cabals, of the need to declare martial law in order to restore Trump's presidency. And in the process, Flynn earned his own pardon from Trump—undoing yet another front in the United States' efforts to crack down on foreign lobbyists. As Trump wrote on Twitter, it was his "Great Honor" to pardon Flynn, who thanked Trump by helping him plot out how to overturn America's 2020 election.[12]

Trump, of course, failed in thwarting the election. And he was soon out of office, facing his own investigations. But those pardons clearly shifted things in Washington. Even as he was on his way out of the White House, Trump's pardons blasted the foundations of the new efforts to stanch foreign lobbying—and, in many ways, set the tone for the range of disappointments that were to come.

*　*　*

As WE SAW in the previous chapter, Joe Biden took a firmer stance on foreign lobbying threats than any major candidate in American history. On the campaign trail, Biden not only pledged to "bar lobbying by foreign governments" but even promised to close the previous loopholes that allowed nominally independent companies to lobby on foreign regimes' behalf. The combined pledges signaled the single greatest shift in American policy toward foreign lobbying since the days of Ivy Lee and the Nazis—and placed Biden as the first president, it appeared, to actually recognize these threats for what they were.

Years into the Biden administration, though, there's no sign that the administration has followed through on its campaign pledges. Even worse, there's little sign the administration even *tried* to follow through—or that Biden even remembers that he made such commitments in the first place.

Part of that, to be fair to the Biden administration, may be structural; there are still a range of legal questions about whether Congress or the administration could actually institute Biden's proposed ban. After all, the "right to petition"—the right that foreign lobbyists rely on for their work and their campaigns—remains constitutionally protected by the First Amendment, and remains at the center of foreign lobbyists' claims of why they should be allowed to continue flacking for the world's worst tyrants. But part of that may also be because Biden, just as with many presidents prior, rose alongside a range of other foreign lobbyists, enshrined as they are in the Washington firmament.

Recall Manafort's network in Ukraine. Not only did it involve a range of Democratic connections—including the Podesta Group, one of the key Democratic lobbying shops through the late 2010s—but Biden's son, Hunter Biden, openly worked for a Ukrainian gas firm controlled by an unabashedly corrupt Ukrainian oligarch.[13] Hunter's hiring, mirrored in his suspect connections to other foreign firms, was predicated not on any expertise in the gas sector but on his connections to his father—and on his potential ability to sway his father toward preferred policy outcomes.[14]

Hunter's multimillion-dollar hire was, unfortunately, hardly unique, but it was of a piece with other crooked foreign firms and regimes recruiting family members of U.S. policymakers, all as a means of influencing American policy. The practice stretches back to at least the days of Jimmy Carter, when the Libyan dictatorship hired Carter's brother as a lobbyist, and when the Marcos dictatorship in the Philippines brought on Carter's son as a consultant.[15] "How could America's leading lights convince themselves—and us—that this is acceptable?" Sarah Chayes, one of the United States' leading anti-corruption researchers, said. "If we want to help our country heal, we must start holding ourselves, our friends, and our allies—and not just our enemies—to its highest standards."[16]

And even outside of his immediate family, some of the country's leading pro-Biden figures likewise spent years making significant sums in the muck of foreign lobbying. For instance, during the 2020 election the largest pro-Biden super PAC—the campaign's primary fundraising committee, bundling donations to help Biden land the White House—was overseen by a figure named Larry Rasky, appointed as the committee's treasurer. Rasky had a lengthy history with Biden, having served as a "longtime Biden advisor," even working as Biden's communications director during his 2008 presidential campaign.[17] He was, as one write-up described, a "legendary Democratic operative."[18]

However, Rasky also had a separate role in the 2010s: joining the onrush of Americans making significant sums while laundering the images and reputations of kleptocratic dictatorships. As federal filings reveal, in early 2019 Rasky and his PR firm, Rasky Partners, inked a six-figure deal with the decades-long dictatorship of Azerbaijan—the same regime that, just a few years before, stood at the center of the greatest foreign lobbying scandal Congress had ever seen. As the filings illustrate, Rasky provided "strategic communications, counsel, and services" to the Azeri regime, with his underlings providing services ranging from "media monitoring" to, curiously, "outreach to influencers."[19]

When I contacted him, Rasky told me that he and his firm's roles with the Azeri dictatorship didn't involve "serv[ing] as lobbyists."[20] (Given that he specifically helped the regime craft its messaging, this is a distinction without a difference.) And to be sure, Rasky committed no crimes; as we've seen, there's nothing illegal in taking hundreds of thousands of dollars to help entrench some of the most heinous regimes around the world.

But the fact that no one surrounding the formation of Biden's biggest super PAC appeared concerned with the involvement of a man who helped flack for one of the most kleptocratic dictatorships on the planet points to the kind of moral rot still gnawing at the heart of the United States' political center. It may also help explain why the Biden administration has effectively dropped its campaign promises about banning foreign lobbyists—and why the administration increasingly seems indifferent to things like foreign lobbying campaigns writ large.

*   *   *

UNFORTUNATELY, IT'S NOT just foreign lobbyists' proximity to Biden's White House that's left this impression. Take some of the Trump administration's few successes on the foreign lobbying transparency front, which we saw in Chapter 14. After the Trump administration uncovered *billions* in unreported foreign donations to a range of American universities—much of that coming directly from brutal dictatorships around the world—the Biden administration effectively dropped the ball on any further inquiries. In October 2022, the White House announced it would not pursue any additional investigations into foreign donations to American universities, with "plans to close the outstanding . . . investigations that remain open."[21]

In and of itself, the move would be a concerning one, given the scope of previous foreign funds uncovered and now reported. But as Department of Education records indicate, reporting of these funds had already fallen off considerably. As one analysis found, "Department of Education records showed that universities reported only a bit over $4 million in foreign gifts throughout part of 2021, compared with over $1.5 billion between July 2020 and January 2021."[22] That is, after the Biden administration entered office, reportage of foreign donations to American universities disappeared almost *entirely.* And with the White House all but writing off any new investigations, there's little reason to think that will change.

Or look at the transparency requirements the Trump administration initiated for American think tanks. Initially, it appeared that the Biden administration would continue this new pressure on think tanks to disclose their foreign patrons. Over the summer of 2022, Biden's Department of Justice released a so-called "Advisory Opinion" arguing that, indeed, organizations that use foreign funds to author publications and "foster . . . cooperation" between foreign governments and the United States should register with FARA.[23] In other words, think tanks should register as what they've long been: vehicles for foreign influence, foreign lobbying, and foreign interests, even if they continue to masquerade as supposedly apolitical, independent bodies.

And yet, even with this "Advisory Opinion," the Biden administration's broader follow-through has been nonexistent. There's no indication that Biden administration officials have pressured think tanks to register with things like FARA, or that the administration even seems interested in the topic.[24] If anything, that pressure has receded—and think tanks have continued to gorge on foreign funding, regardless of the consequences. Even amidst high-profile investigations of figures like Brookings Institution president John Allen, and even as investigations elsewhere continue to reveal how Gulf monarchs and post-Soviet kleptocrats continue to splurge on leading American think tanks, the industry as a whole appears completely unconcerned with examining its own role as a vector of foreign lobbying, let alone providing more disclosures about how their organizations may be furthering foreign regimes' interests.

White House officials, by all appearances, don't seem to care—so little, indeed, that in early 2023 the State Department confirmed to me that they were no longer requesting that think tanks disclose foreign funding. With little fanfare, and with no reasons given, the Biden administration dropped one of the few progressive, pro-transparency moves of the Trump era. The White House's interest in which think tanks were receiving millions from kleptocratic dictatorships—and how that might be affecting American policy—had evaporated.

And in a certain sense, that distinct lack of interest is unsurprising. Because while officials in Washington have largely pulled back from any pressure of their own, there's another development beyond the administration's reach that has eviscerated efforts to finally beat back foreign lobbying networks—and that points to what may have to be done if we're ever to win the war against these foreign lobbyists.

* * *

LAST CHAPTER, WE saw how American prosecutors had forced Skadden—the white-shoe law firm that worked hand in glove with Manafort and his oligarchic allies to keep Yanukovych and pro-Russian figures in power in Ukraine—to divulge the role it played in Ukraine. The law firm's resulting disclosures were, in many ways, a spectacular glimpse into foreign lobbying *in toto*: the meals and the communiqués, the strategy discussions and the loopholes exploited, the payment schemes and the political fallout—all of it overseen by one of the most nominally impressive law firms in America, and all of it predicated on helping Manafort implode Ukraine's democracy.

On its face, the revelations were a clear victory in the broader fight against foreign lobbyists, and especially against the U.S. law firms that had transformed into the go-to vehicles for foreign regimes looking for help. But the Skadden revelations were only part of the story—the rest of which should have given observers pause, and increasing cause for concern.

The key figure overseeing Skadden's efforts in Ukraine was Gregory Craig, whom we met in Chapter 11. An ivory-haired lawyer, Craig was best known for serving as Obama's first White House counsel. Moving from the Oval Office to Skadden, Craig coordinated the broader campaign to spin Skadden's "independent" report, which Yanukovych and Manafort could use for their own benefit. Craig, like Manafort, never bothered to register any of that work with FARA. (As he blithely admitted in one email, "I don't want to register as a foreign agent under FARA.")[25] And unsurprisingly, when federal officials began targeting Skadden with potential prosecution for failing to register its foreign lobbying work, they placed Craig at the center of their allegations.

As prosecutors saw it, Craig had outright lied to American officials about his role in the Skadden assignment. And since he had done so knowingly—since he hadn't just stumbled into his lobbying shenanigans, accidentally becoming an effective pro-Kremlin collaborator—his actions passed the clear threshold for FARA-related criminal prosecution, which requires a willful violation of the law.

The evidence certainly seemed to back them up. As the filings from Skadden indicated, and despite Craig's claims that he was simply a lawyer conducting lawyerly duties, in reality he covertly connected with American media to help spread his pro-Yanukovych work—all while telling U.S. officials he had nothing to do with the media rollout of the report. As we saw earlier, Craig took the lead on connecting with journalists covering Skadden's report, even offering to "hand-deliver" reporters a hard copy if they wanted. All of it was far, far beyond what lawyers who don't register as foreign lobbyists are allowed to do on behalf of foreign clients.[26]

In a certain sense, Craig's work was no different from Manafort's. Both of them worked to entrench the Ukrainian autocrat and disseminate Skadden's pro-Yanukovych work as widely as possible. Craig's spin was a "masterpiece," prosecutors alleged, full of "contempt" for America's lobbying regulations.[27]

But when prosecutors laid out their case in a courtroom in 2019, the jury disagreed. Part of that was because the statute of limitations on Craig's alleged foreign lobbying crimes—generally five years—had already expired. But part of it pointed directly to Craig's defense, which jurors reportedly found "very credible." Convinced by his "reputation as an illustrious Washington lawyer," jurors avoided viewing Craig in the same light as a seedy figure like Manafort. To jurors, Craig may have slipped up from time to time. But, surely, someone who had once served as Obama's White House counsel was hardly guilty of the same kinds of foreign lobbying crimes as Manafort.[28]

After only five hours of deliberation, jurors acquitted Craig. Manafort's primary contact in the American legal sector walked free. As one juror, Michael G. Meyer, said, "I could not understand why so many resources of the government were put into [prosecuting Craig] when in fact actually the republic itself is at risk." Meyer apparently missed the fact that it's *precisely* these kinds of cases—of respectable figures at respectable firms, transforming autocrats abroad into respectable politicians—that helped threaten democracy in the first place, both in America and abroad.[29]

* * *

THE VERDICT WAS a blow for American officials, who'd hoped to use Craig's case, alongside figures like Manafort, as a shot of momentum in their broader prosecutions. But unfortunately, a recalcitrant jury thought otherwise. And prosecutors' failures didn't stop there.

Not long after Craig escaped punishment, prosecutors turned back to those in Trump's immediate orbit, unveiling charges against Barrack. As prosecutors alleged, Barrack had acted as the UAE dictatorship's man in Trump's ear, guiding his administration to pro-UAE policies

across the board.[30] All of the details were there: the back-channel messages, the clandestine meetings, Barrack's claims that the UAE was his
"home team."[31] There, over the course of thousands of messages and
emails and documents, was the playbook for how the Emirati dictatorship gained its man in the White House. As prosecutors outlined, Barrack had "unlocked the back door of the American political system—its
campaigns, its media, its government—to the UAE."[32]

During the trial, Barrack hardly disputed the evidence. But he and
his lawyers had a different frame. As they argued, Barrack's efforts
were simply "in keeping with his views on the region and his work as
a businessman." This may well be true; such "work as a businessman"
earned Barrack's firm some $1.5 billion from Emirati and related Saudi
sources. Barrack went even further, claiming that he was simply interested in building a "web of tolerance" between the United States and
the UAE—and that all of his flattery and his outright pro-UAE efforts
outlined in the indictment about his work were simply part of a "cultural sixth sense."[33]

Once more, the defense, as those who follow foreign lobbying enforcement saw it, was a farce. But once more, jurors lapped it up. They
acquitted Barrack of all charges, sending him free. Upon hearing the
decision, Barrack started to weep.

The decision was yet another setback in the Justice Department's
efforts to use courts to crack down on these foreign lobbying networks,
and to bring even the bare minimum of enforcement to the foreign
lobbying sector. But they didn't give up. In 2022, prosecutors targeted
Wynn, the billionaire Trump ally who allegedly used his perch at the
Republican National Committee to help Beijing bag a dissident hiding
in the United States. Filing a lawsuit against Wynn, the Department of
Justice tried to force him to register with FARA, and to disclose all he'd
done on Beijing's behalf.

As with Craig and Barrack, the government laid out all of the details
of Wynn's operations: stealth meetings, secret phone calls, all of the
efforts to cajole Trump into doing Beijing's bidding. As with Craig and
Barrack, the conclusion—that Wynn had sold out to a foreign power,
planting a foreign agent directly in Trump's ear—was inescapable.

And as with Craig and Barrack, the legal gambit failed. In October

2022, a federal judge ruled in Wynn's favor, declaring that the billion-aire didn't have to register as a foreign lobbyist—or disclose any of the work he'd done on behalf of Chinese officials.[34]

Again, much of the case hinged on technicalities. Citing precedent about statutes of limitations, the presiding judge ruled that Wynn's obligations to disclose his pro-Beijing efforts had expired years earlier, and that the government couldn't force him to do otherwise. The judge did so reluctantly, adding that Wynn should nonetheless "have registered under FARA" while he worked for the Chinese dictatorship.[35] But his hands were tied. And, to prosecutors, a loss on technicalities is still a loss.

For the third time in a row, federal prosecutors bungled a high-profile case against a high-profile foreign lobbyist. For the third time in a row, prosecutors had been publicly humiliated, blowing what appeared to many to be slam-dunk cases—and blowing the momentum built in the Trump era toward finally clamping down on foreign lobbying networks. It was almost anticlimactic when, one month later, federal prosecutors revealed that they wouldn't be bringing foreign lobbying–related charges against Giuliani—despite all of his documented work on behalf of actors in Venezuela, Turkey, and Ukraine.

Combined with Trump's pardons of Manafort and Flynn, all of the progress the Trump era had sparked risked being undone. And the prosecutorial failures couldn't have come at a worse time. Not only because they coincided with the Biden administration pulling back from pressure on universities and think tanks—but also because, by the time Trump left office, new regimes had begun taking the lead in recruiting new foreign agents, and extending their tendrils into new industries wholesale.

*　*　*

FOR YEARS, MCKINSEY was regarded as one of the most prestigious, and one of the most sought-after, consulting firms in the entire country. And with good reason. With deep political connections and with a roster of both remarkable recruits and successful alumni, McKinsey spent years dominating the entire consulting field, inking deals with companies like Coca-Cola and Microsoft, and even steering groups like the Bill & Melinda Gates Foundation. By the mid-2010s, McKinsey maintained a reputation that was, in many ways, unparalleled in the entire history of the consulting industry.

But around the same time, the supposedly pristine firm began scouring for clients beyond America. And as with lobbyists and law firms elsewhere, it didn't take long for McKinsey to intersect with some of the most monstrous regimes on the planet—and realize that there was bottomless money to be made.

Charting McKinsey's broader moral rot could comprise an entire book (and, indeed, it has, as seen in 2022's *When McKinsey Comes to Town*, by Walt Bogdanich and Michael Forsythe, which detailed McKinsey's responsibility for, among other things, America's opioid crisis and controversial immigration detention facilities). But for the sake of this book, it's worth examining one of the key areas where McKinsey grew its business in the 2010s—and the only instance in which McKinsey has publicly declared itself, at long last, as a foreign agent.

As documents filed in 2020 disclosed, McKinsey had a few years earlier inked a deal with something called the Saudi Council of Economic and Development Affairs. The anodyne name of the client pointed directly to its financier: the regime in Saudi Arabia, one of the most anti-democratic forces on the planet. As the findings revealed, McKinsey hoovered up millions while helping the Saudi kleptocracy "grow and diversify" the Saudi economy. As part of its work, McKinsey organized conversations between Saudi officials and American "business leaders and think tank experts."

But it wasn't just meetings that McKinsey helped schedule for the Saudis. Among its other duties, McKinsey tasked employees with surveying American public attitudes toward Saudi Arabia, prepping Saudi officials for conversations with American counterparts, and creating an itinerary for Saudi officials in the United States. The group even helped set up a separate "Strategic Partnership Office," all the better to help the regime in "developing its partnerships" with countries like the United States.[36]

At first blush, McKinsey's relationship with the Saudis was par for the course. Little matter that a firm like McKinsey had become a consigliere for a regime that, back home, launches mass executions, organizes beheadings, and treats women as effective chattel; in the world of foreign lobbying in Washington, this had all been normalized.

But McKinsey didn't stop there. As *The New York Times* later reported, McKinsey had specifically pointed the Saudi regime to three critics who were dragging down the dictatorship's image. Shortly after flagging the dissidents for Saudi authorities, the regime unleashed a new crackdown. Officials arrested either the critics or their family members, jailing them on specious charges. McKinsey denied responsibility for the dictatorship's moves—the organization claimed it was "horrified" that the Saudis may have used the firm's work for such censorship—but the chain of events was clear. The regime tossed millions of dollars at McKinsey, which then fingered a range of dissidents tarnishing the image of the Saudis, who then directed their forces at smothering these critics. McKinsey got paid, and the dissidents got jail time—or worse.[37]

And this is only one instance in a far longer litany of despicable moves McKinsey made abroad. In one remarkable moment, McKinsey organized a staff retreat in China's Xinjiang region—directly amidst China's ongoing genocide of Uyghurs, with Chinese authorities forcing millions of Muslims into the biggest concentration camp system the world has seen since the Second World War.[38] "I think, by the very nature of the business, they are mercenaries," one journalist who's covered McKinsey said. "They will work for anyone."[39]

It's an ethos that many other supposedly esteemed, allegedly prestigious firms in Washington would recognize. And it's an ethos that, at long last, drew McKinsey into becoming what many other firms before them had already transformed into: a foreign agent, and a foot soldier for dictatorship.

* * *

McKINSEY'S TRANSFORMATION WAS just one piece of the far broader evolution of the foreign lobbying space, which has continued well into the 2020s. Stay with the Saudis, for instance. That government hasn't been featured much in this book, but the regime has proven willing and able to fund any number of former American officials, using them not only to launder the government's image but to gain access across

Washington in the process. Spending more than $100 million on American lobbyists alone since 2016, this "army" of pro-Saudi lobbyists and public relations firms has targeted any threats to the reputation of Saudi dictator Mohammed bin Salman (MBS).[40] They've gone so far as to successfully fight lawsuits from families of those killed in the September 11 terrorist attacks, even "orchestrat[ing] a campaign that reportedly duped U.S. military veterans into lobbying against . . . 9/11 victims' families in exchange for a trip to Washington."[41]

Along the way, building out this "extraordinarily well-financed lobbying and influence operation," the Saudi regime began tossing money at prestigious firms like McKinsey.[42] But the Saudis didn't stop there. They've also begun hiring leading American military officers to their sides, carving out yet another area of influence for the regime. Since 2016, at least fifteen retired American generals and admirals have joined the Saudi dictatorship's payroll, including Marine general James L. Jones, who served as Obama's national security advisor. While Jones at least alerted American military brass that he'd inked the deal with the Saudi regime, others ignored even those basic protocols, with some hirings only coming to light because of things like LinkedIn postings.[43]

Because there are no filing requirements to disclose what Jones and the range of other former American military officers are doing on behalf of the Saudi regime, Americans remain in the dark about how they may be affecting U.S. policy. We have no idea what conversations they've been having, what positions they've been pushing, what policies they've stopped or upended or enacted as a result. (As we saw with the case of John Allen and Qatar, former U.S. military officers are hardly strangers to liaising with Gulf dictatorships.)

And this is all from one regime, in Saudi Arabia. The despotic MBS may have overseen the murder of a *Washington Post* journalist, but he's busy authoring a brand-new playbook for lobbying Washington—one that the United States, even if it were to actually enforce the foreign lobbying regulations that are on the books, appears ill-equipped to fight.

Already, other dictatorships have followed suit. For instance, the United Arab Emirates has brought aboard dozens of former American military officials, some of whom have effectively acted as proxies for whitewashing the regime's image in Washington. The most prominent example is former secretary of defense Jim Mattis, who served as a "military advisor" to the UAE before joining the White House—a relationship he never disclosed to the public.[44] Mattis, as *The Washington Post* wrote, became the "most prominent American cheerleader" for Emirati forces—even while the UAE was accused of, among other things, overseeing torture camps and funding Russian mercenaries.

It remains unclear how much money Mattis, or many of the other high-ranking former American military officials, made from their work with foreign dictatorships. And it's a topic that's seen scant attention, with only a handful of articles and investigations in recent years. But it's one more data point in a long line of former American officials selling themselves to kleptocratic regimes—and tilting American policy, without any kind of disclosures along the way.[45]

And it all comes as the momentum of the Trump era—an era in which the threats of unchecked foreign lobbying finally seemed to crest into national consciousness, and into an opportunity to finally push back—has clearly stalled, if not crumbled entirely. Prosecutors may finally be trying to enforce foreign lobbying regulations, but they've lost their cases, with courts and juries ruling time and again against them. Along the way, the Biden administration appears to have dropped the ball more broadly—all while new regimes and new foreign forces unspool their own new foreign lobbying playbooks.

All of which leaves one question: If the United States wants to actually uproot these foreign lobbying networks—and reveal just what effect they're having on democracy in the United States and abroad— what can actually be done?

17

Mr. Lee's Publicity Book

A fundamental mistake of the Americans has been that they considered the revolution as completed when it was just begun.
—Noah Webster[1]

In early 2022, just over a year after Trump had pardoned Manafort of his crimes—and, in so doing, lit the fuse that would obliterate all the progress the United States had made on the foreign lobbying front—Manafort stepped onto an Emirates flight from Miami, bound for Dubai. It would be Manafort's first trip abroad since his pardon—and, as far as anyone knew, his first trip outside of the United States since he and his partners fled Ukraine, toppling that country into a disaster that continues to rupture Europe.

But before the flight could take off, authorities realized that Manafort had boarded via documents that had already been revoked. Officials had specifically canceled his passport after his 2017 arrest, barring him from fleeing the United States. Now, though, Manafort had somehow slipped through the customs check, sending police scrambling. As the red-eye flight began warming up, officers boarded the plane. They found Manafort, and forced him off the flight.[2]

It's unclear what Manafort was planning to do in Dubai. It's not even clear whether Dubai was Manafort's final destination, or simply a stopover to destinations elsewhere. The former Trump campaign manager has never discussed his plans, or whether his trip had anything to do with the UAE's foreign lobbying thrusts[3]—or whether it may have been related to the UAE's transformation in recent years into a center of international, and especially Russian, money laundering networks.[4]

In fact, Manafort hasn't said much of *anything* since his pardon. A single report in April 2022 pointed to his presence in Washington, attempting to provide new clients with "general business consulting," although that appears to have gone nowhere.[5] He released a dull, solipsistic memoir—entitled, appropriately enough, *Political Prisoner*—which skipped over his entire career as a foreign lobbyist.[6] (The book is framed as a woe-is-me prison diary, and is little more than an overweening love letter to Trump.) He's become, both physically and professionally, a shell of his former self; a sagging septuagenarian suffering from supposedly increasing memory loss, which he claims his imprisonment only exacerbated.

And he's watched any legacy of political success decimated, undone by the kind of avarice that propelled him and the broader industry he helped birth in the first place. Indeed, few Americans—few people, either globally or historically—can claim so many links with so many now-ousted despots as Manafort.

Just look at the fates of Manafort's former clients. In the Philippines, Ferdinand Marcos tucked tail and fled, watching his regime crumble and his country rejoice. In Angola, government forces eventually killed Jonas Savimbi, leading to rounds of jubilation in the country's capital. In Nigeria and the Democratic Republic of Congo, both Sani Abacha and Mobutu Sese Seko are widely loathed, viewed as key case studies in the development of modern kleptocracy.

And in the United States, Manafort's most prominent American client, Donald Trump, stands as the most reviled president since at least the mid-nineteenth century. Thanks to Manafort's efforts in 2016 and beyond, Trump can now boast a range of accomplishments, becoming the first American president to be impeached multiple times; the first American president to refuse to recognize an election loss; the first American president whose company was found guilty of tax fraud; the first American president subjected to formal criminal referrals from Congress; and the first former American president indicted and mugshotted. At this point, it should be little surprise if Trump becomes the first former American president jailed after leaving office. (A remarkable accomplishment, considering one of the previous presidents, John

Tyler, left the White House and served on behalf of the Confederacy—becoming, quite literally, a traitor.)

But it is in Ukraine that Manafort has seen his longest—and his most damaging, and his most damnable—legacy continue. Without Manafort, there is no Yanukovych election in 2010. There is no consolidation of arch-kleptocratic and pro-Russian forces in Kyiv in the early 2010s, decimating Ukrainian democracy in the process. There is no buildup of anti-Yanukovych counterprotests, culminating in the blowback and bloodshed of the 2014 Ukrainian revolution. And without that revolution—without Manafort's work in building the tinder, and watching his client light the fire—there is significantly less likelihood of the 2014 Russian invasion, Moscow's expanded invasion in 2022, the catastrophic reality of land war in Europe, and the potential for a great, or even nuclear, war once more.

It's too much to lay the blame for Russia's cataclysmic war in Ukraine on Manafort. Putin's messianism, and his unrepentant revanchism, are the primary propellants of the disaster, as is Russia's broader inability to reckon with its imperial history or recognize the sovereignty of former colonies. But when the history of this era is finally, formally written, there will be an outsized position that Manafort will play in it all. Because without Manafort, Yanukovych's return to power never happens. And without Yanukovych—who continues to hide out in Russia, cowering from the people he once led—there is no war, at least as it's actually played out.

Whatever comes next—however many more bodies are piled, however many more countries are involved, however much devastation remains for Europe, and for the world—much of it can be traced back to one person's peculiar, particular role, and to the career he carved for himself as the most contemptible, condemnable foreign lobbyist extant: Paul Manafort.

* * *

OF COURSE, THE other element of Manafort's legacy is the industry of foreign lobbying itself. And unsurprisingly—as Manafort walks free, and as the United States' efforts to clamp down on foreign lobbying networks crumple elsewhere—the industry itself has purred along, unbroken and unbowed.

If anything, the foreign lobbying industry has *grown* in the years since 2016, when the U.S. realized how much of a threat these foreign lobbying networks actually represent. As tabulated by researchers with OpenSecrets—a pro-transparency organization that's done some of the best work tracking foreign lobbying funding—lobbying expenditures from foreign countries have stretched to nearly $4 billion since 2016.[7] Some of that is from democratic allies, such as Japan and South Korea. But among the top spenders, a gargantuan chunk comes from dictatorial adversaries, from some of the most repugnant regimes on the planet. There's China, taking the top slot, spending nearly $300 million since 2016, vastly more than it allocated before. There's Russia, spending nearly $170 million—also tremendously more than before 2016.[8] And there are the Gulf dictatorships—Qatar, the UAE, and Saudi Arabia—spending nearly a *half billion dollars* cumulatively.

And these are only the numbers disclosed in the FARA database. This isn't even tabulating those supposedly independent companies blowing through the disclosure loopholes—loopholes like those found in the Lobbying Disclosure Act, which allow foreign companies to claim they're apolitical and skirt lobbying transparency requirements, all while spending hundreds of millions more at the behest of their respective dictatorships. This isn't even including the eight- or nine-figure donations to nonprofits and foundations and universities, let alone donations run through proxies. Nor is this including everything that simply *hasn't* been disclosed or discovered elsewhere, either because overstretched regulators don't have the resources to investigate or because such foreign financing networks are hidden behind a lattice of financial tools, like shell companies and trusts, which are saturated in anonymity—and which the United States spent years providing at a far greater clip than any other nation.[9]

In a certain sense, this growth should be expected; even after the storm of 2016, foreign lobbying wasn't going to simply disappear, especially with a president like Trump ensconced in the White House. But the sheer *shamelessness* of some of these foreign lobbyists has been striking, even for those cynical enough to follow things like foreign lobbying for a living. For instance, even after the Kremlin's expanded invasion of Ukraine in 2022, pro-Kremlin entities have continued to find willing lobbyists in Washington, including prominent firms like Squire Patton Boggs and BGR Group.[10] Using things like the loophole in the Lobbying Disclosure Act, these entities—and their American lobbyists—can successfully mask their links with Moscow, all while continuing to push pro-Kremlin policies.

But as we saw in the previous chapter, even when these foreign lobbying networks are identified—and even when they're caught breaking existing laws—that's hardly a guarantee that they'll be brought to justice. Failed prosecutions, inert bureaucracy, a president bent on pardoning his foreign agent allies: all of these ingredients combined to undercut efforts at enforcement in the late 2010s and early 2020s. Foreign lobbyists may have come in for unprecedented scrutiny, thanks in large part to Manafort and Trump. But they then wriggled out once more, slipping law enforcement's grasp, slinking back into the backrooms and threatening to return the world of foreign lobbying to the kind of *status quo ante* that helped land us, and places like Ukraine, in this mess in the first place.

All of which points to one increasingly inescapable conclusion: Should lobbying for these foreign regimes simply be made illegal? If things like FARA continually fall short, should it be scrapped altogether, with—as Biden called for on the campaign trail—outright bans on foreign lobbying instituted instead?

* * *

IT'S NOT AN easy question to answer. We know that FARA, when enforced, *has* been a boon for transparency. And there are certainly tweaks and changes that FARA should see in the near term that could help, from improving its digital database to ending the Lobbying Disclosure Act loophole. Officials could even expand FARA's use of civil injunctions, which would allow the Justice Department to order potential foreign agents to stop their work until they follow the law. Or better yet, they could increase the use of civil fines for FARA violators—something that could hit the pocketbooks of those American firms and American figures skirting even basic transparency requirements. Such an increase in injunctions and fines can target these foreign agents, all while mitigating the risks that come with FARA-related prosecutions, which, as we saw above, all too often fail.

But given the setbacks of the early 2020s, legislators have begun realizing that simply enforcing or updating existing regulations may not be the solution. Instead, it may be time to fulfill the pledge from the American legislators we met previously: those in the 1860s, who said that American officials had no right to sell their talents to foreign regimes, or those in the 1960s, who announced that constitutional rights ended where foreign lobbying began. It may be time, in other words, to finally bar Americans from lobbying for foreign regimes outright.

We've already begun seeing legislators tack in this direction. In 2022, a bipartisan slate of House officials submitted the aptly named Stop Helping Adversaries Manipulate Everything—or SHAME—Act.[11] The bill's text is straightforward: if passed, it would bar Americans from lobbying on behalf of the most anti-American regimes and their related entities. At last, Americans could no longer freely lobby for the Chinese regime, or Russian companies, or Venezuelan kleptocrats, or Iranian proxies. For the first time in U.S. history, American citizens could no longer freely offer their "right to petition" to regimes explicitly trying to use their services for their own anti-American and anti-democratic ends—and make millions of dollars in the process.[12]

The bill wouldn't fully illegalize the foreign lobbying industry as a whole; so far, the only regimes included are those like North Korea, Cuba, and a handful of others officially identified by the U.S. government as "foreign adversaries." But it's a shot across the bow. And it's one that's already proven popular, with the bill endorsed by a broad slate of groups, from the Republican Study Committee to the bipartisan Helsinki Commission to a range of pro-transparency civil society groups.

It's also a bill that forces Americans to ask a simple question: Why *is* it legal for Americans to lobby on behalf of these regimes? Why *is* it legal for Americans to take funds to stump for Chinese genocidaires, or Russian militias, or North Korean officials engaged in some of the most grievous corruption and human rights abuses around the world? And if it shouldn't be legal for Americans to offer this "right to petition" to these monsters, why should Americans be allowed to do so for, say, regimes that butcher investigative journalists (Azerbaijan), or jail women for social media posts (Saudi Arabia), or allow the deaths of thousands and thousands of migrant workers (Qatar)?

Put another way: Why *should* Americans be allowed to offer their constitutional rights, including this right to lobby, to the highest foreign bidders they can find—including the fascistic, authoritarian, and tyrannical regimes now circling the world?

*   *   *

THESE ARE QUESTIONS that, because of the past few years, have begun to roil Washington. But the SHAME Act hasn't yet been passed, let alone been expanded to all dictatorships and despotic governments still employing U.S. firms to do their bidding. And until then, there's little reason to think Americans won't continue selling themselves to Beijing, Moscow, or any other repulsive regime they can find.

And unfortunately, as we've seen throughout this book, traditional lobbying is only part of the picture. With the rise of think tanks, the openness of universities, and the post-government careers of former officials and military officers, whole new classes of Americans and American industries have leapt into the eager arms of these foreign regimes. Beyond the scope of traditional foreign lobbying regulations, beyond even basic transparency requirements, we still have little idea of just how much money foreign governments have tossed at these figures and institutes—let alone what effect it's all had.

But we've begun seeing solutions floated—potential fixes that come, once more, from Congress. In 2022, another bipartisan slate of officials introduced a bill that would go a significant way toward figuring out just how extensive these new networks run, and potentially even preventing them from spreading any further.

Known as the Fighting Foreign Influence Act, the legislation contains some of the boldest proposals the country has ever seen. The bill would force all American nonprofits to disclose any significant donations from foreign governments or foreign political parties, detailing the sources and amounts. Think tanks, universities, foundations: all those American nonprofits processing millions (and potentially more) in wealth linked to foreign regimes, all as a means of opening doors to U.S. policymakers, would finally have to disclose how much they've taken in. That information would then be published by the Treasury Department, allowing insight into which governments and which entities are involved—and what all that unchecked wealth is actually doing.[13]

But the bill doesn't stop there. Another provision would end the loophole that allows foreign lobbyists to act as effective cutouts for foreign money to enter the U.S. political system, corrupting American democracy that much further. This loophole is, as we've seen, a blaring, glaring threat to American elections and American policy, with foreign lobbyists continuing to act as a conduit for kleptocratic wealth to flow directly to legislators' election campaigns.

And the bill would also complete the process begun in the 1860s, when American officials first proposed banning former officials from serving as henchmen for foreign governments. As the legislation details, all major American political figures—presidents, vice presidents, members of presidential administrations, and officials in Congress—would finally, formally be banned from leaving office to work as mouthpieces for foreign regimes. The malignant legacy of figures like Bob Dole would, at last, collapse.[14]

Like the SHAME Act, the Fighting Foreign Influence Act, cosponsored by GOP and Democratic officials alike, hasn't yet passed. But even with its introduction, it's already raised a host of questions. Why have think tanks and universities been allowed to spend years gorging on opaque foreign regime–linked financing? Why have foreign lobbyists—these literal "foreign agents"—been able to donate to American politicians, financing the same officials they're trying to sway? And why have America's most prominent politicians and military officers been allowed to leave office and immediately shop themselves to foreign governments, including those that are explicitly anti-democratic, and even anti-American? And why isn't something like this considered at least similar to the behavior of America's greatest traitors, from Benedict Arnold to Robert E. Lee?

Both pieces of legislation promise to pick up where existing regulations and enforcement efforts have failed. And it should be little surprise that they come from the one body that, thus far, hasn't yet failed in pursuing the fight against foreign lobbying: Congress. While the

executive branch has slowed or thwarted the broader battle against foreign lobbying, and where the courts have proven overwilling to allow
Americans of all stripes to service foreign dictatorships, it is legislators
in the House and the Senate who have picked up the ball. Most remarkably, both chambers have done so on a bipartisan basis.

To be sure, Congress is still partially responsible for the broader
flourishing of foreign lobbying. Dozens and dozens of former members (as well as congressional staffers) have left office and linked up
with other regimes to become foreign agents in their own rights, a
pipeline that current members of Congress have shown little interest in
closing. And as we saw earlier, the House Ethics Committee has helped
stonewall other investigations into how foreign governments access
policymakers in the first place. In early 2023, with Republicans taking
over the House of Representatives, GOP legislators even announced
myopic plans to gut the Office of Congressional Ethics—arguably the
most successful body highlighting how foreign regimes inveigle legislators.[15] Congress has hardly been blameless.

But it was Congress that first investigated America's initial foreign
lobbying scandal, when Russian agents began bribing legislators to flip
votes on Alaska. It was Congress that investigated Ivy Lee's pro-Nazi
work, and then pushed and passed things like FARA. And now, it's
Congress that's at the fore of pushing legislation that can actually clean
up this morass. Especially when viewed with similar legislation already
introduced—including bills that would force other Americans to stop
servicing foreign kleptocratic wealth, and stop providing dictatorial regimes with legal and financial protections—it is Congress that stands
as arguably the last, best hope at preventing Washington from drowning in this flood tide of foreign lobbying.

*   *   *

IF THERE'S ONE thing that's clear, it's that there's one area that can't,
and shouldn't, be trusted as a potential ally: the private sector. Over
and again, the private sector—the firms, the consultancies, all those
profiting from their transformation into lobbyists on behalf of foreign
regimes—has proven itself incapable of policing its own, or of holding itself to even the most basic ethics provisions. Time after time, the

private sector has gleefully chosen profit over patriotism, acting as a handmaiden to the illiberal, autocratic forces goose-stepping around the world.

Indeed, if there's one cohesive story of the post–Cold War era, linking everything from the rise of kleptocracy to the rollback of democracy to the expansion of fascistic dictatorships around the world, it's that the American private sector has been a willing agent in the drive to entrench despotism wherever it can. And when it comes to the world of foreign lobbying, in all of its recent manifestations, that's been especially true.

Look back at the team Manafort cobbled in Ukraine on behalf of Yanukovych. There were the lobbying shops and consultancies, on both sides of the American political aisle, that aided Manafort's laundering efforts. There were the former U.S. officials, transformed into private sector actors whom Manafort could use to lobby their former counterparts. And there, along for much of the ride, was Skadden, appearing to offer its imprimatur to Yanukovych's rule, highlighting how central American law firms have become to the entire process. Providing their supposed stamps of expertise, honesty, and analysis as a means of whitewashing yet another budding dictator. Illustrating just how much the American legal industry has changed—and become a servant to despots around the world.

And that was only one network, in one country, working at the behest of one would-be autocrat—who only lost power thanks to the kinds of democratic energies that Ukrainians have used to topple tyrants, and to inspire the rest of the world. But all of these firms hardly exist in a vacuum. If anything, they're just the unluckiest of the bunch, caught out only for helping Manafort. They're just the tracer dye in the water, underscoring just how many American industries have transformed into key allies of modern dictatorship—and how little Americans and others can rely on the private sector to reform itself.

* * *

BUT PERHAPS NO industry has become more embedded in modern dictatorship—in transforming the world of foreign lobbying, in Washington and elsewhere—than the American public relations industry. A century after Ivy Lee first birthed the industry, public relations firms continue to service dictators around the world, transforming them from despots into democrats, opening doors and enhancing their regimes that much further in the process. It is a legacy, and a line of work, that Lee would firmly recognize—and if his work with the fascists in places like Italy and Germany is any indication, even approve of.

In writing this book, it's clear that at least part of that transformation stems directly from the public relations industry's inability to fully reckon with Lee's legacy. For many in the industry—which now stretches into the millions of employees, with an "annual global economic impact" running into an estimated hundreds of billions of dollars—Lee remains a titan of innovation, the singular figure to whom public relations leaders still look for guidance. Lee not only invented the industry but quite literally wrote the book on it, with the New York–based Museum of Public Relations publishing *Mr. Lee's Publicity Book* as recently as 2017. Billing it as public relations "guidance," the publishers claimed that Lee's book is "just as valuable, perhaps even more so," in the twenty-first century as when Lee first drafted it a century ago.[16]

But cast around for any sign of Lee's downfall—of his decision to flack for Mussolini, to peddle pro-Soviet narratives, to launch himself into the heart of Nazi propaganda—and you'll be left wanting. It's a chapter of Lee's life that those steering the public relations industry appear to ignore, or even actively downplay. As Lee's *Publicity Book* says, there's "no conclusive evidence" that Lee "knowingly worked for the Nazis," as if his entire effort in Germany was just some innocent misunderstanding.[17]

Instead, Lee remains a guiding light, an outstanding figure worth emulating. Lee's "legacy stands out because of [his] constant and repeated concern in establishing professional credibility for himself and his role," one analysis in *Mr. Lee's Publicity Book* reads.[18] In 2021, Shelley Spector, the founder of the aforementioned public relations museum, penned a separate post on Lee's "Code of Ethics," claiming that "PR people have held many roles since the beginning of the profession, none more vital than [being] the guardian of ethics." To Spector, Lee's "most significant contribution to PR" was his "creation of ethical crisis management practices." Spector at least nods at Lee's pro-dictatorship work, but only to note that "some have since come to question Lee's own ethics relative to working with the Germans and the Soviets"—as if his pro-Kremlin or pro-Nazi work is somehow up for debate.[19]

It is all, fittingly enough, spin enough to make you dizzy. Lee was someone who routinely denigrated investigative journalists, routinely obfuscated questions about corporate crimes, and routinely slandered those pushing for transparency or any kind of equitable justice. And once he was done working with American clients, he turned to those regimes set to launch the greatest, and most genocidal, war the world had ever seen. His "Poison Ivy" moniker is not only fitting for the bile he injected into the American body politic but also because his German client, I.G. Farben, refined the kinds of poisonous gas that its Nazi partners unleashed in concentration camps.

It is a legacy the entire industry has done effectively nothing to wrestle with. After *The Economist* described Lee in 2010 as someone who made "verisimilitude [matter] more than veracity,"[20] Public Relations Society of America CEO Gary McCormick raised his hackles, snorting that the magazine's "assessment couldn't be further from the truth." According to McCormick, the industry "has served immeasurable public good." That claim is, by its nature, impossible to measure. But McCormick further pointed to the industry's "strong ethical standards," which include things like "loyalty," "independence," and "fairness," all as a means of "strengthen[ing] the public's trust in the profession."[21]

That's all fine and good. But there is nothing in these "ethical standards" about, say, working for dictators, or laundering the images and reputations of despotic regimes, or even holding other PR firms that follow Lee's pro-fascist lead to account. (Fittingly enough, when I asked both the Public Relations Society of America and the Museum of Public Relations about Lee's work with dictators, or the role that modern PR firms play in helping modern tyrants, I heard nothing back.) Instead, we simply have airy claims about "strong ethical standards"—and nothing about the ethics of choosing whether or not to work with modern fascists, modern authoritarians, and modern dictators.[22]

Which is why it should be wholly unsurprising that, even in the early 2020s, the world's leading public relations firms are still marching in lockstep with foreign dictatorships—and helping them spread their malign influence, their brutal reigns, and their bloodied legacies that much further. In 2022, the Edelman PR agency—the biggest public relations firm in the entire United States, and one that previously worked with Yanukovych—agreed to a substantial deal with a regime we saw in the previous chapter: Saudi Arabia. Little matter that the Saudi government stands as one of the most kleptocratic dictatorships extant, responsible for everything from jailing women for social media posts to executing dozens and dozens of inmates in a single day, all while the Saudi despot MBS authorizes the assassinations of journalists working at American outlets. To Edelman—and to the public relations industry as a whole—none of that mattered.[23]

And what will Edelman be doing for such a regime? According to federal filings, the services they will provide run the gamut, from "planning and strategy" to "media relations" to "monitor[ing] online conversations." Edelman said it would "develop partnerships with celebrities and pursue opportunities that could lead to productions filmed throughout the kingdom," and even "pitched partnering with MTV and teaming up with major institutions" to help whitewash the Saudi regime's image. (Among the celebrities that Edelman lobbed as potential Saudi collaborators were actor Priyanka Chopra, actor Jet Li, and DJ David Guetta.)[24] Edelman also sent out releases claiming that Saudi Arabia maintained a "deep commitment to the empowerment of women"[25]—even as the regime leads a "crackdown" on female campaigners, routinely imprisoning women's rights activists.[26]

It all makes a mockery of claims that the PR industry maintains some kind of airtight ethical standards. Perhaps most remarkably, Edelman signed its contract even after other organizations had been shamed into dropping the Saudis. This, after all, was the original thrust of FARA: the belief that shame could steer lobbyists away from the most grotesque regimes.

It almost never worked—until, at least, MBS oversaw the murder of a *Washington Post* journalist. Following that assassination, numerous American firms dropped the Saudis as a client. For perhaps the first time in American history, the idea that shame could actually deter these firms was no longer an obvious fallacy.[27]

Yet that sense of shame apparently had an expiration date. Only two years after the journalist's assassination, Edelman began rebuilding its Saudi ties, joining not only McKinsey but other firms like Boston Consulting Group and Qorvis who are also helping the Saudis.[28] Whether or not this contravenes Edelman's internal "human rights policy"—which claims the company has a "commitment to uphold human rights in every facet of our business"—is unclear, as the company did not respond to my questions.[29] But by 2023, it was as if the murder, or any of the other horrific crimes associated with the Saudi regime, had never taken place.

But then again, isn't that Edelman's goal? As the firm wrote in its pitch to the regime, they readily acknowledged that people were still concerned with Saudi Arabia's "violations of human rights."[30] And that was a reputation that Edelman would do all it could to fix.[31]

It was, to pick a word, shameless. But it was also a deal firmly in keeping with Lee's legacy, which stalks the industry to this day.

* * *

FOR REASONS HE never explained, Lee never actually published *Mr. Lee's Publicity Book* during his lifetime. It was only in the 2010s when researchers, digging through his archives, discovered his manuscript, and decided to finally release it to the public. The book, billed as a "Citizen's Guide to Public Relations," finally came out in August 2017.[32] And the timing couldn't have been better.

By the time the book was released, Lee's name—and his legacy—was in the news to a greater extent than any time since his death. And it wasn't hard to see why. There was an American president surrounding himself with foreign agents, carrying Lee's work directly into the White House. There was an American populace suddenly realizing the depths and the dangers of foreign lobbying and foreign influence campaigns, a direct outgrowth of Lee's example.

And there was Manafort, the man who carried Lee's torch further than anyone, at the center of it all, tipping the scales of democracy in the United States and elsewhere as he went. Like Lee, Manafort took his domestic innovations abroad, introducing a world of despotic figures to the magic and madness they could take advantage of, if only they hired him. And like Lee, Manafort then watched his career and his influence implode, undone by his witting work on behalf of foreign despots.

It's unclear if Manafort ever read Lee's book. But if he did, the book's final line likely rang true to him. "To appreciate the power of the wielder of publicity it is not necessary to listen to him boasting of his triumphs," Lee wrote. "The complaints of his enemies are a sufficient tribute. They speak only of his power because, until recently, power has been the publicity man's chief weapon. He has only begun to use justice."[33]

America has been waiting a century for the "publicity man" to "use justice," and to give up the work on behalf of dictatorships. And if Lee and Manafort are any example, America will be waiting centuries more for them to finally drop their dictatorial designs.

Because even though Lee and Manafort both lost everything, their legacies still live with us, and continue to infuse despots and their American enablers around the world. They may have watched their personal fortunes crumble, and they may have seen their portfolios and influence implode. But in so many ways, this world—with the American firms and the American officials and the American nonprofits and the American consultants and the American lobbyists helping dictators and tyrants around the globe, smothering democracy wherever they find it, and now turning their sights on the United States itself—is simply the one that Lee and Manafort created, spinning on and on and on.

Afterword: November 2023

There's gold from the grass roots down.
—Joe Milner[1]

In 1999, a pair of researchers poring through recently opened KGB archives in Russia made a startling discovery. There, amid the scattered memos and confessions, was confirmation that the Soviet Union had once slid a mole—a foreign agent, as it were—into the U.S. Congress. It's unclear if the researchers immediately recognized the name, or if they wondered about any connections to the broader history of foreign lobbying writ large. But this agent is someone who would have been known to figures like Ivy Lee—and who will be familiar to those who recall the congressional hearings mentioned toward the beginning of this book: Rep. Samuel Dickstein.

Dickstein, as we saw in this book's earliest section, oversaw the hearings that eventually outed Lee as a courtier to fascism, as the Nazis' go-to megaphone in America. It was Dickstein who laid out the links between I.G. Farben and the Nazi regime, and who, perhaps more than any other congressional official, forced Lee to squirm, and to finally admit to his pro-Nazi work. It was Dickstein who helped jump-start the legislative momentum that would eventually birth FARA.

And it was Dickstein who, a few years after revealing Lee's fascistic work for the world, turned to the Soviets himself, freely offering his services to Moscow. Unlike other Americans recruited by the Soviet Union, he didn't appear to have any overt communist sympathies. Rather, Dickstein—whom Soviet officials nicknamed "Crook"—seemed interested only in money. "'Crook' is completely justifying his code name," Soviet officials wrote. "This is an unscrupulous type, greedy for money . . . a very cunning swindler."

But the Soviets, as the records opened decades later revealed, got their own money's worth. Dickstein used his congressional leverage to expedite Soviet access to American passports—making it far easier for Soviet citizens, and Soviet agents, to travel through the United States. Dickstein also covertly shared "materials on the war budget for 1940, records of conferences of the budget subcommission, reports of the war minister," and more, according to Soviet documents. At one point, Dickstein even passed information about a Soviet defector to his handlers; soon thereafter, the defector was found dead in his hotel room.

Over time, though, Moscow grew fed up with Dickstein's escalating financial requests. The Soviets eventually cut him loose, complaining that he wasn't worth the price he demanded. Dickstein soon left Congress, becoming a New York State Supreme Court justice, serving in public office until his death in 1954. All the while, Dickstein ducked any allegations of his Soviet ties—and dodged any prosecution he would have otherwise faced as an undisclosed foreign agent. It wasn't until Soviet archives opened up that, as author Peter Duffy wrote, Dickstein was revealed as the "only known" elected federal official "to have served as a covert agent for a foreign power."[2]

That was a reality that stood for decades, well into the twenty-first century. Then, in late 2023—after the manuscript for this book had already been finalized—federal prosecutors dropped another bombshell. In a series of shocking indictments, prosecutors alleged that another member of Congress had followed in Dickstein's footsteps and flipped into becoming a foreign agent, all on behalf of a foreign dictatorship.

And this time, this official—Bob Menendez, a Democratic senator from the state of New Jersey—would face the full brunt of the law.

* * *

THE ALLEGATIONS FACING Menendez were a mix of stunning and spectacular, almost bordering on the farcical. They involved everything from hidden gold bars and mob-linked bribery to a sprawling cover-up helping bury the fact that his wife killed a man with her car.

But it was the allegations of Menendez's secret work at the behest of a foreign regime that are most pertinent to this book and that set the Menendez case apart from anything else in American history. For the first time, prosecutors alleged that a sitting senator had conspired to act as a foreign agent—and that he had secretly transformed into a mouthpiece, and into a handmaiden, for a foreign dictatorship, allowing this regime to steer policy at the highest levels of American government.

As prosecutors claimed, Menendez had secretly worked on behalf of the brutal regime in Egypt, offering his services as everything from a mole to a ghostwriter for the kleptocrats in Cairo. There he was, secretly drafting language for Egyptian officials to send around to other unsuspecting American senators. There he was, secretly passing along "highly sensitive" information identifying employees of the U.S. embassy in Cairo—employees who could then be targeted by one of the bloodiest regimes in the region. There he was, secretly sharing texts about upcoming votes on contentious weapons sales to Egypt. (Texts that, as prosecutors detailed, received at least one "thumbs-up" emoji from an Egyptian official.)

There he was, all the while, serving as the head of the Senate Foreign Relations Committee—the highest-ranking senator, perched at the top of Congress's foreign policymaking establishment. Crafting Congress's foreign policy priorities, steering Congress's foreign policy financing, directing Congress's foreign policy decisions—all while allegedly working to "secretly aid the Government of Egypt."[3]

Like Dickstein, Menendez didn't transform into an alleged foreign agent for any ideological reasons; as prosecutors detailed, it was all in return for "hundreds of thousands of dollars of bribes." (Among the alleged bribes were the aforementioned gold bars, which may help explain why Menendez later googled "how much is one kilo of gold worth.") And yet, Menendez's alleged crimes were somehow even more ridiculous, and even more unnerving. For instance, Menendez appeared to operate largely at the behest of his wife, Nadine Menendez—who herself received a paid position at a "low-or-no-show job" from one of Cairo's contacts. Menendez also did all of this while maintaining access, as one write-up said, to "unknown quantities of classified information."[4]

Since this afterword was written before Menendez's trial, it's unclear how much classified information Menendez, who denied any wrongdoing, may have passed along. But one thing at least is clear, and even more galling. All of the FARA reforms mentioned in the previous chapter—the increase of civil injunctions and civil fines, the closing of mile-wide loopholes, and more—have already been bundled into proposed bills in Congress. Legislators have tried to pass these reforms, time and again. But thus far, they've found no success. FARA remains, as it were, unreformed. And as *Bloomberg Law* wrote, there was one legislator who acted as the "primary foil responsible for thwarting" all of these FARA reforms: Menendez.[5]

In other words, an alleged foreign agent amassed such powers that, as the chair of the Senate Foreign Relations Committee, he could—and did—block foreign lobbying reforms, over and over.

It boggles the mind. But it's also something that, a few centuries ago, figures like Alexander Hamilton warned of. There were "so many mortifying examples," Hamilton wrote, "of the prevalence of foreign corruption in republican governments."[6] Thanks to Menendez, we now have perhaps the most mortifying example of that kind of corruption that the United States has ever seen. And we have the final, logical culmination of what these decades of effectively ignoring the threats of foreign agents have led directly to—and what they might have in store for the rest of us, if these foreign agents continue to burrow into the highest reaches of Washington, and far beyond.

ACKNOWLEDGMENTS

First, I'd like to thank my editor, Hannah O'Grady, for shepherding this book from messy, muddled vision into the polished final draft you now hold. Without Hannah's guidance, clarity, and confidence that this book could actually be written—that there was actually a story worth telling, buried in the detritus of FARA filings and convoluted lawsuits and political forces shadowboxing across continents—this book would never exist. That goes likewise for my agent, Samantha Shea, who helped craft the initial pitch that launched this book toward completion. This book is, if nothing else, proof that a writer is nothing without their agent. I'd like to also thank Sue Warga for tackling these endnotes for me.

I want to thank those who've been raising the alarm about un-checked foreign lobbying for far longer than I've ever been interested. Those like Ben Freeman, whose incomparable work on everything from Gulf lobbying networks to think tank funding to kleptocratic wealth entering the American electoral stream threads this book. In the broader swath of the American policy community, Ben's work de-serves as wide a platform as possible. The same should also be said for Ken Silverstein, the writer whose work in the sordid world of foreign lobbyists served as one of my initial—and continuing—inspirations for working on this book. For a significant chunk of the post–Cold War era, Silverstein often seemed to be the only journalist—perhaps even the only American—who recognized the threat of untrammeled foreign lobbying for what it was. He is, as far as I'm concerned, an American hero.

There were plenty of other researchers, scholars, and journalists without whom this book wouldn't be possible. Folks like Tarun Krishnakumar, Meredith McGehee, Craig Holman, Daniel Schuman, Anna Massoglia, Mike Eckel, Tena Prelec, Alexander Cooley, John Heathershaw, Tom Mayne, Paul Massaro, and Nate Sibley—all of whom are leading on this fight, and so much else. And I'd like especially to thank Gigi O'Connell, whose keen eyes and insights made this book far sharper than it would have been otherwise. I'd like to thank Céline Boustani and Thor Halvorssen for making the Human Rights Foundation one of the leaders in the fight against rising dictatorship, as well as the patient archivists at Princeton's Seeley G. Mudd Manuscript Library, who humored my naivete and helped make the process of tackling Ivy Lee's archive far more manageable than it otherwise would have been.

I never would have written this without the consistent support (or consistent trolling) of friends across the country. Some of my oldest friends, including Kyle Holmes, Clement Uduk, Matt Fleskes, and Nick Rischiotto, helped me stomach the Portland Trail Blazers' latest blunders. Some of my dearest friends, like Nick Farris, Sam Woodard, and Justin Young, provided me the mental health breaks I needed, especially at the Puget Sound. Some of my best friends, including Daniel Mollengarden, Matt Youn, Chris Chen, and Chris Tzeng, helped elevate my fantasy football skills into an unstoppable juggernaut, and helped make sure I never forget the taste of a pickleback. And some of my finest friends, like Desmond and Maggie Sermont, Arthur and Nia Wang, Jeremy Blomberg, Cody Hack, and Crystal Vitagliano, helped refine my musical tastes. I also want to thank, as ever, Joe Dwyer for lending his unmatched voice to the audio version of this book, as well as Abe Segura and Natalie Clericuzio, all of whom have willingly signed on to support the Seattle Mariners, wherever and however they can.

And then there are those in New York and nearby who've helped me navigate the newest, and most staggeringly wonderful, chapter of a new life. Those like Amy and Max and Ronan and Zoë, who serve as a model of what a beautiful family can be. Those like Robert and

Marjolein, Amit and Therese, Kanaan and Bristol, Neil and Mariam, and Josh and Molly, who kept us sane during the past few years. Those like Ian and Mel and Zoey (and Ziggy), never hesitating to bring a bit of laughter to things. Those like Doc and Ella (and Vector), helping make the past few years far more fun than otherwise. And those like Walsh and Nastya, whose spectacular journey has only just begun. And I have to thank all the wonderful neighbors who've turned Brooklyn into a home: Jackie and Sarah and Sharon, Eric and KJ and Alex and Liam, and David and Deborah and Taylor.

Most especially, this book wouldn't be possible without the family I have surrounding and supporting me, and making sure I accomplish something with this life. That goes for my wondrous Babu Ji and Ama Ji, whose unfailing support (and willingness to let me marry their daughter) has been an incredible addition to my life. That goes for Jaya, Jacob, and Ari, as well as Pu, Nitu, Mashall, and the rest of the incredible Sharma family. That goes, likewise, for my parents: Jules and Kathy Michel, whose transformation into grandparents has been a seamless, joyful affair. Here's hoping everyone has a chance to try my mother's cookies, and to watch my father slide down the stairs headfirst at some point.

My wife, Versha Sharma, is everything to me. She's steered *Teen Vogue* into a bright, brilliant future, and she's somehow grown even more beautiful in the process. And watching her become a mother to our incomparable, indomitable daughter, Devi Rose, has been the greatest treat of my short life, even with all of the sleeplessness that comes with. Our Gudiya is, without a doubt, the sweetest gift from above—there, with all of her fingers and toes, as the center of our whole world.

This book, though, is dedicated to my younger brother, Norwood. Witnessing Norwood's growth from a lanky teenager into a loving uncle, seeing him become a business wunderkind, and realizing that he hasn't lost any of his empathy or his heart along the way, has made me prouder than I can put into words. I often say that my brother is the best person I know—and that, so long as he is happy, this world will be okay. This holds evermore that we're adults, that he's become my daughter's favorite napping place, and that he's managed to balance family dynamics and business with the work he accomplishes from Montana to the Puget Sound. I admire him deeply, and regard him as the antithesis of some of the individuals cataloged in this book. My brother is proof that there is good in this world.

NOTES

EPIGRAPH

1. "American Graphic: Two Views of Crime and Criminals," *Washington Post,* August 12, 1980.
2. Frank Miller and David Mazzucchelli, *Batman: Year One* (Burbank, CA: DC Comics, 2015).

FOREIGN AGENTS BY THE NUMBERS

1. This data is from the years 1957–2016. Comptroller General of the United States, "Effectiveness of the Foreign Agents Registration Act of 1938, as Amended, and Its Administration by the Department of Justice," report to the Committee on Foreign Relations, U.S. Senate, B-177551, March 1974; Office of the Inspector General, U.S. Department of Justice, "Audit of the National Security Division's Enforcement and Administration of the Foreign Agents Registration Act," Audit Division 16–24, September 2016.
2. This data is from the years 1974–2014. Comptroller General, "Effectiveness"; Office of the Inspector General, "Audit."
3. Ben Freeman, *The Foreign Policy Auction: Foreign Lobbying in America* (n.p.: CreateSpace, 2012).
4. Joseph J. Schatz and Benjamin Oreskes, "Want to Be a 'Foreign Agent'? Serve in Congress First," *Politico,* October 2, 2016.
5. Open Secrets, "Foreign Lobby Watch," https://www.opensecrets.org/fara?cycle=2022, accessed 8 September 2023.
6. Ibid.
7. Ibid.
8. Ibid.

9. "Alaska Investigation," *Reports of Committees of the House of Representatives,* 16th Cong., 3rd Sess. (1869), 1–5.

10. The Clinton Foundation tax documents are found on the IRS's Tax Exempt Organizations Search database, at https://apps.irs.gov/app/eos/details/. For a more legible look at Clinton Foundation finances, see ProPublica Nonprofit Explorer, "Bill Hillary & Chelsea Clinton Foundation," https://projects.propublica.org/nonprofits /organizations/311580204.

11. Elizabeth Redden, "Foreign Gift Investigations Expand and Intensify," *Inside Higher Ed,* February 20, 2020.

PROLOGUE: BAD BUSINESS

1. Orhan Pamuk, *Istanbul: Memories and the City* (New York: Vintage International, 2006).

2. Special Committee on Un-American Activities, House of Representatives, "Investigation of Nazi Propaganda Activities and Investigation of Certain Other Propaganda Activities," Hearings No. 73-DC-4, 73rd Cong., 2nd Sess. (June 5–7, 1934).

3. Ibid.

4. Ibid.

5. Ibid.

6. Ibid.

7. Ibid.

8. David B. Ottaway and Patrick E. Tyler, "Angola Rebel Chief to Receive U.S. Praise, and Possibly Aid," *Washington Post,* January 26, 1986.

9. Franklin Foer, "Paul Manafort, American Hustler," *The Atlantic,* March 2018.

10. Nicholas D. Kristof, "Our Own Terrorist," *New York Times,* March 5, 2002.

11. Ibid.

12. Evan Thomas, "The Slickest Shop in Town," *Time,* March 3, 1986.

13. Phil McCombs, "Salute to Savimbi," *Washington Post,* February 1, 1986.

14. Ottaway and Tyler, "Angola Rebel Chief."

15. McCombs, "Salute to Savimbi."

16. Ottaway and Tyler, "Angola Rebel Chief."

17. Patrick E. Tyler and David B. Ottaway, "The Selling of Jonas Savimbi: Success and a $600,000 Tab," *Washington Post,* February 9, 1986.

18. Sean Braswell, "The Bloody Birth of Corporate PR," OZY, October 24, 2015.

19. Lionel Zetter, *Lobbying: The Art of Political Persuasion,* 3rd ed. (Petersfield, UK: Harriman House, 2014).

20. "Archival Video: 1989: Paul Manafort Admits to Influence Pedaling [*sic*] in Wake of US Department of Housing and Urban Development Federal Investigation," ABC News, April 11, 2016.

21. U.S. Congress, "Amdt1.4.1: Overview of Free Exercise Clause," Constitution Annotated, https://constitution.congress.gov/browse/essay/amdt1-4-1/ALDE_00013221 /, accessed 4 March 2023.

PART I: POISON

1. Everett Dean Martin, *The Behavior of Crowds: A Psychological Study* (New York: Harper, 1920), 235.

1. DIRE CONSEQUENCES

1. Svetlana Alexievich, *Secondhand Time: The Last of the Soviets* (New York: Random House, 2017), 6.
2. Peter Grier, "The Lobbyist Through History: Villainy and Virtue," *Christian Science Monitor*, September 28, 2009.
3. Ibid.
4. Tarun Krishnakumar, "Propaganda by Permission: Examining 'Political Activities' Under the Foreign Agents Registration Act," *Journal of Legislation* 47, no. 2 (2021): 46.
5. Robert C. Byrd, *The Senate, 1789–1989*, vol. 2, *Addresses on the History of the United States Senate*, ed. Wendy Wolff (Washington, DC: U.S. Government Printing Office, 1988), 492.
6. Ibid.
7. Alexander Hamilton, "Federalist No. 21: Other Defects of the Present Confederation" (1787).
8. Thomas V. DiBacco, "150 Years Ago, Russia Bribed Congress to Vote for the Dough to Buy Alaska," *Orlando Sentinel*, November 3, 2017.
9. Ibid.
10. Ronald J. Jensen, *The Alaska Purchase and Russian-American Relations* (Seattle: University of Washington Press, 1975).
11. Ibid.
12. Ibid.
13. Ibid.
14. Ibid.
15. Ibid.
16. Ibid.
17. Tom Kizzia, "William H. Seward, Political Fixer," *AHS Blog*, Alaska Historical Society, March 6, 2013, https://alaskahistoricalsociety.org/william-h-seward-political-fixer/.
18. Milton O. Gustafson, "Seward's Bargain: The Alaska Purchase from Russia," *Prologue Magazine* 26, no. 4 (Winter 1994): 261–269, https://www.archives.gov/publications/prologue/1994/winter/alaska-check.
19. "Alaska Investigation," *Reports of Committees of the House of Representatives*, 16th Cong., 3rd Sess. (1869), 1–5.
20. Lionel Zetter, *Lobbying: The Art of Political Persuasion*, 3rd ed. (Petersfield, UK: Harriman House, 2014).
21. Emily Edson Briggs, *The Olivia Letters: Being Some History of Washington City for Forty Years as Told by the Letters of a Newspaper Correspondent* (New York: Neale, 1906), 91. See https://www.gutenberg.org/files/58604/58604-h/58604-h.htm.

22. Zetter, *Lobbying*.

23. Cited in Nick Ragone, *The Everything American Government Book* (New York: Simon and Schuster, 2004), 194.

24. Adam Hochschild, *King Leopold's Ghost: A Story of Greed, Terror, and Heroism in Colonial Africa* (New York: Houghton Mifflin, 1999).

25. Ibid.

26. Ibid.

27. Ibid.

28. Ibid.

29. Ibid.

30. Ibid.

31. Ibid.

2. WHAT IS A FACT?

1. This quote has been attributed to, among others, George Orwell, William Randolph Hearst, and Malcolm Muggeridge. There is little evidence linking the quote to any of them. See Dorian Lynskey, "The Ministry of Truth," *PowellsBooks.Blog*, June 5, 2019, https://www.powells.com/post/original-essays/the-ministry-of-truth.

2. "The Ludlow Massacre," *American Experience*, PBS, https://www.pbs.org/wgbh/americanexperience/features/rockefellers-ludlow/, accessed 3 March 2023.

3. Ben Mauk, "The Ludlow Massacre Still Matters," *New Yorker*, April 18, 2014.

4. Austin Harvey, "The Bloody Story of the Ludlow Massacre, When Striking Coal Miners and Their Families Were Killed by the National Guard," All That's Interesting, last updated October 14, 2022, https://allthatsinteresting.com/ludlow-massacre.

5. "The Ludlow Massacre."

6. Seamus Finn, "Strikes, Industrial Unrest: All Put in the Shade by the Infamous Ludlow Massacre," *Irish Independent*, May 7, 2009.

7. Mauk, "The Ludlow Massacre Still Matters."

8. "The Ludlow Massacre."

9. Ray Eldon Hiebert, *Courtier to the Crowd: Ivy Lee and the Development of Public Relations in America*, 2nd ed. (New York: PRMuseum Press, 2017).

10. Ibid.

11. Grady's was hardly the only racist voice Lee was exposed to at an early age. Lee's father, James Lee, once contributed to a book called *Anglo-Saxon Supremacy, or, Race Contributions to Civilization*. Lee rarely commented on race in the United States, though there is little indication he veered from the white supremacist rhetoric of his childhood. For instance, he once referred to Asian immigration to the United States as "an invasion from the Orient." Ibid.

12. Ibid.

13. Ibid.

14. Ibid.

15. Scott M. Cutlip, "Public Relations Was Lobbying from the Start," letter to the editor, *New York Times*, January 18, 1991.

16. Hiebert, *Courtier to the Crowd*.
17. "The First Press Release," NewsMuseum (Lisbon), accessed 3 March 2023.
18. "Business School to Hear Ivy Lee," *Harvard Crimson*, January 29, 1924.
19. Timothy Noah, "Mitt Romney, Crybaby Capitalist," *New Republic*, July 16, 2012.
20. "Rise of the Image Men," *The Economist*, December 16, 2010.
21. Hiebert, *Courtier to the Crowd*.
22. "Rise of the Image Men."
23. Ivy Lee with Burton St. John III, *Mr. Lee's Publicity Book: A Citizen's Guide to Public Relations* (New York: PRMuseum Press, 2017).
24. "Rise of the Image Men."
25. Hiebert, *Courtier to the Crowd*.
26. Ibid.
27. Ibid.
28. Upton Sinclair, *The Brass Check: A Study of American Journalism* (Pasadena, CA: Upton Sinclair, 1920).
29. Sarah Laskow, "Railyards Were Once So Dangerous They Needed Their Own Railway Surgeons," Atlas Obscura, July 25, 2018.
30. Hiebert, *Courtier to the Crowd*.
31. Ibid.
32. Emily Atkin, "Big Oil's First Publicist Advised Nazi Germany," *Heated*, January 21, 2020.
33. Hiebert, *Courtier to the Crowd*.
34. Quoted in Katherine H. Adams, *Progressive Politics and the Training of America's Persuaders* (Mahwah, NJ: Lawrence Erlbaum, 1999), 136.
35. Ken Silverstein, *Turkmeniscam: How Washington Lobbyists Fought to Flack for a Stalinist Dictatorship* (New York: Random House, 2008).
36. "Rise of the Image Men."
37. "Rise of the Image Men."
38. Hiebert, *Courtier to the Crowd*.
39. Atkin, "Big Oil's First Publicist."
40. "'Fake News,' Lies and Propaganda: How to Sort Fact from Fiction," University of Michigan Library Research Guides, last updated August 4, 2022, https://guides.lib.umich.edu/fakenews.
41. "Rise of the Image Men."
42. Quoted in Dick Martin and Donald K. Wright, *Public Relations Ethics: How to Practice PR Without Losing Your Soul* (New York: Business Expert Press, 2016).
43. Hiebert, *Courtier to the Crowd*.
44. Ibid.

3. MASTER OF PUBLICITY

1. Quoted in Doug J. Swanson, *Cult of Glory: The Bold and Brutal History of the Texas Rangers* (New York: Penguin Books, 2021).

2. Ray Eldon Hiebert, *Courtier to the Crowd: Ivy Lee and the Development of Public Relations in America,* 2nd ed. (New York: PRMuseum Press, 2017).

3. Ivy Lee Archive, Seeley Mudd Manuscript Library, Princeton University, Box 4, Folder 6.

4. Ibid.

5. Ibid.

6. Hiebert, *Courtier to the Crowd.*

7. "New Yorker Sees Cuno, Stinnes, and Mussolini," *New York Times,* May 27, 1923; "Foreign News: Ivy Lee a-Visiting," *Time,* June 11, 1923.

8. It's unclear if Lee was familiar with Ernest Hemingway's later meeting with Mussolini, in which the dictator sat "frowning over" a French-English dictionary, trying to pose as an erudite scholar—without realizing the book was upside down. See Dennis Mack Smith, *Mussolini* (New York: Knopf, 1982).

9. Ivy Lee with Burton St. John III, *Mr. Lee's Publicity Book: A Citizen's Guide to Public Relations* (New York: PRMuseum Press, 2017).

10. Lee, *Mr. Lee's Publicity Book.*

11. Ibid.

12. Hiebert, *Courtier to the Crowd.*

13. Ivy Lee Archive, Box 4, Folder 2.

14. Hiebert, *Courtier to the Crowd.*

15. Ivy Lee Archive, Box 4, Folder 1.

16. Hiebert, *Courtier to the Crowd.*

17. Ibid.

18. "Ivy Lee Moved to Aid the Soviet," *New York Times,* March 28, 1926.

19. Ibid.

20. Ibid.

21. Ivy Lee, *Present-Day Russia* (New York: Macmillan, 1928).

22. "Ivy Lee Moved to Aid the Soviet."

23. "Ivy Lee Again Fails to Aid Soviet Cause," *New York Times,* July 26, 1927.

24. Lee, *Present-Day Russia.*

25. Ibid.

26. Ibid.

27. Ibid.

28. Ibid.

29. Ibid.

30. Ibid.

31. Ibid.

32. Ibid.

33. Ibid.

34. Ivy Lee Archive, Box 6, Folder 9.

35. Hiebert, *Courtier to the Crowd.*

36. Frederick L. Schuman, review of *Present-Day Russia,* by Ivy Lee, *American Journal of Sociology* 35, no. 1 (July 1929): 144–145.

37. Hiebert, *Courtier to the Crowd.*

38. Ibid.

39. "Fish Sees Demand for Red Trade Ban," *New York Times,* October 29, 1930.

40. "Tinkham Assails Ivy Lee in House," *New York Times,* February 23, 1929.

41. "Opposes Soviet Goods Ban," *New York Times,* June 16, 1931.

42. Hiebert, *Courtier to the Crowd.*

43. Vagit Alekperov, *Oil of Russia: Past, Present and Future,* trans. Paul B. Gallagher and Thomas D. Hedden (Minneapolis: East View Press, 2011).

44. Hiebert, *Courtier to the Crowd.*

4. BROKEN

1. Frantz Fanon, *The Wretched of the Earth,* trans. Richard Philcox (New York: Grove Press, 2007), 48n1.

2. Antony C. Sutton, *Wall Street and the Rise of Hitler* (1976; repr., Forest Row, UK: Clairview Books, 2010).

3. Ibid.

4. Ibid.

5. Special Committee on Un-American Activities, House of Representatives, "Investigation of Nazi Propaganda Activities and Investigation of Certain Other Propaganda Activities," Hearings No. 73-DC-4, 73rd Cong., 2nd Sess. (June 5–7, 1934).

6. Ibid.

7. Ibid.

8. Ibid.

9. Ray Eldon Hiebert, *Courtier to the Crowd: Ivy Lee and the Development of Public Relations in America,* 2nd ed. (New York: PRMuseum Press, 2017).

10. Special Committee on Un-American Activities, House of Representatives, "Investigation of Nazi Propaganda Activities."

11. Sutton, *Wall Street and the Rise of Hitler.*

12. Special Committee on Un-American Activities, House of Representatives, "Investigation of Nazi Propaganda Activities."

13. Ibid.

14. Ibid.

15. Ivy Lee Archive, Seeley Mudd Manuscript Library, Princeton University, Box 5, Folder 7.

16. Ivy Lee Archive, Box 4, Folder 37.

17. Ibid.

18. Hiebert, *Courtier to the Crowd.*

19. William E. Dodd, *Ambassador Dodd's Diary,* ed. William E. Dodd, Jr., and Martha Dodd (London: Victor Gollancz, 1945).

20. Ibid.

21. Ibid.

22. Ibid.

23. Frank C. Hanighen, "Foreign Political Movements in the United States," *Foreign Affairs,* October 1937.

24. Ibid.
25. Ibid.
26. Tarun Krishnakumar, "Propaganda by Permission: Examining 'Political Activities' Under the Foreign Agents Registration Act," *Journal of Legislation* 47, no. 2 (2021): 49.
27. Special Committee on Un-American Activities, House of Representatives, "Investigation of Nazi Propaganda Activities."
28. Ibid.
29. Ibid.
30. Ibid.
31. Special Committee on Un-American Activities, House of Representatives, "Investigation of Nazi Propaganda Activities."
32. Ibid.
33. Ibid.
34. Ibid.
35. Ibid.
36. Ibid.
37. Ibid.
38. Scott M. Cutlip, *The Unseen Power: Public Relations: A History* (Hillsdale, NJ: Lawrence Erlbaum Associates, 1994), 145.
39. Hiebert, *Courtier to the Crowd.*
40. Ibid.
41. "Ivy Lee, as Adviser to Nazis, Paid $25,000 by Dye Trust," *New York Times,* July 12, 1934.
42. "Races: Father and Son," *Time,* July 23, 1934.
43. Cutlip, *The Unseen Power.*
44. Ivy Lee with Burton St. John III, *Mr. Lee's Publicity Book: A Citizen's Guide to Public Relations* (New York: PRMuseum Press, 2017).
45. "Ivy Lee Home from Reich," *New York Times,* August 31, 1934.
46. Ibid.
47. Ibid.
48. Ibid.
49. "Ivy Lee–Farben Link Recounted at Trial," *New York Times,* October 4, 1947.

PART II: MONSTERS

1. Quoted in Anna Reid, *The Shaman's Coat: A Native History of Siberia* (New York: Walker, 2002), 49.

5. SECRET HANDSHAKE

1. Frederick Merk, with Lois Bannister Merk, *Manifest Destiny and Mission in American History: A Reinterpretation* (1963; reprint, Cambridge, MA: Harvard University Press, 1995), 179.

2. Lionel Zetter, *Lobbying: The Art of Political Persuasion,* 3rd ed. (Petersfield, UK: Harriman House, 2014).

3. Robert C. Byrd, *The Senate, 1789–1989,* vol. 2, *Addresses on the History of the United States Senate,* ed. Wendy Wolff (Washington, DC: U.S. Government Printing Office), 504.

4. Quoted in Cynthia Brown, "The Foreign Agents Registration Act (FARA): A Legal Overview," Congressional Research Service report R45037, December 4, 2017, 2n11.

5. Author interview with Krishnakumar.

6. "Foreign Propaganda," U.S. House of Representatives Report No. 1381, 75th Cong., 1st Sess., 2.

7. Tarun Krishnakumar, "Propaganda by Permission: Examining 'Political Activities' Under the Foreign Agents Registration Act," *Journal of Legislation* 47, no. 2 (2021): 55.

8. The bill was remarkable in many ways, and not only for its requirements. "Despite the ominous times, the drafters of FARA produced a remarkably sophisticated piece of legislation," one analysis found. "For one thing, the statute was free of the heated language that had characterized the Congressional reports and hearings preceding its passage." Ava Marion Plakins, "Heat Not Light: The Foreign Agents Registration Act After Meese v. Keene," *Fordham International Law Journal* 11, no. 1 (1987): 191.

9. Ibid., 191–192.

10. "Bookniga Officers Get Prison Terms," *New York Times,* July 15, 1941.

11. Ibid.

12. "Auhagen Convicted as Propaganda Agent; Gets Two Years for Failure to Register," *New York Times,* July 12, 1941.

13. Plakins, "Heat Not Light," 192n56, 192.

14. Plakins, "Heat Not Light," 192n56.

15. "Suspending Statutes of Limitations During War or Emergency," Hearings Before Subcommittee No. 4 of the Committee on the Judiciary, U.S. House of Representatives, 77th Cong., 1st Sess., November 26, 1941, statement of Adolf A. Berle, Jr., 28.

16. FARA would initially be placed with the DOJ's War Division, before moving to the Internal Security Section of the DOJ's Criminal Division in the 1950s. See Matthew T. Sanderson, "A History of the FARA Unit," Caplin & Drysdale, May 5, 2020, https://www.fara.us/a-history-of-the-fara-unit.

17. Plakins, "Heat Not Light," 194.

18. Foreign Agents Registration Act of 1938, as amended April 29, 1942.

19. Plakins, "Heat Not Light," 194–195.

20. Ibid., 195n73.

21. "Foreign Agents Registration Act Amendments," report no. 143, April 1, 1965, U.S. Senate, 89th Congress, 1st Sess., 2.

22. "Foreign Agents Registration Act Amendments," report no. 143, April 1, 1965, U.S. Senate, 89th Congress, 1st Sess., 4.

23. Ibid.

24. Ibid.

25. Plakins, "Heat Not Light," 195.

26. Krishnakumar, "Propaganda by Permission."

27. Interestingly, the nominal spur for these changes came not from concerns about se-
    cret Cold War–related lobbying but from, of all things, sugar quotas. Sparked by
    a rush to fill U.S. sugar quotas following the Cuban trade embargo, sugar cartels
    began throwing money at American political campaigns. They were, as one anal-
    ysis found, "exceptionally organized" and "contributed significant sums of money
    to political campaigns" across the United States, lobbying American politicians
    and shifting American policy in the process. See Ben Freeman, *The Foreign Policy
    Auction: Foreign Lobbying in America* (n.p.: CreateSpace, 2012).

28. Ibid.

29. Quoted in Brown, "The Foreign Agents Registration Act (FARA)," 5. Some regis-
    trants take such requirements that all materials must be disclosed quite literally,
    including an inundation of emails, notes, and other minutiae in their filings. While
    such filings provide transparency, they effectively drown investigators in details—
    and make the filings largely worthless.

30. Ibid., 9.

31. Ibid., 10.

32. Ken Silverstein, *Turkmeniscam: How Washington Lobbyists Fought to Flack for a
    Stalinist Dictatorship* (New York: Random House, 2008).

33. Comptroller General of the United States, "Effectiveness of the Foreign Agents
    Registration Act of 1938, as Amended, and Its Administration by the Department
    of Justice," report to the Committee on Foreign Relations, U.S. Senate, B-177551,
    March 1974.

34. Ibid.

35. Ibid.

36. Ibid.

37. Ibid.

38. "Improvements Needed in the Administration of Foreign Agent Registration," en-
    closure I in J. K. Fasick to Benjamin Civiletti and Edmund S. Muskie, July 31, 1980,
    https://www.gao.gov/assets/id-80-51.pdf.

39. U.S. General Accounting Office, "Foreign Agent Registration: Justice Needs to
    Improve Program Administration," Report to the Chairman, Subcommittee on
    Oversight of Government Management, Committee on Governmental Affairs,
    U.S. Senate, GAO/NSIAD-90-250, July 1990.

40. Ken Silverstein, "Their Men in Washington: Undercover with D.C.'s Lobbyists for
    Hire," *Harper's*, July 2007.

6. WISE MEN

1. Alan Taylor, *American Republics: A Continental History of the United States, 1783–
   1850* (New York: W. W. Norton, 2021).

2. Franklin Foer, "Paul Manafort, American Hustler," *The Atlantic*, March 2018.

3. Ibid.

4. Paul Manafort, *Political Prisoner: Persecuted, Prosecuted, but Not Silenced* (New York: Skyhorse, 2022).

5. Foer, "Paul Manafort, American Hustler."

6. Ibid.

7. Ibid.

8. Ibid.

9. Ibid.

10. Manafort, *Political Prisoner*.

11. Lee Drutman, "How Corporate Lobbyists Conquered American Democracy," *The Atlantic*, April 20, 2015.

12. Quoted in Lee Drutman, *The Business of America Is Lobbying: How Corporations Became Politicized and Politics Became More Corporate* (New York: Oxford University Press, 2015), 51.

13. Joshua Keating, "Get Used to Foreign Interference in Elections," *Slate*, October 7, 2020.

14. John Adams, "Inaugural Address, 4 March 1797," *Founders Online*, National Archives, https://founders.archives.gov/documents/Adams/99-02-02-1878.

15. Dov H. Levin, *Meddling in the Ballot Box: The Causes and Effects of Partisan Electoral Interventions* (New York: Oxford University Press, 2020).

16. The nearest thing to a foreign interference scandal came during the American Civil War, in which both French and British officials openly toyed with recognizing the Confederacy before deciding against it. See Don H. Doyle, *The Cause of All Nations: An International History of the American Civil War* (New York: Basic Books, 2017).

17. The Nazis didn't use only Ivy Lee to target Americans. As Levin discovered, "In October 1940, the Nazis leaked a captured Polish government document, hoping to expose Franklin Roosevelt as a 'criminal hypocrite' and 'warmonger.' The German embassy in Washington gave a U.S. newspaper a bribe to publish the document." The efforts, of course, went nowhere. See Dov H. Levin, "Sure, the U.S. and Russia Often Meddle in Foreign Elections. Does It Matter?," *Washington Post*, September 7, 2016.

18. Author interview with Dov Levin. Years later, KGB archives revealed that Wallace's preferred candidates for both secretary of state and treasury secretary were Soviet agents themselves. Roosevelt's replacement of Wallace with Truman "deprived Soviet intelligence of what would have been its most spectacular success." See Christopher Andrew and Vasili Mitrokhin, *The Sword and the Shield: The Mitrokhin Archive and the Secret History of the KGB* (New York: Basic Books, 1999).

19. "Text of Wallace Letter to Stalin Calling for Peace Program," *New York Times*, May 12, 1948.

20. Author interview with Dov Levin.

21. Jason Daley, "How Adlai Stevenson Stopped Russian Interference in the 1960 Election," *Smithsonian Magazine*, January 4, 2017.

22. Casey Michel, "Russia's Long and Mostly Unsuccessful History of Election Interference," *Politico Magazine*, October 26, 2019.

23. David Shimer, *Rigged: America, Russia, and One Hundred Years of Covert Electoral Interference* (New York: Vintage Books, 2021), 87.

24. Andrew and Mitrokhin, *The Sword and the Shield*.

25. Alexander Feklisov, *The Man Behind the Rosenbergs* (New York: Enigma Books, 2001).

26. Andrew and Mitrokhin, *The Sword and the Shield*.

27. Anatoly Dobrynin, *In Confidence: Moscow's Ambassador to Six Cold War Presidents* (Seattle: University of Washington Press, 2016).

28. Ibid.

29. Andrew and Mitrokhin, *The Sword and the Shield*.

30. Ibid.

31. Peter Baker, "'We Absolutely Could Not Do That': When Seeking Foreign Help Was Out of the Question," *New York Times*, October 5, 2019.

32. Manafort, *Political Prisoner*.

33. Ibid.

34. Ibid.

35. Ibid.

7. EXCESS IS BEST

1. T. J. Stiles, *Custer's Trials: A Life on the Frontier of a New America* (New York: Knopf, 2016), 310.

2. Paul Manafort, *Political Prisoner: Persecuted, Prosecuted, but Not Silenced* (New York: Skyhorse, 2022).

3. Thomas B. Edsall, "Partners in Political PR Firm Typify Republican New Breed," *Washington Post*, April 7, 1985.

4. Manafort, *Political Prisoner*.

5. Edsall, "Partners in Political PR Firm."

6. Meghan Keneally, "The Man Who Got Top Trump Aide into GOP Politics Recalls the Budding Talent," ABC7 Bay Area, April 26, 2016.

7. To take one example: Baker's negotiation with Nursultan Nazarbayev, dictator of the nuclear-armed and newly independent Kazakhstan, took place in the nude, as the two sweated together in a sauna. See J. A. Baker, *The Politics of Diplomacy* (New York: Putnam, 1995), 538–539.

8. "James Baker and the Art of Power," *The Economist*, September 24, 2020.

9. Franklin Foer, "The Quiet American," *Slate*, April 28, 2016.

10. Franklin, "Paul Manafort, American Hustler," *The Atlantic*, March 2018.

11. Bernard Weinraub, "After Nixon and Reagan, Young Republicans Face '88 with Uncertainty," *New York Times*, July 11, 1987.

12. Foer, "Paul Manafort, American Hustler."

13. Ibid.
14. Ibid.
15. Ibid.
16. Edsall, "Partners in Political PR Firm."
17. Kenneth P. Vogel, "Paul Manafort's Wild and Lucrative Philippine Adventure," *Politico Magazine*, June 10, 2016.
18. Foer, "Paul Manafort, American Hustler."
19. Matt Labash, "Roger Stone, Political Animal," *Weekly Standard*, November 5, 2007.
20. Edsall, "Partners in Political PR Firm."
21. In 1981 Atwater authored one of the most infamous quotes in American electoral history, describing the Republicans' so-called Southern Strategy. As Atwater said, "You start out in 1954 by saying, 'N*gger, n*gger, n*gger.' By 1968 you can't say 'n*gger'—that hurts you, backfires. So you say stuff like, uh, forced busing, states' rights, and all that stuff, and you're getting so abstract. Now, you're talking about cutting taxes, and all these things you're talking about are totally economic things and a byproduct of them is, Blacks get hurt worse than whites. . . . 'We want to cut this,' is much more abstract than even the busing thing, uh, and a hell of a lot more abstract than 'N*gger, n*gger.'" See Rick Perlstein, "Lee Atwater's Infamous 1981 Interview on the Southern Strategy," *The Nation*, November 13, 2012.
22. Edsall, "Partners in Political PR Firm."
23. Vogel, "Paul Manafort's Wild and Lucrative Philippine Adventure."
24. Michael Lewis, "Three Words a Lawyer Should Never Say to Clients," Bloomberg, March 27, 1998.
25. Evan Thomas, "The Slickest Shop in Town," *Time*, March 3, 1986.
26. Steven Mufson and Tom Hamburger, "Inside Trump Adviser Manafort's World of Politics and Global Financial Dealmaking," *Washington Post*, April 26, 2016.
27. Manuel Roig-Franzia, "The Swamp Builders," *Washington Post*, November 29, 2018.
28. Thomas, "The Slickest Shop in Town."
29. Roig-Franzia, "The Swamp Builders."
30. One other element of the "swamp" refined by Manafort and his team: the political action committee. According to both Manafort's memoirs and reportage elsewhere, Manafort's colleagues formed the National Conservative Political Action Committee in the 1970s. Per Manafort, it was "the first real political action committee in the United States." It was also a "precursor to the rise of super PACs," according to *The Washington Post*, helping lay the groundwork for deep-pocketed donors to flood American elections with financing. See Manafort, *Political Prisoner*; Roig-Franzia, "The Swamp Builders."
31. Edsall, "Partners in Political PR Firm."
32. Roig-Franzia, "The Swamp Builders."
33. Foer, "Paul Manafort, American Hustler."
34. Katy Daigle, "Trump Criticizes Pequots, Casino," *Hartford Courant*, October 6, 1993.
35. Shawn Boburg, "Donald Trump's Long History of Clashes with Native Americans," *Washington Post*, July 25, 2016.

36. Joseph Tanfani, "Trump Was Once So Involved in Trying to Block Indian Casino That He Secretly Approved Attack Ads," *Los Angeles Times,* June 30, 2016.

37. Marie Brenner, "How Donald Trump and Roy Cohn's Ruthless Symbiosis Changed America," *Vanity Fair,* August 2017.

38. Foer, "Paul Manafort, American Hustler."

39. Alexander Burns and Maggie Haberman, "Mystery Man: Ukraine's US Fixer," *Politico,* March 5, 2014.

8. SHAME IS FOR SISSIES

1. David R. Gayton, "A Letter by Walt Whitman: 'The Spanish Element in Our Nationality,'" *Comparative Literature Undergraduate Journal* (University of California, Berkeley), Fall 2022.

2. *Spy,* February 1992.

3. "Who's the Sleaziest of Them All?," *Spy,* February 1992, 55.

4. Ibid.

5. Filings can be found in the FARA database, available at FARA.gov.

6. Bill Berkeley, "Zaire: An African Horror Story," *The Atlantic,* August 1993.

7. Art Levine, "Publicists of the Damned," *Spy,* February 1992, 55.

8. K. Riva Levinson, "I Worked for Paul Manafort. He Always Lacked a Moral Compass," *Washington Post,* November 1, 2017.

9. Cristina Maza, "Here's Where Paul Manafort Did Business with Corrupt Dictators," *Newsweek,* August 7, 2018.

10. Don Van Natta, Jr., and Douglas Frantz, "Lobbyists Are Friends and Foes to McCain," *New York Times,* February 10, 2000.

11. Tom McCarthy, "Paul Manafort: How Decades of Serving Dictators Led to Role as Trump's Go-To Guy," *The Guardian,* October 30, 2017.

12. Levine, "Publicists of the Damned," 62.

13. Kenneth P. Vogel, "Paul Manafort's Wild and Lucrative Philippine Adventure," *Politico Magazine,* June 10, 2016.

14. Ibid.

15. Ibid.

16. Evan Thomas, "The Slickest Shop in Town," *Time,* March 3, 1986.

17. Mark Fineman and Doyle McManus, "Vote Fraud on Grand Scale Reflected in Manila Area," *Los Angeles Times,* February 16, 1986.

18. Ibid.

19. Vogel, "Paul Manafort's Wild and Lucrative Philippine Adventure."

20. Fineman and McManus, "Vote Fraud."

21. Vogel, "Paul Manafort's Wild and Lucrative Philippine Adventure."

22. J. C. Sharman, *The Despot's Guide to Wealth Management: On the International Campaign Against Grand Corruption* (Ithaca, NY: Cornell University Press, 2017).

23. Pamela Brogan, "The Torturers' Lobby: How Human Rights–Abusing Nations Are Represented in Washington," Center for Public Integrity, Washington, DC,

1992, https://cloudfront-files-1.publicintegrity.org/legacy_projects/pdf_reports/THETORTURERSLOBBY.pdf.
24. Ibid.
25. Ibid.
26. Levine, "Publicists of the Damned."
27. Ibid., 58.
28. Racial realities were an underlying theme of the growing foreign lobbying industry; as one photo caption in the *Spy* investigation, featuring all of the lobbyists and their despotic clients, read, "Rich white lobbyists and the despots who love them." Ibid.
29. Ibid., 59.
30. Ken Silverstein, *Turkmeniscam: How Washington Lobbyists Fought to Flack for a Stalinist Dictatorship* (New York: Random House, 2008), 10.
31. Art Levine, "Shame Is for Sissies," *Mother Jones*, September–October 2005.
32. Adam Bernstein, "Tyrants' Lobbyist, Flamboyant to the End," NBC News, May 2, 2005.
33. Richard Leiby, "Fall of the House of von Kloberg," *Washington Post*, July 31, 2005.
34. Levine, "Publicists of the Damned," 57.
35. Ibid.
36. Levine, "Shame Is for Sissies."
37. "WWYD 2/2," YouTube, posted by UnkownNickelodeon, April 29, 2011, https://youtu.be/-CsOyAzdURM.

PART III: REVOLUTIONS

1. Leo Perutz, *The Marquis of Bolibar,* translated by John Brownjohn (New York: Arcade, 1989).

9. SAFE FOR DICTATORSHIP

1. Quoted in Elizabeth A. Fenn, *Pox Americana: The Great Smallpox Epidemic of 1775–82* (New York: Farrar, Straus and Giroux, 2002).
2. Matthew T. Sanderson, "A History of the FARA Unit," Caplin & Drysdale, May 5, 2020, https://www.fara.us/a-history-of-the-fara-unit.
3. Craig Holman, "Origins, Evolution and Structure of the Lobbying Disclosure Act," Public Citizen, May 11, 2006.
4. Tarun Krishnakumar, "Propaganda by Permission: Examining 'Political Activities' Under the Foreign Agents Registration Act," *Journal of Legislation* 47, no. 2 (2021): 44–74.
5. Cynthia Brown, "The Foreign Agents Registration Act (FARA): A Legal Overview," Congressional Research Service report R45037, December 4, 2017.
6. Lydia Dennett, "Closing the Loophole on Foreign Influence," Project on Government Oversight, April 13, 2018.
7. Office of the Inspector General, U.S. Department of Justice, "Audit of the National

Security Division's Enforcement and Administration of the Foreign Agents Registration Act," Audit Division 16–24, September 2016.

8. Alexander Dukalskis, *Making the World Safe for Dictatorship* (New York: Oxford
University Press, 2021).

9. Ibid.

10. Ibid.

11. Ibid.

12. Ibid.

13. Ibid.

14. "Hotel Rwanda Hero Paul Rusesabagina Convicted on Terror Charges," BBC
News, September 20, 2021.

15. Adele Del Sordi and Emanuela Dalmasso, "The Relation Between External and
Internal Authoritarian Legitimation: The Religious Foreign Policy of Morocco
and Kazakhstan," *Taiwan Journal of Democracy* 14, no. 1 (2018): 95–116.

16. Dukalskis, *Making the World Safe for Dictatorship*.

17. Ibid.

18. Ben Freeman, *The Foreign Policy Auction: Foreign Lobbying in America* (n.p.: CreateSpace, 2012).

19. Ibid.

20. Ibid.

21. Ibid.

22. Ibid.

23. Ibid.

24. Ibid.

25. Ibid.

26. According to DLA Piper, describing the Turkish massacre of the Armenians as
genocide—one of the first of the twentieth century, in which Turkish forces killed
approximately 1.5 million Armenian men, women, and children—is "a matter
of genuine historic dispute." But most Western nations regard it as genocide. See
Thomas de Waal, "What Next After the U.S. Recognition of the Armenian Genocide?," Carnegie Europe, April 30, 2021.

27. Freeman, *The Foreign Policy Auction*.

28. Ibid.

29. Erik Wemple, "Former Congressman and Azerbaijan Advocate Finds Receptive
Audience at Daily Caller," *Washington Post*, April 3, 2015.

30. Freeman, *The Foreign Policy Auction*.

31. Ken Silverstein, *Turkmeniscam: How Washington Lobbyists Fought to Flack for a
Stalinist Dictatorship* (New York: Random House, 2008).

32. Ibid.

33. Ibid.

34. "APCO Wins Agency of the Year at 2006 PRWeek Awards," *PRWeek*, March 3,
2006.

35. Silverstein, *Turkmeniscam*.

36. Ibid.

37. Ken Silverstein, "Alexander Haig's Last Years," *Mother Jones,* September–October 1999.
38. Silverstein, *Turkmeniscam.*
39. Ibid.
40. Ibid.

10. UKRAINIAN COCKTAILS

1. Aodogán O'Rahilly, *The O'Rahilly: A Secret History of the Rebellion of 1916* (Gill, Ireland: Lilliput, 2016).
2. Polina Devitt, Anastasia Lyrchikova, and Katya Golubkova, "Biting the Bullet, Not the Dust: Deripaska Gives Up His Aluminum Empire," Reuters, December 20, 2018.
3. Rosalind S. Helderman and Alice Crites, "The Russian Billionaire Next Door: Putin Ally Is Tied to One of D.C.'s Swankiest Mansions," *Washington Post,* November 29, 2017.
4. "Treasury Designates Russian Oligarchs, Officials, and Entities in Response to Worldwide Malign Activity," press release, U.S. Department of the Treasury, April 6, 2018. To date, Deripaska has not been indicted for bribery, though he has been indicted for sanction evasion and obstruction of justice. Deripaska has denied these allegations.
5. John S. Gardner, "Bob Dole: Soldier, Politician and Republican of the Old School," *The Guardian,* December 5, 2021.
6. Katharine Q. Seelye, "Bob Dole, Old Soldier and Stalwart of the Senate, Dies at 98," *New York Times,* December 5, 2021.
7. "Reaction to Bob Dole's Death from US Dignitaries, Veterans," Associated Press, December 5, 2021.
8. Dole's foreign lobbying filings can be found on FARA's digital database, such as https://efile.fara.gov/docs/5549-Exhibit-AB-20030401-HDWQXY01.pdf.
9. Carrie Levine, "Bob Dole, Trump Campaign Aide to Lobby for Congolese Government," Center for Public Integrity, Washington, DC, May 11, 2017.
10. Glenn R. Simpson and Mary Jacoby, "How Lobbyists Help Ex-Soviets Woo Washington," *Wall Street Journal,* April 17, 2007.
11. "Grave Secrecy: How a Dead Man Can Own a UK Company and Other Hair-Raising Stories About Hidden Company Ownership from Kyrgyzstan and Beyond," Global Witness, London, June 2012.
12. Author interview.
13. Levine, "Bob Dole, Trump Campaign Aide to Lobby."
14. Azure Hall, "Bob Dole's Net Worth at the Time of His Death Might Surprise You," The List, December 5, 2021.
15. Joseph J. Schatz and Benjamin Oreskes, "Want to Be a 'Foreign Agent'? Serve in Congress First," *Politico,* October 2, 2016.
16. Lee Fang, "John Boehner Cashes Out, Joins Corporate Lobbying Firm That Represents China," The Intercept, September 20, 2016.

17. Anna Massoglia and Karl Evers-Hillstrom, "Joe Lieberman Formally Registers as Lobbyist for Chinese Telecom Giant ZTE," Open Secrets, January 2, 2019.

18. Schatz and Oreskes, "Want to Be a 'Foreign Agent'?"

19. Michael Kelly, "Breaking Convention," New Yorker, August 4, 1996.

20. "Press Release—Transcript of Press Conference by Paul Manafort, Dole Convention Manager," July 31, 1996, American Presidency Project, University of California, Santa Barbara.

21. One other foreign, but not necessarily foreign lobbying, scandal that Manafort was involved in by the turn of the century involved a Lebanese national named Abdul Rahman el-Assir. Acting as a global arms broker, el-Assir enlisted Manafort's help on a range of topics, including a financial deal involving a Portuguese bank and an American biometrics company that ended up imploding the bank. El-Assir and Manafort were later accused of taking part in a kickback scheme involving French officials shipping submarines to Pakistan, and then redirecting income from the sales to a French political campaign. It was, as one analyst said, "one of France's biggest political scandals." Manafort allegedly made at least $200,000 from the deal. See Joshua Keating, "Paul Manafort Was Also Involved in One of France's Biggest Political Scandals," Slate, October 31, 2017.

22. Karen Yuan, "A Timeline of Paul Manafort's Career," The Atlantic, February 6, 2018.

23. Paul Manafort, Political Prisoner: Persecuted, Prosecuted, but Not Silenced (New York: Skyhorse, 2022).

24. "Report of the Select Committee on Intelligence, United States Senate, on Russian Active Measures Campaigns and Interference in the 2016 U.S. Election, Volume 5: Counterintelligence Threats and Vulnerabilities," 116th Cong., 1st Sess., Report 116-XXX.

25. Ibid.

26. Seth Hettena, Trump/Russia: A Definitive History (Brooklyn, NY: Melville House, 2018), 148.

27. "Report of the Select Committee on Intelligence."

28. Jim Rutenberg, "The Untold Story of 'Russiagate' and the Road to War in Ukraine," New York Times, November 2, 2022.

29. Associated Press, "Before Trump Job, Manafort Worked to Aid Putin," Florida Times-Union, March 22, 2017.

30. Alayna Treene, "Manafort Memo: 'Can Greatly Benefit the Putin Government,'" Axios, March 22, 2017.

31. Casey Michel, "Ukraine's Corrupt Oligarchs Are Looking Toward the West to Rehab Their Reputations," New Republic, May 12, 2022.

32. Tom Winter, "DOJ: Ex-Manafort Associate Firtash Is Top-Tier Comrade of Russian Mobsters," NBC News, July 26, 2017.

33. Michel, "Ukraine's Corrupt Oligarchs."

34. "How a Putin Ally Is Aiding Giuliani in Ukraine," editorial, Washington Post, December 22, 2019.

35. Laura Kusisto, "Unmasking Three Mismatched Heavies Who Won and Lost the Drake," Observer, June 7, 2011.

36. Robert Waldeck, *The Black Ledger: How Trump Brought Putin's Disinformation War to America* (New York: Cobra y Craneo, 2020).

37. The entire lawsuit can be found here: *Yulia Tymoshenko et al. v. Dmytro Firtash et al.*, U.S. District Court for the Southern District of New York, Civ. No. 11-02794 (RJS), 2011, https://freebeacon.com/wp-content/uploads/2016/03/manafort-complaint-2.pdf.

38. Casey Michel, *American Kleptocracy: How the U.S. Created the World's Greatest Money Laundering Scheme in History* (New York: St. Martin's, 2021).

39. Tom Winter and Ken Dilanian, "Donald Trump Aide Paul Manafort Scrutinized for Russian Business Ties," NBC News, August 18, 2016.

40. Ken Silverstein and Adam Weinstein, "How Trump Aide Paul Manafort Got Ridiculously Wealthy While Aiding a Ukrainian Strongman," Fusion, August 17, 2016, https://web.archive.org/web/20160820050122/http://fusion.net/story/337482/trump-manafort-ukraine-mansions-movies-mobsters/.

41. Waldeck, *The Black Ledger*.

42. Clifford J. Levy, "U.S. Political Strategists Help Shape Ukraine Parliamentary Campaign," *New York Times,* September 28, 2007.

43. Alexander Burns and Maggie Haberman, "Mystery Man: Ukraine's US Fixer," *Politico,* March 5, 2014.

44. Manafort, *Political Prisoner.*

45. Ibid.

46. Adam Weinstein, "Trump Aide Connected to 2006 Attack on US Marines in Ukraine," Task & Purpose, December 23, 2020.

47. Adam Weinstein and Ken Silverstein, "Trump Aide Manafort Implicated in Pro-Russian Protests Against US Troops," Fusion, August 18, 2016, https://web.archive.org/web/20160821164541/http://fusion.net/story/338016/trump-manafort-marines-nato-protests/.

48. Weinstein, "Trump Aide Connected to 2006 Attack."

49. Ibid.

50. Weinstein and Silverstein, "Trump Aide Manafort Implicated."

51. "Ukraine: Opposition Creates Tempest over 'Sea Breeze' in Crimea," June 6, 2006, WikiLeaks, https://wikileaks.org/plusd/cables/06KIEV2190_a.html.

52. Casey Michel, "The Crime of the Century," *New Republic,* March 4, 2015.

53. "Ukraine: Opposition Creates Tempest over 'Sea Breeze' in Crimea."

54. Maxim Tucker, "Trump Campaign Chief Linked to Secret Kiev Cash Payments," *Times* (London), August 17, 2016.

55. Weinstein and Silverstein, "Trump Aide Manafort Implicated."

56. Waldeck, *The Black Ledger.*

57. Barry Meier, "Lawmakers Seek to Close Foreign Lobbyist Loopholes," *New York Times,* June 12, 2008.

58. Silverstein and Weinstein, "How Trump Aide Paul Manafort Got Ridiculously Wealthy."

59. Ibid.

60. Ibid.

61. Kenzi Abou-Sabe, Tom Winter, and Max Tucker, "What Did Ex-Trump Aide Paul Manafort Really Do in Ukraine?," NBC News, June 27, 2017.
62. Meier, "Lawmakers Seek to Close Foreign Lobbyist Loopholes."
63. Burns and Haberman, "Mystery Man."

11. BLOOD MONEY

1. Joshua L. Reid, *The Sea Is My Country: The Maritime World of the Makahs* (New Haven, CT: Yale University Press, 2015).
2. Yanukovych's zoo would not be Manafort's only brush with an ostrich. As investigators later discovered, Manafort owned an ostrich-skin jacket worth $15,000, as well as a separate ostrich-skin vest worth $9,500. He further owned a python-skin jacket worth $18,500. See Ashley Hoffman, "The Internet Can't Stop Plucking at Paul Manafort's $15,000 Ostrich Jacket," *Time*, August 3, 2018.
3. Darmon Richter, "Occupy Mezhyhirya: Squatting the Mansion of Ukraine's Ex-President," Ex Utopia, July 29, 2020.
4. Julia Ioffe, "Of Course the Ousted President of Ukraine Commissioned a Nude Portrait of Himself," *New Republic*, April 30, 2014.
5. "Monument to Corruption: Ukraine's Most-Wanted Man Built $75M Home on a $25G Salary," Fox News, December 5, 2015.
6. Franklin Foer, "Paul Manafort, American Hustler," *The Atlantic*, March 2018.
7. Michael Kranish and Tom Hamburger, "Paul Manafort's 'Lavish Lifestyle' Highlighted in Indictment," *Washington Post*, October 30, 2017.
8. Shortly thereafter, I sat with a friend in a Marquis de Sade–themed café in the western Ukrainian city of Lviv. On the televisions—which were draped by lace stockings, high heels, and whips—played Tymoshenko's prosecution and perp walk on loop. It remains one of the strangest, most surreal meals of my life.
9. It didn't hurt that, around the same time, U.S. attorneys also become key tools in transnational money-laundering networks, providing attorney-client privilege for kleptocratic clients looking to inject their wealth into the American economy. See Alexander Cooley and Casey Michel, "U.S. Lawyers Are Foreign Kleptocrats' Best Friends," *Foreign Policy*, March 23, 2021. As elsewhere, all lobbying-related filings are located in the FARA digital database, such as Baker McKenzie's filing to lobby on behalf of the regime in the Democratic Republic of Congo: https://efile.fara.gov/docs/6821-Exhibit-AB-20200508-1.pdf.
10. Casey Michel and Ricardo Soares de Oliveira, "The Dictator-Run Bank That Tells the Story of America's Foreign Corruption," *Foreign Policy*, July 7, 2020.
11. All filings regarding Skadden's work in Ukraine are located in the FARA digital database, including https://efile.fara.gov/docs/6617-Exhibit-AB-20190118-1.pdf.
12. Sharon LaFraniere, "Trial of High-Powered Lawyer Gregory Craig Exposes Seamy Side of Washington's Elite," *New York Times*, August 26, 2019.
13. Craig initially connected with Manafort because of another bipartisan link. Doug Schoen, a leading Democratic pollster, had offered to help Manafort in Ukraine—and personally recruited Craig to Yanukovych's cause. See ibid.

NOTES 321

NOTES

14. FARA filing regarding Skadden's work in Ukraine: https://efile.fara.gov/docs/6617
-Exhibit-AB-20190118-1.pdf.
15. Greg Farrell and Christian Berthelsen, "Skadden Settlement for Manafort Work
Suggests Ex-Partner's Peril," Bloomberg, January 17, 2019.
16. U.S. Department of Justice, "Prominent Global Law Firm Agrees to Register as an
Agent of a Foreign Principal," press release, January 17, 2019. For the most detailed
examination of Skadden's work for Yanukovych, see the Skadden settlement agreement, January 15, 2019, at https://www.justice.gov/opa/press-release/file/1124381
/download.
17. The entire Skadden report on the Tymoshenko trial can be found at https://s3
.documentcloud.org/documents/538591/tymoshenko.pdf.
18. *U.S. v. Gregory B. Craig*, Grand Jury Indictment, April 11, 2019, www.justice.gov
/usao-dc/press-release/file/1153646/download.
19. *U.S. v. Gregory B. Craig*, Memorandum Opinion and Order, U.S. District Court for
the District of Columbia, Crim. Action No. 19-0125 (ABJ), August 6, 2019, https:
//www.politico.com/f/?id=0000016c-686c-da83-a96c-fafd98ff0000.
20. Skadden's intimate relationship with Manafort didn't end just in Ukraine; around
the same time, Skadden hired Manafort's daughter, placing her in the "same bureau
housing the attorneys who had produced the Tymoshenko report." See Ken Silverstein and Adam Weinstein, "How Trump Aide Paul Manafort Got Ridiculously
Wealthy While Aiding a Ukrainian Strongman," Fusion, August 17, 2016, https:
//web.archive.org/web/20160820050122/http://fusion.net/story/337482/trump
-manafort-ukraine-mansions-movies-mobsters/. Craig initially helped Manafort's
daughter land interviews, and said he was "pissed" when she was initially turned
down. See LaFraniere, "Trial of High-Powered Lawyer Gregory Craig."
21. Skadden settlement agreement, January 15, 2019, https://www.justice.gov/opa
/press-release/file/1124381/download.
22. *U.S. v. Gregory B. Craig*, Notice of Intent to File Motion In Limine to Exclude
Hearsay Testimony from Richard Gates and Jonathan Hawker, U.S. District Court
for the District of Columbia, Case No. 1:19-cr-0125 (ABJ), June 24, 2019, https:
//storage.courtlistener.com/recap/gov.uscourts.dcd.206162/gov.uscourts.dcd
.206162.45.0.pdf.
23. Ibid.
24. Ibid. A separate filing said that Craig did not find Sanger at home, and instead
"left the document behind Sanger's storm door." Josh Gerstein, "Mueller Fallout
Continues as Greg Craig Trial Opens," Politico, August 12, 2019.
25. David M. Herszenhorn and David E. Sanger, "Failings Found in Trial of Ukrainian
Ex-Premier," *New York Times*, December 12, 2012.
26. Gerstein, "Mueller Fallout Continues."
27. Robert Waldeck, *The Black Ledger: How Trump Brought Putin's Disinformation
War to America* (New York: Cobra y Craneo, 2020).
28. Another company that worked on Yanukovych's behalf was the behemoth American consulting company McKinsey. The organization didn't work for Manafort,
but instead served in parallel to Manafort's efforts, helping "polish [Yanukovych's]

battered image" and working toward "resurrecting Mr. Yanukovych's career." Like Manafort, McKinsey connected with Yanukovych via oligarch Rinat Akhmetov. Yanukovych's government was but one of a series of loathsome regimes that McKinsey worked closely with, from China to Saudi Arabia. McKinsey has never disclosed how much money it made from its arrangement with Yanukovych. See Walt Bogdanich and Michael Forsythe, "How McKinsey Has Helped Raise the Stature of Authoritarian Governments," *New York Times,* December 15, 2018.

29. Pinchuk's American lobbyist? The aforementioned Schoen, who had worked as Bill Clinton's political consultant before joining Pinchuk—and, later, Manafort. See Kevin Bogardus, "Ukrainian Billionaire Hires Clinton Pollster," *The Hill,* October 29, 2011.

30. Amy Chozick and Steve Eder, "Foundation Ties Bedevil Hillary Clinton's Presidential Campaign," *New York Times,* August 20, 2016.

31. Maximilian Hess, "Wooing the West: Who Is Ukraine's Viktor Pinchuk?," Eurasianet, February 26, 2020.

32. Katya Soldak, "Ukraine's Victor Pinchuk: The Oligarch in the Middle of the Crisis," *Forbes,* March 3, 2014.

33. LaFraniere, "Trial of High-Powered Lawyer Gregory Craig."

34. "Skadden Stink," editorial, *Kyiv Post,* September 13, 2019.

35. Josh Gerstein, "Democratic Pollster Divulges Details to Jurors About Greg Craig's Ukraine Work," *Politico,* August 16, 2019.

36. Skadden registration statement, January 18, 2019, https://efile.fara.gov/docs/6617 -Registration-Statement-20190118-1.pdf.

37. LaFraniere, "Trial of High-Powered Lawyer Gregory Craig."

38. The entire financing for Skadden's operations in Ukraine was rife with odd, alarming behavior. As *The New York Times* reported: "Publicly, Ukraine's financially strapped government said [Skadden] would be paid only the legal limit for outside contracts of $12,000. In an August 2012 editorial with the headline, 'Skadden Stink,' *The Kyiv Post* called that assertion 'ridiculous,' noting that would cover only about 12 hours of Mr. Craig's services alone at his standard rate. Ms. Tymoshenko's lawyer refused to cooperate with the project unless Skadden disclosed more information. Scrambling, Mr. Craig and Mr. Manafort agreed to raise the 'official' fee to $1.25 million. Bypassing his own firm's billing system, Mr. Craig submitted a new invoice for that amount, although the firm had already collected more than three times that sum from Mr. Pinchuk, routed through offshore bank accounts controlled by Mr. Manafort. At Mr. Manafort's request, Mr. Craig backdated the document to before the newspaper editorial was published." See LaFraniere, "Trial of High-Powered Lawyer Gregory Craig."

39. Skadden settlement agreement, https://www.justice.gov/opa/press-release/file /1124381/download.

40. Foer, "Paul Manafort, American Hustler."

41. Kenneth P. Vogel, David Stern, and Josh Meyer, "Manafort's Ukrainian 'Blood Money' Caused Qualms, Hack Suggests," *Politico,* February 28, 2017.

42. As the *Los Angeles Review of Books* noted, the texts revealed that Manafort was a "sexual abuser" who engaged in "over a decade of coercive and manipulative sexual behavior" regarding his wife. See Maya Gurantz, "Kompromat: Or, Revelations from the Unpublished Portions of Andrea Manafort's Hacked Texts," *Los Angeles Review of Books,* February 18, 2019.

43. Punctuation has been added to make the text messages read more smoothly. The unedited versions of the text messages can be found at https://bit.ly /ManafortDaughterTexts.

12. NOT FOR PROFIT

1. Marlon James, *A Brief History of Seven Killings* (New York: Riverhead Books, 2015).

2. "A Brief History of Nonprofit Organizations (And What We Can Learn)," Nonprofit Hub, n.d., https://nonprofithub.org/a-brief-history-of-nonprofit-organizations/, accessed 3 March 2023.

3. Juliana Kaplan, "Inequality Flamethrower Anand Giridharadas on Why Billionaires Shouldn't Exist and His Hopes for the Biden Administration," Business Insider, December 8, 2020.

4. "President Bill Clinton and Chelsea Clinton Release 2017 Impact Report on the Work of the Clinton Foundation," Clinton Foundation, New York, May 24, 2018.

5. "Clinton Foundation Impact Report 2021," Clinton Foundation, New York.

6. The Clinton Foundation tax documents are found on the IRS's Tax Exempt Organizations Search database, at https://apps.irs.gov/app/eos/details/. For a more legible look at Clinton Foundation finances, see "Bill Hillary & Chelsea Clinton Foundation," Nonprofit Explorer, ProPublica, https://projects.propublica.org /nonprofits/organizations/311580204, accessed 3 March 2023.

7. "Bill Hillary & Chelsea Clinton Foundation."

8. David Hilzenrath, "How Foreign Influence Can Corrupt a President. Legally," Project on Government Oversight, June 7, 2021.

9. Sarah Chayes, *On Corruption in America: And What Is at Stake* (New York: Vintage Books, 2020), 15.

10. "Clinton Foundation Donors," *Wall Street Journal,* December 18, 2008.

11. "A Vast Network for Donors," *Washington Post,* March 18, 2015.

12. United States Attorney's Office, Central District of California, "Lebanese-Nigerian Billionaire and Two Associates Resolve Federal Probe into Alleged Violations of Campaign Finance Laws," press release, March 31, 2021.

13. Rosalind S. Helderman and Tom Hamburger, "Foreign Governments Gave Millions to Foundation While Clinton Was at State Department," *Washington Post,* February 25, 2015.

14. "Donors Tied to Foreign Governments Gave Millions to Clinton Foundation," Philanthropy News Digest, March 23, 2015.

15. Jack Greenberg, "Ethics Experts Alarmed by 93% Decrease in Clinton Foundation Donations Since $250 Million Peak in 2009," Daily Caller, December 5, 2021.

16. Chayes, On Corruption in America.

17. Michael Weiss, "The Corleones of the Caspian," Foreign Policy, June 10, 2014.

18. Accepting funds from a foreign dictatorship to whitewash the regime remains something of a red line for most journalists. However, around this time a number of pro-Azerbaijan lobbyists had begun writing their own op-eds for a series of American media outlets, including The Hill and Roll Call, which never bothered to disclose that the authors were being paid by Azerbaijan's dictatorship—and which were never included in any FARA filings. See Casey Michel, "All the Shills Money Can Buy: How Kazakhstan and Azerbaijan Use Useful Idiots, Crooked Academics, and Law-Breaking Lobbyists to Whitewash Their Police States," MA thesis, Harriman Institute, Columbia University, 2015.

19. Larry Luxner, "Azerbaijan Rolls Out Red Carpet for Visiting U.S. Lawmakers," Washington Diplomat, July 2013.

20. "Ilham Aliyev: 2012 Person of the Year in Organized Crime and Corruption," Organized Crime and Corruption Reporting Project.

21. Will Fitzgibbon, Miranda Patrucić, and Marcos Garcia Rey, "How Family That Runs Azerbaijan Built an Empire of Hidden Wealth," International Consortium of Investigative Journalists, April 4, 2016.

22. Anastasia Tkach, "The Real Scandal of Congressional Junkets to Azerbaijan," Freedom House, May 26, 2015.

23. Casey Michel, "Azerbaijani Kleptocrats Have Been Getting Their Money's Worth in Washington for a Long Time," New Republic, January 26, 2022.

24. Office of Congressional Ethics, U.S. House of Representatives, "Report: Review No. 15-5316," April 22, 2015.

25. Ibid. See also Committee on Ethics, U.S. House of Representatives, "In the Matter of Officially-Connected Travel by House Members to Azerbaijan in 2013," July 31, 2015.

26. In the Matter of Officially-Connected Travel by House Members to Azerbaijan in 2013: Report of the Committee on Ethics, House Report 114-239 (Washington, DC: U.S. Government Publishing Office, 2015).

27. Ibid.

28. Author interview with Meredith McGehee.

29. Casey Michel, "US/Azerbaijan: Lobbyists Continue to Flout Travel Rules," Organized Crime and Corruption Reporting Project, April 24, 2016.

30. Amanda Becker, "Africa Trip Blurs Lines on Travel Propriety," Roll Call, October 18, 2011, https://web.archive.org/web/20170422025553/https://rollcall.com/issues/57_44/Africa-Trip-Blurs-Lines-On-Travel-Propriety-209590-1.html?pg=1&dczone=influence.

31. Eric Lipton and Eric Lichtblau, "Rules for Congress Curb but Don't End Junkets," New York Times, December 6, 2009.

32. Author interview with Jack Abramoff.

33. John Bresnahan, "House Ethics Panel Clears Lawmakers over 2013 Azerbaijan Trip," *Politico,* July 31, 2015.

34. Russ Choma, "Lawmakers Who Traveled to Azerbaijan Urged Action Benefiting State Oil Company That Funded Trip," Open Secrets, May 26, 2015.

35. Casey Michel, "The Man Behind One of the Most Controversial Congressional Trips This Decade Finally Pleads Guilty," ThinkProgress, December 14, 2018.

36. Author interview.

37. Michel, "US/Azerbaijan."

38. Ibid.

39. Author interview.

40. Michel, "US/Azerbaijan."

41. Committee on Ethics, U.S. House of Representatives, "In the Matter of Officially-Connected Travel by House Members to Azerbaijan in 2013," July 31, 2015.

42. U.S. Department of Justice, "Former Non-Profit President Pleads Guilty to Scheme to Conceal Foreign Funding of 2013 Congressional Trip," press release, December 10, 2018.

43. Paul Singer and Paulina Firozi, "Turkish Faith Movement Secretly Funded 200 Trips for Lawmakers and Staff," *USA Today,* October 29, 2015.

44. Author interview.

45. Singer and Firozi, "Turkish Faith Movement Secretly Funded."

46. Alexander Burns and Maggie Haberman, "Mystery Man: Ukraine's US Fixer," *Politico,* March 5, 2014.

47. Rob Crilly, "Can Trump's New Campaign Manager Do for The Donald What He Did for African Tyrants and a Ukrainian Kleptocrat?," *The Telegraph,* April 23, 2016.

48. Paul Manafort, *Political Prisoner: Persecuted, Prosecuted, but Not Silenced* (New York: Skyhorse, 2022).

49. David Voreacos and Chris Dolmetsch, "Manafort Sued by Russian Billionaire Deripaska over TV Deal," Bloomberg, January 10, 2018.

50. The unedited versions of the text messages can be found at https://bit.ly /ManafortDaughterTexts.

51. Franklin Foer, "Paul Manafort, American Hustler," *The Atlantic,* March 2018.

52. The unedited versions of the text messages can be found at https://bit.ly /ManafortDaughterTexts.

PART IV: INSURRECTIONS

1. Gregory P. Downs, *After Appomattox: Military Occupation and the Ends of War* (Cambridge, MA: Harvard University Press, 2015).

13. POT OF GOLD

1. "Will: Disharmony Is Our Creed," *Sarasota Herald-Tribune,* January 23, 2011.

2. Kristen Holmes, "Trump Calls for the Termination of the Constitution in Truth Social Post," CNN, December 4, 2022.

3. Ben Freeman and Lydia Dennett, "Loopholes, Filing Failures, and Lax Enforcement: How the Foreign Agents Registration Act Falls Short," Project on Government Oversight, Washington, DC, December 16, 2014.

4. Ibid.

5. "Sunlight Foundation Recommendations to the Dept. of Justice Regarding the Foreign Agents Registration Act," Sunlight Foundation, Washington, DC, April 8, 2014.

6. Freeman and Dennett, "Loopholes, Filing Failures, and Lax Enforcement."

7. Office of the Inspector General, U.S. Department of Justice, "Audit of the National Security Division's Enforcement and Administration of the Foreign Agents Registration Act," Audit Division 16–24, September 2016.

8. FARA's digital database can be found at https://efile.fara.gov/ords/fara/f?p =1381:1:32995461174955

9. Ibid.

10. Freeman and Dennett, "Loopholes, Filing Failures, and Lax Enforcement."

11. Ken Dilanian, Tom Winter, and Kenzi Abou-Sabe, "Ex-Trump Aide Manafort Bought New York Homes with Cash," NBC News, March 28, 2017.

12. Paul Manafort, *Political Prisoner: Persecuted, Prosecuted, but Not Silenced* (New York: Skyhorse, 2022).

13. Casey Michel, *American Kleptocracy: How the U.S. Created the World's Greatest Money Laundering Scheme in History* (New York: St. Martin's, 2021).

14. Ben Jacobs, "Leader of Pro-Trump Super PAC Had Mortgage on Paul Manafort Property," *The Guardian*, November 1, 2017.

15. "Report of the Select Committee on Intelligence, United States Senate, on Russian Active Measures Campaigns and Interference in the 2016 U.S. Election, Volume 5: Counterintelligence Threats and Vulnerabilities," 116th Cong., 1st Sess., Report 116-XXX.

16. Manafort, *Political Prisoner*.

17. Ibid.

18. Glenn Thrush, "To Charm Trump, Manafort Sold Himself as an Affordable Outsider," *New York Times*, April 8, 2017.

19. Manafort, *Political Prisoner*.

20. Ibid.

21. Ibid.

22. Nolan D. McCaskill, Alex Isenstadt, and Shane Goldmacher, "Paul Manafort Resigns from Trump Campaign," *Politico*, August 19, 2016.

23. Meghan Keneally, "Timeline of Paul Manafort's Role in the Trump Campaign," ABC News, October 30, 2017.

24. Spencer S. Hsu, Rachel Weiner, and Matt Zapotosky, "Roger Stone Trial: Former Top Trump Official Details Campaign's Dealings on WikiLeaks, and Suggests Trump Was in the Know," *Washington Post*, November 12, 2019. Trump later pardoned Stone before he served time in prison.

25. Ken Dilanian, Charlie Gile, and Dareh Gregorian, "Prosecutor Says Roger Stone Lied Because 'the Truth Looked Bad for Donald Trump,'" NBC News, November 6, 2019.

26. Stone sent his email to Manafort on August 3, 2016. The next day, Stone wrote "that he had dinner with Assange the night before," according to CNN. See Andrew Kaczynski and Gloria Borger, "Stone, on Day He Sent Assange Dinner Email, Also Said 'Devastating' WikiLeaks Were Forthcoming," CNN, April 4, 2018; Darren Samuelson and Josh Gerstein, "What Roger Stone's Trial Revealed About Donald Trump and WikiLeaks," *Politico*, November 12, 2019.

27. Rosalind S. Helderman, Tom Hamburger, and Rachel Weiner, "At Height of Russia Tensions, Trump Campaign Chairman Manafort Met with Business Associate from Ukraine," *Washington Post*, June 19, 2017.

28. Aaron Blake, "'How Do We Use [This] to Get Whole?': The Most Intriguing New Paul Manafort–Russia Email," *Washington Post*, September 20, 2017.

29. "Report of the Select Committee on Intelligence."

30. Ibid.

31. Robert Waldeck, *The Black Ledger: How Trump Brought Putin's Disinformation War to America* (New York: Cobra y Craneo, 2020).

32. Ibid.

33. Philip Bump, "New Evidence Revives an Old Question: What Counts as Trump-Russia Collusion?," *Washington Post*, August 18, 2020.

34. Mattathias Schwartz, "Exclusive: Paul Manafort Admits He Passed Trump Campaign Data to a Suspected Russian Asset," Business Insider, August 8, 2022.

35. Ibid.

36. U.S. Department of the Treasury, "Treasury Escalates Sanctions Against the Russian Government's Attempts to Influence U.S. Elections," press release, April 15, 2021.

37. Despite all evidence to the contrary, Manafort has continued to claim that Kilimnik is "*not* a Russian agent." See Manafort, *Political Prisoner*.

38. Jim Rutenberg, "The Untold Story of 'Russiagate' and the Road to War in Ukraine," *New York Times Magazine*, November 2, 2022.

39. "Report of the Select Committee on Intelligence."

40. Federal Bureau of Investigation to Jason Leopold, BuzzFeed News, March 2, 2022 ("Litigation_6th_Release_-_Leopold.pdf"), https://buzzfeed.egnyte.com/dl/gbuL8jn18Z/.

41. Sharon LaFraniere, "Mueller Report Leaves Unanswered Questions About Contacts Between Russians and Trump Aides," *New York Times*, April 18, 2019.

42. Salvador Rizzo, "What Attorney General Barr Said vs. What the Mueller Report Said," *Washington Post*, April 19, 2020.

43. U.S. Department of Justice, "Report on the Investigation into Russian Interference in the 2016 Presidential Election" (Mueller Report), March 2019.

44. Waldeck, *The Black Ledger*.

45. Andrew E. Kramer, Mike McIntire, and Barry Meier, "Secret Ledger in Ukraine Lists Cash for Donald Trump's Campaign Chief," *New York Times*, August 14, 2016.

46. Jonny Wrate, "Trump's Ex-Campaign Chief Accused of Money Laundering in Ukraine," Organized Crime and Corruption Reporting Project, March 21, 2017.

47. Manafort, *Political Prisoner*.

48. Ibid.

49. McCaskill, Isenstadt, and Goldmacher, "Paul Manafort Resigns."

14. BLACK HOLE

1. Alexis de Tocqueville, *Democracy in America* (Chicago: University of Chicago Press, 2002).

2. Brenda Shaffer, "Russia's Next Land Grab," *New York Times*, September 9, 2014.

3. Brenda Shaffer, "Stopping Russia from Cornering Europe's Energy Market," *Washington Post*, November 3, 2014.

4. Casey Michel, "This Professor Refuses to Disclose Her Work for an Autocratic Regime. Here's What Happened When I Confronted Her," *New Republic*, January 22, 2015.

5. Robert Coalson, "Azerbaijan's Opinion-Shaping Campaign Reaches 'The New York Times,'" Radio Free Europe/Radio Liberty, September 18, 2014.

6. Carl Schreck, "Sparks Fly over Scholar's Azerbaijani Ties at Columbia University Event," Radio Free Europe/Radio Liberty, October 24, 2014.

7. Till Bruckner, "How to Build Yourself a Stealth Lobbyist, Azerbaijani Style," Organized Crime and Corruption Reporting Project, June 22, 2015.

8. Collin Binkley, "Feds Say US Colleges 'Massively' Underreport Foreign Funding," Associated Press, October 20, 2020.

9. U.S. Department of Education, "Section 117 of the Higher Education Act of 1965," last modified July 19, 2022.

10. Alexander Cooley, Tena Prelec, John Heathershaw, and Tom Mayne, "Paying for a World-Class Affiliation: Reputation Laundering in the University Sector of Open Societies," working paper, National Endowment for Democracy, May 2021.

11. Brendan O'Brien, "Harvard and Yale Universities Investigated for Possible Non-Disclosure of Foreign Money," Reuters, February 12, 2020.

12. Permanent Subcommittee on Investigations, U.S. Senate, "China's Impact on the US Education System," February 27, 2019.

13. Office of the General Council, U.S. Department of Education, "Institutional Compliance with Section 117 of the Higher Education Act of 1965," October 2020.

14. Ibid.

15. Ibid.

16. Ibid.

17. Phillip Martin, "MIT Abandons Russian High-Tech Campus Partnership in Light of Ukraine Invasion," *All Things Considered*, WGBH, February 25, 2022.

18. Jessica Shi, "MIT Removed Russian Oligarch Viktor Vekselberg from Corporation in April 2018," *The Tech*, January 18, 2019.

19. Cooley et al., "Paying for a World-Class Affiliation."

20. The database can be found at https://sites.ed.gov/foreigngifts/. There remains ample room to improve the database, such as adding contracts, detailing which entities formalized the donations, and noting any additional requests or meetings that accompanied the donations.

21. Office of the General Council, "Institutional Compliance with Section 117."

22. Permanent Subcommittee on Investigations, "China's Impact on the US Education System."

23. Linda Yeung and Ng Kang-chung, "Harvard University Receives Largest Ever Donation from Hong Kong Foundation," *South China Morning Post,* September 8, 2014.

24. Ben Rooney, "Harvard Gets Record $350 Million Donation," CNN Money, September 8, 2014.

25. Cooley et al. "Paying for a World-Class Affiliation."

26. Guillermo S. Hava, "The Other Chan: Donation Sanitization at the School of Public Health," Harvard Crimson, October 19, 2020.

27. Jonathan L. Katzman, "Distasteful Donations," *Harvard Crimson,* September 6, 2019.

28. "Ronnie & Gerald Chan," *Forbes,* https://www.forbes.com/profile/ronnie-gerald-chan/?sh=4704cc285948, accessed 3 March 2023.

29. Author interview.

30. Austin Ramzy, "Asia Society Blames Staff for Barring Hong Kong Activist's Speech," *New York Times,* July 7, 2017.

31. "Statement on PEN Hong Kong Event, Joshua Wong," Asia Society, July 6, 2017.

32. "Asia Society Staff Survey 2019," uploaded by Casey Michel, https://www.scribd.com/document/495683135/Asia-Society-Staff-Survey-2019.

33. Author interview.

34. Casey Michel and David Szakonyi, "America's Cultural Institutions Are Quietly Fueled by Russian Corruption," *Foreign Policy,* October 30, 2020.

35. John de Boer, "What Are Think Tanks Good For?," Centre for Policy Research, United Nations University, March 17, 2015.

36. Ben Freeman, "Foreign Funding of Think Tanks in America," Foreign Influence Transparency Initiative, Center for International Policy, Washington, DC, January 2020.

37. "Our Mission," Aspen Institute, https://www.aspeninstitute.org/what-we-do/#:~:text=The%20Aspen%20Institute%20is%20a,United%20States%20and%20the%20world, accessed 3 March 2023.

38. Freeman, "Foreign Funding of Think Tanks in America."

39. "About the Atlantic Council," Atlantic Council, https://www.atlanticcouncil.org/about/, accessed 3 March 2023.

40. Freeman, "Foreign Funding of Think Tanks in America."

41. Author interview.

42. "International Advisory Board," Atlantic Council, https://www.atlanticcouncil.org/about/international-advisory-board/, accessed 3 March 2023. As mentioned earlier, Pinchuk denies any financial links to Manafort's network.

43. Ryan Grim and Clio Chang, "Amid Internal Investigation over Leaks to Media, the Center for American Progress Fires Two Staffers," The Intercept, January 16, 2019.

44. Eric Lipton, Brooke Williams, and Nicholas Confessore, "Foreign Powers Buy Influence at Think Tanks," *New York Times,* September 6, 2014.

45. Ibid.

46. Ibid.

47. Casey Michel, "Congress Takes Aim at Think Tanks and Their Corrupt Money," *New Republic,* June 27, 2022.

48. Kjølv Egeland and Benoît Pelopidas, "No such thing as a free donation? Research funding and conflicts of interest in nuclear weapons policy analysis," *International Relations,* December 22, 2022.

49. *In the Matter of the Search of Information Stored Within the iCloud Account Associated with DSID/Apple Account Number 1338547227,* Application for a Warrant by Telephone or Other Reliable Electronic Means, U.S. District Court for the Central District of California, Case No. 2:22-MJ-1530, April 15, 2022, https://www .documentcloud.org/documents/22062338-allen-search-warrant?responsive=1 &title=1.

50. Alan Suderman and Jim Mustian, "FBI Seizes Retired General's Data Related to Qatar Lobbying," Associated Press, June 7, 2022.

51. *In the Matter of the Search of Information . . . ,* Application for a Warrant.

52. Michel, "Congress Takes Aim at Think Tanks."

53. Associated Press, "FBI Seizes Retired General's Data Related to Qatar Lobbying," *Politico,* June 7, 2022.

54. Lipton, Williams, and Confessore, "Foreign Powers Buy Influence at Think Tanks."

55. Ibid.

56. Nahal Toosi, "Trump Administration Demands Think Tanks Disclose Foreign Funding," *Politico,* October 13, 2020.

57. Michael R. Pompeo, "On Transparency and the Foreign Funding of U.S. Think Tanks," press statement, U.S. Department of State, October 13, 2020.

58. Secretary Pompeo (@secpompeo), "The @StateDept will henceforth request think tanks that accept money from foreign governments disclose this information to the public. The purpose is simple: to promote free and open dialogue, untainted by the machinations of authoritarian regimes," Twitter, 11:47 a.m. October 13, 2020, https://twitter.com/secpompeo/status/1316042794411196417.

15. YOU'RE FUCKED

1. "Bloomberg: Would Be Godsend if More Billionaires Moved to NYC," NBC 4 New York, September 20, 2013.

2. Paul Manafort, *Political Prisoner: Persecuted, Prosecuted, but Not Silenced* (New York: Skyhorse, 2022).

3. Ibid.

4. U.S. Department of Justice, "Report on the Investigation into Russian Interference in the 2016 Presidential Election" (Mueller Report), March 2019.

5. Another vector of Russian meddling that the Mueller Report overlooked was Moscow's cultivation of American secessionists in places like Texas and California, though this was less an influence or lobbying campaign and more simply a matter of sowing chaos in the United States—and potentially fracturing the United States

outright. This, unexpectedly, was how I initially uncovered the social media prong of Russian interference efforts—including a grammatically challenged post that read, memorably, "IN LOVE WITH TEXAS SHAPE." See Casey Michel, "How the Russians Pretended to Be Texas—and Texans Believed Them," *Washington Post,* October 17, 2017.

6. One area the Mueller Report overlooked, for instance, was how the Kremlin was firmly embedded in leading nonprofit organizations among America's so-called Religious Right. One organization in particular, the US-based World Congress of Families (WCF), offered entrée for a range of pro-Kremlin oligarchs and their proxies—and allowed them to directly access, and lobby, American politicians and allies within the Religious Right. As Alexey Komov, the Russian representative for the WCF—which has accepted funding from multiple now-sanctioned Russian oligarchs—told me, "We're often shown as a strange people like we're homophobic fascists or something." Given the Kremlin's recent manifestation, "homophobic fascist" remains an apt description. See Casey Michel, "How Russia Became the Leader of the Global Christian Right," *Politico Magazine,* February 9, 2017.

7. Unsurprisingly, cultivation of evangelical organizations and groups like the NRA carried significant overlap. For instance, Russian agent Maria Butina originally connected with the NRA because of a Tennessee lawyer named Kline Preston. When I spoke with Preston, he revealed that he believed Putin was, quite literally, a gift from God. "I think there are certain people throughout history . . . who have been placed on this planet, once about every five hundred years, who are difference-makers, without whom things would be much different and worse," Preston told me. "In the history of our nation, I believe firmly that George Washington was one of those people. Had he not lived, this would be a totally different scenario. There are two people in Russian history in the last days that I believe were God-sent. One was Boris Yeltsin, and one was Vladimir Putin. And the reason I say Yeltsin . . . he was the guy that anointed Putin, and, man, that was a world-changer right there. Him. Yeltsin did it. And from whence it came, I can only think, you know, that it was divine."

8. Casey Michel, "Tom Barrack Suggests Trump's White House Was Even More Vulnerable than We Thought," NBC News, July 25, 2021.

9. Sharon LaFraniere and William K. Rashbaum, "Thomas Barrack, Trump Fund-Raiser, Is Indicted on a Lobbying Charge," *New York Times,* July 20, 2021.

10. U.S. Department of Justice, "Former Advisor to Presidential Candidate Among Three Defendants Charged with Acting as Agents of a Foreign Government," press release, July 20, 2021.

11. *U.S. v Rashid Sultan Rashid Al Malik Alshahhi et al.,* Indictment, U.S. District Court, Eastern District of New York, Case No. 1:21-cr-00371, July 15, 2021, https://www.justice.gov/opa/press-release/file/1413381/download.

12. Tom Winter and Dareh Gregorian, "Tom Barrack, Former Trump Inaugural Chair, Released on $250 Million Bond," NBC News, July 23, 2021.

13. Michel, "Tom Barrack Suggests."

14. Rebecca Davis O'Brien, "Trump Adviser's Trial May Shed Light on Foreign Influence Campaigns," *New York Times,* September 17, 2022.

15. Debra J. Saunders, "Steve Wynn Named RNC Finance Chairman," *Las Vegas Review-Journal,* January 30, 2017.

16. Isaac Stanley-Becker and Spencer S. Hsu, "U.S. Sues to Compel Casino Mogul Steve Wynn to Register as Agent of China," *Washington Post,* May 17, 2022.

17. *Attorney General of United States of America v. Stephen A. Wynn,* Complaint for Declaratory and Injunctive Relief, U.S. District Court for the District of Columbia, Civil Action No. 22-1372, May 17, 2022, https://www.justice.gov/opa/press-release/file/1506786/download.

18. U.S. Department of Justice, "Elliott Broidy Pleads Guilty for Back-Channel Lobbying Campaign to Drop 1MDB Investigation and Remove a Chinese Foreign National," press release, October 20, 2020.

19. Spencer S. Hsu, "Major RNC, Trump Fundraiser Elliott Broidy Pleads Guilty to Acting as Unregistered Foreign Agent," *Washington Post,* October 20, 2020.

20. *Attorney General of United States of America v. Stephen A. Wynn,* Complaint for Declaratory and Injunctive Relief.

21. Mark Hosenball, "Trump Ex-Fundraiser Elliott Broidy Pleads Guilty in 1MDB Foreign Lobbying Case," Reuters, October 20, 2020.

22. *Attorney General of United States of America v. Stephen A. Wynn,* Complaint for Declaratory and Injunctive Relief.

23. Ken Dilanian, "Russians Paid Mike Flynn $45K for Moscow Speech, Documents Show," NBC News, March 16, 2017.

24. Carol E. Lee, "Mueller Gives New Details on Flynn's Secretive Work for Turkey," NBC News, December 5, 2018.

25. Isaac Arnsdorf, "Trump's New Spy Chief Used to Work for a Foreign Politician the U.S. Accused of Corruption," ProPublica, February 21, 2020.

26. U.S. Department of the Treasury, "Treasury Targets Corruption and the Kremlin's Malign Influence Operations in Moldova," press release, October 26, 2022.

27. Arnsdorf, "Trump's New Spy Chief."

28. Casey Michel, "The Law That Could Take Down Rudy Giuliani," *New Republic,* October 15, 2019.

29. Jo Becker, Maggie Haberman, and Eric Lipton, "Giuliani Pressed for Turkish Prisoner Swap in Oval Office Meeting," *New York Times,* October 10, 2019.

30. Aram Roston, Matt Spetalnick, and Brian Ellsworth, "Exclusive: Giuliani Told U.S. His Client Deserves Leniency for Financing Venezuela's Opposition—Parnas," Reuters, January 22, 2020.

31. Casey Michel, "The Kleptocrat Who Bankrolled Rudy Giuliani's Drive for Dirt on Biden," *New Republic,* August 4, 2022. Firtash is currently fighting extradition to the United States.

32. Nick Penzenstadler, Steve Reilly, and John Kelly, "Most Trump Real Estate Now Sold to Secretive Buyers," *USA Today,* June 13, 2017.

33. Craig Unger, "Trump's Russian Laundromat," *New Republic,* July 13, 2017.

34. Richard C. Paddock and Eric Lipton, "Trump's Indonesia Projects, Still Moving Ahead, Create Potential Conflicts," *New York Times,* December 31, 2016.
35. "Trump's Luxury Condo: A Congolese State Affair," Global Witness, April 10, 2019.
36. Luke Broadwater and Eric Lipton, "Documents Detail Foreign Government Spending at Trump Hotel," *New York Times,* November 14, 2022.
37. Details of Malaysian government expenditures at Trump International Hotel, Washington, DC, for September 10–19, 2017, prepared December 19, 2018, https://int.nyt.com/data/documenttools/pages-from-malaysian-government-expenditures-trump-hotel/c3e82c1247e1ccc8/full.pdf.
38. Broadwater and Lipton, "Documents Detail Foreign Government Spending."
39. Melissa Zhu, "Najib Razak: Malaysia's Ex-PM Starts Jail Term After Final Appeal Fails," BBC News, August 23, 2022.
40. Broadwater and Lipton, "Documents Detail Foreign Government Spending."
41. Katherine Sullivan, "How a Nigerian Presidential Candidate Hired a Trump Lobbyist and Ended Up in Trump's Lobby—'Trump, Inc.' Podcast," ProPublica, February 27, 2019.
42. Scott Bixby, "Trump's Ukraine Conspiracy Theory Came from Paul Manafort During his 2016 Campaign: Mueller Notes," Daily Beast, November 4, 2019.
43. Jim Rutenberg, "The Untold Story of 'Russiagate' and the Road to War in Ukraine," *New York Times,* November 2, 2022.
44. Radley Balko, "No-Knock Raids Like the One Against Paul Manafort Are More Common than You Think," *Washington Post,* August 10, 2017.
45. *U.S. v. Paul J. Manafort Jr. and Konstantin Kilimnik,* Superseding Indictment, U.S. District Court, District of Columbia, Case No. 1:17-cr-00201-ABJ, June 8, 2018, www.justice.gov/archives/sco/page/file/1070326/download.
46. *U.S. v. Paul J. Manafort Jr. and Richard W. Gates III,* Indictment, U.S. District Court, District of Columbia, Case No. Case No. 1:17-cr-00201-ABJ, October 30, 2017, www.justice.gov/file/1007271/download.
47. Ibid.
48. Sharon LaFraniere, "Paul Manafort's Prison Sentence Is Nearly Doubled to 7½ Years," *New York Times,* March 13, 2019.
49. Dartunorro Clark, Gary Grumbach, and Charlie Gile, "Manafort Gets 7.5 Years in Prison, After Additional 43 Months in Second Sentencing," NBC News, March 13, 2019.
50. Paul Manafort, *Political Prisoner: Persecuted, Prosecuted, but Not Silenced* (New York: Skyhorse, 2022).
51. Theodoric Meyer, "Flynn Admits to Lying About Turkish Lobbying," *Politico,* December 1, 2017. Trump later pardoned Flynn, who was never imprisoned.
52. U.S. Department of Justice, "Elliott Broidy Pleads Guilty."
53. Soo Rin Kim, "Trump Associates Who Have Been Sent to Prison or Faced Criminal Charges," ABC News, January 17, 2020.
54. Skadden settlement agreement, January 15, 2019, https://www.justice.gov/opa/press-release/file/1124381/download.

55. Kenneth P. Vogel and Matthew Goldstein, "Law Firm to Pay $4.6 Million in Case Tied to Manafort and Ukraine," *New York Times,* January 17, 2019.

56. Kenneth P. Vogel, "Skadden Said to Have Paid $11 Million to Settle Ukraine Dispute," *New York Times*, May 10, 2020.

57. David D. Kirkpatrick and Mark Mazzetti, "Prosecutors Add Details to Foreign Lobbying Charges Against Trump Ally," *New York Times,* May 17, 2022.

58. Eric Tucker, "US Sues Casino Mogul Steve Wynn over Relationship with China," Associated Press, May 17, 2022.

59. Erica Orden, "How Federal Prosecutors Are Pursuing Rudy Giuliani," CNN, May 22, 2021.

60. Julia Ainsley, Andrew W. Lehren, and Anna Schecter, "The Mueller Effect: FARA Filings Soar in Shadow of Manafort, Flynn Probes," NBC News, January 18, 2018.

61. Katie Benner, "Justice Dept. to Step Up Enforcement of Foreign Influence Laws," *New York Times,* March 6, 2019.

62. Office of Senator Elizabeth Warren, "Anti-Corruption and Public Integrity Act," August 21, 2018.

63. "The Biden Plan to Guarantee Government Works for the People," https://joebiden.com/governmentreform/#, accessed 3 March 2023.

16. THE REPUBLIC ITSELF IS AT RISK

1. Quoted in Scott Weidensaul, *Living on the Wind: Across the Hemisphere with Migratory Birds* (New York: Farrar, Straus and Giroux, 2000).

2. Paul Manafort, *Political Prisoner: Persecuted, Prosecuted, but Not Silenced* (New York: Skyhorse, 2022).

3. Ibid.

4. Ibid.

5. "Trump Pardons Paul Manafort, Roger Stone and Charles Kushner," BBC News, December 24, 2020.

6. Franklin Foer, "The Triumph of Kleptocracy," *The Atlantic,* December 23, 2020.

7. David L. Stern, "FAQ: Who Is Konstantin Kilimnik and Why Does His Name Appear 800 Times in a Senate Report?," *Washington Post,* August 18, 2020.

8. "Report of the Select Committee on Intelligence, United States Senate, on Russian Active Measures Campaigns and Interference in the 2016 U.S. Election, Volume 5: Counterintelligence Threats and Vulnerabilities," 116th Cong., 1st Sess., Report 116-XXX.

9. Ibid.

10. Aaron Blake, "The Senate's 'Grave' Russia Report: What We Learned, and What It Means," *Washington Post,* August 18, 2020.

11. "Report of the Select Committee on Intelligence."

12. Charlie Savage, "Trump Pardons Michael Flynn, Ending Case His Justice Dept. Sought to Shut Down," *New York Times,* November 25, 2020.

13. Theodoric Meyer, "Emails Give New Detail About Mercury, Podesta Role in Manafort's Lobbying," *Politico,* September 13, 2018.

14. It's worth noting that there's no evidence that Hunter's work in Ukraine or elsewhere affected his father's policies. If anything, in Ukraine, such a scheme appeared to backfire; Biden publicly called for Ukrainian authorities to specifically investigate the firm his son was affiliated with. See Casey Michel, "Trump's Big Lie About Joe Biden, Hunter Biden, and Ukraine Falls Apart," *The Daily Beast,* September 29, 2019.

15. Casey Michel, "The Emerging Artistry of Hunter Biden," *The Atlantic,* September 28, 2021.

16. Sarah Chayes, "Hunter Biden's Perfectly Legal, Socially Acceptable Corruption," *The Atlantic,* September 27, 2019.

17. Theodoric Meyer, "How Lobbyists Are Supporting Biden," *Politico,* April 26, 2019.

18. Mark Paustenbach and Mark Skidmore, "Larry Rasky: A Legendary Democratic Operative Who Boosted Joe Biden," *Politico Magazine,* December 26, 2020.

19. Casey Michel, "Biden's Super PAC Buddy Has a Paul Manafort Problem," *New Republic,* November 1, 2019.

20. Author interview with Larry Rasky.

21. Karin Fischer, "Far-Reaching Investigations of Colleges' Foreign Ties Could Be Closed," letter to the editor, *Chronicle of Higher Education,* October 5, 2022.

22. Jimmy Quinn, "Biden Admin Winds Down Probes into Universities' Foreign Gifts," *National Review,* October 18, 2022.

23. U.S. Department of Justice, National Security Division, email to [addressee redacted], "Re: [Company] Request for Advisory Opinion Pursuant to 28 C.F.R. § 5.2," April 12, 2022, https://www.justice.gov/nsd-fara/page/file/1526096/download.

24. The State Department did not respond to my questions regarding requirements or requests about think tanks and foreign funding disclosure.

25. *U.S. v. Gregory B. Craig,* Grand Jury Indictment, U.S. District Court, District of Columbia, April 11, 2019, https://www.justice.gov/usao-dc/press-release/file/1153646/download.

26. Matthew Continetti, "The Shameful Saga of Greg Craig," *Commentary,* October 2019.

27. Sharon LaFraniere, "Gregory Craig Acquitted on Charge of Lying to Justice Department," *New York Times,* September 4, 2019.

28. Ibid.

29. Ibid.

30. Instead of FARA, Barrack was charged with violating a statute known as Section 951, a related lobbying- and espionage-related regulation. Section 951 was used against others involved in the 2016 interference campaign, such as Maria Butina, the Russian agent who infiltrated the National Rifle Association (NRA). See 18 U.S. Code § 951, "Agents of Foreign Governments."

31. Department of Justice, "Former Advisor to Presidential Candidate Among Three Defendants Charged with Acting as Agents of a Foreign Government," press release, July 20, 2021.

32. Rebecca Davis O'Brien, "Former Trump Adviser Acquitted on Charges of Acting as Emirati Agent," *New York Times,* November 4, 2022.

33. Ibid.

34. Jacqueline Thomsen, "Casino Tycoon Wynn Defeats U.S. Lawsuit over Chinese Agent Claims," Reuters, October 12, 2022.

35. Devan Cole, "Steve Wynn Can't Be Forced to Register as a Foreign Agent of China, Judge Rules," CNN, October 12, 2022.

36. McKinsey's filings can be found in the FARA database, including: https://efile.fara.gov/docs/6852-Registration-Statement-20200810-1.pdf.

37. Katie Benner, Mark Mazzetti, Ben Hubbard, and Mike Isaac, "Saudis' Image Makers: A Troll Army and a Twitter Insider," *New York Times,* October 20, 2018.

38. Walt Bogdanich and Michael Forsythe, "How McKinsey Has Helped Raise the Stature of Authoritarian Governments," *New York Times,* December 15, 2018.

39. Sheelah Kolhatkar, "McKinsey's Work for Saudi Arabia Highlights Its History of Unsavory Entanglements," *New Yorker,* November 1, 2018.

40. Taylor Giorno and Anna Massoglia, "Saudi Arabia Ramped Up U.S. Influence Operations During Biden's Presidency," Open Secrets, October 7, 2022.

41. Ben Freeman, "It's Time to Silence the Saudi Lobbying Machine in Washington," *Washington Post,* October 22, 2018.

42. Ben Freeman, "The Saudi Lobby Builds Back Better," The Intercept, August 25, 2022.

43. Craig Whitlock and Nate Jones, "Retired U.S. Generals, Admirals Take Top Jobs with Saudi Crown Prince," *Washington Post,* October 18, 2022.

44. Jeremy Herb, "Mattis Advised UAE Military Before Joining Trump Administration," CNN, August 2, 2017.

45. Craig Whitlock and Nate Jones, "UAE Relied on Expertise of Retired U.S. Troops to Beef Up Its Military," *Washington Post,* October 18, 2022.

17. MR. LEE'S PUBLICITY BOOK

1. Quoted in Sean Wilentz, *Rise of American Democracy: Jefferson to Lincoln* (New York: W. W. Norton, 2006).

2. Dan Mangan, "Federal Authorities Bar Ex-Trump Campaign Chief Paul Manafort from Dubai Flight Because of Invalid Passport," CNBC, March 23, 2022.

3. John Hudson, "U.S. Intelligence Report Says Key Gulf Ally Meddled in American Politics," *Washington Post,* November 12, 2022.

4. Jonathan Guyer, "Where in the World Are Russians Going to Avoid Sanctions?," Vox, August 9, 2022.

5. Eugene Daniels, "Politico Playbook: Biden Braces for Brutal Inflation Numbers," *Politico,* April 12, 2022.

6. Paul Manafort, *Political Prisoner: Persecuted, Prosecuted, but Not Silenced* (New York: Skyhorse, 2022).

7. "Foreign Lobby Watch," Open Secrets, https://www.opensecrets.org/fara, accessed 3 March 2023.

8. Much of the spike in these Russian expenditures stems from the fact that the federal government forced RT's parent company to register with FARA in 2017. See

Devlin Barrett and David Filipov, "RT Agrees to Register as an Agent of the Russian Government," *Washington Post,* November 9, 2017.

9. Casey Michel, *American Kleptocracy: How the U.S. Created the World's Greatest Money Laundering Scheme in History* (New York: St. Martin's, 2021).

10. Hailey Fuchs, "How Russian Entities Are Retaining Much of Their D.C. Lobbying Influence," *Politico,* March 22, 2022.

11. Josh Rogin, "It's Time to Shut Down the Foreign Dictator Lobbying Racket," *Washington Post,* October 5, 2022.

12. Office of Rep. Steve Cohen, "Representatives Cohen, Wilson, Banks, and Slotkin Introduce the Bipartisan Stop Helping Adversaries Manipulate Everything (SHAME) Act," press release, October 5, 2022.

13. Office of Rep. Jared Golden, "Golden, Bipartisan Colleagues Introduce Legislation to Combat Foreign Influence in Washington," press release, June 16, 2022.

14. Casey Michel, "Congress Takes Aim at Think Tanks and Their Corrupt Money," *New Republic,* June 27, 2022.

15. Emily Wilkins, "GOP Changes Stir Fears About the Future of House Ethics Office," *Bloomberg Government,* January 17, 2023.

16. Ivy Lee with Burton St. John III, *Mr. Lee's Publicity Book: A Citizen's Guide to Public Relations* (New York: PRMuseum Press, 2017).

17. Ibid.

18. Ibid.

19. "#EthicsMatter—Ivy Lee and the First Code of Ethics," Global Alliance for Public Relations and Communication Management, Zurich, February 19, 2021.

20. "Rise of the Image Men," *The Economist,* December 16, 2010.

21. Gary McCormick, "Merely 'Image Men'? Hardly," Public Relations Society of America, December 20, 2010.

22. For instance, the "Code of Ethics" for McCormick's organization is silent as it pertains to American PR specialists aiding dictators. See "Public Relations Society of America (PRSA) Member Code of Ethics," n.d., https://web.archive.org /web/20140115230822/https://www.prsa.org/AboutPRSA/Ethics/CodeEnglish /#.UtcU7XbP23A.

23. Adam Lowenstein, "The American PR Firm Helping Saudi Arabia Clean Up Its Image," *The Guardian,* December 22, 2022.

24. Hailey Fuchs, "The Daily Show Meets Riyadh! How a Giant PR Firm Is Pitching the Saudis," *Politico,* July 17, 2022.

25. Lowenstein, "The American PR Firm Helping Saudi Arabia."

26. Aziz El Yaakoubi, "Saudi Woman Gets 45-Year Prison Term for Social Media Posts, Rights Group Says," Reuters, August 30, 2022.

27. Marcus Baram, "How Saudi Arabia Restored Its U.S. Influence Machine After the Khashoggi Murder," *Foreign Policy,* January 27, 2021.

28. Lowenstein, "The American PR Firm Helping Saudi Arabia."

29. Ibid.

30. Fuchs, "The Daily Show Meets Riyadh!"

31. In May 2022, Edelman CEO Richard Edelman wrote that he was "more convinced than ever about the global rift between democracy and autocracy." A few
days later, the company signed its new deal with Saudi Arabia. It's unclear how
Edelman views its own role in this rift between democracy and autocracy. *See*
Richard Edelman, "Davos Mid-Year," June 2, 2022, https://www.edelman.com
/insights/davos-mid-year-6-am, and Lowenstein, "The American PR Firm Helping Saudi Arabia."

32. Lee, *Mr. Lee's Publicity Book.*

33. Ibid.

AFTERWORD

1. Bob Lee, "They Came for the Gold and Stayed for the Grass," *Rangelands,* October 1996, https://journals.uair.arizona.edu/index.php/rangelands/article/viewFile
/11303/10576.

2. Peter Duffy, "The Congressman Who Spied for Russia," *Politico,* October 6, 2014.

3. Casey Michel, "We've Never Seen Anything Like the Menendez Indictment," *The
Atlantic,* October 26, 2023.

4. Nina Burleigh, "Nadine and Bob Menendez's Flashy, Allegedly Corrupt, Romance,"
New York Magazine, October 31, 2023.

5. Ben Penn, "Menendez Indicted as Foreign Agent After Thwarting Related Bill,"
Bloomberg Law, October 13, 2023.

6. Alexander Hamilton, "Federalist No. 21: Other Defects of the Present Confederation" (1787).

INDEX

ABOUT THE AUTHOR

Versha Sharma

Casey Michel is an author, journalist, and director of the Combating Kleptocracy Program with the Human Rights Foundation. His first book, *American Kleptocracy*, was named by *The Economist* as one of the "best books to read to understand financial crime." His writing on offshoring, foreign lobbying, authoritarianism, and illicit wealth has appeared in *Financial Times*, *The Wall Street Journal*, *The Atlantic*, *Foreign Affairs*, *The Washington Post*, and other publications, and he has appeared on NPR, BBC, CNN, and MSNBC, among other outlets. He has testified in front of the Senate Judiciary Committee on the links between illicit financial networks and national security. He received his master's degree in Russian, Eurasian, and East European studies from Columbia University's Harriman Institute and served as a Peace Corps volunteer in northern Kazakhstan. *Foreign Agents* is his second book.